www.wadsworth.com

www.wadsworth.com is the World Wide Web site for Thomson Wadsworth and is your direct source to dozens of online resources.

At *www.wadsworth.com* you can find out about supplements, demonstration software, and student resources. You can also send email to many of our authors and preview new publications and exciting new technologies.

www.wadsworth.com
Changing the way the world learns®

ANTHOLOGY FOR *Music in Western Civilization*

VOLUME II:
THE ENLIGHTENMENT TO THE PRESENT

ANTHOLOGY FOR *Music in Western Civilization*

Volume II: The Enlightenment to the Present

Timothy Roden
Ohio Wesleyan University

Craig Wright
Yale University

Bryan Simms
University of Southern California

Australia • Brazil • Canada • Mexico • Singapore • Spain • United Kingdom • United States

Anthology for Music in Western Civilization
Volume II: The Enlightenment to the Present
Timothy Roden, Craig Wright, Bryan Simms

Publisher: Clark Baxter
Associate Development Editor: Julie Yardley
Editorial Assistant: Emily Perkins
Executive Technology Project Manager: Matt Dorsey
Executive Marketing Manager: Diane Wenckebach
Marketing Assistant: Marla Nasser
Marketing Communications Manager: Patrick Rooney
Project Manager, Editorial Production: Trudy Brown
Creative Director: Rob Hugel
Executive Art Director: Maria Epes
Print Buyer: Karen Hunt

Permissions Editor: Kiely Sisk
Production Service: Stratford Publishing Services
Text and Cover Designer: Diane Beasley
Copy Editor: Carrie Crompton
Autographers: A-R Editions, Highland Engraving, Dennis Dieterich, and Mark Burgess
Cover Image: Carlo Saraceni (1585–1620), *Saint Cecilia*. Galleria Nazionale d'Arte Antica, Rome, Italy. Scala/Art Resource, NY.
Compositor: Stratford Publishing Services
Text and Cover Printer: Transcontinental Printing/Louiseville

Printed in Canada
3 4 5 6 7 09 08 07 06

Library of Congress Control Number: 2005924658

ISBN 0-495-03000-7

Thomson Higher Education
10 Davis Drive
Belmont, CA 94002-3098
USA

For more information about our products, contact us at:
Thomson Learning Academic Resource Center
1-800-423-0563

For permission to use material from this text or product, submit a request online at **http://www.thomsonrights.com.**
Any additional questions about permissions can be submitted by e-mail to **thomsonrights@thomson.com.**

CONTENTS

VOLUME II

THE ENLIGHTENMENT AND THE CLASSICAL ERA

CHAPTER 43

Music in the Age of Enlightenment: Keyboard Music 824

CHAPTER 45

Joseph Haydn: Instrumental Music 838

CHAPTER 46

Joseph Haydn: Late Symphonies and Vocal Music 858

CHAPTER 47

Wolfgang Amadeus Mozart: Instrumental Music 924

CHAPTER 48

Wolfgang Amadeus Mozart: Vocal Music 989

THE EARLY TWENTIETH CENTURY

COMPOSERS AND TITLES

PREFACE

The anthology that accompanies *Music in Western Civilization* provides students with study scores of representative compositions discussed in the text. By its very nature, an anthology must be selective, excluding some wonderful compositions while incorporating a few obscure ones. These lesser-known compositions uniquely demonstrate a specific aspect of the intersection of music with cultural expression. Whenever possible, however, it has been the intention of the authors to use famous works to ensure that students are familiar with the icons of Western music. It is important that students not simply recognize these masterpieces as sound bites heard in modern mass media, but that they have the opportunity to consider what has contributed to the enduring value of these works of sonic art.

To facilitate the study of each composition, the authors have provided introductions that offer further information about musical structure and historical background for each work. Absorbing all the facts mentioned in the text, anthology, and workbook can quickly become a daunting task for students. One highly recommended way to learn this mass of material is not by attacking the prose with a highlighter, but by transcribing the information about a composition's form, themes, and even specific chords into the score itself. Then, each time students follow the music (hopefully while listening to the CDs), they are reminded of the composition's most salient features, and begin to associate facts with musical sound.

Even the most cursory glance at a music library's catalog of scores will show that numerous editions are available for many works that appear in this anthology. Students (and instructors) may well wonder what criteria were used to select the scores that appear in this volume. We tried to achieve a balance between quality and cost by using scholarly editions that are in the public domain whenever possible. This was done in order to keep the price of the anthology as low as possible for college students. Further, as a special courtesy to students, many publishers and scholars made their editions available at a reduced rate. In a number of instances, piano/vocal editions were used to reduce space, and thereby allow for the inclusion of more compositions. Instructors may prefer a different version of a work from the one included in the anthology, which can provide an opportunity to discuss how editorial principles and practices have evolved over time.

Unless otherwise noted, the authors have provided translations of vocal music. Most Biblical texts are based on *The Holy Bible, translated from the Latin Vulgate and diligently compared with the Hebrew, Greek, and other editions in divers languages* (Philadelphia: John Murphy, 1914). Students may find the numbering of the psalms confusing because the Vulgate reduces the number of many psalms by one from the numbering system used in the King James and other Protestant editions of the Bible. For example, the well-known Twenty-third Psalm is the twenty-second in the Vulgate. Translations of the Mass Ordinary are based on the *Book of Common Prayer* (Boston: Parish Choir, 1899). With the exception of translations that are cited or located within the score, all other translations are by the authors.

This anthology would not have made it to press without the unstinting efforts of many individuals, and it is my pleasure to express my appreciation. It has been a privilege to work with Craig Wright and Bryan Simms. Their drafts and observations of the introductions as well as their generous expenditure of time and unfailing courtesy have made the compilation of the anthology a satisfying endeavor. Several scholars graciously allowed us to use their editions in this anthology: Alexander Blachly (Cordier), Daniel Heartz (Sermisy), Michael Holmes (Merulo), Valerie McIntosh (Jacquet de la Guerre), and Jonathan Zalben (Landini). Professor Heartz's transcription is a classic; the editions by the other scholars in the list represent some of the most recent musical research, and a few are published here for the first time. We are grateful for their contributions.

Without the help of libraries throughout the United States, this anthology would not have been possible. A few libraries were particularly generous in making their collections available for our use. In particular, I wish to thank Faith Hoffman and Deborah Campana of the Oberlin College Conservatory of Music Library, Barry Zaslow from Miami (Ohio) University Music Library, and Julie Niemeyer from Yale University Library. Without the help of Marsha Zavar (Interlibrary Loan, Ohio Wesleyan University), my sanity would have departed long ago for regions unknown. She spent many hours on the Internet and telephone helping to locate rare scores and microfilms, and urging various libraries to expedite their interlibrary loan process.

Our copyeditor, Carrie Crompton, caught countless inconsistencies and made numerous suggestions that improved the text immeasurably. Many music engravers (A-R Editions, Highland Engraving, Dennis Dieterich, and Mark Burgess) reset old scores into digital format, and their efforts will make reading the music much easier. Nancy Crompton of Stratford Publishing Services kept all the various drafts under control and brought what became a vortex of swirling papers to completion. I thank the publisher, Clark Baxter, for the opportunity to participate in this project, and the associate development editor, Julie Yardley, for guiding me through the process. On the editorial staff, Sue Gleason and Abbie Baxter also provided valuable advice. The assistance of Trudy Brown, senior production project manager; Diane Wenckebach, executive marketing manager; and Emily Perkins, editorial assistant, is greatly appreciated.

Closer to home, I thank Ohio Wesleyan University for its liberal support of this project. The provost granted a reduced teaching assignment, the academic dean provided funds for computer hardware and software, a TEW grant provided for travel and the acquisition of material, and the music department generously supported the project by allowing thousands of photocopies to be made on their machine (and budget). Without the patience and enduring support of my wife and sons, to whom I owe a really nice vacation, I would not have been able to complete my work on this anthology.

—Timothy Roden
May 15, 2005

CREDITS

This page constitutes an extension of the copyright page. We have made every effort to trace the ownership of all copyrighted material and to secure permission from copyright holders. In the event of any question arising as to the use of any material, we will be pleased to make the necessary corrections in future printings. Thanks are due to the following authors, publishers, and agents for permission to use the material indicated.

Chapter 41. 738: No. 118— Digli ch'io son fedele. In *Original Vocal Improvisations from the 16th–18th Centuries*. Ed. by Hellmuth Christian Wolff. Cologne: Arno Volk Verlag Hans Gerig KG, 1971. pp. 143–168. **752:** No. 119—John Gay, *The Beggar's Opera*. Larchmont, New York: Argonaut Books, 1961. **757:** No. 120—*La Serva Padrona*. Boca Raton, FL: Edwin F. Kalmus & Co., n.d. pp. 33–52. **777:** No. 121—Prélude [e Duo] "À jamais Colin t'engage" (excerpt from Jean-Jacques Rousseau's Le Devin du village) is published in *Jean-Jacques Rousseau: Le Devin du village*, edited by Charlotte Kaufman, *Recent Researches in the Music of the Classical Era*. Vol. 50 (Madison, WI: A-R Editions, Inc., 1998). Used with permission. **787:** No. 122—Denkmäler der Tonkunst in Österreich. Serie II. Christoph Willibald Gluck Werke. Vol. 1. *Orfeo ed Euridice*. Originalpartitur der Wiener Fassung von 1762. Ed. by Hermann Abert. Vienna: Artaria & Co.; Leipzig: Breitkopf & Härtel, 1914. pp. 59–71, 127–133.

Chapter 42. 808: No. 123—Sammartini, Giovanni Battista. *The Symphonies of G. B. Sammartini. Vol. 1: The Early Symphonies*. Ed. by Bathia Churgin. In *Harvard Publications in Music*. 2: 76–78. **812:** No. 124—Stamitz, Johann. Sinfonia a8. La Melodia Germanica No. 3. In *Mannheim Symphonists: A Collection of Twenty-four Orchestral Works*. Vol. 1. Ed. by Hugo Riemann. New York: Broude Brothers, n.d. pp. 36–47.

Chapter 43. 825: No. 125—*Trésor des Pianistes. Vol. 6. XVIIIe Siècle, 1re Periode: Dominique Scarlatti*. Ed. by Aristide and Louise Farrenc. Paris: Farrenc, 1861–1874. pp. 89–91. **829:** No. 126—Bach, Carl Philipp Emanuel. Fantasia. In *Trésor des Pianistes. Vol. 13. XVIIIe Siècle, 2e Periode: Ch.-Ph.-Emmanuel Bach*. Ed. by Aristide and Louise Farrenc. Paris: Farrenc, 1861–1874. pp. 456–458. **833:** No. 127—Sonata, Op. 5, No. 2. In *Zehn Klavier-Sonaten von Joh. Christian Bach*. Vol. I. Ed. by Ludwig Landshoff. Leipzig: C. F. Peters, 1927. pp. 26–30.

Chapter 45. 839: No. 128—Symphony No. 6, "Le Matin." In *Joseph Haydn: Critical Edition of the Complete Symphonies*. Vol. 1. Ed. by H. C. Robbins Landon. Vienna: Universal Edition, 1965; Revised ed. 1981. pp. 125–134. **849:** No. 129—*Quartet in C. Op. 33, no. 3*. Ed. by Wilhelm Altmann. Leipzig: Ernst Eulenberg, 189. pp. 1–9.

Chapter 46. 859: No. 130—Symphony No. 94, "The Surprise." In *Joseph Haydn: Critical Edition of the Complete Symphonies*. Vol. 11. Ed. by H. C. Robbins Landon. Vienna: Universal Edition, 1966. pp. 74–87. **874:** No. 131—Symphony No. 99. In *Joseph Haydn: Critical Edition of the Complete Symphonies*. Vol. 12. Ed. by H. C. Robbins Landon. Vienna: Universal Edition, 1968. pp. 3–20. **894:** No. 132—*Die Schöpfung [The Creation]*. Ed. by A. Peter Brown. Oxford: Oxford University Press.

Chapter 47. 925: No. 133—Symphony No. 40 in G Minor, K. 550. In *Wolfgang Amadeus Mozart's Werke. Kritisch durchgesehene Gesammtausgabe*. Serie 8. Symphonien. Vol. 3. Leipzig: Breitkopf & Härtel; reprint ed. Ann Arbor: J. W. Edwards, 1955. pp. 181–198. **943:** No. 134—Symphony No. 41 in C Major, K. 551. In *Wolfgang Amadeus Mozart's Werke. Kritisch durchgesehene Gesammtausgabe*. Serie 8. Symphonien. Vol. 3. Leipzig: Breitkopf & Härtel; reprint ed. Ann Arbor: J. W. Edwards, 1955. pp. 264–285. **966:** No. 135—String Quartet in C Major, K. 465. In *Wolfgang Amadeus Mozart's Werke. Kritisch durchgesehene Gesammtausgabe*. Serie 14. Quartette für Streichinstrumente. Leipzig: Breitkopf & Härtel; reprint ed. Ann Arbor: J. W. Edwards, 1955. p. 186. **967:** No. 136—Piano Concerto in A major, K. 488. In *Wolfgang Amadeus Mozart's Werke. Kritisch durchgesehene Gesammtausgabe*. Serie 16. Concerte für das Pianoforte. Vol. 4. Leipzig: Breitkopf & Härtel; reprint ed. Ann Arbor: J. W. Edwards, 1956. pp. 67–88.

Chapter 48. 989: No. 137—*Le Nozze di Figaro*. Ed. and translated by Natalia MacFarren. London: Novello and Company, Ltd., 1872. pp. 21–24, 74–75, 82–84, 139–144. **1011:** No. 138—Requiem. In *Wolfgang Amadeus Mozart's Werke. Kritisch durchgesehene Gesammtausgabe*. Serie 24. Supplement. Leipzig: Breitkopf & Härtel; reprint ed. Ann Arbor: J. W. Edwards, 1955. pp. 42–56.

Chapter 49. 1035: No. 139—Sonate Pathétique, Op. 13. In *Ludwig van Beethoven's Werke. Vollständige kritisch durchgesehene überall herechtigte Ausgabe*. Serie 16. Sonaten für das Pianoforte. Vol. 1. Leipzig: Breitkopf & Härtel; reprint ed. Ann Arbor: J. W. Edwards, 1949. pp. 121–127. **1043:** No. 140—Piano Concerto No. 1, Op. 15. In *Ludwig van Beethoven's Werke. Vollständige kritisch durchgesehene überall herechtigte Ausgabe*. Serie 9. Für Pianoforte und Orchester. Leipzig: Breitkopf & Härtel; reprint ed. Ann Arbor: J. W. Edwards, 1949. pp. 1–36.

Chapter 50. 1072: No. 141—Symphony No. 3 in E♭ major (Eroica), Op. 55. In *Ludwig van Beethoven's Werke. Vollständige kritisch durchgesehene überall herechtigte Ausgabe*. Serie 1. Symphonien für grosses Orchester. Leipzig: Breitkopf & Härtel; reprint ed. Ann Arbor: J. W. Edwards, 1949. pp. 146–163.

Chapter 51. 1092: No. 142—String Quartet in B♭ major, Op. 130. In *Ludwig van Beethoven's Werke. Vollständige kritisch durchgesehene überall herechtigte Ausgabe*. Serie 6. Quartette für Violinen, Bratsche, und Violoncell. Vol. 1. Leipzig: Breitkopf & Härtel; reprint ed. Ann Arbor: J. W. Edwards, 1949. pp. 103–105. **1095:** No. 143—Ludwig van Beethoven, *Missa Solemnis*, vocal score edited by Julius Stern. New York: G. Schirmer, 1905.

Chapter 52. 1118: No. 144—Erlkönig (2nd edition). In *Franz Schubert's Werke. Kritisch durgesehene Gesammtausgabe. Series 20. Lieder und Gesänge*. Vol. 3. August bis Ende 1815. Ed. by Eusebius Mandyczwski. Leipzig: Breitfopf & Härtel, pp. 208–213. **1125:** No. 145—Ganymed. In *Franz Schubert's Werke. Kritisch durgesehene Gesammtausgabe. Series 20. Lieder und Gesänge*. Vol. 5. 1817 u. 1818. Ed. by Eusebius Mandyczwski. Leipzig: Breitfopf & Härtel, pp. 75–79.

Chapter 53. 1134: No. 147—Symphonie fantastique. In *Hector Berlioz Werke. Serie I. Symphonien*. Abtheilung I. Ed. by Felix Weingartner and Charles Malherbe. Leipzig: Breitkopf & Härtel, 1900. pp. 76–96. **1159:** No. 148—Les nuits d'été. In *Hector Berlioz Werke. Serie VI. Gesänge mit Orchesterbegleitung*. Abteilung II. Für eine oder zwei Singstimmen. Ed. by Felix Weingartner and Charles Malherbe. Leipzig: Breitkopf & Härtel, 1900. pp. 121–125. **1165:** No. 149—*Fr. Chopin's Sämmtliche Pianoforte-Werke: Nocturnes*. Ed. by Herrmann Scholtz. Frankfurt: C. F. Peters, [187–]. pp. 37–41.

Chapter 54. 1172: No. 150—*Trio in D minor, Op. 49*. London: Augener Ltd., [1910]. pp. 3–24. **1195:** No. 151—Symphony No. 1 in B♭ Major, Op. 38, "Spring." In *Robert Schumann's Werke. Series I. Symphonien für Orchester*. Ed. by Clara Schumann. Leipzig: Breitkopf & Härtel, 1881. pp. 50–58. **1205:** No. 152—Schumann, Clara. *Zwölf Gedichte aus F. Rückerts Liebesfrühling für Gesang und Pianoforte*. Vol. 2. Leipzig: Breitkopf & Härtel, 1841.

Chapter 55. 1208: No. 153—*Der Freischütz*. Ed. and trans. by Natalia MacFarren and Theodore Baker. New York: G. Schirmer, 1904. pp. 94–112. **1217:** No. 154—*Das Rheingold*. Vocal Score arr. by Karl Klindworth. Trans. by Frederick Jameson. New York: G. Schirmer, 1904. pp. 203–221.

Chapter 56. 1232: No. 155—*Il Barbiere de Siviglia*. [Ed. unknown] New York: G. Schirmer, 1900. pp. 9–29. **1259:** No. 156—*Otello*. Vocal score arr. by Michele Saladino. Translation by Francis Hueffer. London: G. Ricordi, 1887. pp. 341–355.

Chapter 57. 1274: No. 157—Ungarische Rhapsodie No. 15. Rákóczi Marsch. In *Franz Liszts Musikalische Werke. II Pianofortewerke. Band XII. Ungarische Rhapsodien für Pianoforte zu Zwei Händen*. Leipzig: Breitkopf & Härtel, 1926. pp. 167–178. (Gregg Press Ltd., 1966.)

Chapter 58. 1288: No. 158—Symphony No. 3 in F Major, Op. 90. In *Johannes Brahms Sämtliche Werke. Band 2. Symphonien für Orchester. II*. Leipzig: Breitkopf & Härtel, 1926. pp. 1–26. **1334:** No. 159—Feldeinsamkeit. In *Johannes Brahms Sämtliche Werke. Band 25. Lieder Und Gesänge für eine Singstimme mit Klavierbegleitung. III*. Leipzig: Breitkopf & Härtel, 1926. pp. 116–117. **1338:** No. 160—Christus factus est. In *Vier Graduale für Sopran, Alt, Tenor und Bass*. Berlin: Schlesinger'sche Buch-und Musikhandlung (Rob. Lienau), 1910. pp. 3–7.

Chapter 59. 1343: No. 161—In Four Walls (from *Complete Songs for Voice and Piano*), by Modest Mussorgsky. Copyright © 1995 by G. Schirmer, Inc. (ASCAP). International Copyright Secured. All-Rights Reserved. Reprinted by Permission **1346:** No. 162—Tchaikovsky, Peter. "Casse-noisette: ballet férie en 2 actes, opus 71." Madison Heights, WI: Luck's Music Library. pp. 19–.

Chapter 60. 1368: No. 163—"Um Mitternacht" by Gustav Mahler. Vienna: Wiener Philharminscher Verlag A. G., 1926. Used by permission. **1379:** No. 164—*Symphony No. 5*. New York: E. F. Kalmus, n.d. pp. 175–179. **1386:** No. 165—*Die stille Stadt*. In Fünf Lieder. Vienna: Universal. 1910. pp. 3–5.

Chapter 61. 1391: No. 166—*Variations*. Enigma. London: Novello; Ernst Eulenberg, 1899. pp. 1–3, 52–56.

Chapter 62. 1400: No. 167—*Madame Butterfly*. Vocal score ed. by Carlo Carignani. Trans. by R. H. Elkin. New York: G. Ricordi & Co., 1905. pp. 1–25.

Chapter 63. 1405: No. 168—Debussy, Claude. *Fêtes Galantes*. Paris: E. Fromont [1903]. pp. 2–5 **1410:** No. 169—Debussy, Claude. "Reflets dans l'eau" from *Images I*. Paris: A. Durand & Fils, 1905. **1418:** No. 170—*Nocturnes*. Paris: E. Fromont, 1909. pp. 1–17. **1435:** No. 171—Dans la foret de Septembre. Op. 85, no. 1. In *20 mélodies pour chant et piano*. Paris: J. Hamelle, n.d. pp. 72–76. **1441:** No. 172—Lili Boulanger, "Elle est gravement gaie," in *Clairières dans le Ciel* (Paris: Société Anonyme des Éditions Ricordi, 1919). © 1969 Editions Durand.

Chapter 64. 1446: No. 173—Strauss, Richard. *Salome*. Piano edition arr. by Otto Singer. Berlin: Adolph Fuerstner, 1910. pp. 181–203.

Chapter 65. 1466: No. 174—*The Rite of Spring (Le Sacre du Printemps)*. London: Boosey & Hawkes, 1947; re-engraved ed. 1967. © Copyright 1912, 1921 by Hawkes & Son (London) Ltd. Copyright Renewed. Reprinted by permission of Boosey & Hawkes, Inc.

Chapter 66. 1486: No. 175—Schoenberg, Arnold. *Three Piano Pieces (Drei Klavierstücke), Op. 11, No. 1*. New York: Universal Edition; Associated Music Publishers, Inc., n.d. International permission granted by European American Music Distributors LLC. **1486:** No. 175—Schoenberg, Arnold. *Three Piano Pieces (Drei Klavierstücke), Op. 11, No. 1*. New York: Universal Edition; Associated Music Publishers, Inc., n.d. Used by permission of Belmont Music Publishers. **1491:** No. 176—Schoenberg, Arnold. *Pierrot lunaire, Op. 21*. Vienna: Universal Edition, 1941. Used by permission of Belmont Music Publishers. International permission granted by European American Music Distributors LLC. **1495:** No. 177—*Prelude, Op. 74, No. 5*. Moscow: P. Jurgenson; Leipzig: Forberg, 1913.

Chapter 67. 1498: No. 178—Maurice Ravel, "Rigaudon" from *Tombeau de Couperin* (Paris: Durand, 1918). © 1918 Joint Ownership Redfield and Nordice. Exclusive representation by Editions DURAND, France. **1502:** No. 179—Satie, Erik. *2ème Sarabande*. Rouart, Lerolle & Cie, 1911.

Chapter 68. 1507: No. 180—Stravinsky, Igor. *Octet for Wind Instruments. Revised 1952 version*. New York: Boosey & Hawkes, 1952. © Copyright 1924 by Hawkes & Son (London) Ltd. Copyright Renewed. Revised version © Copyright 1952 by Hawkes & Son (London) Ltd. Copyright Renewed. Reprinted by permission of Boosey & Hawkes, Inc. **1518:** No. 181—Milhaud, Darius. "Botofago" from *Saudades do Brazil: Suite de Danses pour Piano*. Paris: Max Eschig, 1921. pp. 4–5.

Chapter 69. 1523: No. 182—Schoenberg, Arnold. *Fourth String Quartet. Op. 37*. New York: G. Schirmer, 1939. Used by permission of Belmont Music Publishers. **1553:** No. 183—Webern, Anton. *Symphonie, Op. 21*. n.p.: Universal Edition, 1921. pp. 8–15

Chapter 70. 1563: No. 184—Wozzeck. Piano edition by Heinrich Klein. Vienna: Universal, 1931. pp. 190–197. **1572:** No. 185—Weill, Kurt. *Die Dreigroschenoper*. Piano ed. by Norbert Gingold. Vienna: Universal Edition, 1928. pp. 7–9.

Chapter 71. 1577: No. 186—Bartók, Béla. Fekete főd from *Eight Hungarian Folksongs*. London: Boosey and Hawkes, 1955. © Copyright 1922 by Hawkes and Son (London) Ltd. Copyright Renewed. Revised edition © Copyright 1955 by Hawkes & Son (London) Ltd. Copyright renewed. Reprinted by permission of Boosey & Hawkes, Inc. **1580:** No. 187—Bartók, Béla. *Concerto for Orchestra*. Rev. ed. London: Boosey & Hawkes, 1993. © Copyright 1946 by Hawkes & Son (London) Ltd. Copyright Renewed. Reprinted by permission of Boosey & Hawkes, Inc.

Chapter 72. 1610: No. 188—Joplin, Scott. *Maple Leaf Rag*. Sedalia, MO: Stark Music Co., 1899.

Chapter 73. 1614: No. 189—Hindemith, Paul. *Mathis der Maler*. Mainz: B. Schott's Soehne, 1970. pp. 302–317.

Chapter 74. 1630: No. 190—Prokofiev, Sergei. Piano Sonata No. 7 in B♭ Major, Op. 83. In *Collected Works of Sergei Prokofiev: Piano Solos in Eleven Volumes*. Vol. 6. Melville, N.Y.: Belwin Mills Publishing Corp., n.d. pp. 199–207. **1639:** No. 191—*Piano Concerto No. 1 in C minor, Op. 35*, by Dmitri Shostakovich. Copyright © 1934 (Renewed) by G. Schirmer, Inc. (ASCAP). International Copyright Secured. All Rights Reserved. Reprinted by Permission.

Chapter 75. 1660: No. 192—Ives, Charles. *114 Songs*. Redding Conn.: C. E. Ives, 1922. pp. 19–22. **1665:** No. 193—Ives, Charles. *114 Songs*. Redding Conn.: C. E. Ives, 1922. pp. 19–22. **1670:** No. 194—*The Unanswered Question*. New York: Southern Music Publishing Co., 1953. **1676:** No. 195—*String Quartet 1931*. Bryn Mawr, PA: Merion Music, Inc (Theodore Presser), 1941. pp. 12–15.

Chapter 76. 1681: No. 196—Copland, Aaron. *Piano Variations*. © Copyright 1932 by The Aaron Copland Fund for Music, Inc. Copyright Renewed. Boosey & Hawkes, Inc., Sole Publisher & Licensee. Reprinted by permission of Boosey & Hawkes, Inc. **1695:** No. 197—Copland, Aaron. *Appalachian Spring*. © Copyright 1945 by The Aaron Copland Fund for Music, Inc. Copyright Renewed. Boosey & Hawkes, Inc., Sole Publisher & Licensee. Reprinted by permission of Boosey & Hawkes, Inc. **1706:** No. 198—"Sea-Snatch" from *Hermit Songs*. Copyright © 1954 (Renewed) by G. Schirmer, Inc. (ASCAP). International Copyright Secured. All Rights Reserved. Reprinted by Permission.

Chapter 77. 1709: No. 199—Gershwin, George. *The Man I Love*. New York: Harms, 1924. **1714:** No. 200—Rodgers, Richard. *Oklahoma!* Vocal score ed. by Albert Sirmay. New York: Williamson Music, n.d. pp. 52–56 (59). 1720: No. 201—Bernstein, Leonard. *West Side Story*. © Copyright 1956, 1957, 1958, 1959 by Amberson Holdings LLC and Stephen Sondheim. Copyright Renewed. Leonard Bernstein Music Publishing Company LLC, Publisher. Boosey & Hawkes, Inc., Sole Agent. Reprinted by permission.

Chapter 78. 1734: No. 202—Britten, Benjamin. *War Requiem*. © Copyright 1961 by Boosey & Hawkes Music Publishers Ltd. Copyright Renewed. Reprinted by permission of Boosey & Hawkes, Inc. **1740:** No. 203—Penderecki, Krzysztof. *Threnody: To the Victims of Hiroshima for 52 strings*. New York: Kalmus; Deshon Music, Inc. & PWM Editions, 1961.

Chapter 79. 1758: No. 204—Composition No. 1 from *Three Compositions for Piano by Milton Babbitt*. Hillsdale, New York: Boelke-Bomart, 1957. **1764:** No. 205—*Agon*. New York: Boosey & Hawkes, 1957. © Copyright 1957 by Hawkes & Son (London) Ltd. Copyright Renewed. Reprinted by permission of Boosey & Hawkes, Inc.. **1769:** No. 206—Boulez, Pierre. *Le marteau sans maître*. London: Universal Edition, 1956. pp. 17–18.

Chapter 80. 1772: No. 207—Cage, John. *Music of Changes. Part I*. New York: Henmar Press Inc., 1961. **1782:** No. 208—Olivier Messiaen, *Mode de valeurs et d'intensités* (Paris: Durand & Cie, 1949). © 1949 by Editions DURAND.

Chapter 82. 1794: No. 209—Berio, Luciano. *Circles*. London: Universal Edition, 1961. pp. 2–8. Reprinted with permission. **1800:** No. 210—*Ancient Voices of Children*. New York: C. F. Peters, 1970. p. 4. **1802:** No. 211—*String Quartet No. 2*, by Elliot Carter. Copyright © 1961 (Renewed) by Associated Music Publishers, Inc. (BMI). International Copyright Secured. All Rights Reserved. Reprinted by Permission. **1816:** No. 212—Reich, Steve. *Clapping Music for Two Performers*. London: Universal Edition, 1980.

Chapter 83. 1817: No. 213—Ligeti, György. *Hungarian Rock*. Mainz: Schott, 1979. **1820:** No. 214—Adams, John. *Nixon in China*. Libretto by Alice Goodman. Piano reduction by John McGinn. New York: Hendon Music: Boosey & Hawkes, 1999. © Copyright 1987 by Hendon Music, Inc., a Boosey & Hawkes company. Reprinted by permission. **1840:** No. 215—*Fanfare for the Uncommon Woman, No. 1*, by Joan Tower. Copyright © 1987 (Renewed) by Associated Music Publishers, Inc. (BMI). International Copyright Secured. All Rights Reserved. Reprinted by Permission. **1851:** No. 216—Pärt, Arvo. *Berliner Messe*. London: Universal Edition, 1990. pp. 27–42.

ANTHOLOGY FOR

Music in Western Civilization

VOLUME II:
THE ENLIGHTENMENT TO THE PRESENT

Part V

THE ENLIGHTENMENT AND THE CLASSICAL ERA

Chapter 41

Music in the Age of Enlightenment
Opera

118

Johann Adolf Hasse
Cleofide (1731)
Aria, "Digli ch'io son fedele"

Johann Adolf Hasse (1699–1783) enjoyed a long and spectacularly successful career. He began his professional life as an opera singer when only nineteen, and two years later his first opera was performed. Like Handel before him, Hasse traveled to Italy, where he studied with Alessandro Scarlatti and Nicola Porpora, a famous voice teacher who later befriended the young and penurious Joseph Haydn. It was not long before Hasse established an enviable reputation and traveled the continent composing and producing his operas. A prolific composer, he created nearly sixty operas, almost all of them of the *opera seria* type, as well as a substantial amount of sacred and instrumental music. *Cleofide* was composed expressly for the Saxon court in Dresden; in fact, it appears that Hasse agreed to certain stipulations that prohibited the performance of this opera in any other venue. Five years later he "rewrote" the opera and gave it a new title: *Alessandro nell' Indie* (*Alexander the Great in India*). This latter opera was performed in Ferrara under the direction of Antonio Vivaldi.

The aria "Digli ch'io son fedele" (Act II, Scene 9) illustrates the typical structure of a Metastasian aria: four lines for the **A** section and five for the **B**. The two stanzas are linked by the rhyming of the final word for each section ("ancor" and "cor"). In another typical feature, the **B** section has a contrasting tone ("weeping" instead of "treasure") that allows the composer to move to a minor key. Hasse expressly wrote this aria for his wife, Faustina Bordoni, who during her younger years was notorious for an exhibition of pugilistic prowess: She and a rival soprano once interrupted a performance by coming to blows on stage. However, she was most famous for her remarkable vocal agility. Audiences of the day expected singers to ornament arias. One observer remarked that Faustina "always sang the first part of an aria exactly as the composer had written it but at the *da capo* repeat introduced all kinds of *doublements* and *manière* without taking the smallest liberties with the rhythm of the accompaniment." The score gives Hasse's original as well as a slightly ornamented version attributed to Bordoni herself, and a far more florid one composed later by King Frederick the Great. On the recording, soprano Emma Kirkby sings the repeat of section **A** with a vocal ornamentation similar but not identical to that of the Prussian king.

Johann Adolf Hasse
Cleofide (1731)
Aria, "Digli ch'io son fedele"
CD 6/16

tr
5
p
(p)
f
(f)
7 5
9 4
8 3
6
6 4
5 3

10
Di - gli ch'io son fe - -
Di - gli ch'io son fe - -
Di - gli ch'io son__ fe - -

de - le, di-gli ch'èil mio te - so-ro, di-gli ch'èil mio te -
de - le, di-gli ch'èil mio te - so-ro, di-gli ch'èil mio te -
de - le, di-gli ch'èil mio te - so - ro, di-gli ch'èil mio te -
so-ro che m'a - - - - - - mi, che
so-ro che m'a - - - - - - mi, che
so - ro che m'a - - - - - - mi, che

15
m'a - mi, ch'io l'a - - do - ro, che non dis - pe - ri an -
m'a - mi, ch'io l'a - - do - ro, che non dis - pe - ri an -
m'a - mi, ch'io l'a - - do - ro, che non dis - pe-ri an -
cor, che non dis-pe - - - - - - - - - - - ri, che
cor, che non dis-pe - - - - - - - - - - - ri, che
cor, che non dis-pe - - - - - - - - - - - ri, che

non dis-pe - ri ancor, che non dis-pe - ri an-cor.
non dis-pe - ri ancor, che non dis-pe - ri an-cor.
non dis - pe-ri an - cor, che non dis - pe - ri an-cor.
20
Di - gli ch'io son fe -
Di - gli ch'io son fe -
Di - gli ch'io son fe -

de - le, di - gli ch'è il mio te - so - ro, che m'a - mi, ch'io l'a -
de - le, di - gli ch'è il mio te - so - ro, che m'a - mi, ch'io l'a -
de - le, di - gli ch'è il mio te - so - ro, che m'a - mi ch'io l'a -
7 6 4 3♯ 7 6 5
do - ro, che m'a -
do - ro, che m'a -
do - ro, che m'a -
4 3♯ 6 4 7 5 6 4

- - mi, che m'a - mi, ch'io l'a - do - ro, ch'io l'a - do - ro, che
- mi, che m'a - mi, ch'io l'a - do - ro, ch'io l'a - do - ro, che
- - mi, che m'a - mi, ch'io l'a - do - ro, ch'io l'a - do - ro, che
non dis - pe - ri an - cor, di - gli ch'è il mio te -
non dis - pe - ri an - cor, di - gli ch'è il mio te -
non dis - pe - ri an - cor, di - gli ch'è il mio te -

ten.
30
so - ro, di-gli ch'io son fe - de - le, che m'a - mi, ch'io l'a - do - ro, che non dis -
so - ro, di-gli ch'io son fe - de - le, che m'a - mi, ch'io l'a - do - ro, che non dis -
so - ro, di-gli ch'io son fe - de - le, che m'a - mi, ch'io l'a - do - ro, che non dis -
pe - ri, che non dis - pe - ri an -
pe - ri, che non dis - pe - ri an -
pe - ri, che non dis-pe-ri an -

(p)
tr
f
Cadenza
cor, che non dis-pe
ri an-cor.
35
p
5♮
6 5

(Fine)
(Fine)
(Fine)
(Fine)
(Fine)
un poco lento
dolce
dolce
dolce
ten.
ten.
Di - gli ch'è la___ mia stel - la, spe - ro pla - car col pian - to,
Di - gli ch'è la___ mia stel - la, spe - ro pla - car___ col pian - to,
Di - gli ch'è la___ mia stel - la, spe - ro pla - car col pian - to,
dolce

50
spe - ro pla - car col pian - to, che lo con - so - li in tan - to
spe - ro___ pla - car col pian - to, che lo con - so - li in tan - to
spe - ro pla - car col pian - to, che lo con - so - li in tan - to
55
l'i - ma - gi - ne___ di___ quel - la che vi - ve nel___ suo cor,
l'i - ma - gi - ne___ di___ quel - la che vi - ve nel___ suo cor,
l'i - ma - gi - ne___ di___ quel - la che vi - ve nel___ suo cor,

60
65
p
p
p
di - gli che lo con - so - li in tan - to l'i - ma - gi - ne di quel - la
di - gli che lo con - so - li in tan - to l'i - ma - gi - ne di quel - la
di - gli che lo con - so - li in tan - to l'i - ma - gi - ne di quel - la
7
5 6 6 6♮ 6 6
70
che vi - ve nel suo cor, che vi - ve nel suo cor.
che vi - ve nel suo cor, che vi - ve nel suo cor.
che vi - ve nel suo cor, che vi - ve nel suo cor.
4 3♯

Dal Segno al Fine

Digli ch'io son fedele
Digli ch'è il mio tesoro:
Che m'ami, ch'io l'adoro,
Che non disperi ancor.

Digli che la mia stella
Spero placar col pianto;
Che lo consoli intanto
L'immagine di quella
Che vive nel suo cor.

Tell him that I am faithful,
Tell him that he is my treasure,
That he can love me, and that I adore him,
That he should not yet despair.

Tell him that I hope
To placate my star with weeping,
That meanwhile the image
Of her who lives in his heart
May console him.

—Pietro Metastasio

119

John Gay

The Beggar's Opera (1728)
Dialogue and Songs from Act I
a. Air XI, "A Fox may steal your hens"
b. Dialogue
c. Air XII, "Oh, ponder well!"
d. Air XIII, "The Turtle thus with plaintive crying"

The decades that followed the death of Henry Purcell in 1695 were a low point in the history of the London theater. The vigorous and rambunctious dramas of the Restoration were followed by plays that wallowed in sentimental twaddle. Aside from occasional examples, such as Purcell's *Dido and Aeneas*, there was no tradition of English opera, so the Italian operas of Handel and others were able to take root. The popularity of this transplanted tradition, replete with its Italian language and castrati, was the object of a satiric essay by Joseph Addison in the daily periodical *The Spectator*. In the 21 March 1711, edition he wrote:

> . . . there is no Question but our great Grand-children will be very curious to know the Reason why their Forefathers used to sit together like an Audience of Foreigners in their own Country to hear whole Plays acted before them in a Tongue which they did not understand. . . . I cannot forbear thinking how naturally an Historian who writes Two or Three hundred Years hence, and does not know the Taste of his wise Fore-fathers, will make the following Reflection, *In the Beginning of the Eighteenth Century the* Italian *Tongue was so well understood in* England, *that Opera's were acted on the publick Stage in that Language*. In short, our *English* Musick is quite rooted out, and nothing yet planted in its stead.

Yet Italian opera was a paper tiger, and on 29 January 1728 this beast was seriously challenged by a native upstart. That evening, Gay's ballad opera began its unprecedented career, with sixty-two performances in its first season alone, and it continued to be performed throughout the English-speaking world every year for the remainder of the century. It deliciously combined humor with social, political, and musical satire. Polly's parents, Mr. and Mrs. Peachum—a play on the word "to peach," or turn informant—are jealous to guard Polly's pecuniary position and their own safety. For their daughter to dally with men would be both laudable and profitable, but for her to marry would be a financial disaster. The character of Macheath, who tries to balance a wife and mistress, was a thinly disguised lampoon of the domestic arrangements of the prime minister, Robert Walpole, as was the amoral greed and self-interest of Mr. Peachum. The musical satire ranges from a parody of Handel's music to broad swipes at the genre of opera in general. At the end of the story, two narrators offer this brief exchange when it appears that the hero Macheath is about to be hanged:

> **Player:** The catastrophe is manifestly wrong, for an Opera must end happily.
>
> **Beggar:** Your objection, Sir, is very just; and is easily remov'd. For you must allow, that in this kind of Drama, 'tis no matter how absurdly things are brought about—So—you rabble there—run and cry a Reprieve—let the prisoner be brought back to his wives in triumph.

Nearly three hundred years after its premiere, Gay's biting humor remains fresh, and his *Beggar's Opera* is still performed in various guises throughout the world.

Scene 9

Mr. Peachum

Dear wife, be a little pacified. Don't let your passion run away with your senses. Polly, I grant you, hath done a rash thing.

Mrs. Peachum

If she had had only an intrigue with the fellow, why the very best families have excus'd and huddled up a frailty of that sort. 'Tis marriage, husband, that makes it a blemish.

Mr. Peachum

But money, wife, is the true fuller's earth for reputations, there is not a spot or a stain but what it can take out. A rich rogue now-a-days is fit company for any gentleman; and the world, my dear, hath not such a contempt for roguery as you imagine. I tell you, wife, I can make this match turn to our advantage.

Mrs. Peachum

I am very sensible, husband, that Captain Macheath is worth money, but I am in doubt whether he hath not two or three wives already, and then if he should [die] in a [Court] Session or two, Polly's dower would come into dispute.

Mr. Peachum

That, indeed, is a point which ought to be consider'd.

John Gay

The Beggar's Opera (1728)

a. Air XI, "A Fox may steal your hens"

CD 6/17

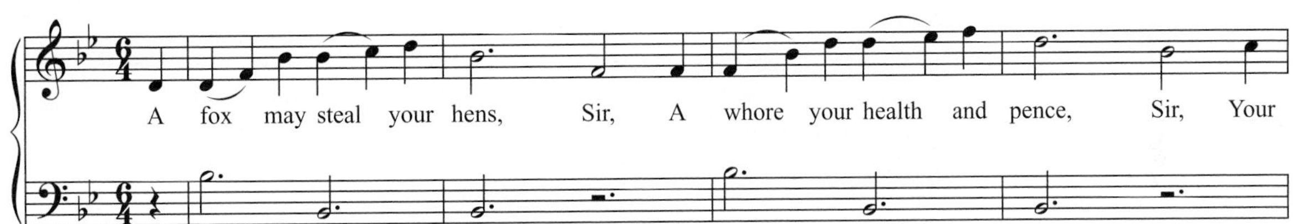

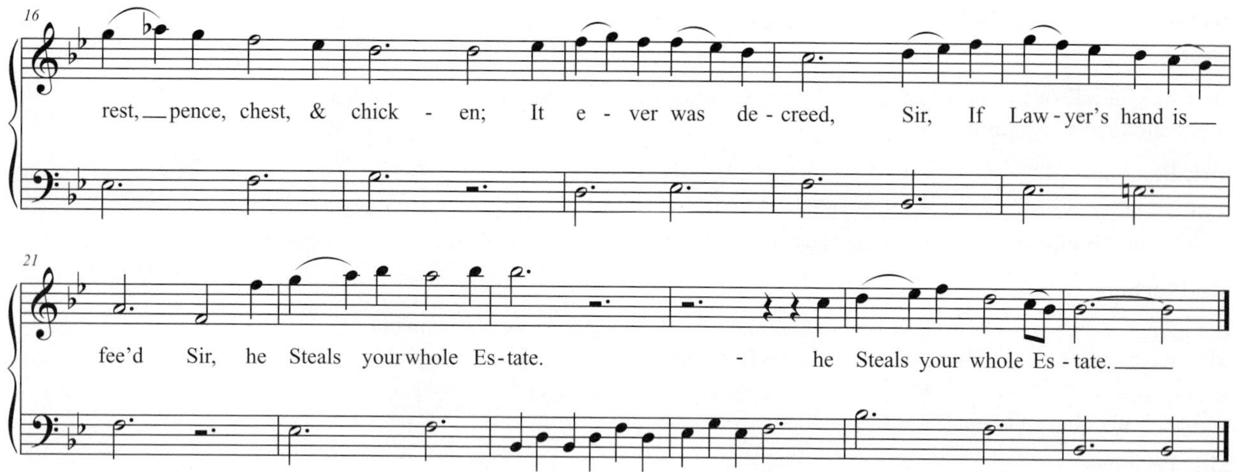

Mr. Peachum

The Lawyers are bitter enemies to those in our way. They don't care that any body should get a clandestine livelihood but themselves.

John Gay
The Beggar's Opera (1728)
b. Dialogue
CD 6/18

Scene 10

Polly

'Twas only Nimming Ned [another member of the gang]. He brought in a damask window-curtain, a hoop-petticoat, a pair of silver candlesticks, a perriwig, and one silk stocking, from the fire that happen'd last night.

Mr. Peachum

There is not a fellow that is cleverer in his way, and saves more goods out of the fire than Ned. But now, Polly, to your affair; for matters must not be left as they are. You are married then, it seems?

Polly

Yes, Sir.

Mr. Peachum

And how do you propose to live, child?

Polly

Like other women, Sir, upon the industry of my husband.

Mrs. Peachum

What, is the wench turn'd fool? A highway-man's wife, like a soldier's, hath as little of his pay, as of his company.

Mr. Peachum

And had not you the common views of a gentlewoman in your marriage, Polly?

Polly

I don't know what you mean, Sir.

Mr. Peachum

Of a [will], and of being a widow.

Polly

But I love him, Sir: how then could I have thoughts of parting with him?

Mr. Peachum

Parting with him! Why that is the whole scheme and intention of all Marriage-articles. The comfortable estate of widowhood, is the only hope that keeps up a wife's spirits. Where is the woman who would scruple to be a wife, if she had it in her power to be a widow whenever she pleas'd? If you have any views of this sort, Polly, I shall think the match not so very unreasonable.

Polly

How I dread to hear your advice! Yet I must beg you to explain yourself.

Mr. Peachum

Secure what he hath got, have him peach'd the next Sessions, and then at once you are made a rich widow.

Polly

What, murder the man I love! The blood runs cold at my heart with the very thought of it.

Mr. Peachum

Fye, Polly! what hath murder to do in the affair? Since the thing sooner or later must happen, I dare say, the Captain himself would like that we should get the reward for his death sooner than a stranger. Why, Polly, the Captain knows, that as 'tis his employment to rob, so 'tis ours to take Robbers; every man in his business. So that there is no malice in the case.

Mrs. Peachum

Ay, husband, now you have nick'd the matter. To have him peach'd is the only thing could ever make me forgive her.

John Gay
The Beggar's Opera **(1728)**
c. Air XII, "Oh, ponder well!"
CD 6/19

Oh, pon - der well! be not se - vere; So save a wretch - ed

4
wife! For on the rope that hangs my Dear, de - pends poor Pol - ly's life

Mrs. Peachum

But your duty to your parents, hussy, obliges you to hang him. What would many a wife give for such an opportunity!

Polly

What is a [will], what is widowhood to me? I know my heart. I cannot survive him.

John Gay

The Beggar's Opera (1728)

d. Air XIII, "The Turtle thus with plaintive crying"

CD 6/20

The tur - tle thus with Plain - tive cry - ing her lov - er____ dy - ing, The tur - tle

8
thus with Plain - tive cry - ing, La - ments her Dove. Down she drops____ quite

15
spent____ with Sigh - ing, Pair'd in death, as____ pair'd in Love.

Polly

Thus, Sir, it will happen to your poor Polly.

Mrs. Peachum

What, is the fool in love in earnest then? I hate thee for being particular: Why, wench, thou art a shame to thy very Sex.

Polly

But hear me, mother.—If you ever lov'd—

Mrs. Peachum

Those cursed Play-books she reads have been her ruin. One word more, hussy, and I shall knock your brains out, if you have any.

Mr. Peachum

Keep out of the way, Polly, for fear of mischief, and consider of what is propos'd to you.

Mrs. Peachum

Away, hussy. Hang your husband, and be dutiful.

120

Giovanni Battista Pergolesi

La serva padrona (1733)
a. Recitative, "Io non so chi mi tien!"
b. Duet, "Lo conosco a quegl'occhietti"

This intermezzo was first performed on 5 September 1733 in the Neapolitan theater of San Bartolomeo, the same opera house where many of Alessandro Scarlatti's operas had received their first public performance. Intended as a light entertainment to be performed between the acts of Pergolesi's tragic *opera seria*, *Il prigioniero superbo* (*The Proud Prisoner*), the intermezzo overshadowed the main offering (much like commercials aired during the Super Bowl) and took on a life of its own, being performed throughout Europe.

La serva padrona consists of two acts. The first opens with Uberto, an old curmudgeon of an aristocrat, complaining that he can no longer find good help. His maid, Serpina, won't bring him his hot chocolate, and she refuses to allow him to leave the house, even going so far as to lock the door on her "master." Tormenting Uberto to the point where he determines to get a wife, who will put this obstinate servant in her place, the wily maid then boldly claims that she shall become the wife of her master! The duet "Lo conosco a quegl'occhietti" concludes the first act with humorous contrasts between Serpina's affirmative "si, si, si" and Uberto's equally adamant "no, no, no." In the second scene of the intermezzo, originally performed after another act of the tragedy, Serpina arouses the old man simultaneously to pity and jealousy by insisting that she will marry a soldier (another servant in disguise), even though he is known to have a vicious temper. Now that she is spoken for, Uberto begins to wax sentimental—until Serpina insists that he pay a handsome dowry to the "Captain." She lets it be known that if Uberto refuses, the "Captain" will require that Uberto marry Serpina or face his wrath. The old man ultimately concludes that if he has to pay the money, he might as well get the girl too. The intermezzo concludes with another duet, in which the unlikely couple sing of the happiness they will enjoy together.

Giovanni Battista Pergolesi
La serva padrona (1733)
a. Recitative, "Io non so chi mi tien!"
CD 6/21

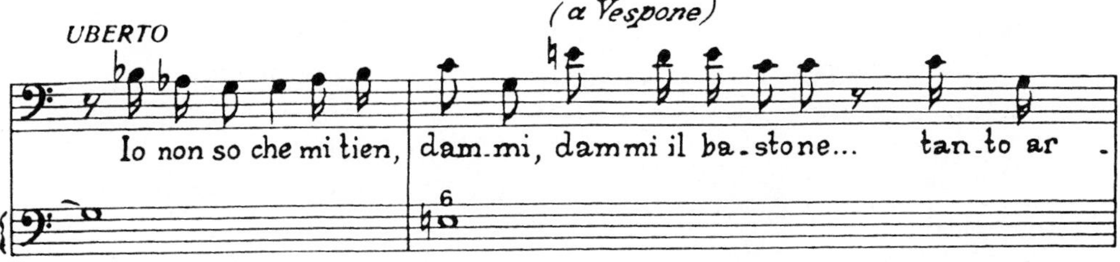

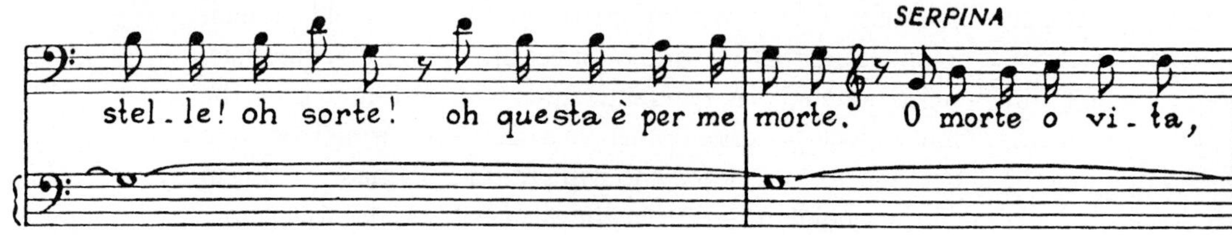

Recitative

Uberto	
Io non so chi mi tien!	I don't know what is keeping me!
Dammi, dammi il bastone!	(to Vespone) Give me the walking stick!
Tanto ardir!	Such impudence!
Serpina	
Oh! voi far e dir potrete	Ah, Sir! you can do and say
Che null' altra che me sposar dovrete.	nothing but that you must marry me.
Uberto	
Vattene, figlia mia.	Get lost, my girl.
Serpina	
Voleste dir: mia sposa.	You meant to say, my bride.
Uberto	
O stelle! o sorte!	My stars! O fate!
O questa è per me morte.	O she is going to be the death of me.
Serpina	
O morte o vita,	Death or life,
così esser dè:	this [marriage] is to be:
L'ho fisso già in pensiero.	I have made up my mind.
Uberto	
Questo è un altro diavolo più nero.	That thought is an even blacker devil.

Giovanni Battista Pergolesi
La serva padrona (1733)
b. Duet, "Lo conosco a quegl'occhietti"
CD 6/22

Allegro

SERPINA
UBERTO
Violini I.
II.
Viole Violoncelli Contrabbassi
Cembalo
f
stacc.
f stacc. UNITI

SERP.
UBER.
Vni I.
II.
Vle Vc. Cb.
Cmb.

7
SERP.
Lo cono-sco, lo co- nosco a quegli occhietti, a quegli oc-
UBER.
I.
Vni
II.
p
Vle
Vc.
Cb.
p
Cmb.
p
SERP.
-chiet-ti fur-bi, la-dri, la-dri, ma-li-gnet - ti, che se
UBER.
I.
Vni
II.
Vle
Vc.
Cb.
Cmb.

13
SERP.
ben voi di-te no, no, no; pur m'ac-cen-na-no di sì, sì,
UBER.
I.
Vni
II.
Vle
Vc.
Cb.
Cmb.
SERP.
sì, sì, sì; pur m'ac-cen-na-no di sì.
UBER.
Si-gno-ri-na, signori-na, v'ingan-
I.
Vni
II.
Vle
Vc.
Cb.
Cmb.

19
SERP.
UBER.
-na - te, v'inganna - te; troppo, troppo, troppo, troppoinalto voi vo -
I.
Vni
II.
Vle
Vc.
Cb.
Cmb.
SERP.
UBER.
-la - - te: glioechied io vi di - con no, no, no, ed è un
I.
Vni
II.
Vle
Vc.
Cb.
Cmb.

25
SERP.
UBER.
so-gno questo qui sì, sì, sì, sì, ed è un so-gno questo qui.
I.
Vni
II.
Vle
Vc.
Cb.
Cmb.
SERP.
Ma per-chè? ma per-chè? Non son i - o bella, gra - zi-o-sa, e
UBER.
I.
Vni
II.
pp
Vle
Vc.
Cb.
Cmb.

32
SERP.
spi - ri - to-sa? Su mi-ra - te: leg - gia - dri - a, leg - gia - dri-a, ve'che brio, che
UBER.
I.
Vni
II.
Vle
Vc.
Cb.
cresc.
Cmb.
SERP.
bri-o, che ma - e - stà! che ma - e - stà!
UBER.
I.
Vni
II.
Vle
Vc.
Cb.
f
Cmb.

40
SERP.
(Ei mi
UBER.
(Ah! co-stei mi va ten-tan-do quan-to va che me la fa, che me la fa.)
I.
Vni
II.
Vle
Vc.
Cb.
Cmb.
SERP.
par che va ca-lan-do, va ca-lan-do,) sì, si-gno-re.
UBER.
Eh! van-ne
I.
Vni
II.
Vle
Vc.
Cb.
Cmb.

47
SERP.
Ri - sol - ve - te.
Son per voi gli af-fet-ti
UBER.
vi - a.
Eh! mat-ta se - i.
I.
Vni
II.
Vle
Vc.
Cb.
Cmb.
SERP.
mie - i, e do-vre-te sposar me do-vre-te, do - vre-te, do-vre-te
UBER.
Oh che im - broglio, ch'im-broglio, ch'imbroglio
I.
Vni
II.
Vle
Vc.
Cb.
Cmb.

53
SERP.
spo - sar me
spo - sar me.
UBER.
e-gl'è per me
e-gl'è per me.
I.
Vni
II.
Vle
Vc.
Cb.
Cmb.
SERP.
Lo co-nosco sì a que -
UBER.
I.
Vni
II.
Vle
Vc.
Cb.
Cmb.

59
SERP.
-gliocchietti fur - bi, la-dri, ma - li-gnet-ti.
UBER.
Signo-rina, signorina;
I.
Vni
II.
Vle
Vc.
Cb.
Cmb.
SERP.
No, no, no, no, che se ben, che se ben che se ben mi di-te
UBER.
v'in-gan-na - te.
I.
Vni
II.
Vle
Vc.
Cb.
Cmb.

67
SERP.
no, pur m'accenna-no di sì.
Ma perchè, ma perchè?
UBER.
V'in-gan - na - te.
I.
Vni
II.
Vle
Vc.
Cb.
Cmb.
SERP.
Io — son bel-la, gra - zi-o-sa, spi - ri-to-sa.
UBER.
(Ah! co - stei mi
I.
Vni
II.
Vle
Vc.
Cb.
Cmb.

75
SERP.
(Va ca - lando, sì, sì.) Ve'che brio, che bri-o, che ma - e -
UBER.
va ten-tando.)
I.
Vni
II.
Vle
Vc.
Cb.
Cmb.
SERP.
-stà! che ma - e - stà!
UBER.
Quanto va, quanto va, quanto va che me la
I.
Vni
II.
Vle
Vc.
Cb.
Cmb.

83
SERP.
UBER.
Via, si-gno-re,
fa, la-ral-là la-ral - là la-ral-là la-ral - là. Eh! van-ne
I.
Vni
II.
Vle
Vc.
Cb.
Cmb.
sf
ri-sol-ve-te. Son per voi gl'af - fet-ti
vi - a. Eh! mat-ta se - i. Si-gno - ri-na, v'ingan -
p

89
SERP.
mie-i, e do-vre-te sì
sì...
e do-vre-te sposar-
UBER.
-na-te.
Si-gno-ri-na, no
no. (Oh! che imbroglio egli è per
I.
Vni
coi I. Violini
II.
Vle
Vc.
Cb.
Cmb.
SERP.
me.
Io son
UBER.
me! quanto va, quanto va, quanto va che me la fa.)
I.
Vni
II.
Vle
Vc.
Cb.
Cmb.

95
SERP.
bel-la, gra-zi - o-sa, spi-ri - to-sa.
Ve' che brio, ve' che
UBER.
La-rallà la-ral - là.
I.
Vni
II.
Vle
Vc.
Cb.
Cmb.
SERP.
bri-o!
(Va ca-lando sì, sì,) son per voi, son per
UBER.
Si - gnori - na, si - gnori - na...
si-gnori . si-gno
I.
Vni
II.
Vle
Vc.
Cb.
Cmb.

103
SERP.
voi, son per voi gl'affetti mie-i e dovre-te sì, sì, sì, sì,
UBER.
-ri... signori-na, matta siete, signori-na, no no no
I.
Vni
II.
Vle
Vc.
Cb.
Cmb.
SERP.
sì, sì, do-vre-te do-vre-te do-vre-te spo-sar
UBER.
no... Oh! che im-broglio, ch'imbroglio, ch'im-broglio e-gli è per
I.
Vni
II.
Vle
Vc.
Cb.
Cmb.
cresc.

110
SERP.
me, spo - sar me.
UBER.
me, e-gli è per me.
I.
Vni
II.
Vle
Vc.
Cb.
Cmb.
SERP.
UBER.
I.
Vni
II.
Vle
Vc.
Cb.
Cmb.

Duet

Serpina	
Lo conosco a quegl'occhietti Furbi, ladri, malignetti, Che seben voi dite no, Pur m'accennano di si.	I know by your little eyes (winks?)— sly, roguish, malicious— that even though you say no, they show signs to me of yes.
Uberto	
Signorina, v'ingannate. Troppo in alto voi volate, Gl'occhi ed io vi dicon no, Ed un sogno è questo si.	Young lady, you are mistaken. You fly much too high; these eyes and I say no, and your "yes" is a dream.
Serpina	
Ma perchè? Non sono io bella, Graziosa e spiritosa? Su, mirate, leggiadria, Vè che brio, che maestrà.	But why? Am I not beautiful, charming, and lively? Look at my elegance, my spirit, my presence.
Uberto	
(Ah! costei Mi va tentando Quanto da che me la fa.)	(Ah, the woman is tempting me; she can try as much as she likes.)
Serpina	
(Ei mi par Che va calando.) Risolvete! Eh! vanne via. Risolvete. Eh! matta sei. Son per voi gl'affetti miei E dovrete sposarme. O ch'imbroglio egl' è per me!	(It appears his resistance to me is dropping.) Yes, my Lord. Make up your mind! What! Go away. Make up your mind. What! you are crazy. My affections are for you and you should marry me. Oh what a fine mess this is!

121

Jean-Jacques Rousseau
Le Devin du village (1752)
Duet, "À jamais Colin"

Like *La serva padrona*, Rousseau's *intermède* (the French translation of the Italian intermezzo) was given between the acts of a traditional *tragédie lyrique*. Louis XV, who was in the audience, was so captivated by the opening air that he sang it continuously the next day. It was reported that the royal intonation was exceedingly deficient. Like Pergolesi's intermezzo, *Le Devin du village* was spectacularly successful and the composer was extraordinarily proud of his achievement. It continued to be performed until 1829, when some irreverent soul—Berlioz protested his innocence of the action, but in a manner intimating that he was the perpetrator—tossed a periwig (an oversized, old-fashioned powdered wig) on the stage during a performance, an act of satire that drove the work from the repertoire.

In his *Lettre sur la musique* (1753), and his *Dictionnaire de musique* (1768), as well as his articles on music for the French *Encyclopédie*, Jean-Jacques Rousseau voiced many distinctive, indeed unique, opinions about music. According to Rousseau's theories, all music sprang from natural melody (not harmony as Rameau had declared). He believed that in primitive times humans had only a natural musical language, a kind of inarticulate chant uniting language and melody. According to his theory, language and melody gradually diverged, and harmony eventually evolved from melody. It was essential that melody should maintain a direct and spontaneous quality, because it is the principal means of musical expression. Consequently, melodious airs should provide the basic material of opera. Within the airs, individual words should not be highlighted at the expense of the overall feeling of the text. So, too, with duets—and here Rousseau differed with the Italians. In Italian *opera buffa*, duets expressing different points of view (with different music) were becoming common (see "Lo conosco" by Pergolesi). For Rousseau, however, a duet should develop a single, unified effect. This is clearly Rousseau's aim in the duet "À jamais Colin" from his comic opera *Le Devin du village*. A young shepherd, Colin, has been attracted by the fancy clothes of a woman in town and has been unfaithful to his true love, the shepherdess Colette. Distraught, Colette seeks the help of the village Soothsayer. Instead of conjuring up some magic incantation, he suggests she prey upon Colin's jealousy and pretend to have a lover herself. Her ruse is successful, Colin sees the folly of his ways, and the two pledge their love and fidelity in the duet "À jamais Colin."

Jean-Jacques Rousseau
Le Devin du village (1752)
Duet, "À jamais Colin"
CD 6/0

6
Ob. 1, 2
Bn.
Vn. 1
Vn. 2
Va.
B.
mf
13
20
f

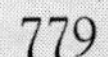

27

Ob. 1, 2 — mp

Bn. — mp

Vn. 1

Vn. 2

Va. — mp

COLIN

A ja- mais Co- lin t'en- ga- ge son coeur et sa foi, son coeur et __ sa __

B. — mp

34

Ob. 1, 2 — mf

Bn. — mf

Vn. 1 — mf

Vn. 2 — mf

Va. — mf

COLETTE — mf

A ja- mais Co- lin je t'en- ga- ge mon coeur et ma foi, mon

(COLIN) — mf

foi, ______ son coeur et sa foi, ______ son coeur et sa foi.

B. — mf

41
Reprise
coeur et ma foi. Qu'un doux ma- ri-
Qu'un doux ma- ri- a- ge m'u- nisse a- vec toi,
48
mp
-a- ge, qu'un doux ma- ri- a- ge m'u- nisse a- vec toi, qu'un doux ma- ri- a- ge m'u-
qu'un doux ma- ri- a- ge m'u- nisse a- vec toi, qu'un doux ma- ri- a- ge m'u-

55
mp
mf
mf
mp
-nisse a- vec toi, m'u- nisse a- vec toi,
-nisse a- vec toi, m'u- nisse a- vec toi,
62
m'u- nisse a- vec toi. A ja- mais Co- lin je t'en-
m'u- nisse a- vec toi.

69
-ga- ge mon coeur et ma foi, mon coeur et ma foi,
A ja- mais Co- lin t'en-
5 6
77
mp
p
à demi voix
mon coeur et ma foi. Qu'un doux ma- ri- a- ge, m'u- nisse a- vec toi. Qu'un
à plein voix
mf
-ga- ge, son coeur et sa foi, son coeur, son coeur et sa foi. Qu'un
7 7 4 ♯ ♮ 7 4 3

84
doux ma- ri- a- ge m'u- nisse a- vec toi. A ja-
doux ma- ri- a- ge m'u- nisse a- vec toi. A ja- mais Co- lin t'en-
91
-mais Co- lin je t'en- ga- ge mon coeur et ma foi. Qu'un doux ma- ri- a- ge m'u-
-ga- ge son coeur, son coeur et sa foi. Qu'un doux ma- ri- a- ge m'u-

98
mf
mp
-nisse a- vec toi. Qu'un doux ma- ri- a- ge m'u- nisse a- vec toi,
-nisse a- vec toi. Qu'un doux ma- ri- a- ge m'u- nisse a- vec toi,
105
p
f
m'u- nisse a- vec toi, m'u- nisse a- vec toi.
m'u- nisse a- vec toi, m'u- nisse a- vec toi.
Fin

Colin

À jamais Colin t'engage Son Coeur et sa foi.	For always Colin gives you His heart and his faith.

Colette

À jamais Colin je t'engage Mon Coeur et ma foi.	For always, Colin, I give you My heart and my faith.

Together

Qu'un doux mariage M'unisse avec toi.	Since a sweet marriage Unites me with you.

122

Christoph Willibald Gluck

Orfeo ed Euridice (1762)
a. Aria, "Deh placatevi"
b. Chorus, "Misero giovane"
c. Obbligato recitative, "Ahimè! Dove trascorsi?"
d. Aria, "Che farò senza Euridice"

Gluck composed his *Orfeo ed Euridice* to an Italian libretto for a German-speaking Viennese audience in 1762. Continuing the tradition of Baroque *opera seria,* he assigned the role of the male lead, Orfeo, to a castrato who sang in the alto range. When Gluck took the opera to Parma in 1769, however, he rewrote the part for a soprano castrato. Five years later, when he brought it to Paris, Gluck transposed the part yet again, now downward for high tenor voice—the castrato had almost no place in French opera and was often an object of ridicule. Castrati disappeared from opera in the early nineteenth century, and in 1813 a woman (alto) adopted and performed the original alto castrato part. Today the role of Orfeo is usually performed by a female alto or a male countertenor singing in falsetto voice. This latter voice, heard on the present recording, has the range but not the power of the castrato, a voice that is now virtually extinct.

Act II, Scene I

Orfeo descends into the Underworld to reclaim his beloved Euridice. A demonic host of furies and shades blocks his way, but gradually yields to the power of his song. Much of the force of this aria/chorus is derived from the accompaniment. In fact, Gluck requires two orchestras, one for the furies (violins, cornetts, and trombones) and a second for Orfeo (strings and harp). Note particularly how Gluck has worked the chorus into the action. The chorus engages in a virtual shouting match with the hero and the scene concludes with a dialogue between the protagonists. This greater unity of action is a hallmark of reform opera. In the French tradition of serious opera, choruses and ballets interrupted the flow of the drama; even the name for them, "divertissements," suggests that they were diversions from the drama. As part of his reform, Gluck instructed the dancers to avoid traditional choreography and make their movements coincide with the emotion and drama depicted on stage. In his reform operas, the dramatic forces—recitative, aria, chorus, and ballet—are better integrated into a unified whole.

Orfeo

Deh placatevi con me
Furie! Larve! Ombre sdegnose!

Oh! have mercy on me
You furies, you specters, angry shades!

Chorus

No! No! No!

No! No! No!

Orfeo

Vi renda almen pietose
Il mio barbaro dolor!

At least take pity
On my wrenching grief!

Chorus

Misero giovane,
Che vuoi, che mediti?
Altro non abita
Che lutto e gemito
n queste orribili
Soglie funeste!

Wretched youth,
What do you want?
Here there is nothing
But wailing and lamentation
In these harrowing
Mournful regions!

Orfeo

Mille pene, ombre moleste,
Come voi sopporto anchi'io!
Ho con me l'inferno mio,
Me lo sento in mezzo al cor.

A thousand pains I suffer,
Like you, o angry shades!
An inferno lies within me,
I feel it to the depths of my heart.

Chorus

Ah, quale incognito
Affetto flebile
Dolce a sospendere
Vien l'implacabile
Nostro furor?

Ah, what unknown,
Mournful compassion
Comes tenderly
To suspend
Our implacable fury?

Orfeo

Men tiranne, ah! voi sareste
Al mio pianto, al mio lamento,
Se provaste un sol momento
Cosa sia languir d'amor!

Ah, you would be less callous
To my weeping, to my lament,
If for a single moment you could experience
What it is to languish for love!

Chorus

Ah, quale incognito
Affetto flebile
Dolce a sospendere
Vien l'implacabile
Nostro furor?
Le porte stridano
Su i neri cardini
E il passo lascino
Sicuro e libero
Al vincitor!

Ah, what unknown,
Mournful compassion
Comes tenderly
To suspend
Our implacable fury?
Screech open gate,
On black hinges,
And permit
The victor to pass
Safe and free!

—Raniero de Calzabigi

Christoph Willibald Gluck

Orfeo ed Euridice (1762)

a. Aria, "Deh placatevi"

b. Chorus, "Misero giovane"

CD 7/12

f
f
f I. Orch.
Fu - rie, Lar - ve, Om - bre sde - gno - se! Vi ren - daal - men pie - to - se il mio
Nò! Nò! Nò!
Nò! Nò! Nò!
Nò! Nò! Nò!
f I. Orch.
f I. Orch.
f I. Orch.
f
f
bar - ba - ro do - lor, vi ren - da al - men pie - to - se il mio bar - ba - ro do -

(p)
II. Orch.
(p)
(p)
(p)
I. Orch.
Viol.
Cornetto
e Tromb. Viol.
Cornetto
e Tromb.
(f)
lor!
Deh pla -
Nò!
Nò!
Nò!
Nò!
Nò!
Nò!
Nò!
Nò!
Nò!
(f) I. Orch.
(f)
(f)
f
f
f
ca - te - vi, pla - ca - te - vi con me!
Fu - rie, Lar - ve,
I. Orch.
I. Orch.
f
f
f
f

I. Orch.
Om - bre sde - gno - se! Vi ren - da al - men pie - to - se il mio bar - ba - ro do -
Nò!
Nò!
Nò!
f I. Orch.
I. Orch.
lor! Fu - rie, Lar - ve, om - bre sde - gno - se! Vi ren - da al - men pie -
Nò!
f I. Orch.

to - se il-mio bar - ba - ro do - lor, il mio bar - ba - ro do - lor!
Andante.
Più mosso.
Oboi e Cornetti.
Violini.
Viola.
Soprano.
Alto.
Tenore.
Basso.
Mi - se-ro gio - va-ne, che vuoi, che me - di-ti? Al-tro non a - bi-ta che lut - to e ge - mi-to in que - ste or -
Fagotti, Violoncelli e Bassi.
Cembalo.

ri - bi - li so - glie fu - ne - ste! Che vuo - i, mi - se - ro gio - va - ne? Che?
ri - bi - li so - glie fu - ne - ste! Che vuo - i, mi - se - ro gio - va - ne? Che?
ri - bi - li so - glie fu - ne - ste! Che vuo - i, mi - se - ro gio - va - ne? Che?
ri - bi - li so - glie fu - ne - ste! Che vuo - i, mi - se - ro gio - va - ne? Che?
Al - tro non a - bi - to che lut - to e ge - mi - to, che lut - to e ge - mi - to, che lut - to e
Al - tro non a - bi - to che lut - to e ge - mi - to, che lut - to e ge - mi - to, che lut - to e
Al - tro non a - bi - to che lut - to e ge - mi - to, che lut - to e ge - mi - to, che lut - to e
Al - tro non a - bi - to che lut - to e ge - mi - to, che lut - to e ge - mi - to, che lut - to e

ge - mi - to in que - ste or - ri - bi - li so - glie fu - ne - - - - ste.
ge - mi - to in que - ste or - ri - bi - li so - glie fu - ne - - - - ste.
ge - mi - to in que - ste or - ri - bi - li so - glie fu - ne - - - - ste.
ge - mi - to in que - ste or - ri - bi - li so - glie fu - ne - - - - ste.
II. Orchestra.
Moderato.
Harpa.
(p)
pizz.
Violini.
(p)
pizz.
(p)
pizz.
Viola.
(p)
Orfeo.
Mil - le pe - ne, om - bre mo - le - ste, co - me voi sop -
pizz.
Violoncello e Basso.
(p)

por - to anch'-i - o, sop - por - to anch'-i - o! Ho con me l'in - fer - no mi - o,
me lo sen - to in mez - zo al cor, me lo sen - to, lo sen - to in mez - zo al cor.

a) Con maggior dolcezza.

dol - cea so - spen - de-re vien l'im-pla - ca - bi-le no - stro fu - ror?
dol - cea so - spen - de-re vien l'im-pla - ca - bi-le no - stro fu - ror?
dol - cea so - spen - de-re vien l'im-pla - ca - bi-le no - stro fu - ror?
dol - cea so - spen - de-re vien l'im-pla - ca - bi-le no - stro fu - ror?
II. Orchestra.
Andante.
Harpa.
Violini.
Viola.
Orfeo.
Violoncello e Basso.
(p)
Men ti - ran - ne, ah! voi sa - re - ste al mio pianto, al mio la - men - to. se pro - va - ste un' sol mo - men - to co - sa
sia lan-guir d'a - mor, se pro - va - ste un'sol-mo-men-to co-sa si - a lan - guir d'a - mor, co-sa sia lan - guir d'a-mor!

I. Orchestra.

Andante.

Oboi e Cornetti.
Violini.
Viola.
Soprano.
Alto.
Tenore.
Basso.
Fagotti, Violoncelli e Bassi.
Cembalo.

Sempre più raddolcito.

Ah qua-le in-co-gni-to af-fet-to fle-bi-le dol-ce a so-spen-de-re vien l'im-pla-ca-bi-le no-stro fu-ror?

Allegro.

Le por-te stri-da-no sui ne-ri car-di-nie

il pas - so la - sci - no si - cu - roe li - be - ro al vin - ci -
il pas - so la - sci - no si - cu - roe li - be - ro al vin - ci -
il pas - so la - sci - no si - cu - roe li - be - ro al vin - ci -
il pas - so la - sci - no si - cu - roe li - be - ro al vin - ci -
(dim. poco a poco)
tor! E il pas - so la - sci - no si - cu - roe li - be - ro
tor! E il pas - so la - sci - no si - cu - roe li - be - ro
tor! E il pas - so la - sci - no si - cu - roe li - be - ro
tor! E il pas - so la - sci - no si - cu - roe li - be - ro

al vin - ci - tor! Le por - te stri - da - no su i ne - ri car - di - ni
al vin - ci - tor! Le por - te stri - da - no su i ne - ri car - di - ni
al vin - ci - tor! Le por - te stri - da - no su i ne - ri car - di - ni
al vin - ci - tor! Le por - te stri - da - no su i ne - ri car - di - ni
il pas - so la - sci - no si - cu - ro e li - be - ro al vin - ci - tor!
il pas - so la - sci - no si - cu - ro e li - be - ro al vin - ci - tor!
il pas - so la - sci - no si - cu - ro e li - be - ro al vin - ci - tor!
il pas - so la - sci - no si - cu - ro e li - be - ro al vin - ci - tor!

p
un poco p
(un poco p)
E il pas - so la - sci - no si - cu - ro e li - be - ro al vin - ci -
E il pas - so la - sci - no si - cu - ro e li - be - ro al vin - ci -
E il pas - so la - sci - no si - cu - ro e li - be - ro al vin - ci - tor!
E il pas - so la - sci - no si - cu - ro e li - be - ro al vin - ci - tor!

(un poco p)
più p
tor, al vin - ci - tor!
tor, al vin - ci - tor!
al vin - ci - tor!
al vin - ci - tor! al vin - ci - tor!

Act III, Scene 1: Obbligato recitative and aria, "Che farò senza Euridice"
Impelled by Euridice's pleading and his own desire, Orfeo finally turns back to reassure his beloved. This rash act forces the gods to reclaim her again, and Orfeo now laments his folly and loss. With its chordal exclamations and agitated tremolos, the orchestra provides a fine example of *recitativo obbligato*—without the orchestra this recitative would be far less effective. The following aria, "Che farò senza Euridice," is justifiably considered one of the greatest laments in the operatic repertoire. After Orfeo sings this aria, he determines to forsake life, commit suicide, and join his beloved as she returns to the underworld. He is prevented from this tragedy by Cupid, who takes away his knife and, since Orfeo has proved his fidelity, restores Euridice to life. They return to earth—amid much dancing by shepherds and shepherdesses—for the requisite "happy ending."

Christoph Willibald Gluck
Orfeo ed Euridice (1762)
c. Obbligato recitative, "Ahimè! Dove trascorsi?"
d. Aria, "Che farò senza Euridice"
CD 7/3–4

cresc.
f
fp
(La souote.)
di - ce! Eu-ri di - ce! Con - sor - te! Ah più non vi-ve, la
chia - mo in van! Mi-se-ro me! La per-do, e la
più f
per - do per sem - pre! Oh Leg - ge! Oh mor - te! Oh ri - cor - do cru - del! Non hò soc -
(p)
(f)

(p)
(mf)
cor - so, non m'a-van - za con - sig-lio! Io veg-go so - lo (Ah fie-ra vi-sta!) il lut-tu - o - so as-pet-to dell'
p
mf
f
or - ri-do mio sta - to! Sa - zia-ti, sor - te rea! Son dis - pe - ra - to!
Andante espressivo.
Violini.
spiccato assai.
Viola.
Orfeo.
Violoncello e Basso.
Andante espressivo.
Cembalo.

Che fa-rò senza Eu-ri - di - ce? Do-vean - drò sen-za il mio ben? Che fa -
rò dove an - drò, che fa - rò sen - za il mi-o ben, do - ve an - drò sen - za il mi-o
ben? Eu-ri - di - ce, Eu-ri - di - ce! Oh Di - o! Ri -

un poco lento
spon - di! Ri - spon - di! I - o son pu - re il tu - o fe -
un poco lento
Tempo I.
del, io son pu - re il tuo fe - del, il tuo fe - del! Che fa - rò sen - za Eu ri - di - ce? Do - vean
Tempo I.
drò sen - za il mio ben? Che fa - rò, do - ve an - drò, che fa - rò sen - za il mi - o

(Più lento.)
(Adagio.)
ben? Do - vean_ drò_ sen - zail mi - o ben? Eu - ri - di - ce! Eu - ri - di - ce! Ah non m'a-
(Più lento.)
(Adagio.)
(Tempo I.)
van - za, più soc - cor - so, più spe - ran - za, ne dal mon - do, ne dal ciel! Che fa-
(Tempo I.)
rò sen - za Eu - ri - di - ce? Do - vean - drò sen - zail mio ben? Che_ fa - rò_ do - ve an - drò,_ che fa -

Recitative

Orfeo

Ahimè! Dove trascorsi? Ove mi spinse Un delirio d'amor?	Alas! What have I done? Where has the delirium of love Led me?

Aria

Orfeo

Che farò senza Euridice? Dove andrò senza il mio ben? Euridice! Euridice! Oh Dio! Rispondi! Io son pure il tur fedel! Euridice! Euridice! Ah, non m'avanza Più soccorso più speranza, Né dal mondo, né dal ciel!	What shall I do without Euridice? Where will I go without you, my beloved? Euridice! Euridice! Oh God! Answer! I am still faithful to you! Euridice! Euridice! Ah, for me There is no more assistance, no more hope, Neither from earth, nor from heaven!

Music in the Age of Enlightenment
Orchestral Music

123

Giovanni Battista Sammartini
Symphony in D Major (c1740)
First movement, *Allegro*

Imagine a musical world that had never heard nor even imagined the symphonies of Haydn, Mozart, or Beethoven. It was into such a milieu that Sammartini's compositions appeared in the early 1740s, when Corelli's compositions were the most widely circulated instrumental music, copies of Vivaldi's *The Four Seasons* (1725) were being reprinted and arranged for various instruments—even the hurdy-gurdy—and Handel had yet to compose his *Music for the Royal Fireworks* (1749). In this age of the suite and concerto grosso, Sammartini's symphonies were truly something new, and Englishman Charles Burney, who went to Mass in Milan in order to hear them performed, considered them "very ingenious and full of the spirit and fire peculiar to that author."

Sammartini's works have a distinctive energy and charm, even for modern listeners. The simple harmony so characteristic of the *galant* style is enriched in the Symphony in D Major through contrast between major and minor modes. Sammartini also uses contrasts of monophonic, homophonic, and polyphonic texture to good effect, not unlike the "Hallelujah" chorus from Handel's *Messiah* (1741), which was composed at about the same time. While in the light of history Sammartini's compositions may appear slight and insubstantial, in his time they were in high demand and were published and performed throughout Europe. Compositions such as this one laid the foundation for the symphony as an independent instrumental genre.

Giovanni Battista Sammartini
Symphony in D Major (c1740)
First movement, *Allegro*
CD 7/5

7
13
19
26
33

40
48
54
60

124

Johann Stamitz
La Melodia Germanica, No. 3 (c1755)
Symphony in E♭ Major
First movement, *Allegro assai*

Johann Stamitz was a remarkable musician: an innovative composer, a virtuoso violinist, an inspiring and demanding conductor, a shrewd judge of musical talent, and an influential teacher (his two sons also became notable composers). His success was further enhanced by a political acumen that enabled him to gain and maintain the patronage of rich and powerful aristocrats. Unfortunately for the history of the symphony, Stamitz's promising career was cut short when he died suddenly at the age of thirty-nine.

In 1754, at the height of his fame, the composer was invited to Paris for a year. He resided in the home of a rich aristocratic banker, La Pouplinière, who had been the patron of Rameau for the past twenty-two years and whose houseguests frequently included Rousseau and Voltaire. There, amid the opulent surroundings of a suburban palace as well as at public performances offered by the *Concert spirituel*, Stamitz's symphonies were introduced to Parisian society.

During the mid-1750s, a Parisian publishing firm released a collection of six symphonies, entitled *La Melodia Germanica*. Half of the works in the set, of which this symphony was the third, were written by Stamitz. (The other composers were Franz Xaver Richter, his Mannheim colleague, and the Austrians Georg Wagenseil and

Karl Kohaut.) The War of the Buffoons had recently erupted (see MWC, Chapter 41), and this collection of German symphonies added to the heady artistic ferment then bubbling in the French capital. So successful were these works that the Mannheim style of symphony reigned in the Parisian concert hall until supplanted by that of Haydn in the 1780s. The first movement of the Symphony in E♭ illustrates typical traits of the Mannheim style. Energetic rhythms abound, the exposition is not repeated, the recapitulation omits the first theme—opening instead with the second theme in the tonic key—and the movement concludes with a return of the opening gesture.

Johann Stamitz
La Melodia Germanica, No. 3 (c1755)
Symphony in E♭ Major
First Movement, *Allegro assai*
CD 7/6

Fp
F
p
(decres)
fp
f
13
dim.
pp

p
cres
F
crescendo
rinf
cresc.
23
FF
dim.

cres
cres
cres
cres
F
F
FF
FF
FF
F
F
cresc.
f
32
p
p
p
p
p

p
p
Fp
Fp
F
p
F
p
F
p
F
p
fp
41
Fp
Fp
Soli
F
p
F
p
F
p
F
F
p
F
p
F
p
F
p
F
F
F
p
F
p
F
p
F
F
p
F
p
F
fp
sf
p
sf
p
f

F
F
F
F
F
dolce
f
dim.
p
55
p
F
F
F
F
f
p

a 2.
p
cres
a 2.
p
cres
pp
cres
p
cres
p
cres
p
cres
pp
cresc.
70
F
FF
F
FF
a 2.
F
FF
F
FF
F
FF
FF
(allarg...)

80
ff
p
p
f
p
f
p

(cres)
(cres)
(cres)
(cres)
f
p
cre - - scen - - do
92
FF
FF
FF
FF
FF
FF
f

p
Fp
F
Soli
101
sf
fp
f

F
p
dolce
f
117

132
p
cres
pp
F
rinf
FF
cresc.
ff
f

Music in the Age of Enlightenment
Keyboard Music

125

Domenico Scarlatti
Essercizi (1738)
Sonata No. 26 in A Major

Throughout the history of music, there have been numerous families that have produced multiple generations of musicians. While the Bach family is most notable, other clans would include such names as Mozart, Stamitz, Couperin, Gabrieli, de Lassus, and of course Scarlatti. In most instances, the sons wrote in the same genres as their fathers, but not in the case of Domenico Scarlatti. Although Domenico did compose thirteen works in the métier of his father—opera—his attention and reputation were centered on music for the keyboard. According to the most recent count, he composed 555 keyboard sonatas, but only thirty of these, those that appeared in the *Essercizi,* were published during his lifetime. The rest were collected and copied by a devoted pupil during the last years of Scarlatti's life. Today these manuscripts survive in various libraries around Europe. Unlike the sonatas of Mozart or Beethoven, or even Baroque sonatas for that matter, all of Scarlatti's are in just one movement. However, he developed the habit of ordering the sonatas in pairs that contrasted different modes (major and minor). Thus, Sonata No. 26 in A major is preceded by No. 25 in the relative-minor key of F♯.

The *Essercizi* was published in 1738, when the composer was fifty-three. In his dedication, he states that the sonatas were composed between 1719 and 1728, while he was serving King João V of Portugal. The king had recently elevated him to a knighthood, in effect allowing his composer to join the ranks of the nobility. Scarlatti described these sonatas in the preface to the collection as "an ingenious Jesting with Art"; the historian Charles Burney called them "original and happy freaks."[1]

What was it about these compositions that drew forth such descriptions? First, Scarlatti seemed infatuated with crossing the hands, a technique Franz Liszt would later use to great effect. Second, the sonatas are saturated with figurations that imitate the guitar. While the most famous technique is the acciaccatura (see MWC, p. 388), others include pedal points that suggest strumming on the guitar's open strings, and the left hand crossing over the right as if to pluck the top string before returning to the bass. Third, the harmony is often surprising, with major and minor modes contrasted in unexpected ways, and colorful, if nontraditional, chords. While Scarlatti's sonatas use binary instead of sonata forms, invariably the **A** and **B** sections conclude with the same theme. His music is certainly not as technically demanding as the fugues of Johann Sebastian Bach or the sonatas of Beethoven, and, from the performer's viewpoint, playing Scarlatti is sheer delight.

Domenico Scarlatti
Essercizi (1738)
Sonata No. 26 in A Major
CD 7/7

[1] Charles Burney, *A General History of Music*, vol. 2 (New York: Harcourt, Brace and Co., 1935), 706.

*left hand

60
68
79
l.h.
88
96
104

126

Carl Philipp Emanuel Bach

Fantasia in C Minor for clavichord (1753)

When you listen to C.P.E. Bach's Fantasia in C Minor, the strangeness of the work—its wandering, unpredictable nature—immediately becomes apparent. This is typical of the eighteenth-century fantasia generally. In this genre, the composer could give free rein to the imagination without having to shape the music to fit a prescribed musical form. If the fantasia were a literary form, it would stand close to the meditation or the soliloquy. Indeed, in 1787 a German poet, Heinrich Wilhelm von Gerstenberg (1737–1823), took Bach's by then well-known fantasia and assigned two separate texts to be declaimed to the music. The first was the famous "To be or not to be" speech from *Hamlet,* in which Shakespeare's tragic hero meditates on the uncertainty of life. The second is the final speech of Socrates. Socrates had been condemned to death for his supposed crimes against the young minds of Athens, and gave his memorable soliloquy just prior to drinking a cup filled with hemlock, a lethal poison. He concluded his address with the words: "The hour of the departure has arrived, and we go our separate ways—I to die and you to live. Only God knows which is better" (Plato, Apology, 42a). Serious business—yet both are appropriate texts for Bach's serious fantasia.

Just as contrast is an important element in the two meditations, so it is in Bach's Fantasia. The minor key; sudden juxtapositions of tonal areas and dynamics; and contrasting rhythms, melodic gestures and phrase lengths emphasize the composition's solemn "voice" and conflicting moods. Often the clavichord seems to want to speak its personal message through recitative style. We can be sure that Bach intended a clavichord here because above several long notes he placed the *Bebung* sign (see the last three measures of the middle *Largo* section), instructing the performer to play that note with a vibrato—a unique feature of the clavichord that sets it apart from all other keyboard instruments. Finally, given the several enharmonic modulations that occur in this fantasia, it seems certain that C.P.E. Bach had his clavichord tuned in equal temperament or a tuning very close to it. Without this type of intonation system, his imaginative and idiosyncratic harmonic modulations would not have been possible.

Carl Philipp Emanuel Bach
Fantasia in C Minor for clavichord (1753)
CD 7/8

Largo.
Allegro moderato

127

Johann Christian Bach

Piano Sonata in D Major, Opus 5, No. 2 (1766)
First movement, *Allegro di molto*

"I suppose you have heard that the English Bach is dead? What a loss to the musical world!" Thus Wolfgang Amadeus Mozart wrote to his father in 1782 upon learning of the premature death of J.C. Bach in London. Indeed, next to his father, perhaps the single most important influence upon Mozart during his growth to compositional maturity was Johann Christian Bach.

Although J.C. was born in Leipzig, Germany, and was taught by C.P.E. Bach in Berlin, his musical style is more Italianate than Germanic—closer in style to Sammartini than to C.P.E. The reason for this is clear: Bach also spent five years in Milan studying with Italian teachers and absorbing the Italian dialect of *galant* style. (In fact, he absorbed so much of Italy that he broke with centuries of family tradition and converted to Catholicism, much to the dismay and sneering disapproval of Emanuel.) Yet although Bach's music is *galant,* it goes beyond the often diminutive scope of *galant* musical forms. The first movement of Opus 5, No. 2, is a weighty piece with clear-cut sections and the well-defined thematic functions that will come to be associated with sonata form: strong first theme, transitional passage, contrasting second theme, and closing idea. It also has a full-blown development section such as one might find in a piano sonata from the Classical period. In fact, to the untrained ear, this movement by the "London" Bach could easily pass as one from an early piano sonata by Mozart.

Johann Christian Bach

Piano Sonata in D Major, Opus 5, No. 2 (1766)

First movement, *Allegro di molto*

Thomson-Schirmer Website

Allegro di molto

3

f *p* *f* *p* tr tr *f* tr *p* *f* *ff* dolce *p*

cresc.
f
p
poco rit.
ff

a tempo
p
f
tr
p
f
tr
ff
p

mf
p
poco rit.
a tempo
f
p
f
p
f
dolce
ff
p

cresc.
mf
p
cresc.
f
p
f
p
f
ff

Joseph Haydn
Instrumental Music

128

Joseph Haydn
Symphony No. 6 in D Major, *Le Matin* (1761)
First movement, *Adagio; Allegro*

In 1761 Joseph Haydn entered the service of a powerful Austrian family: the Esterházys. While the Esterházy princes had a splendid palace in Vienna, their wealth was derived from agricultural estates to the southeast of the city, and the family spent much of their time in the country. Soon after Haydn's arrival, Prince Paul Anton asked his new servant to write a trilogy of programmatic compositions illustrating morning, noon, and night. Haydn determined to show the performing abilities of his newly hired court orchestra to the best advantage. Thus these three symphonies, entitled *Le Matin, Le Midi,* and *Le Soir,* are in concertante style, meaning that they include solos for members of the string and woodwind families.

The first movement of *Le Matin,* which features the woodwinds as the concertante instruments, seems to radiate with the sunny optimism that the youthful Haydn brought to his new position. The slow introduction, written in a style similar to the opening of a French overture, is meant to suggest the rising of the sun. A particularly interesting passage occurs in measures 58–70, where the chromatically ascending line played by the first violins provides for a colorful progression of chords. His Serene Princely Highness was evidently pleased with Haydn's trilogy, for he soon rewarded his resident composer with an increase in salary.

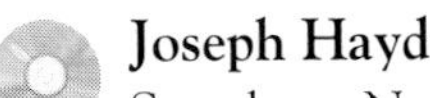

Joseph Haydn

Symphony No. 6 in D Major, *Le Matin* (1761)

1st movement, *Adagio-Allegro*

CD 7/9

Adagio

Flauto

2 Oboi

Fagotto

2 Corni in D/Re

Adagio

Violino I

Violino II

Viola.

Violincello e Basso

pp p cresc.

10
tr
[Tutti]
[f]
[p]
p
f
16
a2

22
f
f
f
f
f
f
f
f
28
tr
tr
tr

32
tr
tr
f p
f p
tr
f p
f p
f p
f p
f p
f p
f p
f p
37
f p
f p
f
f p
f p
f p
f
f p
f p
f p
f
f p
f p
f p
f
f p
f p
f p
f

42
a2
48
Solo
[p]
Soli
[p]
p
tr

55
[Tutti]
59
a2
a2

67
72
a2
Solo
pizz.
pizz.
pizz.
pizz.

79
tr
I Solo
col' arco
col' arco
87
Solo
[p]
[Tutti]
[f]
Soli
[p]
[f]
p
[f]
col' arco
p
f
col' arco
p
f
p
p

95
f
f
f
101
tr

106
112
a2
a2
[Vc.]
[Tutti]

129

Joseph Haydn

Opus 33, No. 3, The "Bird" Quartet (Hob.III:39; 1781)
First movement, *Allegro moderato*

The great German poet Johann Wolfgang von Goethe (1749–1832) compared the string quartet to a conversation among four intelligent people. This new genre differed dramatically from the trio sonata, which was at best a dialogue monopolized by the violin and cello, and at worst a soliloquy by the violin. What was Haydn's innovation? He dropped the harpsichord and replaced the top- and bottom-heavy texture with one that was distributed more equally among all the instruments. Haydn began this process of "musical equality" in earnest in his string quartets Opus 20 (1772) and continued it in the quartets of Opus 33 (1781).

What makes Haydn's quartets different from his symphonies? In the quartets, Haydn emphasized motivic expansion, and that expansion is carried out in all parts and registers of the texture. We can observe this equality of texture in measures 32–37, where the first violin and viola exchange motive, and in measures 43–59, where the melodic gesture descends through all four parts. By contrast, his symphonies rely less on motivic development and more on impressive and dramatic contrasts between instruments, textures, and dynamics. When there is motivic expansion in a symphony, it is usually expressed in the upper ranges of the texture (by violins and higher woodwinds).

Joseph Haydn
Opus 33, No. 3, The "Bird" Quartet (Hob.III:39; 1781)
First movement, *Allegro moderato*
CD 7/10

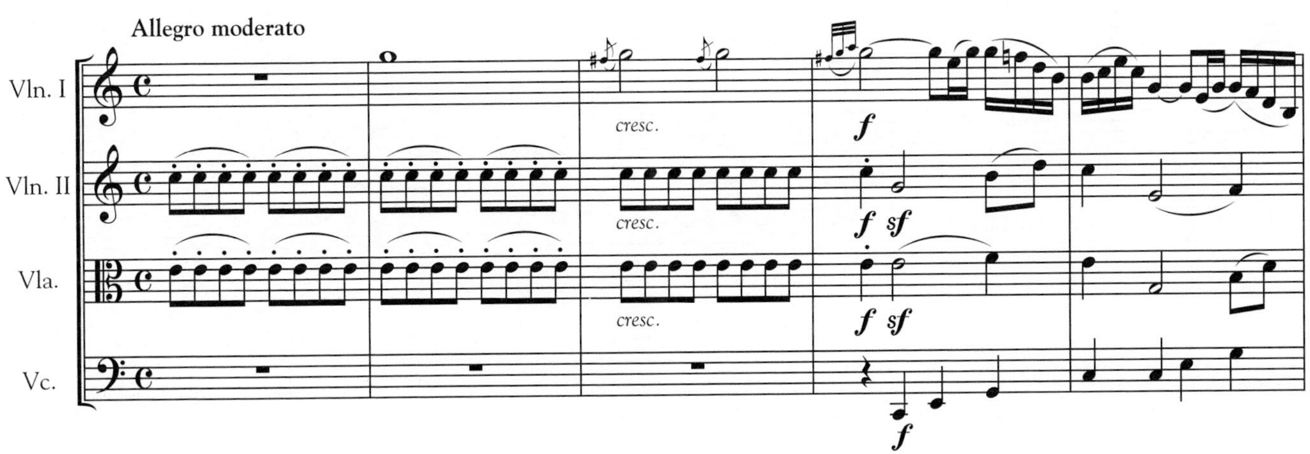

p
cresc.
f
sf
20
tr

30
40
dolce
semplice

50
1.
2.
60
p
cresc.
f
sf

70
semplice
semplice
semplice
80

cresc.
decresc.
90
pp
cresc.
f
p
100
sf

sf
sf
sf
sf
sf
sf
sf
sf
110
p
cresc.
f
p
cresc.
f
sf
p
cresc.
f
sf
p
cresc.
f
p
cresc.
p
p
cresc.
p
cresc.
f
f
sf
f
sf
f
p
p

130
dolce
140
semplice

p
p
150
cresc.
cresc.
cresc.
f
f
f
p
p
p
1.
2.
p
p
p
p cresc.
cresc.
cresc.
cresc.
poco f
poco f
dolce

Joseph Haydn
Late Symphonies and Vocal Music

130

Joseph Haydn
Symphony No. 94, The "Surprise" (1791–1792)
Second movement, *Andante*

Joseph Haydn was the first composer to write a symphonic movement using theme-and-variations form; before his time, a theme-and-variations piece was an independent, one-movement work. The theme of this *Andante* may be Haydn's most famous melody—certainly it is the one we usually associate with the image of kindly "Papa Haydn." The melody is shaped in binary form (**AB**), with each of the two sections eight bars in length. After the theme is stated, four variations ensue, followed by a coda that serves to recall the theme's original statement. With its simple construction and the surprising *fortissimo* chord, the opening bars of this movement possess two traits typical of Haydn's music: popular accessibility and novel effect.

Joseph Haydn
Symphony No. 94, The "Surprise" (1791–1792)
Second movement, *Andante*
CD 7/11

9
[Tutti]
Tutti
pp
pizz.
ten.
ff
col'arco
17
p
[ten.]

23
[Solo]
[p]
p
p
23
29
ten.
ten.
[Tutti]
f
f
f[Tutti]
f
f
f
f
29
ten.
[ten.]
[ten.]
[ten.]
ten.
ten.
p
f
fz
fz

36
[Solo]
[p]
[fz]
36
fz
ten.
ten.
ten.
ten.
fz
41
41
p
ten.
ten.

47
[Tutti]
ten.
[Solo]
[ten.]
55
[Tutti]

59
59
63
a 2
a 2
63

66
66
69
69
p

75
Solo
[ten.]
[ten.]
[p]
[Solo]
p
75
p
p
p
80
Solo
[ten.]
[p]
80
ten.
pp
ten.
pp

86
tr
f
86
[ten.]
[ten.]
[ten.]
[ten.]
92
92
[ten.]
[ten.]

98
p
98
104
[Tutti]
f
f [Tutti]
[f]
ff
ff
f
104
[ten.]
[ten.]
ff
f
f
Vlc.
f
B.
f

109
109
113
[Solo]
p
113
pianissimo e dolce
p
p
p
p

118
118
124
124

130
[Tutti]
f
130
135
135
Vlc.
B.

139
139
144
[Solo]
[p]
ten.
Solo
[p]
ten.
ten.
ten.
[Solo]
[p]
p
pp
144
[pp]
[pp]
pp
6
6
6
6

131

Joseph Haydn

Symphony No. 99 in E♭ Major (1794)
First movement, *Adagio; Vivace assai*

The London Symphonies mark the high point of Haydn's career as a symphonic composer. The premiere performance of this symphony was given on 10 February 1794 in London's Hanover Square rooms. At this concert, inaugurating his second trip to London, the composer conducted from the pianoforte. After a career devoted to serving his patron, Haydn was always conscious of his audience and used strong contrasts and the element of surprise to capture its attention as well as gratify its insatiable desire for novel entertainment. Immediately, in the opening *Adagio*, we hear a stark contrast between full orchestra and solo line, and between *fortissimo* and *piano*. The introduction is full of tonal surprises as well. These unexpected tonal movements are not whimsical, however, for they foreshadow some of the melodic and harmonic material in the ensuing exposition and development. To illustrate this, observe how the opening measures are reworked into the first theme. In the first two measures, the first violins play two descending seconds, followed by the skip of a fourth. (These important notes are marked by the symbol +.) When the exposition begins, the first theme outlines the same basic motive, although the intervals have been adjusted slightly for the sake of the harmony. Yet the melodic character of the first theme sounds substantially different. This is due to the fast tempo and alteration of the melodic shape.

Introduction (vln. I, mm. 1–2)

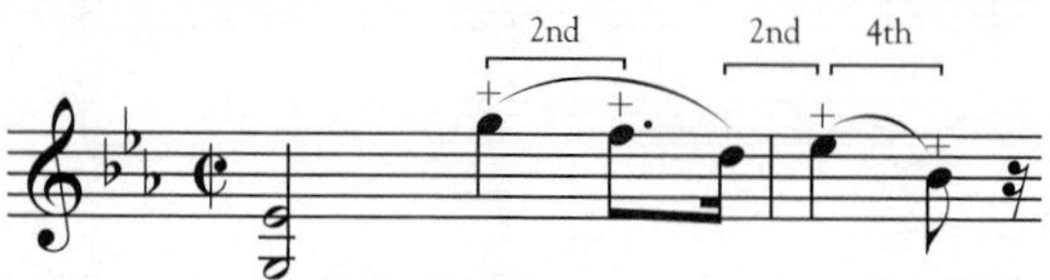

Theme 1 (vln. I, mm. 19–20)

Joseph Haydn

Symphony No. 99 in E♭ Major (1794)

First movement, *Adagio; Vivace assai*

CD 7/12

1 Adagio

2 Flauti

2 Oboi

2 Clarinetti in Si♭/B

2 Fagotti

2 Corni in Mi♭/Es

2 Clarini in Mi♭/Es

Timpani in Mi♭-Si♭/Es-B

1 Adagio

Violino I

Violino II

Viola

Violoncello

Basso

ten. f ff p [Tutti] tenuto

5
[1mo Solo]
[Tutti]
(ten.)
a 2
2do Solo
[a 2]
Tutti
Vlc.
12
[1mo Solo]
1mo [Solo]
[sim.]

19 Vivace assai
19 Vivace assai
p
p
p
Vlc.
p
25
(a 2)
f
f
f
[a 2]
f
f
f
f
25
f
f
f
Vlc.
f
Basso
f

32
a 2
a 2
fz
32
Tutti
37
fz
(fz)
a 2
a 2
37

42
42
47
(Solo)
(Tutti)
47

52

a 2

a 2

a 2

a 2

52

Vlc.

Tutti

58

fz

fz

[*fz*]

fz

58

fz

fz

fz

[*fz*]

63
a 2
a 2
f
f
f
fz
fz
fz
69
1mo Solo
[p]
p
pizz.

76
1mo Solo
[p]
[p]
1mo Solo
(p)
(Tutti)
f
fz
[fz]
76
col'arco
83
a 2
[tr]
tr

90
1mo Solo
(p)
Soli
(p)
1mo Solo
p
90
p
p
p
p
[p]
[p]
[p]
pizz.
[p]
96
1mo Solo
[p]
1mo Solo
(p)
2do
p
96

*) 107 - 117 *fz* Oboi, Fagotti; ⌒ Oboi - Birchall

111
fz
(fz)
a 2
111
[fz]
116
1mo [Solo]
[p]
a 2
116
p
Tutti

121
[1mo Solo]
(p)
1mo Solo
[p]
121
p
126
[1mo Solo]
[p]
p
126
p

132
132
[Tutti]
138
[Tutti]
(f)
138
Vlc.
Basso

143
a 2
a 2
fz
(fz)
[fz]
143
Tutti
149
149

153
ff
153
157
[p]
p
1mo Solo
pizz.

164
[Tutti]
Tutti
col' arco
170
[1mo Solo]
a2
1mo Solo

177
1mo Solo
p
[p]
2do
p
177
[p]
[p]
pizz.
[p]
183
(a 2)
f
ff
[f] fz
fz
fz
183
f
[f]
col'arco
[f]

190
2do
[a 2]
190
196
196

132

Joseph Haydn
The Creation (1796–1798)
"The Heavens Are Telling" ("Die Himmel erzählen")

Joseph Haydn was a devout Roman Catholic who wrote some fourteen polyphonic Masses. He was also, however, a man of the Enlightenment, and in the mid 1780s joined a lodge of freemasons in Vienna. His oratorio *The Creation* was compatible with the theology of the church as well as with Masonic ideals; each group could read in its own interpretation. The oratorio emphasizes not a redeemer, as does Handel's, but rather a timeless god of cosmic grandeur who has set in motion an earth full of wondrous beauty. From the outset Haydn conceived this oratorio for the concert hall, not the church. This was not music for a particular sect or denomination, but for all humanity. Haydn published the score of *The Creation* setting English and German texts simultaneously.

The Creation commences with an Overture entitled "Chaos," a meandering passage that avoids cadences because, as Haydn said, "there is no form yet." There follow the famous words "In the beginning God created the heaven and the earth." The oratorio proceeds with the biblical story of creation from the book of Genesis. From time to time this account is embellished with newly created poetry inspired by Milton's *Paradise Lost,* which provides the textual basis for the arias. The three archangels, Gabriel (soprano), Uriel (tenor), and Raphael (bass), as well as Adam (bass) and Eve (soprano), sing the arias and recitatives. One of Haydn's innovations was to integrate the soloists into several of the choral movements. Thus it is that the three archangels appear as a trio in the chorus "The Heavens Are Telling."

In the recording, an English conductor directs an English ensemble, singing not in their native language, but in German—something the composer did not envision.

Joseph Haydn

The Creation (1799)

"The Heavens Are Telling" ("Die Himmel erzählen")

CD 7/13

Allegro

Flute 1 2, Oboe 1 2, Clarinet in C 1 2, Bassoon 1 2, Contra Bassoon, Horn in C 1 2, Trumpet in C 1 2, Trombone 1, Trombone 2, Bass Trombone, Timpani in C, G

Allegro

Violin 1, Violin 2, Viola

CHORUS

SOPRANO: Die Him - mel er - zäh - len die Eh - re Got - tes; / *The hea - vens are tell - ing the glo - ry of God;*

ALTO: Die Him - mel er - zäh - len die Eh - re Got - tes; / *The hea - vens are tell - ing the glo - ry of God;*

TENOR: Die Him - mel er - zäh - len die Eh - re Got - tes; / *The hea - vens are tell - ing the glo - ry of God;*

BASS: Die Him - mel er - zäh - len die Eh - re Got - tes; / *The hea - vens are tell - ing the glo - ry of God;*

Cello & Double Bass (Vc.) (D.B.)

7
Fl. 1/2
Ob. 1/2
III/1, 2
Cl. 1/2
III/1, 2
Bn. 1/2
C. Bn.
Hn. 1/2
Tpt. 1/2
II/1, 2
Tbn. 1
Tbn. 2
B. Tbn.
Timp.
fz
Vn. 1
Vn. 2
Va.
S.
und seiner Hän-de Werk zeigt an das Fir-ma-ment,
the won-der of his works dis-plays the fir-ma-ment,
A.
und sei-ner Hän-de Werk zeigt an das Fir-ma-ment,
the won-der of his works dis-plays the fir-ma-ment,
CHORUS
T.
und sei-ner Hän-de Werk zeigt an das Fir-ma-ment,
the won-der of his works dis-plays the fir-ma-ment,
B.
und sei-ner Hän-de Werk zeigt an das Fir-ma-ment,
the won-der of his works dis-plays the fir-ma-ment,
Vc. & D.B.

14
Fl.
Ob.
Cl.
Bn.
C. Bn.
Hn.
Tpt.
Tbn. 1
Tbn. 2
B. Tbn.
Timp.
Vn. 1
Vn. 2
Va.
CHORUS
S.
und_ sei-ner Hän-de Werk zeigt an das Fir-ma-ment.
the_ won-der of his works dis-plays the fir-ma-ment.
A.
und sei-ner Hän-de Werk zeigt an das Fir-ma-ment.
the won-der of his works dis-plays the fir-ma-ment.
T.
und sei-ner Hän-de Werk zeigt an das Fir-ma-ment.
the won-der of his works dis-plays the fir-ma-ment.
B.
und sei-ner Hän-de Werk zeigt an das Fir-ma-ment.
the won-der of his works dis-plays the fir-ma-ment.
Vc. & D.B.
I/1
cantabile

21
Fl. 1 2
Ob. 1 2
Cl. 1 2
Bn. 1 2
C. Bn.
Hn. 1 2
Tpt. 1 2
Tbn. 1
Tbn. 2
B. Tbn.
Timp.
Vn. 1
Vn. 2
Va.
GABRIEL
GAB.
Dem kom - men-den Ta - ge sagt es der Tag;
To day that is com - ing speaks it the day;
URIEL
UR.
Dem kom - men-den Ta - ge sagt es der Tag;
To day that is com - ing speaks it the day;
RAPHAEL
RAPH.
Dem kom - men-den Ta - ge sagt es der Tag;
To day that is com - ing speaks it the day;
pizz.
Vc. & D.B.

29
Fl.
Ob.
Cl.
Bn.
C. Bn.
Hn.
Tpt.
Tbn. 1
Tbn. 2
B. Tbn.
Timp.
Vn. 1
Vn. 2
Va.
GAB.
p sotto voce
die Nacht die ver-schwand der fol - gen-den Nacht, die Nacht die ver-
the night that is gone to fol - low-ing night, the night that is
UR.
p sotto voce
die Nacht die ver-schwand der fol - gen-den Nacht, die Nacht die ver-
the night that is gone to fol - low-ing night, the night that is
RAPH.
p sotto voce
die Nacht die ver - schwand der fol - gen-den Nacht, die Nacht die ver-
the night that is gone to fol - low-ing night, the night that is
Vc. & D.B.

36
A
III/1, 2
Fl.
Ob.
Cl.
Bn.
C. Bn.
Hn.
Tpt.
Tbn. 1
Tbn. 2
B. Tbn.
Timp.
Vn. 1
Vn. 2
Va.
GAB.
- schwand der fol - gen - den Nacht.
gone to fol - low - ing night.
UR.
- schwand der fol - gen - den Nacht.
gone to fol - low - ing night.
RAPH.
- schwand der fol - gen - den Nacht.
gone to fol - low - ing night.
CHORUS
S.
Die Him - mel er - zäh - len die Eh - re
The hea - vens are tell - ing the glo - ry of
A.
Die Him - mel er - zäh - len die Eh - re
The hea - vens are tell - ing the glo - ry of
T.
Die Him - mel er - zäh - len die Eh - re Got - tes; und
The hea - vens are tell - ing the glo - ry of God; the
B.
Die Him - mel er - zäh - len die Eh - re Got - tes; und
The hea - vens are tell - ing the glo - ry of God; the
Vc. & D.B.
arco

42
Fl. 1 2
Ob. 1 2
III/1, 2
Cl. 1 2
III/1, 2
Bn. 1 2
C. Bn.
Hn. 1 2
Tpt. 1 2
Tbn. 1
Tbn. 2
B. Tbn.
Timp.
Vn. 1
Vn. 2
Va.
CHORUS
S.
Got - tes; und sei - ner Hän - de Werk, und sei - ner Hän - de Werk zeigt an das Fir - ma -
God; the won - der of his works, the won - der of his works dis - plays the fir - ma -
A.
Got - tes; und sei - ner Hän - de Werk zeigt an, zeigt an das Fir - ma -
God; the won - der of his works dis - plays, dis - plays the fir - ma -
T.
sei - ner, und sei - ner Hän - de Werk zeigt an, zeigt an das Fir - ma-
won - der, the won - der of his works dis - plays, dis - plays the fir - ma-
B.
sei - ner, und sei - ner Hän - de Werk, und sei - ner Hän - de Werk zeigt an das Fir - ma-
won - der, the won - der of his works, the won - der of his works dis - plays the fir - ma-
Vc. & D.B.
fz
6 6 9 3 3 3 6 5 10 9 3 3 3 5 3 3 4+ 6 6 4 3

48
Fl. 1 2
Ob. 1 2
III/1, 2
Cl. 1 2
III/1, 2
I/1
I/1
Bn. 1 2
C. Bn.
Hn. 1 2
Tpt. 1 2
Tbn. 1
Tbn. 2
B. Tbn.
Timp.
Vn. 1
Vn. 2
Va.
fz
fz
S.
-ment, und sei - ner Hän - de Werk zeigt an das Fir - ma -
-ment, the won - der of his works dis - plays the fir - ma -
A.
-ment, und sei - ner Hän - de_ Werk zeigt an, zeigt an das Fir - ma -
-ment, the won - der of his_ works dis - plays, dis - plays the fir - ma -
CHORUS
T.
-ment, und sei - ner Hän - de - Werk zeigt an, zeigt an das Fir - ma -
-ment, the won - der of his_ works dis - plays, dis - plays the fir - ma -
B.
-ment, und sei - ner Hän - de Werk zeigt an das Fir - ma -
-ment, the won - der of his works dis - plays the fir - ma -
Vc. & D.B.
fz
fz
9 3 3 5 ♮ 4+ 6 6 3

54
Fl.
Ob.
Cl.
Bn.
C. Bn.
Hn.
Tpt.
Tbn. 1
Tbn. 2
B. Tbn.
Timp.
Vn. 1
Vn. 2
Va.
GAB.
UR.
RAPH.
S.
A.
T.
B.
CHORUS
Vc. & D.B.
I/1
I/2
I
pp
p
pizz.
GABRIEL
In al - le Welt er -
In all the lands re -
URIEL
In al - le Welt er - geht das Wort,
In all the lands re - sounds the word,
RAPHAEL
In al - le Welt er - geht das
In all the lands re - sounds the
- ment.
- ment.

61
Fl.
Ob.
Cl.
Bn.
C. Bn.
Hn.
Tpt.
Tbn. 1
Tbn. 2
B. Tbn.
Timp.
Vn. 1
Vn. 2
Va.
GAB.
- geht das Wort, je - dem Oh - re klin - gend, kei - ner Zun - ge fremd, kei - ner,
- sounds the word, ne - ver un - per - cei - ved, e - ver un - der - stood, e - ver,
UR.
je - dem Oh - re klin - gend, kei - ner Zun - ge fremd, kei - ner,
ne - ver un - per - cei - ved, e - ver un - der - stood, e - ver,
RAPH.
Wort, je - dem Oh - re klin - gend, kei - ner Zun - ge fremd, kei - ner,
word, ne - ver un - per - cei - ved, e - ver un - der - stood, e - ver,
Vc. & D.B.

68
Fl.
Ob.
Cl.
Bn.
C. Bn.
Hn.
Tpt.
Tbn. 1
Tbn. 2
B. Tbn.
Timp.
Vn. 1
Vn. 2
Va.
GAB.
kei - ner, kei - ner Zun - ge fremd.
e - ver, e - ver un - der - stood.
UR.
kei - ner, kei - ner Zun - ge fremd. In al - le
e - ver, e - ver un - der - stood. In all the
RAPH.
kei - ner, kei - ner Zun - ge fremd.
e - ver, e - ver un - der - stood.
Vc. & D.B.
arco

75
I/1
tr
Fl. 1 2
Ob. 1 2
Cl. 1 2
Bn. 1 2
C. Bn.
Hn. 1 2
Tpt. 1 2
Tbn. 1
Tbn. 2
B. Tbn.
Timp.
Vn. 1
Vn. 2
Va.
GAB.
In al - le Welt er - geht das Wort, je - dem Oh - re klin - gend,
In all the lands re - sounds the word, ne - ver un - per - cei - ved,
UR.
Welt er - geht das Wort, je - dem Oh - re klin - gend,
lands re - sounds the word, ne - ver un - per - cei - ved,
RAPH.
In al - le Welt er - geht das Wort, je - dem Oh - re klin - gend,
In all the lands re - sounds the word, ne - ver un - per - cei - ved,
pizz.
Vc. & D.B.

82
Fl.
Ob.
Cl.
Bn.
C. Bn.
Hn.
Tpt.
Tbn. 1
Tbn. 2
B. Tbn.
Timp.
Vn. 1
Vn. 2
Va.
GAB.
UR.
RAPH.
Vc. & D.B.
III/1, 2
[III]
[III/1, 2]
III
II
arco
kei-ner Zun-ge fremd, kei-ner, kei-ner, kei - ner Zun - ge fremd, kei-ner,
e - ver un-der - stood, e - ver, e - ver, e - ver un - der - stood, e - ver,

89
B
Più allegro
Fl.
Ob.
Cl.
Bn.
C. Bn.
Hn.
Tpt.
Tbn. 1
Tbn. 2
B. Tbn.
Timp.
B
Più allegro
Vn. 1
Vn. 2
Va.
GAB.
kei-ner, kei - ner, kei - ner Zun - ge fremd.
e - ver, e - ver, e - ver un - der - stood.
UR.
kei-ner, kei - ner, kei - ner Zun - ge fremd.
e - ver, e - ver, e - ver un - der - stood.
RAPH.
kei-ner, kei - ner, kei - ner Zun - ge fremd.
e - ver, e - ver, e - ver un - der stood.
CHORUS
S.
Die Him - mel er -
The hea - vens are
A.
Die Him - mel er -
The hea - vens are
T.
Die Him - mel er - zäh - len die
The hea - vens are tell - ing the
B.
Die Him - mel er - zäh - len die
The hea - vens are tell - ing the
Vc. & D.B.

97
Fl.
Ob.
III/1, 2
Cl.
III/1, 2
Bn.
C. Bn.
Hn.
Tpt.
Tbn. 1
Tbn. 2
B. Tbn.
Timp.
Vn. 1
Vn. 2
Va.
CHORUS
S.
-zäh - len die Eh - re Got - tes; und sei - ner Hän - de Werk, und sei - ner Hän - de
tell - ing the glo - ry of God; the won - der of his works, the won - der of his
A.
-zäh - len die Eh - re Got - tes; und sei - ner Hän - de Werk zeigt
tell - ing the glo - ry of God; the won - der of his works dis-
T.
Eh - re Got - tes; und sei - ner, und sei - ner Hän - de Werk zeigt
glo - ry of God; the won - der, the won - der of his works dis-
B.
Eh - re Got - tes: und sei - ner, und sei - ner Hän - de Werk, und sei - ner Hän - de
glo - ry of God; the won - der, the won - der of his works, the won - der of his
Vc. & D.B.

103
Fl. 1 2
Ob. 1 2
III/1, 2
Cl. 1 2
III/1, 2
Bn. 1 2
C. Bn.
Hn. 1 2
Tpt. 1 2
II/1, 2
Tbn. 1
Tbn. 2
B. Tbn.
Timp.
Vn. 1
Vn. 2
Va.
CHORUS
S.
Werk zeigt an das Fir - ma - ment.
works dis - plays the fir - ma - ment.
A.
an, zeigt an das Fir - ma - ment.
- plays, dis - plays the fir - ma - ment.
T.
an, zeigt an das Fir - ma - ment.
- plays, dis - plays the fir - ma - ment.
B.
Werk zeigt an das Fir - ma - ment.
works dis - plays the fir - ma - ment.
Vc. & D.B.
tasto solo
3
6
5

109
C
Fl.
Ob.
Cl.
Bn.
C. Bn.
fz
Hn.
Tpt.
Tbn. 1
Tbn. 2
B. Tbn.
fz
Timp.
C
Vn. 1
Vn. 2
Va.
fz
S.
A.
CHORUS
T.
Und sei - ner Hän - de Werk zeigt an das Fir - ma -
The won - der of his works dis - plays the fir - ma -
B.
Und sei - ner Hän - de Werk zeigt an das Fir - ma - ment, zeigt an das Fir - ma -
The won - der of his works dis - plays the fir - ma - ment, dis - plays the fir - ma -
Vc. & D.B.
fz
fz

115
Fl.
Ob.
Cl.
Bn.
C. Bn.
Hn.
Tpt.
Tbn. 1
Tbn. 2
B. Tbn.
Timp.
Vn. 1
Vn. 2
Va.
fz
S.
Und sei - ner Hän - de Werk zeigt an das Fir - ma - ment, das Fir - ma - ment.
The won - der of his works dis - plays the fir - ma - ment, the fir - ma - ment.
A.
Und sei - ner Hän - de Werk zeigt an das Fir - ma - ment.
The won - der of his works dis - plays the fir - ma - ment.
CHORUS
T.
- ment, das Fir - ma - ment. Und
- ment, the fir - ma - ment. The
B.
- ment. Und sei - ner
- ment. The won - der
Vc. & D.B.

121
Fl.
Ob.
Cl.
Bn.
C. Bn.
Hn.
Tpt.
Tbn. 1
Tbn. 2
B. Tbn.
Timp.
Vn. 1
Vn. 2
Va.
fz
CHORUS
S.
Und sei - ner Hän - de Werk zeigt an das Fir - ma - ment, das Fir - ma -
The won - der of his works dis - plays the fir - ma - ment, the fir - ma -
A.
Und sei - ner Hän - de Werk zeigt an das Fir - ma - ment.
The won - der of his works dis - plays the fir - ma - ment.
T.
sei - ner Hän - de Werk zeigt an das Fir - ma - ment. Und sei - ner Hän - de Werk zeigt an das Fir - ma -
won - der of his works dis - plays the fir - ma - ment. The won - der of his works dis - plays the fir - ma -
B.
Hän - de Werk zeigt an, zeigt an das Fir - ma - ment. Und sei - ner Hän - de Werk, und sei - ner Hän - de
of his works dis - plays, dis - plays the fir - ma - ment. The won - der of his works, the won - der of his
Vc. & D.B.

128
Fl.
Ob.
Cl.
Bn.
C. Bn.
Hn.
Tpt.
Tbn. 1
Tbn. 2
B. Tbn.
Timp.
Vn. 1
Vn. 2
Va.
CHORUS
S.
-ment.
-ment.
Und sei-ner Hän-de Werk, und sei-ner
The won-der of his works, the won-der
A.
Und sei-ner Hän-de Werk zeigt an das Fir - ma-ment. Und sei-ner Hän-de Werk zeigt
The won-der of his works dis-plays the fir - ma-ment. The won-der of his works dis-
T.
-ment. Und sei-ner Hän-de Werk zeigt an das Fir-ma-ment, das Fir-ma-ment. Und sei-ner Hän-de
-ment. The won-der of his works dis - plays the fir-ma-ment, the fir-ma-ment. The won-der of his
B.
Werk zeigt an das Fir - ma-ment, zeigt an, zeigt an das Fir-ma-
works dis-plays the fir - ma-ment, dis - plays, dis - plays the fir-ma-
Vc. & D.B.

135
Fl. 1 2
Ob. 1 2
Cl. 1 2
Bn. 1 2
fz
C. Bn.
Hn. 1 2
Tpt. 1 2
Tbn. 1
fz
Tbn. 2
fz
B. Tbn.
Timp.
Vn. 1
fz
Vn. 2
fz
Va.
CHORUS
S.
Hän-de Werk zeigt an, zeigt an das Fir-ma-ment. Und sei-ner Hän-de Werk zeigt
of his works dis-plays, dis-plays the fir-ma-ment. The won-der of his works dis-
A.
an das Fir-ma-ment. Und sei-ner Hän-de Werk zeigt an, zeigt
-plays the fir-ma-ment. The won-der of his works dis-plays, dis-
T.
Werk zeigt an, zeigt an das Fir-ma-ment, sei-ner Hän-de Werk zeigt an das Fir-ma-
works dis-plays, dis-plays the fir-ma-ment, won-der of his works dis-plays the fir-ma-
B.
-ment. Und sei-ner Hän-de Werk zeigt an das Fir-ma-ment,
-ment. The won-der of his works dis-plays the fir-ma-ment,
Vc. & D.B.

142
Fl. 1 2
Ob. 1 2
Cl. 1 2
Bn. 1 2
C. Bn.
Hn. 1 2
Tpt. 1 2
Tbn. 1
Tbn. 2
B. Tbn.
Timp.
Vn. 1
Vn. 2
Va.
CHORUS
S.
an das Fir - ma-ment.
-plays the fir - ma-ment.
Und sei-ner Hän-de Werk, und
The won-der of his works, the
A.
an das Fir - ma-ment.
-plays the fir - ma-ment.
Und sei-ner Hän-de Werk, und
The won-der of his works, the
T.
-ment, das Fir - ma - ment.
-ment, the fir - ma - ment.
Und sei-ner Hän-de
The won-der of his
B.
— das Fir - ma - ment.
— the fir - ma - ment.
Und sei-ner Hän-de Werk, und
The won-der of his works, the
Vc. & D.B.

148
D
Fl.
Ob.
Cl.
Bn.
C. Bn.
Hn.
Tpt.
Tbn. 1
Tbn. 2
B. Tbn.
Timp.
Vn. 1
Vn. 2
Va.
S.
sei - ner Hän - de Werk zeigt an, zeigt an das Fir - ma-ment. Die
won - der of his works dis - plays, dis - plays the fir - ma-ment The
A.
sei - ner Hän - de Werk zeigt an, zeigt an das Fir - ma - ment.
won - der of his works dis - plays, dis - plays the fir - ma - ment.
CHORUS
T.
Werk zeigt an das Fir - ma - ment, das Fir - ma - ment. Die Him - mel er -
works dis - plays the fir - ma - ment, the fir - ma - ment. The hea - vens are
B.
sei - ner Hän - de Werk zeigt an, zeigt an das Fir - ma - ment. Die
won - der of his works dis - plays, dis - plays the fir - ma - ment. The
Vc. & D.B.

154
Fl.
Ob.
Cl.
Bn.
C. Bn.
Hn.
Tpt.
Tbn. 1
Tbn. 2
B. Tbn.
Timp.
Vn. 1
Vn. 2
Va.
CHORUS
S.
Him - mel er - zäh - len die Eh - re Got - tes; und sei - ner Hän - de Werk zeigt
hea - vens are tell - ing the glo - ry of God; the won - der of his works dis -
A.
Die Him - mel er - zäh - len die Eh - re Got - tes;
The hea - vens are tell - ing the glo - ry of God;
T.
- zäh - len die Eh - re Got - tes; und sei - ner Hän - de Werk zeigt
tell - ing the glo - ry of God; the won - der of his works dis -
B.
Him - mel er - zäh - len die Eh - re Got - tes; und sei - ner Hän - de Werk
hea - vens are tell - ing the glo - ry of God; the won - der of his works
Vc. & D.B.
fz
ff
tasto solo

160
Fl. 1 2
Ob. 1 2
Cl. 1 2
Bn. 1 2
C. Bn.
Hn. 1 2
Tpt. 1 2
Tbn. 1
Tbn. 2
B. Tbn.
Timp.
Vn. 1
Vn. 2
Va.
CHORUS
S.
an das_ Fir - ma - ment, zeigt __ an das_ Fir - ma - ment, zeigt an ___ das Fir - ma -
- plays the_ fir - ma - ment, dis - plays the_ fir - ma - ment, dis - plays ___ the fir - ma -
A.
und sei - ner_ Hän - de Werk zeigt an das_ Fir - ma - ment, das Fir - ma -
the won - der_ of his works dis - plays the_ fir - ma - ment, the fir - ma -
T.
an das_ Fir - ma - ment, zeigt an das_ Fir - ma - ment, zeigt an ___ das Fir - ma -
- plays the_ fir - ma - ment, dis - plays the_ fir - ma - ment, dis - plays ___ the fir - ma -
B.
— zeigt an, ___ zeigt an ___ das Fir - ma -
— dis - plays, ___ dis - plays ___ the fir - ma -
Vc. & D.B.

166
Fl. 1 2
Ob. 1 2
Cl. 1 2
Bn. 1 2
C. Bn.
Hn. 1 2
Tpt. 1 2
Tbn. 1
Tbn. 2
B. Tbn.
Timp.
Vn. 1
Vn. 2
Va.
fz
CHORUS
S.
- ment. Und sei - ner Hän - de Werk, und sei - ner Hän - de Werk zeigt an, zeigt
- ment. The won - der of his works, the won - der of his works, dis - plays, dis -
A.
- ment. Und sei - ner Hän - de Werk, und sei - ner Hän - de Werk zeigt an, zeigt
- ment. The won - der of his works, the won - der of his works dis - plays, dis -
T.
- ment. Und sei - ner Hän - de Werk zeigt an das Fir - ma - ment, das
- ment. The won - der of his works dis - plays the fir - ma - ment, the
B.
- ment. Und sei - ner Hän - de Werk, und sei - ner Hän - de Werk zeigt an, zeigt
- ment. The won - der of his works, the won - der of his works dis - plays, dis -
Vc. & D.B.
3 4 2 6 6 2 6 6

172
E
Fl.
Ob.
Cl.
Bn.
C. Bn.
Hn.
Tpt.
Tbn. 1
Tbn. 2
B. Tbn.
Timp.
E
Vn. 1
Vn. 2
Va.
S.
an das Fir - ma - ment. Die Him - mel er - zäh - len die Eh - re
- plays the fir - ma - ment. The hea - vens are tell - ing the glo - ry of
A.
an das Fir - ma - ment. Die Him - mel er - zäh - -
- plays the fir - ma - ment. The hea - vens are tell - -
CHORUS
T.
Fir - ma - ment. Die Him - mel er - zäh - len die Eh - - - - - re
fir - ma - ment. The hea - vens are tell - ing the glo - - - - - ry of
B.
an das Fir - ma - ment. Die Him - mel er - zäh - len die Eh - re
- plays the fir - ma - ment. The hea - vens are tell - ing the glo - ry of
Vc. & D.B.

178
Fl. 1 2
Ob. 1 2
Cl. 1 2
Bn. 1 2
C. Bn.
Hn. 1 2
Tpt. 1 2
Tbn. 1
Tbn. 2
B. Tbn.
Timp.
Vn. 1
Vn. 2
Va.
S.
Got - tes; und sei - ner Hän - de Werk zeigt an, zeigt -
God; the won - der of his works dis - plays, dis -
A.
-len, er - zäh - len die Eh - re Got -
-ing, are tell - ing the glo - ry of God;
CHORUS
T.
Got - tes; und sei - ner
God; the won - der
B.
Got - tes; und sei - ner Hän - de Werk zeigt
God; the won - der of his works dis -
Vc. & D.B.

184
Fl. 1 2
Ob. 1 2
Cl. 1 2
Bn. 1 2
C. Bn.
Hn. 1 2
Tpt. 1 2
Tbn. 1
Tbn. 2
B. Tbn.
Timp.
Vn. 1
Vn. 2
Va.
CHORUS
S.
an das Firmament, zeigt an das Firma-
-plays the firmament, displays the firma-
A.
-tes; und seiner Hände Werk zeigt an das Firma-
the wonder of his works displays the firma-
T.
Hände Werk zeigt an das Firma-
of his works displays the firma-
B.
an das Firmament, zeigt an das Firma-
-plays the firmament, displays the firma-
Vc. & D.B.

190
Fl. 1 2
Ob. 1 2
Cl. 1 2
Bn. 1 2
C. Bn.
Hn. 1 2
Tpt. 1 2
Tbn. 1
Tbn. 2
B. Tbn.
Timp.
Vn. 1
Vn. 2
Va.
S.
- ment, zeigt an das Fir - ma - ment, zeigt an das Fir - ma - ment.
- ment, dis - plays the fir - ma - ment, dis - plays the fir - ma - ment.
A.
- ment, zeigt an das Fir - ma - ment, zeigt an das Fir - ma - ment.
- ment, dis - plays the fir - ma - ment, dis - plays the fir - ma - ment.
CHORUS
T.
- ment, zeigt an das Fir - ma - ment, zeigt an das Fir - ma - ment.
- ment, dis - plays the fir - ma - ment, dis - plays the fir - ma - ment.
B.
- ment, zeigt an das Fir - ma - ment, zeigt an das Fir - ma - ment.
- ment, dis - plays the fir - ma - ment, dis - plays the fir - ma - ment.
Vc. & D.B.

Wolfgang Amadeus Mozart
Instrumental Music

133

Wolfgang Amadeus Mozart
Symphony No. 40 in G Minor (K. 550; 1788)
First movement, *Allegro*

As early as 1793, this symphony was advertised in Vienna as "one of the last and most beautiful of the master." Since then it has become *the* Mozart symphony, one of the most frequently played and analyzed compositions in the repertoire of Western music. While today we view this work as the epitome of Viennese classicism, early nineteenth-century writers, such as E.T.A. Hoffmann, viewed Mozart's compositions as works of expressive romanticism. Certainly the minor key, the drooping "sigh" motive, and intense chromaticism lend a melancholy tinge to the sophisticated elegance of K. 550. Centuries of Western musical tradition have associated the descending minor second with lamentation and sorrow, and this interval pervades the entire movement. It quickly becomes evident that the major/minor second guided many of Mozart's compositional choices, from the sequential repetition of phrases in the first theme to the key that opens the development section. When Mozart composed this symphony in July 1788, he did not include clarinets in the orchestration. Later, possibly for two concerts that were given on 16 and 17 April 1791, conducted by Antonio Salieri, Mozart rewrote the woodwind parts to include a pair of clarinets.

Wolfgang Amadeus Mozart

Symphony No. 40 in G Minor (K. 550; 1788)

First movement, *Allegro*

CD 7/14

16
f
p
a 2.

33
a 2.

p
p
p
p
p
cresc.
cresc.
cresc.
cresc.
a 2.
cresc.
cresc.
cresc.
cresc.
cresc.
cresc.
cresc.
f
tr
sf

a 2.
a 2.

86
a 2.
a 2.
a 2.
p
p
p
p
p
p

105
a 2.

119
a 2.

Vcl.

Bassi

p
p
p
p
p
f
f
f
f
f
f
f
f
f
p
p
p

a 2.
a 2.

199

215
a 2.
p
sf

p
p
p
p
p
p
cresc.
cresc.
cresc.
cresc.
cresc.
cresc.
cresc.
cresc.
cresc.
cresc.
f
f
f
f
f
f
f
f
f
f
tr
tr
tr
tr

a 2.
a 2.

267
p
p
p
p
a 2.
p
p
p
p
f
p
p
f
f
f
f
f
f
f
f
a 2.
f
f

p
sf
f

134

Wolfgang Amadeus Mozart
Symphony No. 41 in C Major (K. 551; 1788)
Fourth movement, *Molto allegro*

Which is the better play, Shakespeare's *Romeo and Juliet* or *Hamlet*? Of course it is impossible to say; each is wonderful in its own way. So, too, are Mozart's last two symphonies. The G minor (K. 550) is dark and brooding, while the C major (K. 551) is bright, even triumphant. Surely the most remarkable movement of his very last symphony is its highly complex finale. Like some but by no means all finales, this is in sonata form. It uses five different themes combined in a variety of patterns. In the development, Mozart resurrects some contrapuntal techniques associated with J.S. Bach (retrograde, inversion, and stretto) to work out his themes. It therefore comes as no surprise to encounter another Baroque musical procedure hovering above this music: fugue. Indeed, in Germany K. 551 was known as "the symphony with the fugal finale" ("mit dem Schlussfuge"). The coda is an elaborate five-part fugue with one very special moment when all five subjects sound simultaneously (mm. 385–401). The term "Jupiter" was coined by Johann Peter Salomon in England, and ultimately this English term stuck.

Wolfgang Amadeus Mozart
Symphony No. 41 in C Major (K. 551; 1788)
Fourth movement, *Molto allegro*
CD 7/15

8
a 2.
a 2.
f
18
a 2.

28
a 2.
p
39
p
p
Vcl.
p
p

51
f
a 2.
Bassi
tr
61
a 2.

70
a 2.
p
p
p
p
p
p
79
I.
tr
tr
tr
tr

00
tr
f
97

106
a 2.
115

122
129
a 2.
a 2.

138
146
p
I.
I.
p
p
p
p
p

155
p
p
p
p
p
p
p
166
p
f
f
f
f
f
f
f
f
f
f

178
187
I.
p
f

198
p
p
p
p
p
p
f
f
f
f
f
p
p
209
f
f
a 2.
f
f
f
f
f

218
228
a 2.
a 2.

236
246

256
a 2.
tr.
265
p

274
a 2.
p
p
I.
283
I.
p
p
p

292
302
a 2.

310

318

326
a 2.
a 2.
336

345
p
I.
tr
355
1.
2.
f
Vcl.

370
a 2.
f
a 2.
f
a 2.
f
f
f
f
f
384
f
f
f
f
Vcl.
Basso
f

395
a 2.
405
a 2.
Bassi

135

Wolfgang Amadeus Mozart

String Quartet in C Major, the "Dissonance" (K. 465; 1785)
Introduction

Four years after Haydn published his six "Russian" quartets (Op. 33; 1781), Mozart came out with a half-dozen quartets of his own. Mozart dedicated these compositions (which he referred to as his "six children") not to a wealthy aristocrat, who might be expected to return the compliment with a monetary gift, but to Haydn, "his dearest friend." Wolfgang and his father, as well as two aristocrats, played these quartets for Haydn, who then declared to Leopold that Wolfgang was "the greatest composer known to me either in person or by reputation." While Haydn was deeply moved, others were not so favorably impressed and complained that the set was composed with too much "harmonic spice." Although K. 465 is one of Mozart's finest quartets, its fame derives not so much from the overall quality of the work as from the remarkably daring introduction to the first movement. The opening is filled with startling cross-relations (for example, an A♭ is heard against an A♮), which we hear as dissonant intervals—hence the name, the "Dissonance" Quartet. If we are inclined sometimes to think of Mozart's music as being all sweetness and light, this introduction demonstrates just how intensely chromatic and harmonically complex it can be. However, the musicologist Charles Rosen has noted that the tonality of C major is never far away. One can play any chord in this introduction and follow it with a C-major chord, and it appears to be a perfect resolution. Try this on the piano if you don't have a string quartet handy. Needless to say, after compressing such a harrowing tonal journey into twenty-two measures, the bright, unclouded C-major theme comes as a welcome relief. This score is offered for study purposes only; there is no recording.

Wolfgang Amadeus Mozart

String Quartet in C Major, the "Dissonance" (K. 465; 1785)

Introduction

136

Wolfgang Amadeus Mozart

Piano Concerto in A Major (K. 488; 1786)

First movement, *Allegro*

Mozart had a special affection not only for the pianoforte, the instrument on which he had established his reputation as a child prodigy, but also for the clarinet. For this concerto, he added two clarinets to the orchestra, an unusual step at the time. In a letter to a longtime acquaintance, Prince von Fürstenburg, Mozart wrote that if clarinets were not available to an orchestra, the parts could be rescored and played, not by the oboes or bassoons, but by a violin and viola! However, this new orchestration was not the only surprising feature of this composition. While the concerto-sonata (double-exposition) form guides our expectations of musical structure, Mozart treated this thematic model with great flexibility in his concertos. The first movement of K. 488 comes closest to matching this "standard" formula, yet even here there is an important surprise: A new theme is added at the end of the second exposition. This lyrical melody offers a quiet close to the exposition and simultaneously serves as the transition into the development, for which it provides the primary musical material.

Exposition 1			Exposition 2			
Theme 1	Theme 2	Closing	Theme 1	Theme 2	Closing	New Theme
m. 1	m. 31	m. 49	m. 67	m. 83	m. 117	m. 143

Development	Recapitulation						Coda
New Theme	Theme 1	Theme 2	Closing	New Theme	Theme 1	Cadenza	Closing
m. 156	m. 199	m. 214	m. 230	m. 255	m. 278	m. 291	m. 292

Wolfgang Amadeus Mozart
Piano Concerto in A Major (K. 488; 1786)
First movement, *Allegro*
CD 8/1

11
f
a 2.
22

29
p
p
p
Vcl.
p
Bassi
p
37
p
p
p
p

46
f
p
53
cresc.
f

60
SOLO
76

82
TUTTI
SOLO
a 2.
legato
tr

94
sf
p
sf a 2.
f
dolce

113
p
p
legato

124

134
TUTTI
tr
a 2.
f
p
SOLO
tr

153
TUTTI
SOLO
p
p
p
p
TUTTI
SOLO

164
TUTTI
SOLO
legato

175
TUTTI
SOLO
p
TUTTI
SOLO

187
TUTTI
3
3
6
6
p
p
p
p

200
SOLO
TUTTI
a 2.

214
SOLO
legato
p
p
p
p
f
p
f
p
f
p
fp

224
f
p
f
p
f
p
f
f
f
f
f
f
p
p
p
p
p
p
p
p

243
legato

253

265
Clar.
Fag.
legato
Clar.
Fag.
Cor.

281
TUTTI
cresc.
a 2.
f
p

294
TUTTI
SOLO
Cadenza

Wolfgang Amadeus Mozart
Vocal Music

137

Wolfgang Amadeus Mozart
Le nozze di Figaro (1786)
a. Aria, "Se vuol ballare"
b. Aria, "Porgi, amor"
c. Aria, "Voi, che sapete"
d. Ensemble, "Vostre dunque"

Musically, Mozart's *Le nozze di Figaro* (1786) is important because it replaces the virtuosic aria of the traditional Italian opera with a generally simpler aria style that emphasizes the natural qualities of the characters. Socially, *Figaro* was a revolutionary document, in which a cunning and manipulative barber was portrayed as morally superior to a nobleman.

Pierre-Augustin Beaumarchais, the author of the original play, wrote two comedies featuring not the typical aristocratic hero, but Figaro, a commoner who cannot trace his ancestry back any further than he can remember—he was born out of wedlock and never knew his parents. In the first play, an amorous aristocrat, Count Almaviva, hires the conniving Figaro to bring about his marriage with the beautiful Rosina, which the ever-resourceful barber accomplishes through disguises, lies, and bribery. In the sequel, it is the barber himself who desires marriage. In 1816 Rossini (1792–1868) based his most famous opera, *The Barber of Seville*, on the first play. Mozart, however, chose to set *The Marriage of Figaro*. In outwitting the philandering Almaviva, Figaro not only reunites the Count and Countess, but also discovers his own parents. The plots of both operas are filled with twists and turns, suitably highlighted in quicksilver musical changes. The action of Mozart's opera is sketched below.

Act I: As Figaro and Susanna are preparing for their wedding, Figaro becomes uneasy when he realizes that the Count has designs on his fiancée, and that the bedroom the couple will occupy is immediately next to the Count's (Figaro has been hired as the Count's valet). Singing "Se vuol ballare," Figaro declares that he will manipulate the Count, frustrating the illicit desires of his master. Cherubino, Almaviva's page, enters and arouses the suspicion of the Count, who correctly perceives that the boy is infatuated with the Countess. Later, in his first ploy to fend off the Count's designs on Susanna, Figaro arrives with a group of peasants and asks the Count to immediately conduct the wedding ceremony of his "vassals." The Count hesitates, and comes up with the brilliant idea of announcing his intention of sending Cherubino off to join the army, thereby deferring the marriage and eliminating his youthful rival in one stroke.

Act II: The Countess, singing "Porgi, amor," laments that her husband no longer regards her with love and devotion. However, not one to relinquish her claims when she can achieve her goals through intrigue, she hatches a scheme—with the assistance of Figaro and Susanna—to entrap the Count. They decide on a bait and switch: Susanna will agree to meet the Count that night, but the tryst will actually be with Cherubino, whom they will dress as a girl, hoping that the resulting embarrassment will teach the Count to remain faithful to, if not love, his wife. Meanwhile, an amorous Cherubino (ironically enough, his name means "cherub," a chubby, innocent angel), who has been busy composing a song cataloguing his tumultuous emotions, enters and sings "Voi, che sapete." Expecting sympathy and perhaps a few caresses, he is instead whisked into female garb; yet he is nothing if not persistent, and still woos the Countess. As her broken heart warms to his tenderness, the boy is just about to steal a kiss when, of course, the Count knocks on the door. The standard "hide in the closet" routine follows, but the Count is not fooled. When Almaviva, enraged by jealousy, briefly retires to find a tool to break down the door, Cherubino escapes through a window and Susanna takes his place. Other characters are gradually added, and the plot thickens accordingly. In the ensemble finale, part of which includes "Vostre dunque," Figaro—who delayed Cherubino's departure for the army and is therefore responsible for the current mess—manages to free himself from the Count's wrath with a little fast talking and creative embellishment of the truth.

Acts III and IV: Events occur quickly in the last half of the opera. Figaro accidentally discovers the identity of his parents—Dr. Bartolo and Marcellina: two characters who have plotted to disrupt his matrimonial plans. Not only will they now support the wedding of their son to Susanna, but they will also tie the knot on the same day. Cherubino is discovered and palmed off on a peasant girl who desires to marry the lad. In the final act, the Count is reunited with his wife, all hindrances preventing the marriage of Figaro and Susanna are removed, and everyone lives happily ever after.

Wolfgang Amadeus Mozart
Le nozze di Figaro (1786)
a. Aria, "Se vuol ballare"
CD 8/2

Allegretto

FIGARO

Voice

Se vuol bal - la - re, si - gnor Con - ti - no, se vuol bal - la - re,

Strings pizz. & Corni

Piano

p

staccato

7

si - gnor Con - ti - no, il chi - tar - ri - no le suo - ne - rò, il chi - tar -

14

ri - no le suo - ne - rò, sì, le suo - ne - rò, sì, le suo - ne -

20

rò. Se vuol ve - ni - re

Vln. arco

Ob.

Cor.

arco

25
nel - la mia sco - la, la ca - pri - o - la le in - se - gne -
30
rò, se vuol ve - ni - re nel - la mia sco - la, la ca - pri - o - la
Tutti
Strings
37
le in - se - gne - rò, si, le in - se - gne - rò, si, le in - se - gne - rò.
Tutti, Wind sustain
43
Sa - prò, sa - prò, sa -
48
prò, sa - prò, sa - prò, ma pia - no,

53
— pia-no, pia-no, pia-no, pia-no, pia-no, pia - no;
Cor.
58
me - gl'o - gni ar - ca - - - no dis - si - mu - lan - - do
62
Presto
sco - prir po - trò. L'ar - te scher-men - do, l'ar - te a-do-pran - do,
p
Strings, Fag. sustain
68
di quà pun-gen - do, di là scher-zan - do, tut - te le mac-chi-ne ro - ve-scie-
Ob.
75
rò, ro - ve - scie - rò. L'ar - te scher-men - do, l'ar - te a-do - pran-do,
Tutti
cresc.
f
f
p

84
di quà pun - gen - do, di là scher - zan - do, tut - te le mac - chi-ne ro - ve-scie - rò,
Strings
92
tut - te le mac-chi-ne ro - ve - scie - rò, tut - te le mac - chi-ne ro - ve-scie-rò, ro -
Tutti
Strings
p Vln. 2 & Viola
Tutti
100
Tempo I⁰
ve - scie - rò, ro - ve - scie - rò. Se vuol bal - la - re, si - gnor Con -
Strings pizz. & Cor.
cresc.
p staccato
107
ti - no, se vuol bal - la - re, si - gnor Con - ti - no, il chi - tar - ri - no le
114
suo - ne - rò, il chi - tar - ri - no le suo - ne - rò, si, le suo - ne -

Se vuol ballare, Signor Contino
Il chitarrino le suonerò. Si.
Se vuol venire nella mia scuola,
La capriola le insegnerò. Si.
Saprò, ma piano meglio ogni arcano
dissimulando scoprir potrò.
L'arte schermendo, l'arte adoprando,
Di quà pungendo, di là scherzando,
Tutte le macchine rovescierò.
Se vuol ballare . . .

If you want to dance, "Mister Count"
I'll play the guitar. Yes!
If you come to my school,
I'll teach you to dance. Yes!
I'll sneak up quietly, all the better
To uncover your secret plan.
Sometimes parrying, sometimes thrusting,
Sometimes pricking, sometimes tricking
I'll upset your applecart.
If you want to dance . . .

Wolfgang Amadeus Mozart
Le nozze di Figaro (1786)
b. Aria, "Porgi, amor"
CD 8/3

9
Cl.
Vln.
Fag.
14
Cl.
Cor.
Fag.
18 COUNTESS
Por - gi a - mor, qual - che ri - sto - ro Al mio
Strings
Viola
duo - lo, a' miei so - spir!
Cl.

28
O mi ren - di il mio te - so - ro, O mi
Viola
Fag.
33
la - scia almen mo - rir, o mi la - scia almen mo - rir! por - gi a-mor, qual-che ri -
Strings
cresc.
f p
37
sto - ro al mio duo - lo, a' miei so - spir! o mi ren - di il mio te - so - ro, o mi
Fag.
41
la - - - - - - - scia al - men mo - rir, al - men mo -
Tutti
p

Porgi, amor, qualche ristoro Al mio duolo, a' miei sospir! O mi rendi il mio tesoro, O mi lascia almen morir!	O love, offer some relief to my sorrow, to my sighing! Oh return to me my treasured one, or at least let me die!

Wolfgang Amadeus Mozart
Le nozze di Figaro (1786)
c. Aria, "Voi, che sapete"
CD 8/4

6
CHERUBINO
Voi, che sa - pe - te che co - sa è a-
Fl. & Cl.
12
mor, Don - ne, ve - de - te, s'io l'ho nel cor,
Fl. & Fag.
Fl. & Ob.
Cl. & Fag.
Fl. & Ob.
Cor. sustain
3
3
17
Don - ne, ve - de - te, s'io l'ho nel cor. Quel - lo ch'io pro - vo,
Fl.
23
vi - ri - di - rò, E per me nuo - vo ca - pir non so.
Ob. & Fag.
Fl. & Cl.

29

Sen - to un af - fet - to pien di de - sir, Ch'o - ra è di - let - to,

Wind

35

ch'o - ra è mar - tir, Ge - lo, e poi sen - to l'al - ma avvam -

Fl. *Wind sustain*

40

par, E in un mo - men - to tor - no a ge - lar;

45

Ri - cer - co un be - ne fuo - ri di me, Non so chi il

50
tie - ne non so cos' è, So-spir-o e ge - mo sen-za vo - ler, pal - pi-to e
fp
55
tre - mo sen-za sa - per, Non tro-vo pa - ce not - te, nè dì, Ma pur mi pia - ce
mfp
60
lan - guir co - sì. Voi, che sa - pe - te che co - sa è a -
65
mor, Don - ne, ve - de - te, s'io l'ho nel cor,
3
3

Voi, che sapete che cosa è amor,
donne, vedete s'io l'ho nel cor.
Quello ch'io provo viridirò;
è per me nuovo, capir non so.
Sento un affetto pien di desir,
ch'ora è diletto, ch'ora è martir.
Gelo, e poi sento l'alma avvampar,
e in un momento torno a gelar.
Ricero un bene fuori di me,
non so chi'l tiene, non so cos'è.

Sospiro e gemo senza voler,
palpito e tremo senza saper.
Non trovo pace notte, nè dì
ma pur mi piace languir così.
Voi, che sapete che cosa è amor,
donne, vedete s'io l'ho nel cor.

You ladies who know the nature of love,
see if I have it within my heart.
What I experience I will explain;
it's so new to me I don't understand it.
I have a feeling full of desire,
sometimes delightful, sometimes tormenting.
At first I freeze, and then my spirit burns,
and then in a moment I turn to ice.
I seek a treasure outside myself,
I don't know who holds it, I don't even
know what it is.
I sigh and groan without wanting to,
I shake and tremble and know not why.
I find no peace night or day,
yet it only pleases me to languish so.
You ladies who know the nature of love,
see if I have it within my heart.

Wolfgang Amadeus Mozart
Le nozze di Figaro (1786)
d. Ensemble, "Vostre dunque"
CD 8/5

16

(COUNT)

que-sto fo-glio cos' è?

FIGARO

To - - - sto, to - sto, n'ho tan - te, a-spet-

21

ANTONIO

Sa-rà for-se il som-ma-rio dei de - bi-ti!

COUNT

Par

FIGARO

ta-te! No, la li - sta de-gli o-sti.

Wind sustain.

cresc.

f *p*

cresc.

f *p*

26

SUSANNA

La - scia-lo, e par-ti;

COUNTESS

La - scia-lo, e par-ti;

(COUNT)

la - te! e tu la-scia-lo.

FIGARO

La - scia-lo, e par-ti;

ANTONIO

Par-to sì, ma se tor - no a -

cresc.

f *p*

31
la - scia-lo,
la - scia-lo,
la - scia-lo, e
la - scia-lo,
la - scia-lo,
la - scia-lo, e
la - scia-lo,
la - scia-lo,
la - scia-lo, e
FIGARO
Van-ne, van-ne, non te - mo di te,
van-ne, van - ne, non
(ANTONIO)
var - ti
par - to si, ma se tor - no a - tro - var - ti
f
p
f
p
cresc.
36
par - - - ti!
par - - - ti!
O ciel! la pa-ten-te del
par - - - ti!
Dun - que?
dun - que?
(Exit Antonio.)
te - mo di te!
f p

42
Giu-sti Dei! la pa - ten - te!
COUNT
FIGARO
pag-gio! Co - rag - gio! O che te - - - - sta! o che
cresc.
47
te - sta! quest' è la pa - ten - te, che poc' an - zi il fa-ciul-lo mi diè.
f p
52
COUNT
FIGARO
COUNT
Per che fa - re? Vi man - ca Vi
57
SUSANNA
Il su-gel-lo.
COUNTESS
Il su-gel-lo.
FIGARO
man - ca? ri - spon - di! E l'u - san - za
cresc.

62
COUNT
FIGARO
Sù via, ti con - fon - di?
E l'u - san - za di por - vi il su -
f
67
SUSANNA
Se mi sal - vo da que - sta tem -
COUNTESS
Se mi
COUNT
FIGARO
gel - lo.
Que - sto bir - bo mi to - glie il cer - vel - lo, Sbuf - fa in
p
72
pe - - - - - - - - - - - - - - sta,
se mi
sal - vo da que - sta tem - pe - sta, Più non hav - vi nau - fra - gio per me,
se mi
Tut - to tut - to è un mi - ste - ro per me,
que - sto
va - no e la ter - ra cal - pe - sta! Po - ve - ri - no, ne sa men - di me,
sbuf - fa in -
fp

77
sal - vo da que - sta tem - pe - sta, più non hav - vi nau-
sal - vo da que - sta tem - pe - sta, più non hav - vi nau-
bir - bo mi to - glie il cer - vel - lo, tut - to, tut - to è un mi-
va - no, e la ter - ra cal - pe - sta! po - ve - ri - no, ne
fp
f p
82
f p
fra - gio per me, no, più non hav - vi nau - fra - gio per
fra - gio per me, no, più non hav - vi nau - fra - gio per
ste - - - per me, si, tut - to, tut - to è un mi - ste - - - per
sa men - di me, si, po - ve - ri - no, ne sa men - di
f p

Antonio Vostre dunque saran queste carte, che perdeste.	Well then, these must be your papers that you lost.
Count Olà, porgile a me!	Hey, hand them over to me!
Figaro Sono in trappola.	I'm in a trap.
Susanna and Countess Figaro, all' erta!	Figaro, take care!
Count Dite un po', questo foglio cos'è?	Tell me one thing, what is this document?
Figaro Tosto, tosto, n'ho tante, aspettate!	Certainly, immediately, I have so many, wait a moment!
Antonio Sarà forse il sommario dei debiti?	Is it, perhaps, the list of your debts?
Figaro No, la lista degli osti.	No, a list of innkeepers.
Count *(to Figaro, then Antonio)* Parlate! e tu lascialo.	Speak! and you let him be.
Susanna and Countess *(to Antonio)* Lascialo, e parti;	Leave us alone and go;
Antonio Parto si, ma se torno a trovarti—	Yes, I'm leaving, but if I catch you again—
Figaro Vanne, vanne, non temo di te,	Shoo, shoo, I am not afraid of you,

Count *(to Figaro)* Dunque?	Well then?
Countess *(to Susanna)* O ciel! la patente del paggio!	Heavens! the page's commission!
Susanna *(to Figaro)* Giusti Dei! la patente!	Lord have mercy! the commission!
Count *(ironically, to Figaro)* Coraggio!	Courage!
Figaro O che testa! quest' è la patente, che poc'anzi il faciullo mi diè.	Where's my head! it is the commission that the lad gave me a little while ago.
Count Per che fare?	Because?
Figaro Vi manca—	It was missing—
Count Vi manca?	It was missing?
Countess *(to Susanna)* Il suggello.	The seal.
Susanna *(to Figaro)* Il suggello.	The seal.
Count Rispondi!	Answer me!
Figaro È l'usanza—	It's the custom—
Count Sù via, ti confondi?	Go on, are you confused?
Figaro È l'usanza di porvi il suggello.	It's the custom to seal a commission.
Count Questo birbo mi toglie il cervello, tutto, tutto è un mistero per me, si.	This knave addles my brain, Everything, everything is a mystery to me.
Susanna and Countess Se mi salvo da questa tempesta, più non havvi naufragio per me, no.	If I save myself from this tempest, I will never again risk shipwreck.
Figaro Sbuffa invano e la terra calpesta! Poverino, ne sa mendi me, si.	In vain he fumes and stomps the ground! Poor fellow, he knows even less about it than I do.

138

Wolfgang Amadeus Mozart
Requiem Mass (1791)
a. "Confutatis"
b. "Lacrimosa" (completed by Süssmayr)

Mozart composed a significant amount of church music when he worked for the Archbishop of Salzburg during the 1770s, but little after he moved to Vienna in 1781—elaborate religious music was out of favor at the imperial court and with the Enlightenment generally. His Requiem (1791), which proved to be his very last composition, was the result of a private commission from a nobleman living outside Vienna. As work progressed, Mozart became obsessed with the composition, and was convinced he was composing it for his own death. The heart and soul of this requiem, like most, is the setting of the chant *Dies irae*, an extended prayer for mercy during the final Day of Judgment. The text opens with a vivid recitation of the events that will occur on that momentous occasion and concludes with the soul of the deceased begging for mercy, asking to be placed among the elect in Heaven and not cast with the wicked into the torments of Hell. Mozart, as did most composers of requiems, divided the *Dies irae* into sections, of which the "Confutatis" and "Lacrimosa" are the concluding portions. The "Confutatis" describes a scene that was carved in stone over the central door of many medieval cathedrals. A majestic Christ sits in judgment; on his left side the damned, writhing in pain, are dragged off to Hell, while on his right the elect look appropriately beatific as they prepare to enter the gates of Heaven. The "Lacrimosa" opens with the dead, full of sorrow, tears, and mourning, called to stand before the Judge and receive their verdict; it concludes with a final petition for mercy. On 4 December 1791, three singers from the court theater visited the composer and they, along with Mozart, sang the completed portions of the Requiem. When they came to the "Lacrimosa," Mozart, knowing his end was near, broke down in tears. Hours later, he was dead.

Wolfgang Amadeus Mozart
Requiem Mass (1791)
a. "Confutatis"
CD 8/6

Confutatis maledictis, Flammis acribus addictis, Voca me cum benedictis.	When the accursed have been confounded And given over to the bitter flames, Call me with the blessed.
Oro supplex et acclinis, Cor contritum quasi cinis: Gere curam mei finis.	I pray in supplication on my knees. My heart contrite as the dust, Safeguard my fate.

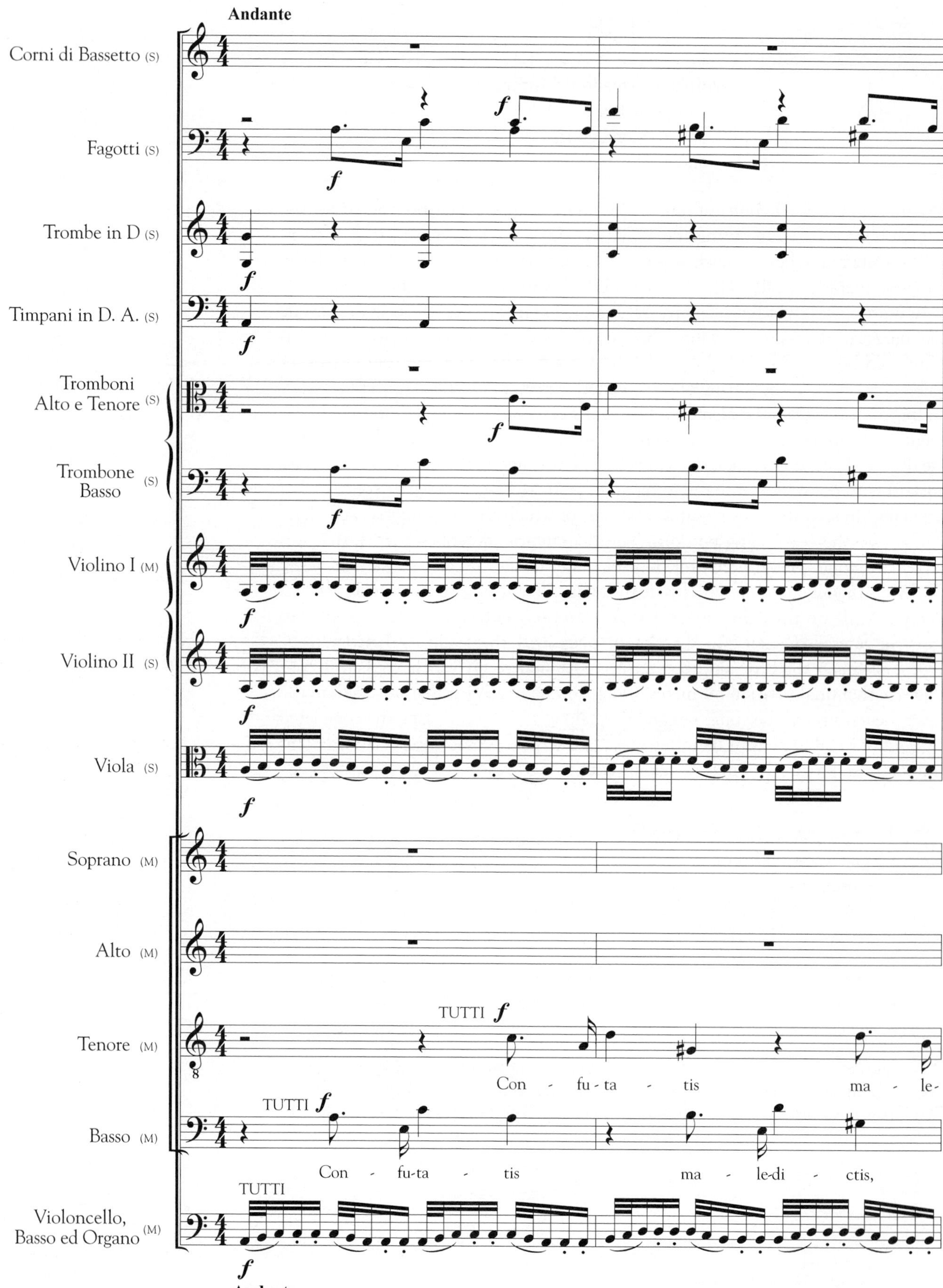
Andante
Corni di Bassetto (S)
Fagotti (S)
Trombe in D (S)
Timpani in D. A. (S)
Tromboni Alto e Tenore (S)
Trombone Basso (S)
Violino I (M)
Violino II (S)
Viola (S)
Soprano (M)
Alto (M)
Tenore (M)
TUTTI
Con - fu - ta - tis ma - le-
Basso (M)
TUTTI
Con - fu-ta - tis ma - le-di - ctis,
TUTTI
Violoncello, Basso ed Organo (M)
Andante

3
di - ctis,
flam - mis a - cri-bus ad-
flam - mis a - cri-bus ad - di - ctis,
ma - le-

5
p
p
p
p
p
p
TUTTI
sotto voce
Vo - - - - - ca,
TUTTI
sotto voce
Vo - - - - - ca,
di - ctis, flam - mis a - cri-bus ad - di - ctis.
di - ctis, flam - mis a - cri-bus ad - di - ctis.

8
vo - ca me, vo - ca me cum be-ne-di - - - - ctis.
vo - ca me, vo - ca me cum be-ne-di - - - - ctis.
Con - fu-

11
Con - fu - ta - tis ma - le - di - - ctis,
ta - tis ma - le - di - ctis, flam - mis

13
(S)
flam - - - mis a - cri - bus ad - di - ctis, con - fu - ta - tis ma - le -
a - cri-bus ad - di - ctis, con - fu - ta - tis ma - le - di - ctis, ma - le -

15
p
p
p
p
(M)
p
p
sotto voce
Vo - - - - - ca,
sotto voce
Vo - - - - - ca,
di - ctis, flam - mis a - cri-bus ad - di - ctis.
di - ctis, flam - mis a - cri-bus ad - di - ctis.
p

18
vo - ca me cum be-ne - di - ctis, cum be - ne - di - ctis, vo - - - ca me,
vo - ca me, vo - ca me cum be-ne - di - ctis. vo - - - ca

22
p
p
p
p
vo - ca me, vo - ca me cum be-ne - di - - - - - ctis.
me, vo - ca me cum be - ne - di - - - - - ctis.
p

26
p
O ro - sup - plex et ac - cli - - - - - - - -
p
O ro - sup - plex et ac - cli - - - - - - - -
p
O ro - sup - plex et ac - cli - - - - - - - -
p
O ro - sup - plex et ac - cli - - - - - - - -
6 4 2♯
7♭ 5♭ 3
6♭ 5♭ 4♭ 5♭ 7♭ 3

29
nis,
cor con - tri - tum qua - si
nis,
cor con - tri - tum qua - si
nis,
cor con - tri - tum qua - si
nis,
cor con - tri - tum qua - si
3♭
6♮ 4 2♯
7 5♮ 3♯

32
ci - - - - - - - - nis.
Ge - re
ci - - - - - - - - nis.
Ge - re
ci - - - - - - - - nis.
Ge - re
ci - - - - - - - - nis.
Ge - - - - - - re
6♭ 5 7
5 4♮
3♯
3♭
6♭
4
2

35
cu - - - ram, ge - re - cu - ram me - i
cu - - - ram, ge - re - cu - ram me - i
cu - - - ram, ge - re - cu - ram me - i
cu - - - - - ram, cu - - - - - ram me - - - i
7♭ 5♭ 6♭♭ 4♭ 6 4 2♯ 7♭ 5 3 6♭ 4

38
fi - - - - - - - - - nis!
fi - - - - - - - - - nis!
fi - - - - - - - - - nis!
fi - - - - - - - - - nis!
5
3
7♭
♮

Wolfgang Amadeus Mozart

Requiem Mass (1791)

b. "Lacrimosa" (completed by Süssmayr)

CD 8/7

4
cresc.
p
di - es il - la, qua re - sur - get ex fa - vil - la ju - di - can - dus

8
f
(Tromb. colla Parte)
sotto voce
p
(S)
ho - mo re - us. La - cri-mo - sa di - es il - la, qua re-sur - get
ho - mo re - us. La - cri-mo - sa di - es il - la, qua re-sur - get
ho - mo re - us. La - cri-mo - sa di - es il - la, qua re-sur - get
ho - mo re - us. La - cri - mo - sa di - es il - la, qua re - sur - get
6♭ 5♭ 4
2

12
ex fa-vil - la ju - - - di-can - dus ho - - mo re - us.
ex fa-vil - - la ju - - - di-can - dus ho - - mo re - us.
ex fa-vil - la ju - - - di-can - dus ho - - mo re - us.
ex fa - vil - la ju - di - can - dus ho - mo re - us.
6 7 5 8 7♭ 7♭ 6 5 4 3♮ 7♭ 6 9 8
4 3♯ 4♮ 3 3 5 4 3

15
p
Hu - ic er - go par - ce, De - us, pi - e Je - su,___ Je - su, Do - mi-
Hu - ic er - go par - ce, De - us, pi - e Je - su, Je - su, Do - mi-
Hu - ic er - go par - ce, De - us, pi - e Je - su, Je - su, Do - mi-
Hu - ic er - go par - ce, De - us, pi - e Je - su, Je - su, Do - mi-

19
(Tromb. c. P.)
ne!
Do - na e - is
ne!
Do - na e - is
ne!
Do - na e - is
ne!
Do - na e - is

23
re - qui-em!
Do - na e - is, do - na e - is re -
re - qui-em!
Do - na e - is, do - na e - is
re - qui-em!
Do - na e - is, do - na e - is re -
re - qui-em!
Do - na e - is, do - na e - is re -
5 6 5 3♭ 7 5 ♮ ♮ 6 5 7 5 5 ♯ 6 4

27
- - - - - qui - em!
A - - - - - - men.
re - - - - qui - em!
A - - - - - - men.
- - - - - qui - em!
A - - - - - - men.
- - - - - qui - em!
A - - - - - - men.
5 6 5
♯ 4 4 ♯
♯
6 6
4
♯

Lacrimosa dies illa, Qua resurget ex favilla Judicandus homo reus: Huic ergo parce Deus.	Mournful that day When from the dust shall rise Guilty man to be judged. Therefore spare him, O God.
Pie Jesu, Domine, Dona eis requiem. Amen.	Merciful Jesus, Lord Grant them rest. Amen.

The Early Music of Beethoven

139

Ludwig van Beethoven
Piano Sonata in C Minor ("Pathétique") (1798)
First movement, *Grave; Allegro molto e con brio*

While it frequently took Beethoven years to complete a composition, the *Pathétique* was finished in a matter of months and published in 1799—the year marked by the death of George Washington; Napoleon's successful coup d'état, which brought him to power in France; and the first public performance of Haydn's *The Creation*. Many of Beethoven's piano sonatas are known by fanciful names, such as the "Moonlight," "Appassionata," or the "Hammerklavier," but these did not originate with the composer. He provided titles to only two of his sonatas, "Pathétique" (Op. 13) and *Lebewohl* (*Farewell*, Op. 81a). The title "Pathétique," which suggests a mood of deep emotional suffering, was a stroke of promotional genius on Beethoven's part. It appealed to turbulent young hearts and sold more copies than Beethoven's other compositions. Later, in 1852, the Russian music critic Wilhelm von Lenz lamented that young women—the market for whom most piano sonatas were published—would massacre this composition upon the least pretext in order to demonstrate the depths of their emotional attachments. However, it was also a favorite work among professional musicians. One nineteenth-century virtuoso, Ignaz Moscheles (Eeg´-nahtz Mosh´eh-lehs), was so taken with the sonata when he first encountered it during his youth that he copied it out by hand because he lacked the money to purchase the score. More recently, the opening of the second movement served as the theme song for a long-running nightly radio show, *Adventures in Good Music*, hosted by the late Karl Haas. It is a mark of Beethoven's compositional skill that it still wears well, despite its familiarity.

The thematic character of this movement is not melodic, but energetic in its scales and arpeggios. The first theme shoots up two octaves in about as many seconds, and the second theme is not much different. One interesting aspect of the second theme is that it begins not in the relative key of E♭ major, but in E♭ minor. The expected relative major does not arrive until the end of this thematic group, in measure 88. Beethoven further alters our expectations by the return of the introductory motive from the *Grave*. Not only does the music return—unpredictably—in measures 132 and 294, but there are also slight modifications to its presentation that keep it sounding fresh.

Ludwig van Beethoven
Piano Sonata in C Minor ("Pathétique") (1798)
First movement, *Grave; Allegro molto e con brio*
CD 8/8

11
Allegro di molto e con brio.
p
sf
cresc.
p
sf
cresc.
p
sf
sf
sf
cresc.
sf
sf
sf
sf
sf
sf
sf
p
E♭
sf
sf
sf
sf
sf
sf
sf

78
sf
decresc.
pp
p
cresc.
f
p
cresc.
f
p
cresc.
f
sf
sf
sf
ff
sf
ff
1.
2.

133
Tempo I.
fp
fp
fp
p
decresc.
pp
attacca subito Allegro molto e con brio.
Allegro molto e con brio.
p
cresc.
f
p
cresc.
f
p
cresc.
p
pp
cresc.

183
sf
pp
cresc.
sf
sf
sf
fp
Recap.
p
sf
cresc.
Trans.
p
sf
cresc.
p
cresc.
p
cresc.
p

221
decresc.
pp
p
cresc.
f
p

268
cresc.
f
p
cresc.
f
f
ff
ff
Grave.
p
cresc.
sf
decresc.
pp
Allegro molto e con brio.
p
sf
cresc.
ff
ff

140

Ludwig van Beethoven

Piano Concerto No. 1 in C Major (1795)

Third movement, *Allegro*

Beethoven's Piano Concerto No. 1 was composed after his Piano Concerto No. 2 in B♭ Major (Op. 19). Although the C-major concerto was published in 1801, Beethoven may have performed the work as early as 1795 and again in concerts at Prague and Vienna in 1798. This last concert included the overture to Mozart's *The Magic Flute* and a symphony by Joseph Haydn (probably no. 94, "The Surprise") as well as opera arias. Haydn himself was in the audience and was accompanied by his younger brother, Michael, a notable composer of sacred music during the Classical period.

The movement's humorous, lighthearted character results from the vivacious rhythmic drive of the rondo theme. Further, there is an angularity and unexpected quality in the phrase structure that is almost impish in the way it diverts our expectations. The twenty-bar rondo theme opens with a measure-long motive that is repeated twice. While the answering figure would logically conclude with a balancing two-bar phrase, it is teased out, and the harmonic progression extends the melodic phrase to six measures. We might expect another answering phrase to balance the opening six measures, but we find instead two additional four-bar phrases. The cadence of the last phrase (m. 14) recalls that of the first phrase (mm. 4–5), but on the tonic rather than the dominant. Yet another phrase is elided onto this cadence. This phrase could cadence in only three bars or again in five, but is extended to six. In the end, the rondo theme is perfectly balanced, with two six-bar phrases separated by two four-bar phrases. The wit derives from the unexpected manner in which this symmetry is achieved.

Ludwig van Beethoven
Piano Concerto No. 1 in C Major (1795)
Third movement
CD 8/9

RONDO.

(A)

Allegro.

Flauto.
Oboi.
Clarinetti in C.
Fagotti.
Corni in C.
Trombe in C.
Timpani in C.G.

Allegro.
SOLO.

Pianoforte.

Violino I.
Violino II.
Viola.
Violoncello e Basso.

20
TUTTI.
Fl.
Ob.
a 2.
Clar.
Fag.
Cor.
Trom.
Timp.
TUTTI.
TUTTI.

35
a 2.
a 2.
ff
a 2.
sf
f
Ob.
Clar.
Fag.
Cor.
SOLO.
SOLO.
SOLO.
p

50
Piano
Strings
Strings
Piano
Strings
TUTTI.
Fl.
Ob.
Clar.
Fag.
Cor.
Winds
SOLO.
Piano
TUTTI.
SOLO.
Strings
TUTTI.
SOLO.

Ob.
Fag.
Fl.
Fag.
TUTTI.
a 2.
cresc.
TUTTI.
SOLO.
SOLO.
cresc.
cresc.
cresc.
cresc.
Ob.
m.s.

97
Fl.
Ob.
Cor.
p
Ob.
Fag.
p
cresc.

121
cresc.
Fl.
TUTTI.
Ob.
a2.
Fag.
TUTTI.
SOLO.
SOLO.
pp
decresc.
pp
pp
pp
pp

147
pp
Ped.
p
TUTTI.
Fl.
f
Ob.
a2.
Clar.
Fag.
Cor.
Trom.
Timp.
TUTTI.
TUTTI.

178
a 2.
SOLO.
SOLO.
SOLO.

192
ben marcato e sempre stacc.
pizz.
Fl.
Fag.
Cor.
cresc.
arco
Ob.
TUTTI.
cresc.
TUTTI.
TUTTI.

218
Fl.
Ob.
Fag.
Cor.
SOLO.
SOLO.
SOLO.
pp
ben marcato e stacc.
pizz.
Cor.
cresc.

247
Fl.
TUTTI.
Ob.
Fag.
TUTTI.
TUTTI.
arco
cresc.
SOLO.
Cor.
SOLO.
bēn marcato e stacc.
SOLO.
pizz.

268
Fl.
Ob.
Fag.
TUTTI.
a 2.
a 2.
a 2.
cresc.
TUTTI.
TUTTI.
arco
SOLO.
SOLO.

296
Fl.
Ob.
Fag.
Cor.
pp
cresc.
p
pp
cresc.
p
pp
pp

A
311
Fl.
TUTTI.
Ob.
a 2.
Clar.
Fag.
Cor.
Trom.
Timp.
TUTTI.
TUTTI.

337
a2.
a2.
a2.
a2.
a2.

353
Ob.
SOLO.
Clar.
Fag.
Cor.
SOLO.
SOLO.

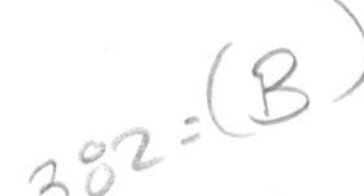

375

Fl.

Ob.

Clar.

Fag.

Cor.

TUTTI

TUTTI.

TUTTI.

SOLO.

SOLO.

SOLO.

394
TUTTI.
Fl.
p
cresc.
p
SOLO.
Fag. a2.
p
cresc.
p
m.s.
TUTTI.
SOLO.
TUTTI.
SOLO.
p
cresc.
p
p
cresc.
p
p
cresc.
p
cresc.
p
Ob.
p
Fag.
p
Cor.
p
p
p
p
m.s.
m.d.

423
Cor.
cresc.
p
Fl.
TUTTI.
p cresc.
Ob.
Clar.
Fag.
Cor.
Trom.
Timp.
TUTTI
TUTTI.

441
a 2.
a 2.

455
457
Cadenza.
Cadenza.
Cadenza.
cresc.

465
Fl.
pp
Oh.
Fag.
Cor.
Timp.
tr
Ped.

485
TUTTI.
Fl.
Ob.
a 2.
Clar.
Fag.
Cor.
Tr.
Tim.
TUTTI.
a 2
a 2.

500
CODA
a 2.
SOLO.
SOLO.
SOLO.
p
Fl.
Ob.
Fag.
Cor.
sf
pp

516
p
cresc.
sf
pp
fp

530
f
decresc.
cresc.
fp
p
ff
decresc.
p
pp
decresc.
pizz.
pp
decresc.
pizz.
pp
decresc.

557
Ob.
Cor.
Cadenza.
TUTTI.
cresc.
TUTTI.
Cadenza.
arco
arco
Adagio.
Tempo I°
Fl.
Ob.
Clar.
Fag.
Cor.
Trom.
Timp.
Adagio.
Tempo I°
Adagio.
Tempo I°

Beethoven's Middle Period *1802–1814*

141

Ludwig van Beethoven
Symphony No. 3 ("Eroica," 1802–1805)
Second movement (Funeral March), *Adagio assai*

Music has always played an important role in funerals, particularly for heads of state. We have seen a Baroque example in Henry Purcell's Funeral March for Queen Mary (no. 108). Another composition, the "Dead March" from Handel's oratorio *Saul*, was used to accompany the journey of Lincoln's body to Springfield, Illinois, in 1865. When Beethoven died, Vienna paid tribute with a funeral that would have done honor to a king. The music that accompanied the procession to the cemetery was his own *Marcia funebre*—the one from his Piano Sonata in A♭ Major (see MWC, Chapter 50).

Aside from the title, *Marcia funebre*, what makes this movement a funeral march? Certainly the *Adagio* tempo contributes to the solemnity, as does the generally low range of the melody and the minor key. Furthermore, the movement observes the typical ternary form of eighteenth-century funeral marches, and thirty-second-note rhythms (mm. 9–15 and 76–77) suggest the roll of muffled drums. It is curious, however, that Beethoven imitated drum rolls in the string section when he could have had the timpani actually play them. Recently, scholars have proposed that the program of the second movement is meant to reflect the hero's anguish over the death of a comrade.[1] By suggesting muffled drums, rather than writing these rhythms for percussion instruments, the music conveys the inner emotions of grief rather than simply reproducing a funeral march. Other intimations of the hero's sorrow are apparent in the coda, where the theme is punctuated as if by sobs (see MWC, Chapter 50); the statement of the **A** theme in measure 154 that occurs in the "wrong" key of G minor; and the wrenching harmonic modulation to A♭ major a few bars later. This symphony is programmatic music at its best, doing what no other art form can do—conveying emotional content without the hindrance of text or literal representation. We do not see the horse-drawn caisson or the coffin, but instead feel the solemn tug of mourning.

[1] Thomas Sipe, *Beethoven: Eroica Symphony*, Cambridge Music Handbooks (Cambridge: Cambridge University Press, 1998), 104–105.

Section	A						B			
Theme	a	b	a	b	a	closing	c	d	c	retrans.
Key	C minor						C major			
Measure	1	17	31	37	51	56	69	80	90	102

A							Coda
a	fugato	a	development	a	b	a	a
C minor							
105	114	154	158	173	181	195	209

Ludwig van Beethoven
Symphony No. 3 ("Eroica," 1802–1805)
Second movement (Funeral March), *Adagio assai*
CD 8/10

12
cresc.
decresc.
p cresc.
pp
sf
p

p
pp
sf
espressivo decresc.
33
cresc.
f
p cresc.

47
cresc.
decresc.
sf cresc.
p
f
sf

63
Maggiore.
a 2.

cresc.
76

cre
scen
do
p
cresc.
87
sempre p
6

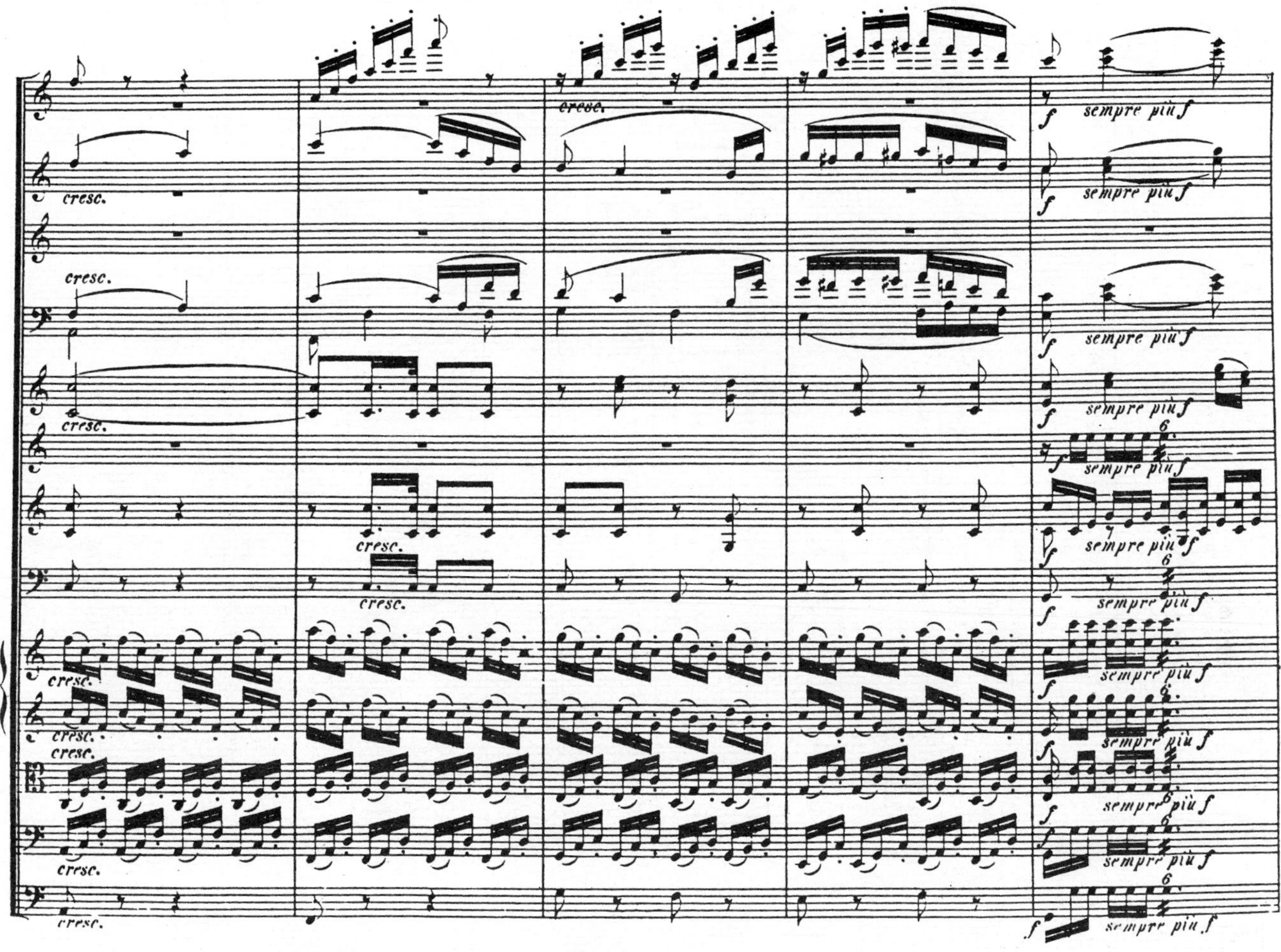
cresc.
cresc.
cresc.
cresc.
cresc.
cresc.
cresc.
sempre più f
sempre più f
sempre più f
sempre più f
sempre più f
sempre più f
sempre più f
sempre più f
sempre più f
sempre più f
sempre più f
sempre più f

f cresc.
ff
sf
fp
cresc.
p
sotto voce
p

a 2.

129

a 2.
a 2.
sf
ff
tr
p
sotto voce
decresc.
decresc.p

1084

p
12?
cresc.
decresc.
f
sf

p
cresc.
sf
pp
6
f

p
cresc.
f
a 2.
sf

f
sf
p
decresc.
cresc.
pp

pp
pp
pp
pp
pp
sf
sf
sf cresc.
sf cresc.
cresc.
p cresc.
cresc.
p
p cresc.
p
p cresc.
p
cresc.
p cresc.
decresc.
pp
pp
cresc.
p cresc.
p
decresc.
pp
pp
cresc.
p cresc.
p
p cresc.
p
decresc.
pp
pp
cresc.
p
p
pp
pp
cresc.
p
p

espressivo
espressivo
pp
pp
p cresc.
decresc.
decresc.
cresc.
decresc.
cresc.
decresc.
cresc.
decresc.
cresc.
decresc.
cresc.
decresc.
pp
pp
sf
sf
sf
pp
sf
sf
p
sotto voce
sempre più p
pp
f
pizz.
arco.
decresc.
decresc.

After the Congress of Vienna
Beethoven's Late Music

142

Ludwig van Beethoven
String Quartet in B♭ Major (1826)
Fifth movement (Cavatina)

When Haydn and Mozart composed their string quartets, the genre was intended primarily for the personal enjoyment of the performers themselves or for a small, select audience. This began to change in the early years of the nineteenth century. During the winter months of 1804–1805, the Austrian violinist Ignaz Schuppanzigh (1776–1830) began offering public concerts of quartet music. Indeed, he was the first musician whose reputation and livelihood were based primarily upon his skill in playing chamber music. Schuppanzigh's ensemble, which had long been at Beethoven's disposal, premiered a number of the composer's quartets, including Opus 130.

The fifth movement of this quartet is labeled "Cavatina," a vocal form that was then popular in the operas of Rossini and Weber. While there was great variety in the Italian style of cavatina, the German cavatina emphasized slow tempos, and it is this latter style that Beethoven used in this movement (*Adagio molto espressivo*). A performance instruction often encountered in operatic music, *sotto voce*—that is to say, in an undertone or a subdued manner—occurs four times in this short movement. This cavatina is true to its name; the first violin part could easily be sung as a vocalise by a soprano or tenor voice. There are a few examples where the second violin soars over the first (such as in mm. 19, 51, and 61) or where the second violin extends the phrase by repeating the figure just played by the first. The sudden modulation to C♭ major in the middle section ("*Beklemmt*") is further set apart by the triplet rhythms in the accompaniment and the sobbing syncopations in the melody. When the tonic key returns in measure 49, so does the opening melody. The emotionalism of this movement is not the hyperbolic lamentation of Tchaikovsky's *Pathétique* Symphony or an aria by Puccini. It is rather the intensely private tears of a soul—perhaps one isolated from humanity by deafness—experiencing an anguish of spirit not meant for public display.

Ludwig van Beethoven
String Quartet in B♭ Major (1826)
Fifth movement (Cavatina)
CD 8/11

cresc.
p
f
Beklemmt.
pp
sempre pp
sotto voce

143

Ludwig van Beethoven
Missa solemnis (1823)
Kyrie

Unlike Haydn or Mozart, Beethoven rarely wrote sacred music. So when he began work on a *Missa Solemnis* to be sung as part of the consecration of his friend and patron Archduke Rudoph as Archbishop, Beethoven felt the need to examine the liturgical traditions of the Mass. He studied dusty books of chant as well as the music of Palestrina, Bach, Handel, and many others. The result is apparent even in the opening of the *Kyrie*. Its slow tempos and static melody, harmony, and rhythm recall the devices used by numerous composers to suggest the unhurried, timeless character of God. Composers likewise used musical symbolism in the "Christe" to suggest the second person of the Trinity. In his B-Minor Mass, Bach set this passage as a duet, but Beethoven did not do anything quite so obvious. Instead he filled the section with parallel thirds, a technique that Beethoven scholar Martin Cooper has suggested the composer used to emphasize Christ as "friend and helper."[1] When the third section of the *Kyrie* begins in measure 128, it recapitulates the themes of the first section, but emphasizes the subdominant key of G major before settling into the tonic of D major.

The spaciousness of the musical setting puts this composition on a par with Bach's B-Minor Mass: It is sacred music, but not for liturgical use. Beethoven himself came to think of his great Mass as something more akin to an oratorio; that is to say, a composition meant to instruct and uplift the spirit and moral character of the audience, but not to be used for church services—even for the consecration of an archbishop.

[1] Martin Cooper, *Beethoven: The Last Decade, 1817–1827* (London: Oxford University Press, 1970), 226.

Ludwig van Beethoven

Missa solemnis (1823)

Kyrie

CD 8/12

27
Ky - - ri - e.
Ky - - ri - e e - lei -
p
ff
-e, Ky - ri - e
-e, Ky - ri - e
-e, Ky - ri - e
-e, Ky - ri - e
p W.–w.
ff Tutti
p W.–w.
Ped.

35
A
-son.
p
cresc.
f
e - lei - son, Ky - ri - e, Ky - ri -
e - lei - son, Ky - ri - e e - lei -
e - lei - son, Ky - ri - e, e - lei -
e - lei - son, e - lei - son, Ky - ri - e e - lei -
Tpt.

43
B
Ch.
-e e - lei - son, Ky - ri-e e - lei - - son,
-son, e - lei - son, e - le - i - son,
-son, e - lei - son, e - le - i - son,
-son, e - lei - son, e - lei - son,
50
cresc.
Ky - ri-e e - lei - son, e - lei - son, Ky - ri - e, Ky -
Ky - ri-e e - lei - son, e - lei - son, Ky - ri - e,
Ky - ri-e e - lei - son, e - lei - son, Ky - ri - e,
Ky - ri-e e - lei - son, e - lei - son, Ky - ri - e, Ky -
Organ

57
C
p
-ri-e e-lei - son, e - lei - son,
Ky - ri-e e - lei - son, e - lei - son, Ky -
Ky - ri-e e - lei - son, e - lei - son, e - lei - son, Ky -
- ri-e e - lei - son, e - lei - son, e - lei - son, Ky -
pp senza Org.
cresc.
64
Ky ri - e e - lei - son, e - lei - son, Ky - ri -
- ri - e e - lei - son, e - lei - son, Ky - ri -
- ri - e e - lei - son, e - lei - son, Ky - ri -
- ri - e e - lei - son, Ky - ri - e, Ky - ri -
f Org. sf
senza Org.
p cresc.
Cl.
f W.-w.

71
D
p
pp
- e e - lei - son, Ky - ri - e e - lei - son,
- e e - lei - son, Ky - ri - e e - lei - son,
- e e - lei - son, e - lei - son, e - lei - son,
- e e - lei - son, e - lei - son, e - lei - son,
Bssn.
Cl.
Bssn.
78
e - lei - son.
e - lei - son.
e - lei - son.
e - lei - son.
cresc.
Vla.

86
Andante assai ben marcato.
D'
Chri - ste, Chri - ste e - lei - - son,
Soli
Chri - ste, Chri - ste
e - lei - - - - - - - - - - - son,
Chri - ste, Chri - ste,
Andante assai ben marcato.
D'
sf Bsn. sf Hns. sf sf
Cl.
cresc.
sf sf sf
92
Chri - ste, Chri - ste, Chri - ste, Chri - ste e - lei - - - - - -
e - lei - - - - - - son, Chri - ste e - lei - - - - - - - son,
Chri - ste, Chri - ste, Chri - ste e - lei - - son, Chri - ste, Chri - ste
Chri - ste, Chri - ste e - lei - - - son, Chri - ste, Chri - ste
Ob.
p

98
cresc.
son, e - lei - son, e - lei
cresc.
Chri - ste, Chri - ste e - lei - son, Chri - ste e - lei
cresc.
e - lei - son, e - lei - son, Chri - ste e - lei
cresc.
e - lei - son, Chri - ste e - lei - son, e - lei
cresc.

104
E
Soli
- son, Chri - ste, Chri - ste, Chri - ste e - lei-son,
- son, Chri - ste, Chri - ste, Chri - ste e - lei-son,
- son, Chri - ste, Chri - ste
- son, Chri - ste, Chri - ste,
Ch.
p
Chri - ste, Chri - ste, Chri - ste e - lei
Chri - ste, Chri - ste, Chri - ste e - lei-son, Chri - ste e - lei -
e - lei - son, e - lei - son, Chri - ste
e - lei - son, Chri - ste,
E
Fl.
Tpt.
cresc.
f più f
ff
sf

109
Chri - ste, Chri - ste
Chri - ste, Chri - ste
e - lei - - -
Chri - ste, Chri - ste
sf p
- son, e - lei - son, Chri - ste e - lei - - - - - - - - - - -
sf p
- son, Chri - ste, Chri - ste, Chri - ste e - lei - - son, Chri - ste, Chri - ste e -
sf p
e - lei - son, Chri - ste, Chri - ste e - lei - - son, Chri - ste, Chri - ste e -
sf p
Chri - ste e - lei - - - - - - - - - - - - - - - - - -
sf sf p
sf sf

115
e - lei
e - lei
- son, e - lei
son, Chri - ste, Chri - ste e - lei
e - lei son, Chri - ste, Chri - ste, Chri - ste, Chri - ste, Chri - ste e -
son,
- lei son,
- lei son,
son,
Cl.
cresc.
decresc.

121
F
son, e - lei - son.
son, e - lei - son.
son, e - lei son, e - lei - son.
- lei - son, e-lei - son, Chri - ste e - lei - son.
ppp
Chri - ste, Chri - ste, Chri - ste e - lei -
Chri - ste, Chri - ste, Chri - ste, Chri - ste, Chri - ste e - lei -
Chri - ste, Chri - ste, Chri - ste, Chri - ste, Chri - ste e - lei -
Chri - ste, Chri - ste, Chri - ste e - lei -
F
p
pp
ppp

128
Tempo I
-son.
-son.
-son.
-son.
Tempo I
Full Orch. f
p
Ped.
Cl.
p

137
G
Ky - ri - e,
Ky - ri - e, Ky -
Ky - ri - e, Ky -
Ky - ri - e, Ky -
Ky - ri - e, Ky -
G
Fl.
cresc.
f Tutti
p
Cl., Bsn.
f

145
Ky - ri -
Ky - - ri - e,
Ky - ri -
Ky - - ri - e, e - lei -
e - lei -
- ri - e,
Ky - ri - e,
- ri - e,
Ky - ri - e,
- ri - e,
Ky - ri - e,
- ri - e,
Ky - ri - e,
Ob., Bsn,
Cl., Bsn.
Ob.
p
ff
p
p
Ped.

154
H
- e, e - lei - son.
- e, e - lei - son.
- son.
- son.
p cresc.
f
dim.
p f
e - lei - son, Ky - - ri - e e - lei - son, Ky -
e - lei - son, Ky - - ri - e e - lei - son, Ky -
e - lei - son, Ky - - ri - e e - lei - son, Ky -
e - lei - son, Ky - - ri - e e - lei - son, Ky -
H
p cresc.
f Tutti
decresc.
p f

161
p
p
- ri - e e - lei - - son,
Ky - ri-e
p
- ri - e e - lei - - son,
p
- ri - e e - lei - - son,
p
- ri - e le e - lei - son,
Fl., Cl.
Ob., Hn.
p
dolce
sempre
p
168
p
Ky - ri-e e - lei - son, Ky - ri - e e -
Ky - ri-e e - lei - son, Ky -
Ky - ri-e e - lei - son, e -

175
K
e - lei - son, Ky - - - ri - e e - lei
- ri - e, Ky - - - ri - e e - lei - son,
- lei - son, Ky - - - ri - e e - lei - son, e -
- lei - son, Ky - - - ri - e e - lei - son, e -
K
f
sf
sf
182
sf
sf
sf
dim.
son, Ky ri - e e - lei
e - lei
- lei son, e - lei
- lei son, e lei
sf
sf
sf
dim.

189
L
son, Ky - ri - e e-
son, Ky - ri - e e - lei -
son, Ky - ri - e e - lei -
son, Ky - ri - e e - lei - - - - -
Ob.
p cresc.
Bsn.
196
M
cresc.
lei - - - son, e - lei - son, Ky - ri e e - lei -
- - - son, e - lei - son, Ky - ri e e-
son, e - lei - son, e - lei - son, Ky - ri e e - lei -
son, e - lei - son, e - lei - son, Ky - ri e e - lei -
Ob.
cresc.

203
cresc.
p
N
più p
- son, e - lei - - - - - - - - - - - - - son, Ky -
- lei - son, e - lei - - - - - - - - - - son, Ky -
- - son, e - lei - - - - - - - - - - son,
- - son, e - lei - - - - - - - - - - son,
Ob.
cresc.
p dim.
210
pp
- ri - e e - lei - son,
- ri - e e - lei - son,
più p
Ky - ri - e e - lei - son,
Ky - ri - e e - lei - son,
Bsn.
p sempre dim.
pp dim.
più pp

217
pp
f
p
pp
e - lei - son, Ky - ri - e e - lei - - son.
e - lei - son, Ky - ri - e e - lei - - son.
e - lei - son, Ky - ri - e e - lei - - son.
e - lei - son, Ky - ri - e e - lei - - son.
cresc.
Tutti
dim.

Chapter 52

Franz Schubert

Franz Schubert
"Erlkönig" (1815)

Unlike most *Lieder* composed during the early years of the nineteenth century, "Erlkönig" was not written for amateur musicians. This famous song requires the skills of highly trained and talented professionals. The vocal range may not be excessive (spanning only an octave and a fifth), but the singer must rapidly shift between the upper and lower ranges with little preparation, and alter the style of his or her voice to portray the different characters. In fact, during the nineteenth century, it was not unheard of to have a quartet perform the song as a mini-melodrama. The solo part is not the only one that is difficult: With its continuous, driving, triplet rhythms, the accompaniment requires a pianist blessed with uncommon powers of endurance. Schubert, a competent pianist but by no means a virtuoso, found the accompaniment nearly impossible to play and altered the triplets to eighth-notes in performance. Franz Liszt, however, was known to make it even more difficult by playing certain passages in octaves.

Schubert gave his setting of Goethe's tale of horror a more dramatic twist than earlier song composers such as Johann Friedrich Reichardt. Casting his setting in a through-composed form freed Schubert to write in a manner that would reflect the attitudes and emotions of the three main characters. The father, who continually tries to calm his anxious child, sings in the lower part of the soloist's range, and his harmony is either static or moves relatively slowly. In contrast, the son sings in the upper range, and, after hearing the voice of the erlking, with a more chromatic line. Schubert's characterization of the demonic erlking is especially precise. While the erlking tries to entice the child, the accompaniment plays in a light triplet pattern and diatonic harmony. But when he loses patience and snatches at the boy, the accompaniment returns to the rhythm associated with the pounding hooves of the horse—we can almost see the erlking running alongside. The diminished seventh-harmonies convey the boy's anguish.

This song was such a favorite among nineteenth-century audiences that numerous arrangements were made of it. Both Berlioz and Liszt arranged the accompaniment for orchestra, and an enterprising Viennese musician turned each section into a waltz for use on All Hallow's Eve.

Section	A	B	C	D	E	D¹	F	D²	G
Stanza	I	II	III	IV	V	VI	VII.1–2	VII.3–4	VIII
Key	g	mod.	B♭	mod.	C	mod.	E♭ to d	d to g	g
Measure	1	33	58	73	87	98	117	124	131

Franz Schubert
"Erlkönig (1815)
CD 9/1

Schnell. ♩ = 152.

Singstimme.

Pianoforte.

Wer rei - tet so spät durch Nacht und Wind? Es ist der Va - ter mit sei - nem

Kind; er hat den Kna - ben wohl in dem Arm, er fasst ihn
sicher, er hält ihn warm. Mein
Sohn, was birgst du so bang dein Ge-sicht? Siehst, Va - - ter,
du den Erl - kö - nig nicht? den Er - len -
kö - nig mit Kron' und Schweif? Mein Sohn, es ist ein
f
pp
f
(pp)
mf
p
mf

54
Ne - belstreif.
„Du lie - - bes Kind, komm,
(ppp)
geh mit mir! gar schö - - - ne Spie - - le
spiel' ich mit dir; manch bun - - - - te Blu - men sind
an dem Strand; mei - ne Mut - - ter hat manch'
gül - - den Ge - wand".
Mein Va - ter, mein Va - ter, und hö - rest du
f

76
nicht, was Er-len-könig mir lei - se verspricht? Sei ru-hig, bleibe
p
decresc.
ru-hig, mein Kind; in dür-ren Blättern säu-selt der Wind. „Willst,
fei - ner Kna - be, du mit mir gehn? mei-ne Töch - ter sol - len dich
ppp
war - ten schön; mei-ne Töch - ter füh - ren den nächt - li-chen Reihn, und
wie - gen und tan - zen und sin - gen dich ein, sie wie - gen und tan - zen und sin - gen dich ein".
f

97
Mein Va - ter, mein Va - ter, und siehst du nicht dort Erl - kö-nigs Töchter am dü - stern Ort?
decresc.
Mein Sohn, mein Sohn, ich seh' es ge - nau; es scheinen die al - ten Wei - den so grau.
cresc.
ff
„Ich lie - be dich, mich
p
pp
reizt dei-ne schö-ne Ge-stalt; und bist du nicht wil - lig, so brauch' ich Ge-

123
walt". Mein Va - ter, mein Va - ter, jetzt fasst er mich an! Erl - kö - nig
fff
fz
fz
hat mir ein Leids ge - than! Dem Va - ter
fz
fz
fz
fz
f
accelerando
grau - set's, er rei - tet geschwind, er hält in Ar - men das
cresc.
äch - zen - de Kind, er - reicht den
ff
fz
Recit.
Hof mit Müh und Noth; in seinen Armen das Kind war todt.
Andante.
fz
fp
pp
p
f

I	Wer reitet so spät durch Nacht und Wind? Es ist der Vater mit seinem Kind; er hat den Knaben wohl in dem Arm, er faßt ihn sicher, er hält ihn warm.	A	Who rides so late through night and wind? It's the father with his child. He holds the boy close in his arm, he grasps him tight, he keeps him warm.
II	Mein Sohn, was birgst du so bang dein Gesicht? Siehst, Vater, du den Erlkönig nicht? Den Erlenkönig mit Kron' und Schweif? Mein Sohn, es ist ein Nebelstreif.	B	My son, why do you hide your face so fearfully? Don't you see, father, the erlking? the erlking with crown and train? My son, it's just a wisp of fog.
III	"Du liebes Kind, komm, geh mit mir! gar schöne Spiele spiel' ich mit dir; manch bunte Blumen sind an dem Strand; meine Mutter hat manch gülden Gewand."	C	"You dear child, come, go with me! many a fine game I'll play with you; lots of pretty flowers are on the bank, my mother has a robe full of gold."
IV	Mein Vater, mein Vater, und hörest du nicht was Erlenkönig mir leise verspricht? Sei ruhig, bleibe ruhig, mein Kind, In dürren Blättern säuselt der Wind.	D	My father, my father, don't you hear what erlking softly promised me? Be quiet, stay quiet, my child, the wind is only rustling the dry leaves.
V	"Willst, feiner Knabe, du mit mir gehn, meine Töchter sollen dich warten schön; meine Töchter führen den nächtlichen Reihn, und wiegen und tanzen und singen dich ein."	E	"Don't you want to go with me, handsome boy, my daughters will wait on you, my daughters lead the nightly dances, and with you will rock, dance, and sing."
VI	Mein Vater, mein Vater, und siehst du nicht dort Erlkönigs Töchter am düstern Ort? Mein Sohn, mein Sohn, ich seh' es genau; es scheinen die alten Weiden so grau.	D^1	My father, my father, don't you see erlking's daughters in that dark place? My son, my son, I see it quite well; it's just the old willow so gray.
VII	"Ich liebe dich, mich reizt deine schöne Gestalt; und bist du nicht willing, so brauch' ich Gewalt!" Mein Vater, mein Vater, jetzt fasst er mich an. Erlkönig hat mir ein Leids gethan!	F D^2	"I love you, your beautiful body charms me; and if you're not willing, then I'll use force!" My father, my father, he is grabbing me. Erlking has done me great harm!
VIII	Dem Vater grauset's, er reitet geschwind, er hält in Armen das ächzende Kind, erreicht den Hof mit Müh' und Noth; in seinen Armen das Kind war todt.	G	The father was terrified, he rode like the wind, he clutched the groaning child in his arms, he barely made it to the courtyard— in his arms the child was dead.

—Johann Wolfgang von Goethe

145

Franz Schubert

"Ganymed" (1817)

Johann Wolfgang von Goethe (1749–1832) occupies a place in German literature not unlike that of Shakespeare in English letters. His novel *The Sorrows of Young Werther* was a blockbuster, and many composers turned to his *Faust* as a source for their own operas, instrumental works, and songs. Schubert's appreciation of Goethe's poetry was immense. Around ten percent of his songs, including the much-admired "Erlkönig" and "Gretchen am Spinnrade," are set to texts by Goethe. The youthful Schubert not only dedicated "Ganymed" to Goethe, but also sent him two copies after it was printed in 1821. Alas, the famous author did not acknowledge its receipt, even though both copies were found among Goethe's personal effects after his death.

Like "Erlkönig," "Ganymed" is through-composed. The ecstatic language and contrasting images are matched by a flexible setting that at one moment is like a recitative, while at another it soars with a lyricism that matches the rapturous text. Its harmonic structure moves through many tonal areas and the song does not conclude in same key that was heard at the beginning. The second section in particular runs through a partial circle of fifths before settling into F major for the conclusion.

A				B					C	Coda
A♭	E♭	C♭	V/C♭	F♯	B	E	A/a	V/F	F	
1	19	31	46a	46b	52	56	64	71	75	116

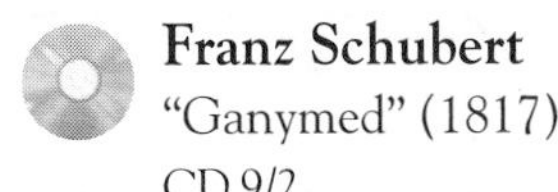

Franz Schubert
"Ganymed" (1817)
CD 9/2

Etwas langsam.

Singstimme.

Pianoforte.

pp

Wie im Mor - gen - glan - - ze

du rings mich an - glühst, Früh - ling, Ge - lieb - -

ter! Mit tau - sendfacher Liebes - won - ne sich an mein Herze
23
drängt dei - ner e - - - wigen Wär - me hei - - - lig Ge -
p
cresc.
fühl, un - - end - - - li - che Schö - - - ne!
f
cresc.
p
Dass ich dich fas - sen möcht' in die - sen Arm! Ach, an dei - nem
Bu - - sen lieg' ich, und schmach - te, und dei - - - ne

Blu - men, dein Gras drän - gen sich an mein Herz.
46
Du kühl'st den bren - nenden Durst
p
52
mei - nes Busens, lieb - li - cher Mor - gen - wind!
decresc.
Ruft drein die Nach - ti - gall lie - bend nach mir aus dem

Ne - bel-thal.
dimin.
68
Ich komm'! ich kom - me! ach! wo -
pp un poco accelerando
cresc.
f
hin, wo - hin?
Hin - auf strebt's, hin -
decresc.
p
stacc. cresc.
auf! Hin - auf strebt's, hin - auf! Es schwe-ben die Wol-ken
f
ff
p
ab - wärts, die Wol - ken nei - gen sich der seh - nen - den Lie - be.

Mir! Mir! In eurem Schoo - sse auf - wärts! Um - fan-gend umfan-gen!
p
cre - scen - do -
90
Auf-wärts an dei-nen Bu - sen, all - lie-bender Va-ter! Die
f
p
p
Wol - ken nei-gen sich der seh - nen-den Lie - be. Mir! Mir! In
eu - rem Schoosse auf - wärts! Um - fan-gend umfan-gen! Auf-wärts an dei-nen
cre - scen - do
f
Bu - sen, all - lie-bender Va - ter, all -
ff
p
fp
fp

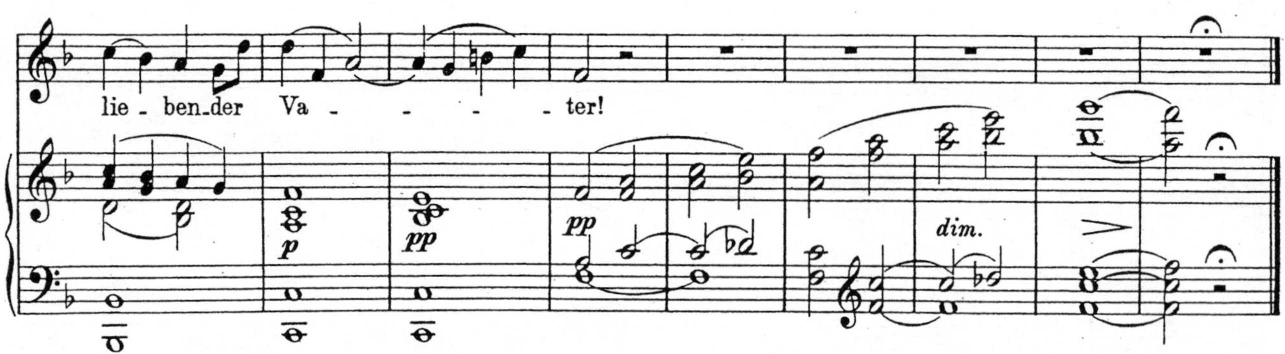

Wie im Morgenglanze du rings mich anglühst, Frühling, Geliebter! Mit tausendfacher Liebeswonne sich an mein Herze drängt deiner ewigen Wärme heilig Gefühl, unendliche Schöne!	As in the morning light you gleam about me, spring, beloved! With a thousandfold rapture of love presses to my heart your eternal warmth, holy feeling endless beauty!
Daß ich dich fassen möcht' in diesen Arm!	O that I could grasp you in these arms!
Ach, an deinem Busen lieg' ich, und schmachte, und deine Blumen, dein Gras drängen sich an mein Herz. Du kühlst den brennenden Durst meines Busens, lieblicher Morgenwind! Ruft drein die Nachtigall liebend nach mir aus dem Nebelthal.	O, on your breast I lie and languish and your flower, your grass I press to my heart. You cool the burning thirst of my bosom, dear morning wind! The nightingale calls lovingly to me from the valley mists.
Ich komm'! ich komme! ach! wohin, wohin?	I come, I come! O, to what place?
Hinauf strebt's hinauf! Es schweben die Wolken abwärts, die Wolken neigen sich der sehnenden Liebe. Mir! Mir! In eurem Schoße aufwärts! Umfangend umfangen! Aufwärts an deinen Busen, all-liebender Vater!	Upward it surges, upward! The clouds waft down, the clouds bend over with yearning love. To me! To me! Into their lap, upwards! Embrace upon embrace, upward toward your bosom, all-loving father!

—Johann Wolfgang von Goethe

146

Franz Schubert

"Nähe des Geliebten" (1815)

Today the *Lied* is a staple of vocal recitals performed in concert settings. However, that was not usually the case in Schubert's day, when the middle class purchased such songs to entertain their family and friends in the intimacy of their own homes. Certainly, elaborate compositions such as "Erlkönig" or "Ganymed" would have been beyond the musical capabilities of most amateurs. Strophic settings like that of "Nähe des Geliebten" were more consistent with the popular conception of the *Lied:* a simple rendition of the text that enabled anyone, regardless of talent, to express the yearnings of their heart. Modestly skillful pianists can get through the accompaniment of this song with reasonable facility, and an untrained tenor or soprano voice can manage the melody quite nicely. Yet even while maintaining a simple musical style, this song of longing for an absent love touches the heart.

As if to emphasize the physical distance between the poet and the beloved, the introduction opens with a strikingly chromatic progression that starts on a chord distant from the tonic. With the entrance of the voice, the tonic chord is reached, the harmony becomes diatonic, and the chord progressions are quite standard. The vocal melody itself divides into two parts, just like each stanza of the text, and both phrases begin and end on the tonic harmony. In the second phrase (m. 7), where the poet describes his vision of the beloved in the flickering moonlight and on the narrow path, chords reminiscent of the introduction return, although compressed into a single measure. So, in hindsight, the unusual opening is meant to show that the beloved is appearing to the soloist just before she sings "Ich denke dein" ("I think of you"). The tonal stability of the final measures—in contrast to the introduction—suggests that the poet is at rest. The beloved is nearby, even if only in spirit.

Franz Schubert

"Nähe des Geliebten (1815)

CD 9/3

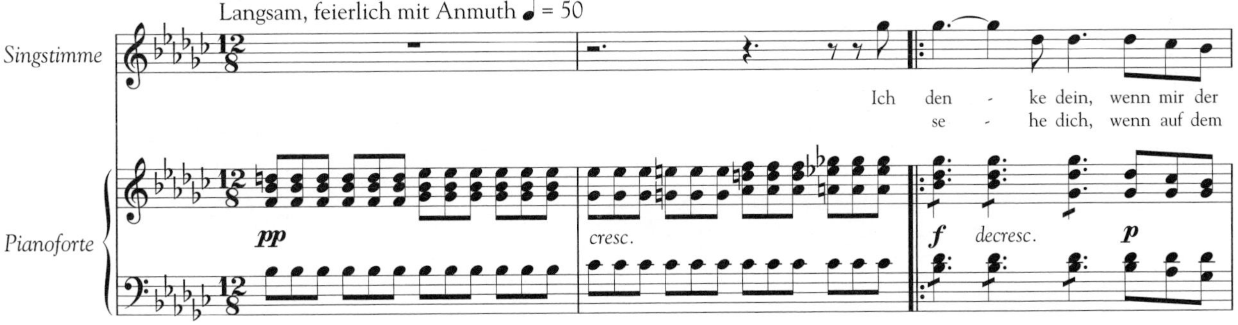

Ich denke dein, wenn mir der Sonne Schimmer
 Vom Meere strahlt;
Ich denke dein, wenn sich des Mondes Flimmer
 In Quellen malt.

Ich sehe dich, wenn auf dem fernen Wege
 Der Staub sich hebt;
In tiefer Nacht, wenn auf dem schmalen Wege
 Der Wandrer bebt.

Ich höre dich, wenn dort mit dumpfem Rauschen
 Die Welle steigt!
Im stillen Hain, da geh' ich oft zu lauschen,
 Wenn alles schweigt.

Ich bin bei dir; du seist auch noch so ferne,
 Du bist mir nah!
Die Sonne sinkt, bald leuchten mir die Sterne.
 O, wärst du da!

—Johann Wolfgang von Goethe

I think of you when I see the sunlight
 radiate from the sea;
I think of you when the flickering moonlight
 paints itself in the spring.

I see you when on the distant path
 the dust rises up;
In the depths of night, when on the narrow path
 the traveler shivers.

I hear you when with dull roar
 the waves rise up!
Into the quiet woods I often go to listen,
 when all is still.

I am with you. Though you are still far away,
 you are close to me!
The sun sets; soon the stars will gleam down to me.
 O, would that you were here!

Music in Paris Under Louis Philippe
Berlioz and Chopin

147

Hector Berlioz
Symphonie fantastique (1830)
Fourth movement, "March to the Scaffold"

Berlioz was a raconteur *par excellence*. The tale he wrote to underlie the *Symphonie fantastique* combines personal ambitions, frustrations, and bizarre imaginings that show the composer in his most "fantastic" frame of mind. The symphony is important not primarily because of the lurid story it portrays, but because it is a superb work of art that opened a new chapter in the history of the symphonic gēnre. Ever since the first performance, the fourth movement has been a favorite; Berlioz recalled it taking the audience "by storm." This may be due in part to the vividness of the program that the composer wrote to explain his music:

> Part four: March to the Scaffold
>
> Having realized that his love goes unrecognized, the artist poisons himself with opium. The dose of the narcotic, too weak to kill him, plunges him into a sleep accompanied by the most horrible visions. He dreams that he has killed the one he loved, that he is condemned, led to the scaffold, and now witnesses his own execution. The procession [of the execution squad] advances to the sounds of a march that is sometimes dark and savage, sometimes brilliant and solemn, in which the muffled sounds of solemn steps suddenly give way to the [crowd's] noisiest clamor. At the end of the march, the first four measures of the *idée fixe* reappear like a last thought of love interrupted by the fatal blow.

Yet it is not so much the program as the orchestration that gives life to this movement about an execution. When the first theme enters in measure 17 (the march that is sometimes dark, sometimes brilliant), we hear it repeated five times in succession, and each time the orchestration is varied, giving the theme a slightly different twist. The short second theme (m. 62) recalls the syncopated rhythms of the introduction and suddenly gives way to the second half of the movement, invoking, perhaps, the noisy clamor of a crowd gathered to watch the spectacle. Although this passage is uniformly loud, the composer's genius for orchestration shines forth, especially in the momentary *piano* passages.

The orchestra prepares for the entrance of the *idée fixe* with a half-cadence, and the clarinet enters with its truncated version of the beloved's theme in the bright key of G major. When the orchestra administers the coup de grâce, it is by a single blow of a G-minor chord. We then hear the head bounce down the scaffold and the crowd erupt in celebration during the nine bars of unremitting G major.

Hector Berlioz

Symphonie fantastique (1830)

Fourth movement, "March to the Scaffold"

CD 9/4

* In this movement the wind instruments may be doubled. (Note by H. Berlioz)

7
Cl.
Corni
Fag.
Cor.
Tr.
Tbn. I & II
Tbn. III
Tube
Timp. I
Timp. II
Vln. I
Vln. II
Vla.
Vcl.
Cb.
2.
pp
p
1.
p
cresc. poco a poco

14
Cl.
Corni
Fag.
Cor.
Tr.
Tbn. I & II
Tbn. III
Tube
Timp. I
Timp. II
Vln. I
Vln. II
Vla.
Vcl.
Cb.
(a4)
ff
mf
cresc. molto
pizz.
arco
f
unis.
dim.

Fag.
Vln. I
Vln. II
Vla.
Vcl.
Cb.
(a2)
(a4)
p
mf
f
cresc.
dim.
Corni
Timp. I
Timp. II
a4
pp

37
Fl.
Ob.
Cl.
Corni
Fag.
Cor.
Tr.
Tbn. I & II
Tbn. III
Tube
Timp. I
Timp. II
Vln. I
Vln. II
Vla.
Vcl.
Cb.
ff
mf
p
f
dim.

44
Fl.
Ob.
Cl.
Corni
Fag.
(a2)
(a4)
Timp. I
Timp. II
Vln. I
Vln. II
Vla.
Vcl.
Cb.
pizz.
51
a4
dim.
pp

59
Fl.
Ob.
Cl.
Corni
Fag.
Cor.
Tr.
Tbn. III
Tube
Timp. I
Timp. II
Vln. I
Vln. II
Vla.
Vcl.
Cb.
f
p
cresc.
mf
p
arco
ff
f < ff

66
Fl.
Ob.
Cl.
a2
Corni
Fag.
a2
Cor.
Tr.
2.
Tbn. I & II
mf
Tbn. III
1.
Tube
mf
f
mf
Timp. I
f
mf
Timp. II
f
mf
Vln. I
ff
Vln. II
ff
Vla.
ff
Vel.
ff
Cb.
ff

73
Fl.
Ob.
Cl.
Corni
Fag.
Cor.
Tr.
Tbn. III
Tube
Timp. I
Timp. II
Vln. I
Vln. II
Vla.
Vcl.
Cb.
cresc.
poco f
pizz.
arco

80
Fl.
Ob.
Cl.
Corni
Fag.
Cor.
Tr.
Tbn. III
Tube
Timp. I
Timp. II
Tamb.
Cin.
Vln. I
Vln. II
Vla.
Vcl.
Cb.
(a2)
1.
pizz.
arco

87
Fl.
Ob.
Cl.
Corni
Fag.
a4
Cor.
Tr.
Tbn. III
Tube
Timp. I
Timp. II
Vln. I
Vln. II
Vla.
Vel.
Cb.
poco f
f cresc.
ff
mf
pizz.
arco
cresc.
(mf) cresc.

92
Fl.
Ob.
Cl.
a2
Corni
Fag.
Cor.
a2
Tr.
Tbn. I & II
2.
mf
Tbn. III
Tube
2.
div.
f
mf
Timp. I
f
Timp. II
f
Vln. I
f
ff
ff
Vln. II
f
ff
ff
Vla.
ff
ff
Vcl.
ff
ff
Cb.
ff
ff

97
Fl.
Ob.
Cl.
Corni
Fag.
Cor.
Tr.
Tbn. III
Tube
Timp. I
Timp. II
Vln. I
Vln. II
Vla.
Vcl.
Cb.
mf
cresc.
f

101
Fl.
Ob.
Cl.
Corni
Fag.
Cor.
Tr.
Tbn. III
Tube
Timp. I
Timp. II
Vln. I
Vln. II
Vla.
Vcl.
Cb.
cresc.
poco f
1.

107
Fl.
Ob.
Cl.
Corni
Fag.
Cor.
Tr.
Tbn. III
Tube
Timp. I
Timp. II
Tamb.
Cin.
Vln. I
Vln. II
Vla.
Vcl.
Cb.
a2
(a2)
1.
pizz.
arco

114
Fl.
Ob.
Cl.
Corni
Fag.
Cor.
Tr.
Tbn. I & II
Tbn. III
Tube
Timp. I
Vln. I
Vln. II
Vla.
Vel.
Cb.
a2
mf
cresc.
(a4)
arco
ff
sempre più forte

* This remark leads to the conclusion that the composer desired the kettle-drums to be muffled at the beginning of this piece. (Note by the editors)

123
Fl.
Ob.
Cl.
Corni
Fag.
Cor.
Tr.
Tbn. I & II
Tbn. III
Tube
Baguettes de bois
Wooden drum-sticks
Timp. I
Timp. II
Tamb.
Cin.
Vln. I
Vln. II
Vla.
Vcl.
Cb.
a2
1.
dim.

130
Fl.
Ob.
Cl.
Corni
Fag.
Cor.
Tr.
Tbn. I & II
Tbn. III
Tube
Timp. I
Tamb.
Cin.
Vln. I
Vln. II
Vla.
Vcl.
Cb.
ff
mf

139
Fl.
Ob.
Cl.
Corni
Fag.
Cor.
Tr.
Tbn. I & II
Tbn. III
Tube
Timp. I
Timp. II
Tamb.
Cin.
Vln. I
Vln. II
Vla.
Vcl.
Cb.
a2
1.
sul G
ff
f

145
Fl.
Ob.
Cl.
Corni
Fag.
Cor.
Tr.
Tbn. I & II
Tbn. III
Tube
Timp. I
Timp. II
Tamb.
Cin.
Vln. I
Vln. II
Vla.
Vcl.
Cb.

151

Fl.

Ob.

Cl.

Corni

Fag.

Cor.

Tr.

Tbn. I & II

Tbn. III

Tube

Timp. I

mute in B

Timp. II

Vln. I

Vln. II

Vla.

Vcl.

Cb.

* This is no clerical error; the G-minor chord is immediately neat to the D♭-major chord. The composer requests the violinists and violaplayers no to "correct" their parts by placing a ♭ before the D of the fifth of the G-minor chord. (Note by H. Berlioz)

158

Fl. — p, pp, ff, a2

Ob. — p, pp, ff

Cl. — p, pp, ff, 1. pp dolce assai ed appassionato

Corni — ff; p, pp, ff

Fag. — p, pp, (a4) ff

Cor. — ff

Tr. — ff

Tbn. I & II — ff

Tbn. III — ff

Tube — ff

Timp. II — ff

Vln. I — p, pp, ff

Vln. II — p, pp, ff

Vla. — p, pp, ff

Vcl. — p, pp, ff

Cb. — p, pp, ff

165
rall. poco a tempo
Fl.
Ob.
Cl.
Corni
Fag.
1., 2.
3., 4.
Cor.
Tr.
Tbn. I & II
Tbn. III
Tube
Timp. I
Timp. II
Timp. III
Three drummers
Tamb.
Cin.
G. Tamb.
Muffle the tone.
Muffle the tone with the hand.
Rall. poco a tempo
Vln. I
Vln. II
Vla.
Vcl.
Cb.
pizz.
a2

172
Fl.
Ob.
Cl.
Corni
1., 2.
Fag.
3., 4.
Cor.
Tr.
Tbn. I & II
Tbn. III
Tube
Timp. I
Timp. II
Timp. III
Tamb.
Cin.
G. Tamb.
Vln. I
Vln. II
Vla.
Vcl.
Cb.
arco
ff
f

148

Hector Berlioz

"Absence" from *Les nuits d'été* (1840)

Berlioz composed this song in 1840, before—it is believed—he began his liaison with the soprano Marie Recio. It quickly became "her" song, and she performed it regularly on the concert tours she and Berlioz made together. Later, when she finally stopped singing in his concerts, she allowed him to let other sopranos sing the work, although he tactfully waited eight years before doing so. At the end of his life (Marie had died six years before), partially paralyzed from a stroke and unable to speak, he inscribed the opening line—text and music—of "Absence" in the autograph book of a friend, as a final farewell.

The numerous open octaves and widely spaced chords that characterize the accompaniment to this song are perhaps more appropriate for an orchestral performance than for the keyboard. Yet it is that very barrenness that illustrates the unfulfilled desire and vast distance that separates the lovers. Note especially the tritone that occurs three times (mm. 3, 29, and 55), always on the word "bien-aimée" ("beloved"). The effect is to underscore a yearning desire that finally dissolves into resolution. Berlioz turned the three stanzas of the poem into a five-part rondo by repeating the first stanza after the second and third of Théophile Gautier's original poem (see translation). While the first stanza describes the poet's emotions, the second and third stanzas describe the distance in time and space that separates the two lovers. Berlioz set these two stanzas in a more recitative-like style and each passage concludes with an unresolved dominant-seventh chord. With each return of the **A** section (stanza I) the harmony is wrenched back to the tonic key of F♯ major.

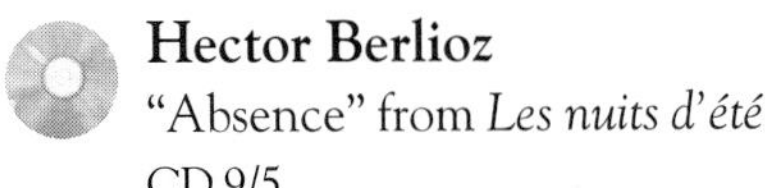

Hector Berlioz

"Absence" from *Les nuits d'été* (1840)

CD 9/5

5
(p)
Com-me une fleur loin du so-leil, La fleur de ma vie est fer-
pp
11
mf
dim.
-mé-e Loin de ton sou-ri-re ver-meil.
mf
dim.
pp
16
1 poco più animato
(p)
En-tre nos cœurs quel-le dis-tan-ce! Tant d'es-pace en-tre nos bai-
poco più animato
pp

con agitazione
(mf)
sers! O sort a - mer! ô dure ab - sen - ce!
mf
poco cresc.
f
O grands dé - sirs i - na - pai - sés!
Tempo I
ppp
p
Ped.
mf
Re - viens, re - viens, ma bien - ai - mé - e!
pp
p
mf
Ped.

31
(p)
Comme u - ne fleur loin du so - leil, La fleur de ma
pp
36
mf
dim.
p
vie est fer - mé - e Loin de ton sou - ri - re ver - meil.
mf
dim.
pp
42
2
poco più animato
cresc.
D'i - ci là - bas que de cam - pa - gnes, Que de vil - les et de ha -
poco più animato
pp
cresc.

46
rit.
Tempo I. e largo
meaux, Que de val - lons et de mon - ta - gnes, A las -
rit.
Tempo I. e largo
poco f
Ped.
Ped.
50
ppp sotto voce
ser le pied des che - vaux! Re-viens, re -
p
p
ppp
dim.
Ped.
Ped.
54
ed estinto ppp
(ppp)
- viens, ma bien - ai - mé - - é! Comme u - ne
(ppp)
Ped.
Ped.

Reviens, reviens, ma bien-aimée; Comme une fleur loin du soleil, La fleur de ma vie est fermée Loin de ton sourire vermeil.	Come back, come back, my beloved; Like a flower far from the sun, my life's flower is closed far from your rosy smile.
Entre nos coeurs quelle distance! Tant d'espace entre nos baisers! Ô sort amer! ô dure absence! Ô grands désirs inapaisés!	What distance between our hearts! How long between our kisses! O bitter fate! Oh pitiless absence! Oh great unsatisfied desires!
D'ici là-bas, que de compagnes, Que de villes et de hameaux, Que de vallons et de montagnes, À lasser le pied des chevaux!	How many fields there are from here to there, How many towns and villages, How many hills and valleys, Enough to weary horses' feet.

149

Frédéric Chopin
Nocturne in D♭ Major, Opus 27, No. 2 (1835)

The two nocturnes that make up Opus 27 were published in May 1836. Chopin dedicated the set to the Countess d'Apponyi, the wife of Austria's ambassador to Paris. The Countess belonged to the set of Parisian socialites—between two and three thousand strong—who, due to their wealth and sophistication, spent their days and nights in diversion: attending concerts, parties, dinners, and any other activity that provided amusement. Every Monday evening, the Countess opened her mansion to this well-acquainted and sophisticated crowd, and on Sunday afternoons she sponsored concerts where various artists, including Chopin and Rossini, performed. During inclement weather, she held these musicales in her large, flower-filled greenhouse. As an habitué of these soirées, Chopin not only performed in the Countess's urbane setting, but also encountered a bevy of wealthy women who, having ample time and money, were willing to pay handsome fees for the privilege of taking piano lessons from this young, elegant, and fine-looking musician.

Chopin's nocturnes are noted for their great lyrical beauty, and have often been compared with the arias of the Italian opera composer Vincenzo Bellini. This nocturne has two themes that alternate smoothly without any transitional passagework. Each time the themes return, they are ornamented, much in the manner that an operatic diva would embellish her aria. Harmonically, these works are full of subtle surprises, such as unresolved cadences and sudden movements between remote tonal areas (for example, the juxtaposition of D♭-major and A-major chords in mm. 33–34). The coda introduces a new motive, but one that is related to the parallel sixths of the **B** section.

A	B	A	B'	A	B'	Coda
1	10	26	34	46	54	62

Frédéric Chopin
Nocturne in D♭ Major, Opus 27, No. 2 (1835)
CD 9/6

espressivo
cresc.
17
con forza
cresc.

f
pp
fz
mf
a tempo
ritenuto
dolce
leggieriss.
dolce
32
34

cresc.
cresc.
dimin.
rit.
46
a tempo
dolce

cresc.
con forza
con anima
con forza
cresc.
appassionato
60
ritard.
a tempo
dolciss.
mini cadenza ?
Coda

dimin.
p
dolciss.
dim.
calando
smorzando
dolciss. e dimin.
pp

Leipzig and the Gewandhaus
Felix Mendelssohn and the Schumanns

150

Felix Mendelssohn
Piano Trio in D Minor, Opus 49 (1839)
First movement, *molto allegro ed agitato*

Mendelssohn composed his Trio for piano, violin, and cello, Opus 49, in the summer of 1839, during a sojourn in the city of Frankfurt, where he had directed the Lower Rhine Music Festival. The work, like most of Mendelssohn's mature chamber compositions, effortlessly merges a classical form with a modern and thoroughly romantic expression—qualities plainly seen in the first movement. The work's unique resolution of opposing historical and stylistic streams was underscored by Robert Schumann when he reviewed the composition in 1840, shortly after its publication. "There's little to be said, since it is by now in everyone's hands," Schumann confessed.

> It is the master trio of the present day, just like Beethoven's Trio in B♭ [Op. 97] and D [Op. 70, No. 1], or the Schubert E♭ [D. 939] were in their time. It is a beautiful composition that will bring pleasure to our grandchildren and great-grandchildren in years to come. . . .
>
> What can I add about this Trio that is not already apparent to all who have heard it? Certainly, its praises are sung best by listening to it played by Mendelssohn himself. There may be bolder virtuosos than him, but no others can with such magical freshness play Mendelssohn's works as he can. (*Neue Zeitschrift für Musik*, 19 December 1840)

What were the classic and romantic elements of sonata form that Mendelssohn brought together when composing this movement? In general, the movement retains the proportions, thematic clarity, and melodic abundance of a sonata by Mozart, along with the contrasting themes and subtle methods of motivic unity characteristic of Beethoven's music. The expressive quality of the themes, as well as the long phrases and harmonic color, are more romantic in character. The exposition consists of two themes that are each divided into contrasting parts and concludes with a closing theme that recalls the opening idea. As is typical of the classical style, the development begins with its own introduction, which begins a long process of modulation. The recapitulation and coda do not repeat themes literally, but provide an opportunity for further elaboration.

Section	Exposition						Development		
Theme	Ia	Ib	Trans.	IIa	IIb	Closing	Ia	IIa	IIb
Measure	1	39	67	119	163	187	222	250	284

Dev., cont.		Recapitulation					Coda		
Closing	IIa	Ia	Trans.	IIa	IIb	Closing	Closing	IIa	Ia
297	312	368	427	435	479	503	540	558	604

Felix Mendelsshohn
Piano Trio in D Minor, Opus 49 (1839)
First movement, *molto allegro ed agitato*
CD 9/7

f
dim.
p
A
cresc.
6
sf
41
f
p
52
sfp

sf cresc.
sf
f
sf cresc.
sf
f
cre
sf
scen
sf
do
sf
più forte
64
ff
ff
B
ff
marcato
sf
ff
ff
75
sf
sf
sf
marcato
sf

sf
ff
87
cre
scen
espressivo
do
102
dim.
espress.
C
p

112
pp
p
espressivo
dim.
pp
sempre pp
122
130
pp
pp
p
p
cantabile
cresc.
138
sf
p
sf
p

145
pp
pp
dim.
pp
153
dolce
sf
dim.
pp
dim.
pp
sf
pp
pp
D
agitato
pp
164
pp
cresc.
pp
cresc.
cre
scen
tr
169
f
f
do
tr
f
sf

174
più f
più f
sf
sf
sf
sf
179
f
f
f
sf
sf
sf
sf
sf
sf
185
p
p
E
sf
sf
p
cresc.
f
191
cresc.
cresc.
sf
sf
ff
ff
sf
sf
cresc.
sf
ff

197
sf
sf
ff
ff
ff
203
sf
sf
sf
sf
sf
sf
sf
sf
211
marcato
marcato
f
f
F
f marcato
ff
217
fp
p
Ped.

223
p
sf
cresc.
sf
p
Ped.
231
sf
p
p
G
cresc.
sf
p
cresc.
Ped.
239
cresc.
sf
p
cresc.
sf
p
cresc.
f
dimin.
Ped.
248
dim.
dim.
p
sf
sf

260
p
p
p
pp e legato
268
sempre p
sempre pp e legato
276
sf
sf cresc.
sf
sf
cresc.
cresc.
284
p
p
H
pp agitato
sempre p

289
cresc.
cresc.
cre - - scen -
294
f
sf
f
sf
sf
- do
f
299
sf
sf
sf
sf
sf
sf
più f
sf
304
sf
marcato assai
sf
sf
f
sempre più f

310
p
p
I
pp leggiero
Ped.
316
marcato
sempre pp
cresc.
321
sf
sf
f
più f
326
p
p
pp leggiero
Ped.

331
336
K
cresc.
sf
343
p
cre
scen
do
f
357
dimi
nu
en
dimin.
dimin

358
do
pp
pp
pp
pp
p
u
en
do
pp
368
cantabile
L
pp
Ped.
375
sf
sf
382
sf
cresc.
cresc.
cre
scen
do
Ped.

390
ritard.
a tempo
ritard.
a tempo
Adagio.
Tempo I.
sf
ritard.
399
410
cre
scen
do
418
dimin.
dimin.
cresc.

425
M
p
dim.
433
dolce
pp
dimin.
440
dimin.
448
sf
cantabile
N
sf

456
sf
f
p
463
pp
pp
pp
sf espress.
sf
473
p
p
pp
agitato
pp
482
p
cresc.
sf
p
cresc.
cre- scen - do

487
f
f
f
sf
3
sf
sf
491
più f
più f
3
sf
sf
sf
495
f
f
8
3
f.
sf
sf
8
sf
sf
sf
500
p
p
P
sf
sf
sf
sf
p cre
scen

505
sf
cresc.
do
f
510
ff
515
sf
521
marcato

529
Q
sf
3
f
535
sempre più f
ff
più f
Ped.
543
sempre più f
sempre
sf
R

561
568
sf
mf
f
Ped.
576
assai animato
p
583
cre - - - scen - do
ff

588
mf
S
p
cre
scen
do
593
sf
sf
ff
cresc.
cresc.
f
598
f
f
sf
sf
sf
603
ff
ff
sf
sf
ff
sf
Ped.

151

Robert Schumann

Symphony No. 1 (1841)

Second movement, *Largetto*

Robert Schumann sketched his Symphony No. 1 in B♭ in January 1841, in a burst of creative energy that spanned only four days. The work was soon orchestrated, and it received its first performance by Leipzig's Gewandhaus Orchestra under the direction of Felix Mendelssohn in March of the same year.

The symphony was conceived with an illustrative character, in the manner of Beethoven's "Pastoral Symphony." The subject was nature during springtime, and, like Beethoven, Schumann originally gave descriptive titles to each of the four movements: "Spring's Beginning," "Evening," "Happy Games," and "Spring Bursting Out." But Schumann was also sensitive to the dangers of a composer being too specific in establishing a work's meaning, so he dropped these titles when the work was published in 1841. Still, the B♭ symphony retains its descriptive nickname, "Spring" Symphony.

The second movement, *Larghetto,* in E♭, paints a soothing musical portrait of a spring evening. Cast in a rondo-like form, the movement repeatedly returns to its inspiring opening theme—one that consists of three phrases (**abb**), all supported by a syncopated accompaniment. In the movement's first contrasting section (**B**), the violas lead into the theme with a motive first played by the second violins as an accompaniment figure in measure 7, thereby providing a hint of musical unity between the two sections. However, rondos are noted for differentiation between sections, so in addition to the new theme, Schumann sets this section apart by dividing the melodic interest more evenly between the strings and winds. When the **A** section returns in measure 41, the cello plays an abbreviated version of the theme, but in the dominant key of B♭ major rather than in the tonic one would expect. The **C** section is different in style from either **A** or **B**. Whereas the earlier sections were notable for the lyrical beauty of their themes, the melodic character of **C** is more fragmentary and the harmonic plan more unstable, allowing for a development-like passage.

When the **A** section returns for the final time, the main melody recurs in its full form and in the home key of E♭ major. The motive that unified the **A** and **B** sections is brought back and given prominence in the coda. To conclude the movement, Schumann follows the example of Beethoven's "Pastoral" by linking movements together without pause, and the final twelve measures of the *Larghetto* constitute a transition to the symphony's third movement.

A	B	A[1]	C	A[2]	Coda	Transition
1	25	41	55	78	100	113

Robert Schumann
Symphony No. 1 (1841)
Second movement, *Largetto*
CD 9/8

I.
dol.
dim.
cresc.
a 2.
fp
sf
34

E
tr
p sempre e dolce
p sempre e dolce
p sempre e dolce
p sempre e dolce
p pizz.
p cresc.
dim.
div.
sempre p
p
cresc.
dim.
p
cresc.
dim.
cantabile
pizz.
f
p
f
p
p
E
47
fp
fp
f
p
f
p
f
p
fp
f
p
fp
f
p
f
p
f
p
tr
cresc.
arco
f
p

F
I.
cresc.
sf
p
arco
poco
marcato
a
tr
60
poco a poco
F

cresc.
sf
p
fp
f
73
I Solo
dol.
p cresc.
pp espressivo
dim.
divisi
pp sempre
tr

84
cresc.
cresc.
cresc.
cresc.
p
p
p
p
p
p
p
cresc.
cresc.
cresc.
cresc.
cresc.

sf
dim.
92
f
dol.

sf
p
tr
cresc.
dim.
3
100
I.
p dol.
f
pp
fp
pp dol.
divisi
pizz.

152

Clara Schumann

"Liebst du um Schönheit" (1841)

Although there had been a handful of notable piano virtuosos prior to the nineteenth century, during the Romantic era the number of concert pianists increased as fast as a warren of rabbits: They were everywhere. Yet a few names—Frédéric Chopin, Franz Liszt, and Clara Schumann—stood above the rest and are renowned even today. Like her peers, Clara Schumann composed as well as performed, and her works—almost all of which involve piano—reveal the diversity and depth of her genius. Her songs are especially distinguished. She began to compose songs in earnest in 1840, shortly after her marriage to Robert Schumann, who had poured forth a torrent of great songs in the months preceding their marriage. Robert hatched the idea of a joint collection, expressing their mutual love, with poetry drawn from Friedrich Rückert's *Liebesfrühling (Springtime of Love)*. The project was completed in the summer and fall of 1841 and given the title *Twelve Songs from F. Rückert's "Springtime of Love."* Robert secretly arranged to have the songs published and presented a printed copy to Clara on her twenty-second birthday.

Nine of the songs were written by Robert and three by Clara. To underscore that *Liebesfrühling*—like love itself—was the combined work of two individuals, they gave the composition two opus numbers: It is listed on the title page as Opus 37/12. The first number is Robert's, the second, Clara's. One of Clara's contributions to the joint composition is the touching "Liebst du um Schönheit" ("If You Love Beauty"), the fourth song in the collection. The melody has a simple artlessness but the harmony provides great warmth and subtlety. Rückert's poem has four stanzas, and Clara set the *Lied* in a modified strophic form (**A A**[1] **A A**[1]). The vocal setting for each of the four stanzas is based upon two alternating versions of a single melody. The accompaniment is nearly the same for all four stanzas, although there are some important modifications (for example, compare mm. 7–10 with mm. 15–18). For the last stanza, the accompaniment intensifies the mood by expanding the texture to include octave doublings (compare mm. 26–27 with mm. 2–3, 10–11, and 18–19). The result is a beautiful, tender song that asks for and commits to love for a lifetime.

Clara Schumann

"Liebst du um Schönheit" (1841)

CD 9/9

mf
Lie - be den Früh - ling der jung ist je - des Jahr! Liebst du um
Schä - tze, o nicht mich lie - be. Lie - be die Meer - frau, sie
11
rit.
Bewegter
hat viel Per - len klar. Liebst du um Lie - be, o ja mich
f
16
lie - be! Liebst du um Lie - be, o ja mich lie - be, lie - be mich im - mer, dich lieb' ich
p
rit.

Liebst du um Schönheit
O nicht mich liebe!
Liebe die Sonne,
Sie trägt ein gold'nes Haar!

Liebst du um Jugend,
O nicht mich liebe!
Liebe den Frühling
Der jung ist jedes Jahr!

Liebst du um Schätze,
O nicht mich liebe!
Liebe die Meerfrau,
Sie hat viel Perlen klar.

Liebst du um Liebe,
O ja mich liebe!
Liebe mich immer,
Dich lieb' ich immerdar!

—Friedrich Rückert

If you love for beauty,
you won't love me.
Love the sun instead,
she has golden hair.

If you love for youth,
you won't love me.
Love springtime instead,
she stays young each year.

If you love for money,
you won't love me.
Love the mermaid instead,
she has many fine pearls.

If you love for love,
then, yes, love me.
Love me forever,
and I will love you as long.

German Opera of the Nineteenth Century *Weber and Wagner*

153

Carl Maria von Weber
Der Freischütz (1821)
Act 2, Wolf's Glen Scene, concluding section

It is a dark and stormy night when the hunters Max and Caspar meet in the haunted Wolf's Glen to cast magic bullets. What brings about the fearful meeting, which everyone in the audience knows is fraught with peril to Max's immortal soul? Love, of course. Max is in desperate need of these bullets to win a shooting contest the next day, so as to gain the hand of his beloved Agathe. But unknown to him, Caspar is in league with the devil, called Samiel, who seeks to entrap Max in a tangled web of evil.

This is the setting for the Wolf's Glen Scene, the dramatic high point of Carl Maria von Weber's opera *Der Freischütz* (*The Bewitched Marksman*). The opera itself is close in form to *Singspiel*—an older type of German-language opera in which simple musical numbers are inserted into a spoken play. The Wolf's Glen Scene itself is a finale, a long and multipartite number occurring at the end of an act that alternates ensemble, choral, and solo singing. In addition to these musical resources, Weber also brings in "melodrama," in which speaking is accompanied by, or alternates with, music from the orchestra.

At the end of the Wolf's Glen Scene, Caspar puts the proper ingredients—including lead and shards of glass broken from a church window—into the pot and, after the orchestra intones Samiel's motive, the first bullet is cast. The excitement rises as other bullets are tossed from their mold, and following the seventh bullet both Max and Caspar are thrown to the ground in a great eruption of nature. As a distant church bell strikes one, the storm abates and the curtain falls.

The premiere of *Der Freischütz* took place in Berlin. It was a smash hit, and whenever it was performed, it played to a full house. It was staged in New York City as early as 1825. In Berlin, the excitement was so great that crowds formed in front of the theater four hours before the curtain went up. The management finally opened the doors to relieve the congestion and in the ensuing rush even people who did not have tickets were swept into the theater. In the audience that night were the 12-year-old Felix Mendelssohn (along with his parents) and E.T.A. Hoffmann—the author who provided the stories for Offenbach's *Tales of Hoffmann* and Tchaikovsky's *The Nutcracker*. The Wolf's Glen Scene was a sensation.

Carl Maria von Weber

Der Freischütz (1821)

CD 9/10

CASPAR. Hier, erst das Blei; etwas Glas von zerbrochenen Kirchenfenstern, das findeth sich. Etwas Quecksilber. Drei Kugeln, die schon einmal getroffen.

CASPAR. First the lead; some broken glass of church-windows, that can always be got; some quicksilver; three bullets that have hit their mark.

CASPAR. Das rechte Auge eines Wiedenhopfs; das linke eines Lucheses. Probatum est!

CASPAR. The right eye of a lapwing, the left of a lynx; a powerful charm.

CASPAR. Und nun den Kugelsegen!

CASPAR. And now a blessing on the bullets!

(At the three rests he prostrates himself three times to the earth.)

CASPAR. Schütze, der im Dunkeln wacht, Samiel! Samiel! hab, acht! Steh mir bei in dieser

Thou who roam'st at midnight hour, Zamiel, Zamiel, thy pow'r, Spirit dread, be near this

Nacht, Bis der Zauber ist voll- bracht! Salbe mir so Kraut als Blei, Segn'es sieben, neun und drei, dass die Kugel tüchtig sei!

night, And complete the mystic rite. By the shade of of murderer's dead, Do thou bless the charmed lead. Seven the number we revere:

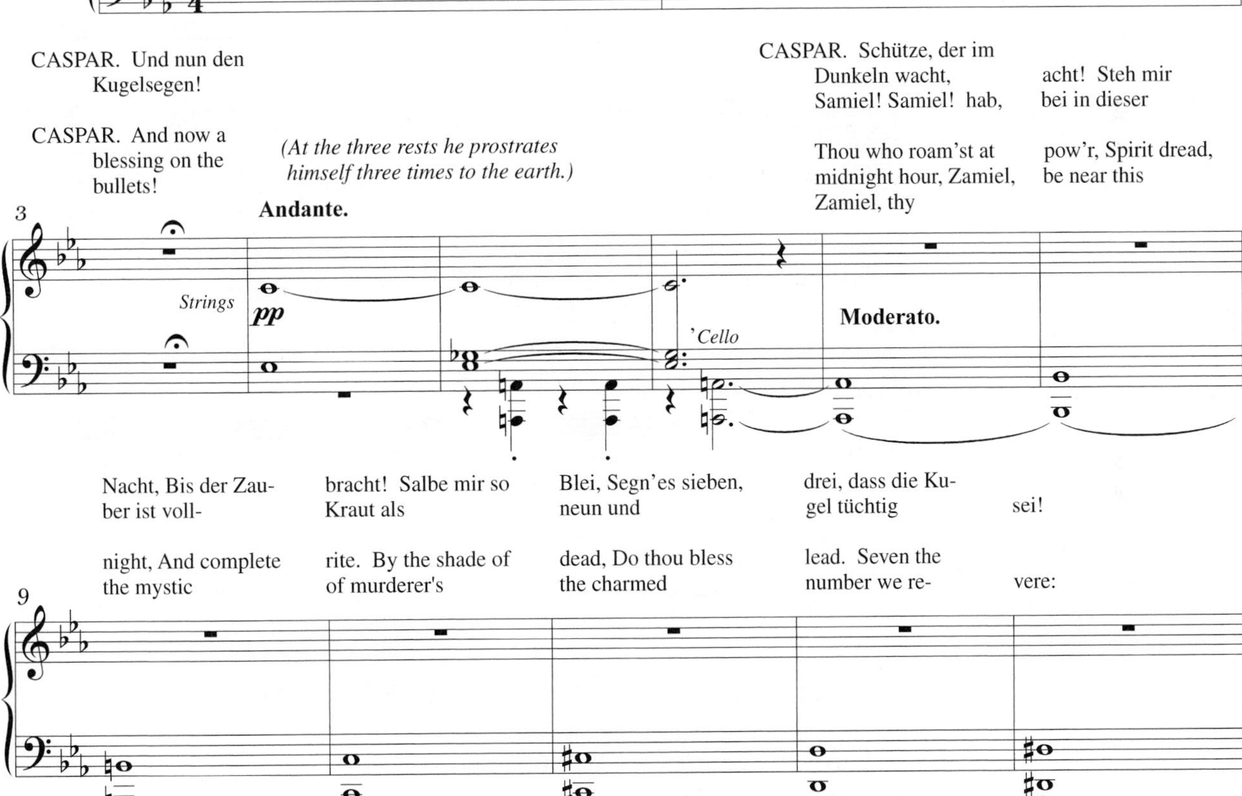

(The contents of the ladle ferment and hiss, with a greenish flame. A cloud passes entirely over the moon. The scene is now lighted only by the fire on the hearth, the owl's eyes, and the decayed wood of the oak-tree.)

Samiel! Samiel! herbei!

Zamiel! Zamiel! appear!

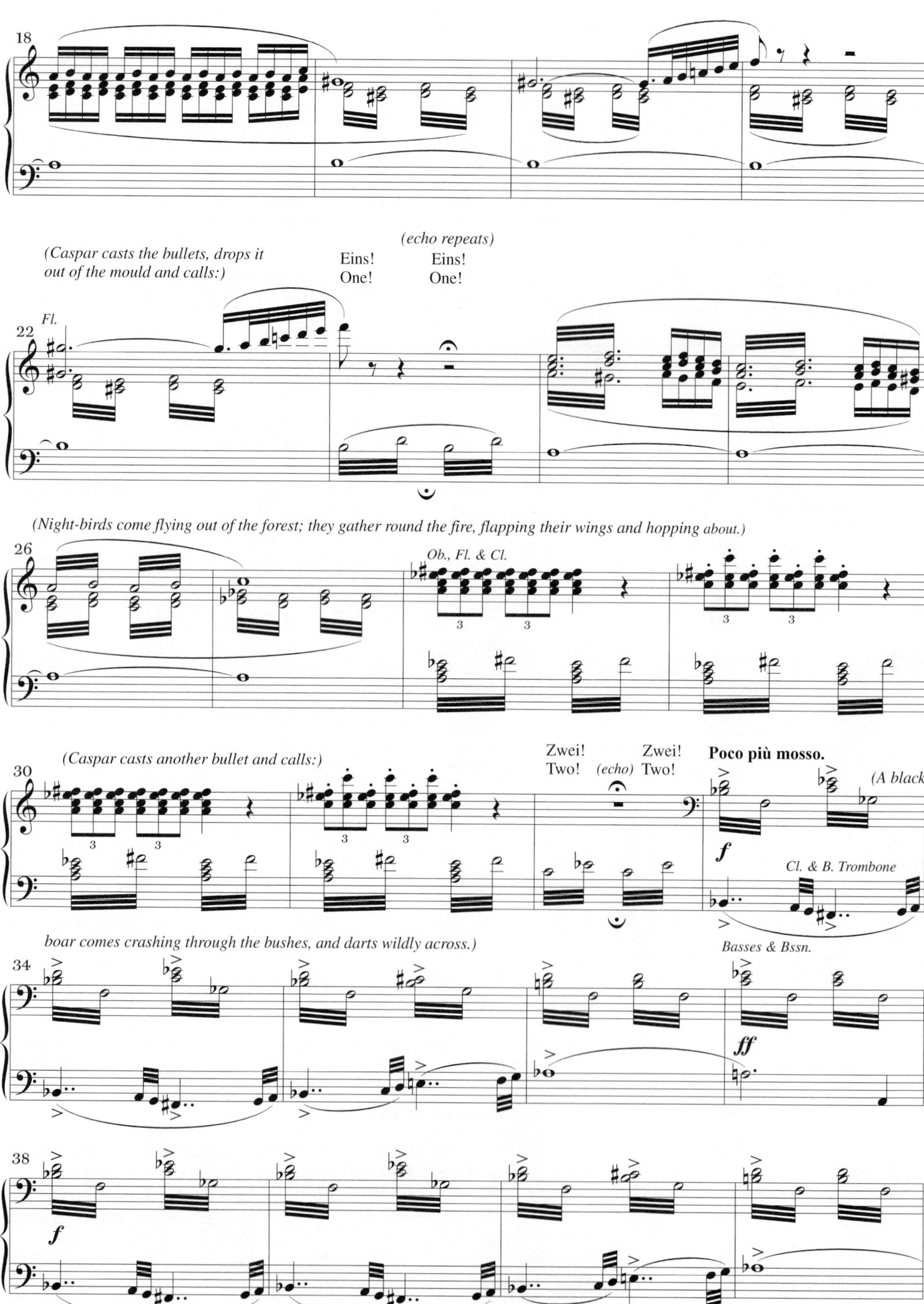
18
(Caspar casts the bullets, drops it out of the mould and calls:)
(echo repeats)
Eins!
One!
Eins!
One!
22
Fl.
(Night-birds come flying out of the forest; they gather round the fire, flapping their wings and hopping about.)
26
Ob., Fl. & Cl.
(Caspar casts another bullet and calls:)
30
Zwei!
Two!
(echo)
Zwei!
Two!
Poco più mosso.
(A black
Cl. & B. Trombone
boar comes crashing through the bushes, and darts wildly across.)
34
Basses & Bssn.
38

42
ff
(Caspar becomes agitated and calls:)
Drei!
Three!
(echo)
Drei!
Three!
(A hurricane rises, bends and breaks the tops
46
Strings & K.-dr. p roll
Cl., Horns & Bssn.
of the trees, sparks fly from the fire, etc., etc.)
49
cresc.
f
52
Strings
ff
Wind
55
58

CASPAR. (counts fearfully):
Vier!
Four!
(echo)
Vier!
Four!
(Rattling of wheels, cracking of
fp
ff
Strings, Ob., Cl. & Bassn.
whips, and trampling of horses, are heard. Four wheels darting fire roll across the stage.)
Fl.
ff
(Neighing and barking are heard in the air; misty forms of hunters on foot
CASPAR. (becoming more
and more agitated:)
Fünf!
Five!
(echo)
Fünf!
Five!
CASPAR. Wehe! das wilde Heer!
Ah! The Wild Huntsman!
4 Horns (in E, F, and B flat alti).
fp
ff
Bssn. & Trombone
and on horseback, with stags and hounds, rush through the air.)

INVISIBLE CHORUS. Tenor and Bass.
85
ff
Durch Berg und Thal, durch Schlucht und
Thro' hill and dale, Thro' glen and
90
Schacht, durch Thau und Wol - ken Sturm und Nacht, durch Thau und Wol - ken,
mire, Thro' dew and cloud, thro' storm and fire, Thro' dew and cloud, thro'
94
Sturm und Nacht!
storm and fire!
ff Strings
Durch Höl - le.
To hol - low
100
Sumpf und Er - den kluft, durch Feu - er, Er - de, See and Luft, jo
caves where de - mons loom, We lure our prey to death and doom, yo

105
ho, wau wau! jo ho, wau wau! ho, ho, ho, ho, ho, ho,
ho, wow wow! yo ho, wow wow! ho, ho, ho, ho, ho, ho,
ten.
110
ho, ho!
ho, ho!
CASPAR. Sechs! Six!
(echo)
Sechs! Six!
(Total darkness obscures the sky. Storm of thunder, lightning and hail; flames start from the earth; meteors appear on the hills, etc.)
Presto.
ff
Tutti, Trombones, Trumpets, & c.
115
120
124
ff

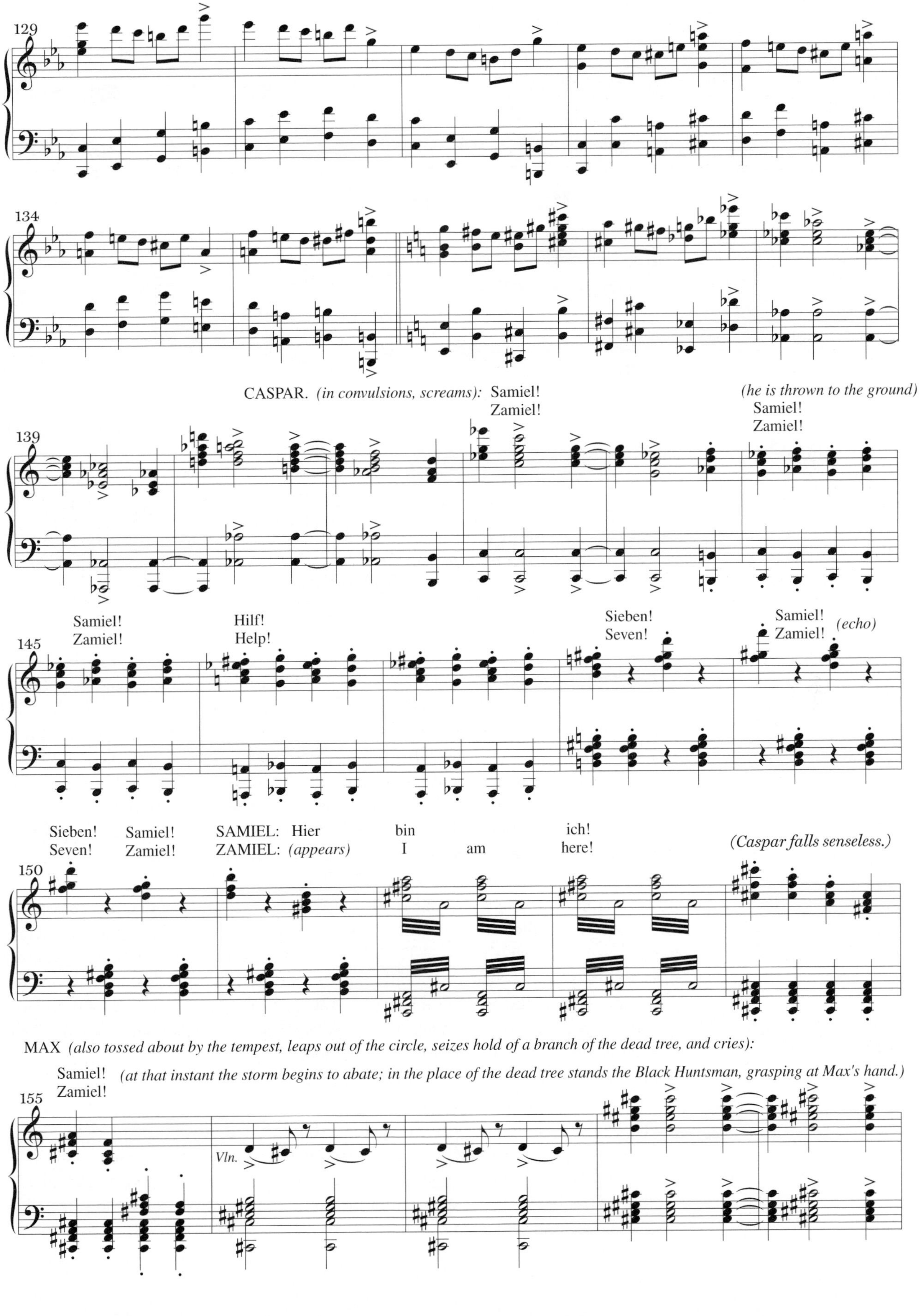

CASPAR. *(in convulsions, screams):* Samiel! Zamiel!

(he is thrown to the ground) Samiel! Zamiel!

Samiel! Zamiel!

Hilf! Help!

Sieben! Seven!

Samiel! Zamiel! *(echo)*

Sieben! Seven!

Samiel! Zamiel!

SAMIEL: Hier bin ich!

ZAMIEL: *(appears)* I am here!

(Caspar falls senseless.)

MAX *(also tossed about by the tempest, leaps out of the circle, seizes hold of a branch of the dead tree, and cries):*

Samiel!
Zamiel!
(at that instant the storm begins to abate; in the place of the dead tree stands the Black Huntsman, grasping at Max's hand.)
Vln.

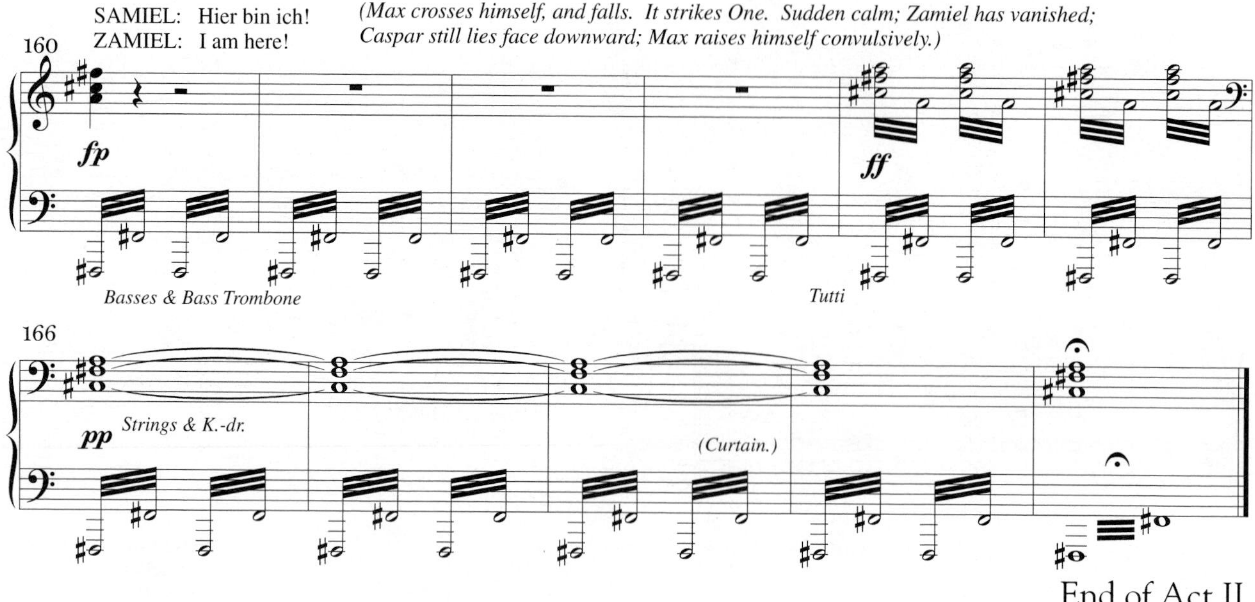
SAMIEL: Hier bin ich!
ZAMIEL: I am here!
(Max crosses himself, and falls. It strikes One. Sudden calm; Zamiel has vanished; Caspar still lies face downward; Max raises himself convulsively.)
160
fp
ff
Basses & Bass Trombone
Tutti
166
pp
Strings & K.-dr.
(Curtain.)

End of Act II.

154

Richard Wagner
Das Rheingold (1854)
Entrance of the Gods into Valhalla

Das Rheingold (*The Rhine Gold*) is the first installment in Richard Wagner's epic cycle of four operas, *Der Ring des Nibelungen* (*The Ring of the Nibelung*). Wagner called this first part a *Vorabend*—a prelude of sorts—and at a mere three hours' duration it is by far the shortest of the cycle. The opera is populated by ancient gods, led by Wotan, and other creatures inhabiting the prehistoric universe. At the beginning, Alberich—one of the dwarfish Nibelungs who inhabit the middle of the earth—steals a horde of gold that he has discovered in the Rhine River. He uses its magical power to enslave his own people, but the gold is subsequently stolen by Wotan to pay for the building of a magnificent castle, called Valhalla.

The following excerpt from *Das Rheingold* occurs near the end of opera, as part of a passage often called the "Entrance of the Gods into Valhalla." This famous excerpt opens with Donner, the god of Thunder (also known as Thor), swinging his hammer to gather the mists that surround the rainbow bridge leading to Valhalla. When the hammer strikes, the mists disappear amid the flash of lightning and roll of thunder—a sound effect created in Wagner's day by pouring steel balls down a metal chute. The radiant bridge shines forth in the evening sunlight and the gods admire their new home from a distance. Wotan, in high spirits, prepares to lead his wife, Fricka, and other gods over the splendid bridge to inhabit Valhalla. (At the first performance in Bayreuth, one critic complained that the walkway looked more like a decorative ornament belonging in a backyard garden than a shimmering walkway to heaven.) But his advisor, Loge (god of fire), views the situation more realistically. In spite of the heroic music and appearance of invulnerability, Wotan and his fellow gods, Loge says, are doomed.

Richard Wagner
Das Rheingold (1854)
Entrance of the Gods into Valhalla
CD 9/11

(Donner besteigt einen hohen Felsstein am Thalabhange, und schwingt dort seinen Hammer; mit dem Folgenden ziehen die Nebel sich um ihn zusammen.)
(Donner has mounted on a high rock by the precipice and now swings his hammer; during the following the mists collect round him.)

9
Don - ner, der Herr, ruft euch zu Heer!
Don - ner, your lord, call - eth his hosts!
allmählich immer stärker
ff
11
(Er schwingt den Hammer)
(He swings his hammer)
Auf des
At his
marcato
13
Ham - mers Schwung schwe - bet her - bei!
ham - mer's swing hith - er-ward sweep!
ff
15
marcato

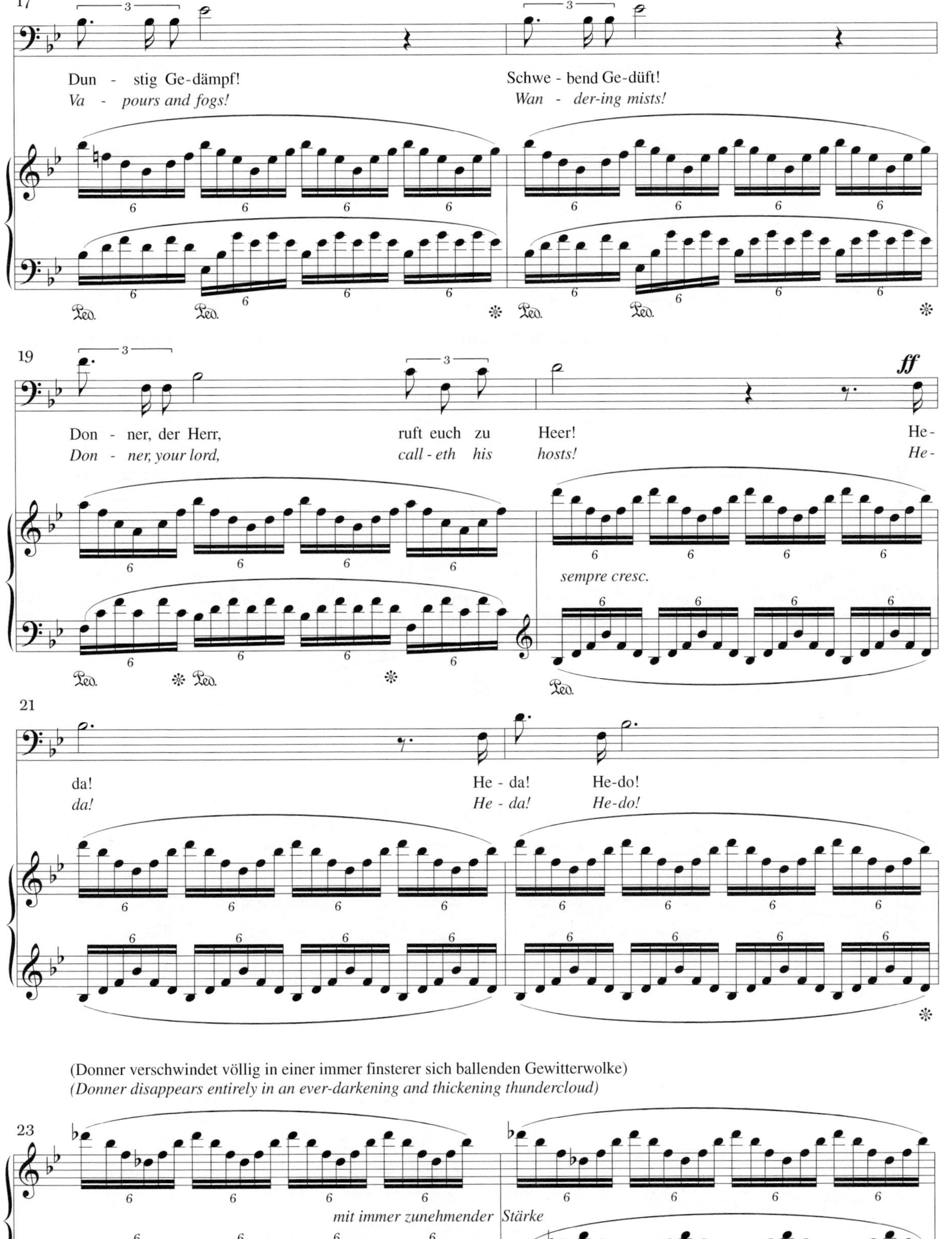
17
Dun - stig Ge-dämpf!
Va - pours and fogs!
Schwe - bend Ge-düft!
Wan - der-ing mists!
19
Don - ner, der Herr,
Don - ner, your lord,
ruft euch zu
call - eth his
Heer!
hosts!
ff
He-
He-
sempre cresc.
21
da!
da!
He - da!
He - da!
He-do!
He-do!
(Donner verschwindet völlig in einer immer finsterer sich ballenden Gewitterwolke)
(Donner disappears entirely in an ever-darkening and thickening thundercloud)
23
mit immer zunehmender Stärke

(Man hört seinen Hammerschlag schwer auf den Felsstein fallen.)
(The stroke of his hammer is heard to fall heavily on the rock.)
8va
più f

DONNER
(mit dem Hammer)
(with the Hammer)
35
ff
8va
ff
sf
12
Ped.
(Ein starker Blitz entfährt der Wolke; ein heftiger Donnerschlag folgt.)
(A vivid flash of lightning comes from the cloud; a violent clap of thunder follows.)
ff
(Froh ist mit ihm im Gewölk verschwundern.)
(Froh has also disappeared in the clouds.)
37
sempre ff
dim.
DONNER
(unsichtbar)
(unseen)
39
Bru - der, hei-her! Wei - se der Brü-cke den Weg!
Bro - ther, to me! Shew them the way o'er the bridge!
(Plötzlich verzicht sich die Wolke; Donner und Froh werden sichtbar; von ihren Füssen aus zieht sich mit
(Suddenly the clouds disperse; Donner and Froh become visible; from their feet a rainbow-bridge stretches with
blendendem Leuchten eine Regenbogen–Brücke über das Thal hinüber bis zur Burg, die jetzt im Glanze der Abendsonne strahlt.)
blinding radiance across the valley to the castle which now glows in the light of the setting sun.)
41
più p
Mässig bewegt
pp dolce

43
46
49
52
FROH
(Froh, der der Brücke mit der ausgesteckten Hand den Weg
(Froh, who points with outstretched hand to the bridge as the
Zur Burg führt die
The bridge leads you
sempre dolce
55
über Thal angewiesen, zu den Göttern:)
way across the valley—to the gods:)
Brü - cke leicht doch fest eu - rem
home - ward, light yet firm to your

58
Fuss: be - schrei - - - - tet kühn ih - ren
feet: now tread un - daunt - - - - ed its
61
schreck - lo - - - sen Pfad!
ter - ror - - - less path!
Erste Viol.
(Zweite Viol. in tieferer Lage, dazu die Harfen in, durch 4 Oktaven auf–und aharpeggierender akkordlicher Sextolen–bewegung)
weich
più p
(Wotan und die andern Götter sind sprachlos in den prächtigen Anblick verloren)
(Wotan and the other gods contemplate the glorious sight, speechless)
65
ten.
ten.

68
8va
cresc.
ten.
ten.
poco cresc.
ten.
71
(8va)
dim.
ten.
mf
dim.
74
WOTAN
A - bend-lich strahlt der Son - - - ne
Gold - en at eve the sun - - - light
più p
pp
p
dim.
weich
più p
78
Au - ge; in präch - - - - ti - ger Gluth
gleam - eth; in glo - - - - ri - ous light
pp

81
prangt glän - zend die Burg.
glow fast - ness and fell.
In des
In the
pp
Ped.
85
Mor - gens Schei - - - ne mu - thig er schim-merndlag sie
morn - ing's ra - - - diance, brave - ly it glis-tened, ly - - - ing
dim.
88
her - ren-los, hehr ver - lo - ckend vor mir.
lord - less there, proud - ly lur - ing my feet.
più p
pp

92
Von Mor - - - - gen bis A - bend, in
From morn - - - - ing till eve - ning, in
95
Müh' und Angst, nicht won - nig ward sie ge -
care and fear, un - blest, I worked for its
più p
99
won - - - nen!
win - - - ning!
Es naht die Nacht: vor ih-rem
The night is nigh: from all its
dim.
pp cresc.
f
pp
104
Neid bie - te sie Ber - gung nun.
ills shel-ter it of - fers now.
cresc. molto
ff
(Wie von einem grossen Gedanken ergriffen, sehr entschlossen)
(As though seized by a great thought, very firmly)
sehr energisch

109
So grüss' ich die Burg,
So greet I the home,
ff
p
112
si - cher vor Bang' und Grau'n!
safe from dis - may and dread!
fp
p
cresc.
(Er wendet sich feierlich zu Fricka)
(He turns solemnly to Fricka)
114
Fol - ge mir, Frau! In Wal -
Fol - low me, wife! In Wal -
f
ff
dim.
p
119
FRICKA
Was deu - tet der Na - me?
What mean-eth the name, then?
- hall woh - - - ne mit mir.
- hall dwell now with me.
più p
p
(nich gebunden, aber gut gehalten)

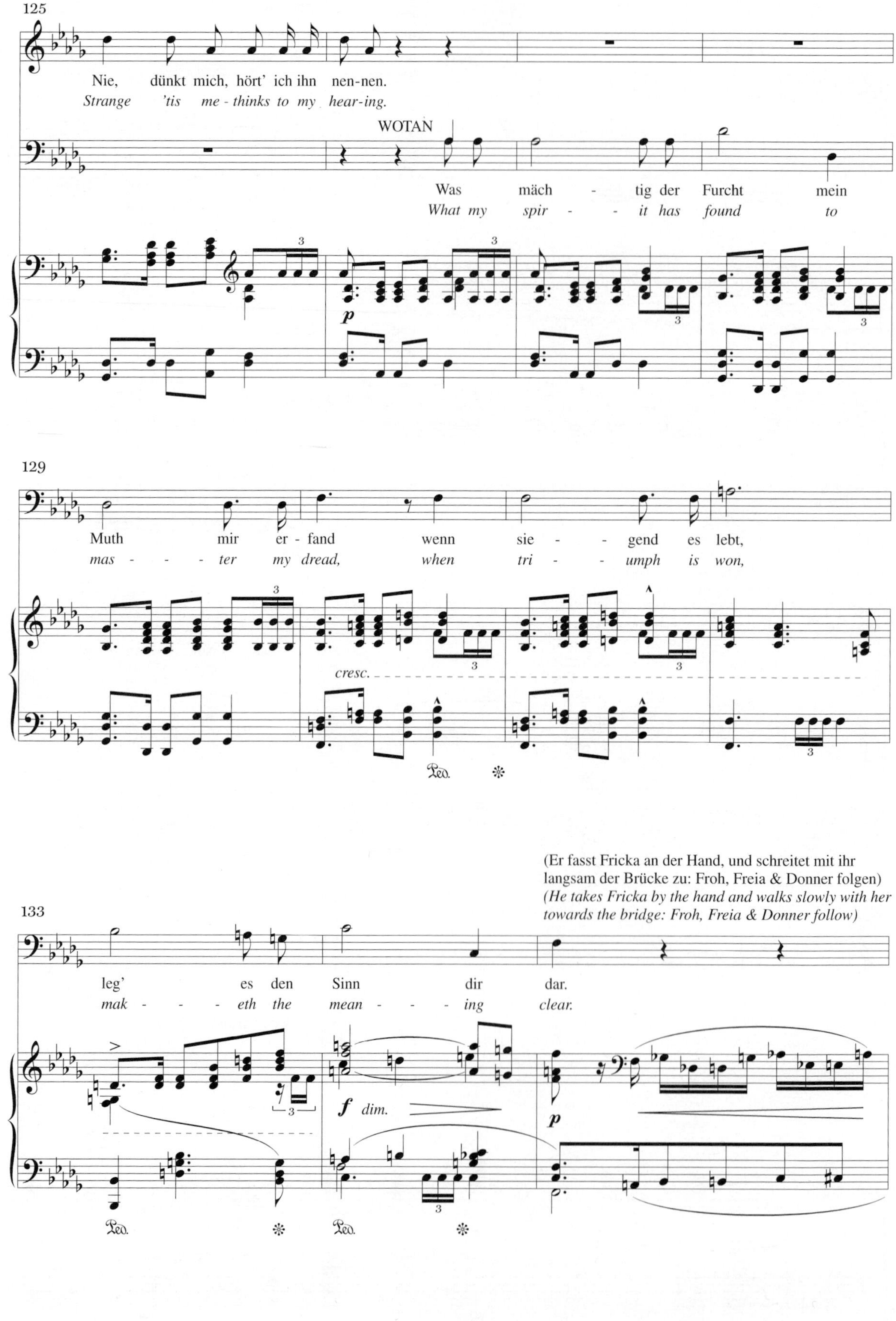

125
Nie, dünkt mich, hört' ich ihn nen-nen.
Strange 'tis me - thinks to my hear-ing.
WOTAN
Was mäch - tig der Furcht mein
What my spir - - it has found to
p
129
Muth mir er - fand wenn sie - - gend es lebt,
mas - - - ter my dread, when tri - - umph is won,
cresc.
(Er fasst Fricka an der Hand, und schreitet mit ihr langsam der Brücke zu: Froh, Freia & Donner folgen)
(He takes Fricka by the hand and walks slowly with her towards the bridge: Froh, Freia & Donner follow)
133
leg' es den Sinn dir dar.
mak - - - eth the mean - - - ing clear.
f dim.
p

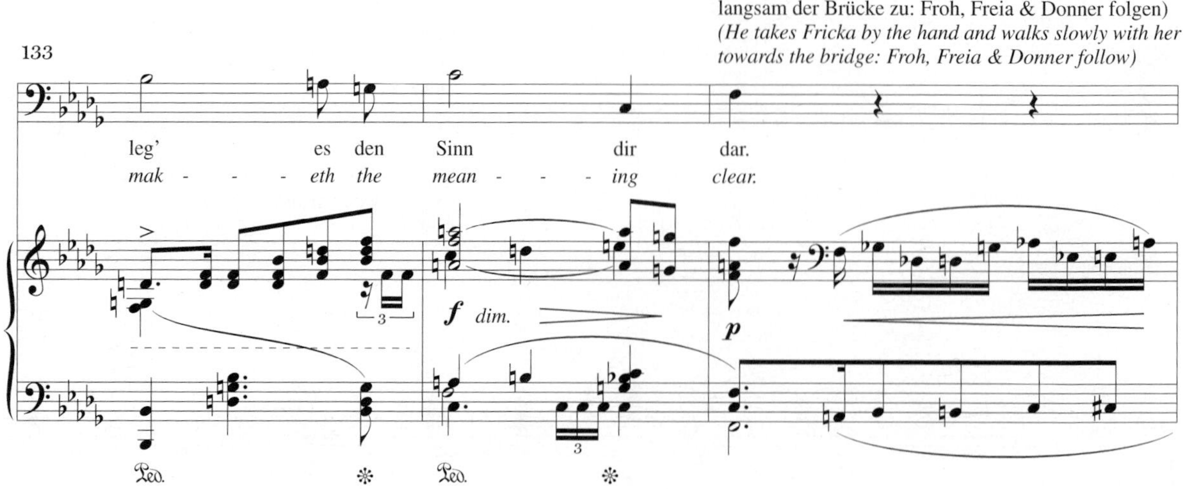

LOGE (im Vodergrunde verharrend, und den Göttern nachblickend)
(remaining in the foreground and looking after the gods)
136
Ih-rem En - de ei-len sie zu, die so
They are hast - ing on to their end, who now
p
Ped.
138
stark im Be-steh - en sich wäh - nen. Fast
deem them-selves strong in their great - ness. A -
p
140
schäm' ichmich mit ih-nen zu schaf-fen; zur le - cken-den Lo - - - he mich
shamedam I to share in their deal-ings; to flick - er-ing fire a -
p
p
Ped.
143
wie - der zu wan - - - deln, spür' ich lo - cken de Lust: sie
gain to trans-form me, fan - cy lur - eth my will: to
poco cresc.
Ped.

145
auf - zu-zeh - ren, die einst mich ge - zähmt, statt mit den Blin - den
burn and waste them who bound me ere - while, ra - ther than blind - ly
cresc.
147
blöd zu-ver-geh'n und wä - ren es gött - lich-ste Göt - ter nicht
sink with the blind e'en were they of gods the most god - like not
ff
149
dumm dünk-te mich das! Be-den-ken will ich's: wer weiss, was ich thu'?
ill were it, me-seems! I must be-think me: who knows what may hap?
p
più p
p
(Er geht, um sich den Göttern in nachlässiger Haltung anzuschliessen)
(He goes, assuming a careless manner, to join the gods)
152
poco cresc.
pp

Opera in Italy
Rossini and Verdi

155

Gioachino Rossini
The Barber of Seville (1816)
Act 1, No. 1
a. *Introduzione*, "Piano, pianissimo"
b. Cavatina, "Ecco ridente"; Seguito dell'Introduzione, "Ehi, Fiorello"

Rossini's *Il barbiere di Siviglia* (*The Barber of Seville*) has remained, since the time of its first hearing in 1816, one of the most successful and admired of comic operas. The work maintains the traditional form of comic opera inherited from the Classical era. Following a spirited overture, each act is subdivided into a succession of musical numbers (arias, duets, other ensembles, and a few choruses) that are connected by simple recitative. The libretto by Cesare Sterbini is based on a timeless French comedy of the same title by Beaumarchais. In it, young lovers finally win out over daunting odds and a madcap series of escapades.

In the first section of *Barber*, following the overture, the young Court Almaviva—disguised as a poor student—tries to attract the attention of the lovely Rosina, who lives in Seville with her guardian, Dr. Bartolo. The Count has hired musicians to accompany him in a dawn serenade, which he sings in the street outside her bed chamber. Musically, this opening section is a special type of operatic number called an *Introduzione* (Introduction). Typically, introductions are multi-sectional and mix together several types of singing. The audience is brought into the middle of an action—the background will be filled in later. In the middle of the *Introduzione*, the Count sings his first aria—or "cavatina," as Rossini termed an entrance aria—"Ecco ridente in cielo" ("Look, Smiling in Heaven"). The introduction concludes with the Count sadly admitting defeat—his lady love did not so much as even show a light at the window—and he orders his valet, Fiorello, to pay the band. At the prospect of obtaining some ready money, the penurious musicians become as excited as young pups. Erupting in a riot of joy, they inadvertently frustrate the Count's desire to slip away without calling more attention to his ineffectual wooing. Although this entire opening scene consists of a continual dramatic progression, Rossini provided it with a symmetrical and self-contained ternary form. The Count's cavatina is the central **B** section and the chaotic final passage, the stretta, acts as a coda.

Section	**A**	**B**	**A'**	**Stretta**
Measure	1	99	185	216

Gioachino Rossini
The Barber of Seville (1816)
Act 1, No. 1
a. *Introduzione*, "Piano, pianissimo"
b. Cavatina, "Ecco ridente"; Seguito dell'Introduzione, "Ehi, Fiorello"
CD 9/12–13

Introduzione, "Piano, pianissimo"

Time of the action, near dawn; place, an open square in Seville. At the left the house of Bartolo, its windows having practicable bars and closed blinds, which can be unlocked and locked at the proper time. Fiorello, lantern in hand, ushers in a number of musicians with their instruments. Later, Count Almaviva, wrapped in a cloak.

Moderato

Vln. Fag. & 'Cello

Piano

p

Str.

6

f

p

Wind sustain

11

p

Fag. & Viola

FIORELLO
(coming forward cautiously)

16

F.

Pia - no, pia -
Hush, let us

p

22

F.

nis - si - mo, sen - za par - lar, tut - ti con me ve - ni - te
soft - ly tread, breathe not a word, No one must see, no one must

f

27
F.
qua, ve-ni-te qua.
see, no one must hear.
TENOR (sotto voce)
CHORUS
Pia - no, pia - nis - si-mo, ec - co - ci
Hush, let us soft - ly tread, breathe not a
BASS (sotto voce)
p
32
FIORELLO
F.
Ve - ni - te qua, pia -
Breathe not a word. Soft -
qua, ec - co - ci qua,
word, No one must see,
p
37
F.
no, ve - ni - te qua.
ly, no one must hear.
pia - no, ec - co - ci qua.
soft - ly, no one must hear.
Strings pizz.
p
staccato

42
F.
Tut - to è si - len-zio,
No sound is stir-ring,
Cl.
47
nes - sun, qui sta,
all here is still,
che i no - stri
Till we with
Cl.
p
52
can-ti
singing
pos - sa tur - bar;
night's si - lence fill.
Tut-to è si-
No sound is
Wood
Cl.
57
len-zio, nes-sun qui sta, che i no-stri can-ti pos-sa tur-bar; Tut-to è si-
stir-ring, all here is still, Till we with sing-ing night's si-lence fill. No sound is

61
F.
len - zio, nes-sun qui sta, che i no - stri can - ti pos - sa tur - bar.
stir - ring, all here is still, Till we with sing - ing night's si - lence fill.
Vln.
pp
65
COUNT (sotto voce)
C.
Fio - rel - lo, O - là! Eb -
Fio - rel - lo, Ho - la! Your
FIORELLO
F.
Si - gnor, son qua.
My lord, I'm here.
Strings arco
p
Viola & Basso
pp
71
C.
ben! gli a - mi - ci? Bra - vi, bra -
friends, where are they? All to my
F.
Son pron - ti già.
They're stand - ing near.
Ob. & Fag.

76
C.
vis - si - mi! fa - te si - len - - - zio, pia - no, pia -
wish has sped, none have ob - serv'd you, But let them
Viola
cresc.
80
C.
nis - si - mo, sen - za par - lar, sen - za par - lar.
soft - ly tread, no one must see, no one must hear.
FIORELLO
F.
Sen - za par-
No one must
p
CHORUS Pia - no, pia - - -
Yes, we will
p
f
p

84
C.
Pia - - - no,
Soft - - - ly.
F.
lar, sen-za par-lar, ve - ni - te
see, no one must hear. Breathe not a
nis - si-mo, sen - za par - - - lar,
soft - ly tread, no one shall hear,
88
C.
sen - za par lar, pia - no,
No one must see, soft - ly
F.
qua,
word,
sen - za par - lar, pia - no,
No one shall see, soft - ly,

CD 9/13

Cavatina, "Ecco ridente"

110
112
C.
COUNT
Ec - co ri-den - te in cie - 6 - lo
Dawn, with her ro - sy man - - - - tle,
pp Strings & Guitars
116
spun - ta la bel - la au - ro - - - ra,
Stands at the gate of morn - - - - ing,
e tu non sor - gi an -
Night's gloom a - far is
119
co - ra, e 6 puoi dor - mir co - sì?
driv - en, Yet thou art slum - b'ring still!
Sor - gi, mia dol - ce
Wake, and a - rise, my
123
spe - - 6 - me,
fair - - - est,
vie - ni, bel - l'i - dol mi - o,
Look forth in beau - ty beam - ing,
ren - di men cru - do oh
Brigh - ter than sun - shine
Trombe

127
a piacere
C.
Di - o! lo stral, lo stral che mi fe - ri, lo
gleam - ing With joy, with joy my heart to fill, with
131
Allegro
stral che mi fe - rì.
joy my heart to fill.
Oh
Oh
Wood
mf
Cor. Strings pizz. & Guitars
135
sor - te! già veg - go quel ca - ro sem - bian - te:
mo - ment of rap - ture! Her fair hand ap - pear - eth;
arco
p
mf
139
que - st'a - ni-ma a - man - te ot -
My sigh - ing she hear - eth, My
p

143
C.
ten - - - - - - - - ne pie - - - tà!
pray'r she grants.
Wind
p
146
Oh i - stan - te d'a - - - -
Bliss - ful mo - ment, She ap -
sf
sf
149
mo - re! Fe - - - li - ce
pear - eth! My sigh - ing
cresc.
sf
f
152
mo - - - men - to! i - - - - stan - te d'a - - -
she hear - eth! Ye mo - ments, oh
sf
p

155
C.
mo - re! fe - li - - - ce mo - - - men - - - - to!
has - ten, Un - til I be - - - hold her!
mf
158
C.
oh dol - ce con - ten - to, che e-
Un - til I have told her My
p
162
C.
gual, no, non ha, no,
heart she en - - - - chants. Un -
p
165
C.
no, che e - gual non ha, che e - gual non ha!
til I've told her my heart, my heart she en - chants,
cresc.
f

a piacere
168
C.
oh dol - ce con - ten - - - - - - to, che e -
un - til I have told her my
p
172
gual non ha! che e - gual non
heart she en - chants, my heart she en -
Tutti.
f
175
ha! che e - gual non ha! che e - gual non
chants, my heart she en - chants, yes, she en -
p
f
178
ha! che e - gual non ha! che e - gual che e - gual non ha!
chants, yes, she en - chants, my, heart she en - chants!
ff
182

Seguito dell' Introduzione, "Ehi, Fiorello"

198
C.
che fa - rò?
All is vain–
Tut - to è van - no –
I'll dis - miss them:
Buo - na
Friends, come
pizz.
p
p stacc.
203
(The count give his purse to Fiorello, who distributes
gente! –
hither,
CHORUS (sotto voce)
A - van - ti, a - van - ti!
Come near - er, come near - er!
Mio si - gnor–
Sir, we come.
p
208
money to the musicians.)
Pìu di suo - ni, pìu di can - ti, pìu di
Here I need no more de - tain ye, Take my

213
C.
suo - ni, io bi - so - gno or - mai non ho.
thanks, yes, my good friends, take my thanks and go.
FIORELLO
F.
Buo-na not - te a tut - ti
Here no long - er we will de -
217
F.
quan - ti, più di voi che far non sò, buo-na not - te buo-na
tain ye, So good - bye, my friends, now go, Here no long - er we'll de -
221
F.
not - te più di voi che far non sò.
tain ye, So good - bye, my friends, now go.
pp
pp
(The musicians surround the Count, thanking him and kissing his hands and the hem of his cloak; he, annoyed by their noisy
Allegro vivace
226
Vlns. & Fag.
Cl.
Fl.
p
demonstrations, tried to chase them off, as does also Fiorello.)
230

234
C.
COUNT
Bas - ta,
Si - lence,
CHORUS
Mil - le gra - zie, mio si - gno - re, del fa - vo - re, del - l'o -
Sir, we humb - ly thank your ho - nor, No - ble pa - tron, gen'rous
238
C.
ba - sta, non par - la - te! ma non ser - ve, non gri - da - te!
gent - ly, I dis - miss ye, 'Tis suf - fi - cient, pray now cease ye!
no - re, mil - le gra - zie, mio si - gno - re, del fa - vo - re, del - l'o -
do - nor, Sir, we humb - ly thank your ho - nor, No - ble pa - tron, gen' rous

242
C.
Ma - le - det - ti! an - da - te
Oh con - found ye! be still, ye
FIORELLO
F.
Zit - ti, zit - ti, che ru - mo - re!
Pray, be si - lent, hush, ye ras - cals!
no - re! Ah, di tan - ta cor - te - si - a, ah, di tan - ta cor - te -
do - nor, For your boun - ty we are grate - ful, for your boun - ty we are
Vlns. Cl. & Fag.
p
246
vi - a! ah ca - na - glia, via di
ras - cals! was such up - roar ev - er
ma - le - dit - ti! via di qua!
was such up - roar ev - er heard!
si - a, ob - bli - ga - ti, ob - bli - ga - ti, ob - bli - ga - ti in ve - ri -
grate - ful, Thou - sand, thou - sand, thou - sand, thanks, a thou - sand, thanks, to you,– my
Ob.
p

250
C.
qua! Tut - to quan - to il vi - ci - na - to, tut - to quan - to il vi - ci -
heard! All the neigh - bors will be flock - ing, all the neigh - bors will be
F.
Ve' che chias - so in - dia - vo - la - to, ve' che chias - so in - dia - vo -
Friends, the noise you make is shock - ing, yes, the noise you make is
tà! Oh che in - con - tro for - tu -
lord. Gold - en pie - ces, what good
Fl. & Vln. I
Vln. II
p
Tutti
254
C.
na - to que - sto, chias - so, que - sto, chias - so, que - sto, chias - so, sve - glie -
flock - ing, To be - hold this scene ab - surd, yes, to be - hold this scene ab -
F.
la - to! ah che rab - bia, ah che rab - bia, ah che rab - bia, che mi
shock - ing, Have a care, yes, have a care lest to chas - tise ye I am
na - to! È un si - gno - re di qua - li -
for - tune! We're most luck - y, up - on my
cresc.

258
C.
rà, si, tut - to quan - to il vi - ci - na - to que - sto, chias - so, sve - glie-
surd, yes, all the neigh - bors will be flock - ing, To be - hold this scene ab-
F.
fa! ma ve' che chias - so in - dia - vo - la - to! ah che rab - bia che mi
stirr'd! Be - gone, the noise you make is shock - ing, To chas - tise ye I am
tà. Oh che in - con - tro for - tu - na - to! è un si - gnor di qua - li -
word! Gold - en pie - ces, what good for - tune! We're most luck - y, 'pon my
mf
262
C.
rà! Ah ca - na - glia, via di qua!
surd, Go, ye ras - cals, ser - vile herd!
F.
fa! Ma - le - det - ti, an - da - te vi - a, ma - le - det - ti, an - da - te vi - a, ah ca -
stirr'd! Go, ye ras - cals, 'tis suf - fi - cient, go, ye ras - cals, 'tis suf - fi - cient, Was such
tà. sì, sì, è un si - gnor di qua - li - tà!
word, yes, this is luck, up - on my word!
f

267
C.
ff
Tut - - - - to quan - to il vi - ci -
All the neigh - bors will be
F.
ff
na - glia, via di qua! ca - - - - - na - glia, ah ca -
up - roar ev - er heard! I tell ye go, ye
ff
È un si - - - - - gnor di qua - li -
This is luck, up - on my
ff
ff
272
C.
na - to que - sto, chias - so, sve - glie - rà! Bas - ta,
flock - ing, To be - hold this scene ab - surd, Si - lence,
F.
na - glia, ah ca - na - glia, via di qua!
ras - cals! Was such up - roar ev - er heard!
tà, sì, gra - zie, gra - zie, del fa - vor.
word, A thou - sand, thou - sand thanks, my lord.
Strings only

277
C.
ba-sta! Bas-ta, ba-sta!
si-lence! si-lence, si-lence!
F.
Zi-ti, zit-ti! Zit-ti, zit-ti! Oh che rab-bia che mi
Hush, ye ras-cals, hush, ye ras-cals, Was such up-roar ev-er
Gra-zie! gra-zie!
Thank you! thank you!
282
C.
Ah ma-le-det-ti, an-da-te vi-a, ma-le-det-ti, an-da-te vi-a, ah ca-
Ah, go, ye ras-cals, I dis-miss ye, go, ye ras-cals, I dis-miss ye, Was such
F.
fa!
heard!
p

287
C.
na - glia, via di qua! Ma - le - det-ti! an-da - te
up - roar ev - er heard! Go, ye ras-cals, I dis-
F.
Zit - ti, zit-ti, che ru - mo-re!
Hush, ye rascals, 'tis suf - fi-cient,
Ah di tan - ta cor - te - si - a, ah di tan - ta cor - te-
For your boun - ty we are grate - ful, for your boun - ty we are
as before
p
292
vi - a! ah ca - na - glia, via di
miss ye, Was such up - roar ev - er
ma - le - det-ti! via di qua!
Was such up-roar ev - er heard!
si - a, ob - bli - ga - ti, ob - bli - ga - ti, ob - bli - ga - ti in ve - ri -
grate - ful, Thou - sand, thou - sand, thou - sand thanks, a thou - sand thanks to you, my
p

296
C.
qua! Tut - to quan - to il vi - ci - na - to, tut - to quan - to il vi - ci -
heard! All the neigh - bors will be flock - ing, all the neigh - bors will be
F.
Ve' che chias - so in-dia - vo - la - to, ve' che chias - so in-dia - vo -
Go, the noise you make is shock - ing, yes, the noise you make is
tà. Oh che in - con - tro for - tu -
lord. Gold - en pie - ces, what good
p
300
C.
na - to que - sto, chias - so, que - sto, chias - so, que - sto, chias - so, sve - glie -
flock - ing, To be - hold this scene ab - surd, yes, to be - hold this scene ab -
F.
la - to! oh che rab - bia, oh che rab - bia, oh che rab - bia che mi
shock - ing, Have a care, oh, have a care, Lest to chas - tise ye I am
na - to! È un si - gno - re di qua - li -
for - tune! We are luck - y, up - on my
cresc.

304
C.
rà, si, tut - to quan - to il vi - ci - na - to que - sto, chias - so, sve - glie-
surd, yes, all the neigh - bors will be flock - ing, To be - hold this scene ab -
F.
fa! ma ve' che chias - so in - dia - vo - la - to! Oh che rab - bia che mi
stirr'd, Be - gone, the noise you make is shock - ing, To chas - tise ye I am
tà. Oh che in - con - tro for - tu - na - to! è un si - gnor di qua - li -
word. Gold - en pie - ces, what good for - tune! We are luck - y, 'pon my
308
C.
rà, si, tut - to quan - to il vi - ci -
surd, yes, all the neigh - bors will be
F.
fa! Ma ve' che chias - so in - dia - vo -
stirr'd! Be - gone, this noise you make is
tà– si - gno - re gra - zie, gra - zie,
word! Oh thank you, thank you, thank you,

312
C.
na - to que - sto, chias - so, sve - glie - rà, si,
flock - ing, To be - hold this scene ab - surd, yes,
F.
la - to! oh che rab - bia che mi fa! ma
shock - ing, To chas - tise ye I am stirr'd! Be -
gra - zie, è un si - gnor di qua - - li - tà– si -
thank you, This is luck, up - on my word, Oh
317
C.
tut - to quan - to il vi - ci - na - to que - sto,
all the neigh - bors will be flock - ing, To be -
F.
ve' che chias - so in dia - vo - la - to! oh che
gone, the noise you make is shock - ing, To chas -
gno - re– gra - zie, gra - zie, gra - zie, è un si -
thank you, thank you, thank you, thank you, This is

322
C.
chias - so, sve - glie - rà, que - sto, chias - so, sve - glie - rà, que - sto,
hold this scene ab - surd, hence, be - gone ye ser - vile herd, hence, be -
F.
rab - bia che mi fa! oh che rab - bia che mi fa! oh che
tise ye I am stirr'd! to chas - tise ye I am stirr'd to chas-
gnor di qua - - - li - tà, di qua - li - tà, di
luck, up - on my word, up - on my word, up -
327
C.
chias - so, sve - glie - rà! ma - le - det - ti, via di qua, via di qua, via di qua!
gone ye ser - vile herd, hence, be - gone ye ser - vile herd, ser - vile herd, ser - vile herd!
F.
rab - bia che mi fa! ma - le - det - ti, via di qua, via di qua, via di qua!
tise ye I am stirr'd Was such up - roar ev - er heard! ev - er heard! ev - er heard!
qua - li - tà, qua - li - tà, qua - li - tà, qua - li - tà, qua - li - tà!
on my word, 'pon my word, 'pon my word, 'pon my word, 'pon my word!

156

Giuseppe Verdi
Otello (1887)
Act 4, scene 3

Verdi completed his great operatic adaptation of Shakespeare's tragedy *Othello* at the age of seventy-three. One would think that after a spectacularly successful forty-year career, he would have felt confident of its reception by the public. Instead, he was apprehensive: He was old and perhaps the audience was tired of his compositions. The reviews, while noting the lack of text repetition and standard forms that were a traditional element of Italian opera, observed that *Otello* had the lyricism that was the heart and soul of the Italian style. Those in the audience, however, did not need the critics to tell them what to think. Not content with expressing their delight through repeated ovations (reports of curtain calls vary between eight and twenty), they unhitched the horses from Verdi's carriage and pulled it by hand through the streets to his hotel. There, the beloved composer was called out to the balcony several more times to acknowledge the adulation of the crowd.

The opera rises to its musical and dramatic climax in the murder scene near the conclusion. The general Othello is controlled by his emotions, which are manipulated by his lieutenant, Iago, out of jealousy and scorn. Using contrived evidence and playing on Othello's weaknesses, Iago convinces Othello that his wife, Desdemona, has been unfaithful to him.

In the first part of Act 4, scene 3, Othello quietly enters his wife's bed chamber, his mind torn between jealous rage and tender love. The forty-five-measure introduction by the orchestra conveys his conflicting emotions, concluding with the passionate music that closed Act 1 when, moved by the intensity of his love for Desdemona, he had kissed her. We realize at this moment that love still burns in his breast—murder is not a foregone conclusion. The second part of the scene, the dialogue between the tragic pair, is in a recitational style with a constantly changing tonal center. As taut as a tiger about to spring, Othello interrogates Desdemona, misinterprets her reaction to Cassio's death, and strangles his wife despite her protestations of fidelity. No sooner is the deed done than Iago's plot is unmasked (part 3 of the scene). Othello is filled with grief and remorse and shortly afterwards kills himself.

This scene is notable in the history of Italian opera for its use of the orchestra—not primarily the voice—to convey the heightened dramatic moment. The emotional conflicts that simmer in Othello's soul are depicted by its opposing motives, and his lack of control is ingeniously underscored by its fragmented phrases and tonal disjunctions.

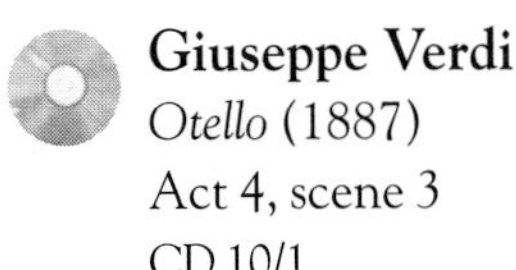

Giuseppe Verdi
Otello (1887)
Act 4, scene 3
CD 10/1

16
(Guarda Desdemona)
(He looks at Desdemona)
X (Spegna la face)
(He extinguishes the candle)
O.
X
pp
20
(movimento di furore)
(gesture of fury)
O.
dim.
p
un poco pùi marcato e cresc.
staccate
24
(Si avvicina al letto)
(He goes towards the bed)
(S'arresta)
(He stops)
O.
8va
f
ff
28
Y (Rialza le cortine, comtempla lungamente Desdemona che dorme)
(He raises the bedcurtains and looks for a long time on the sleeping Desdemona.)
O.
Y
ppp

32
O.
Z
36
(Da un bacio a Desdemona)
(He kisses Desdemona.)
(altro bacio)
(second kiss)
Più animato. ♩ = 88.
dolce
pp
40
DESDEMONA (si desta)
(she awakes)
(Si alza)
(She raises herself)
D.
Chi è là?
Who's there?
(un altro ancora)
(third kiss)
pp
44
AA
Lo stesso Movimento. ♩ = 80.
O - tel - lo?
O - thel - lo?
Si!
Ay!
un poco accent.
pp e staccato

47
50
DESDEMONA dolciss.
O - rai
I prayed
OTELLO
Di - ce - ste que - sta se - ra le vos - tre pre - ci?
Say, have you prayed to - night? tell me, Des - de - mo - na?
senza misura
51 morendo
Se vi sov - vie - - - ne di qual - che col - pa com-
If you be - think your - self of a - ny crime un - for-
pp
53
mes - sa che atten - da gra - zia dal ciel, im - plo - ra - te - la to -
gi - ven as yet by heav'n and by grace, then so - li - cit straight for

Lo stesso Movimento.
55 BB DESDEMONA
D.
Per-chè?
My lord?
O.
sto. T'af-fret-ta! Uc-ci-de-re non vo-glio l'a-ni-ma
it. Well, do it! For heav'n for-fend, I would not kill your
BB Lo stesso Movimento.
f
58
D'uc-ci-der par-li?
You talk of kil-ling?
Pie-tà di me, mio
Then Lord have mer-cy
tua.
soul.
Si!
Ay!
f
60
Dio.
on me.
E ab-bia-te pie-
Ah, then you
A-men.
A-men.
f

62
CC
D.
tà voi pu - - - - - - - - - - re.
too have mer - - - - - - - - - - cy!
O.
Pen - sa a' tuoi pec -
Think u - pon your
CC
p
64
Mio pec - ca - to è l'a - mor.
They are loves borne to you.
ca - ti.
sins!
Per ciò tu
For that thou
marcate
f
66
E per - chè t'a - mo m'uc - ci - di?
Be - cause I love you, you kill me?
No! sul - l'a - ni - ma
No! I swear by my
3
muo - ri.
di - est.
ff
A mi Cas - sio.
You love Cas - sio.
ff
dim.

69
D.
mia!!
soul!
cupo
O.
Quel faz-zo-let - to ch'io ti do-nai gli
That hand-ker-chief I gave you, you gave to
m.d.
m.s.
71
D.
Non è ve - ro! Io rea non so - no!
'Tis a false - hood. And yet I'm guilt - less.
O.
de - sti Nel - la sua man lo vi - di. Con-fes - sa!
Cas-sio. In his own hands I saw it. Con-fess thee!
73
DD
D.
Giu - ro!
Guilt - less!
O.
Ba-da al-lo sper-giu - - - ro... Pen - - - sa che
Pray take heed of per - - - - ju - ry Think, thou art
DD
f

75
D.
Non per mo-rir.
But not to die.
A -
Lord
O.
sei sul tuo let - to di mor - te.
ly - ing u-pon thy death-bed.
Per mo-rir to-sto.
Yes, pre-sent-ly.
77
D.
i - - - ta!
help me!
Cas-sio non a-mo...
Cas-sio I love not!
ch'ei qui ven-ga...
Call him hi-ther,
ei
and
79
ppp lunga
ff
D.
par-li.
ask him.
Cie-lo! Mor-to?
Heav'n dead?
Son per-du - - ta! ei tra-
He be-trayed, I un-
OTELLO
cupo
(freddo)
(coldly)
O.
Mu-to è per sempre.
He's mute for e-ver.
Mor-to.
Dead
col canto
ff

83
D.
di - to!
done!
O-tel - - - lo non uc-
Oh, ba - - - nish me but
con forza
O.
E pian-ger l'o - si?
Dost weep thou strum - pet?
ppp
85
(con disperazione)
(in despair)
ci - der-mi…
kill me not!
Ch'io vi - - - va an-
Oh spare me, oh
Tu in-va - - - no ti di-fen - di.
Nay no - - thing now will save thee.
Giù!
Ha!
cresc. poco a poco
87
EE Tempo doppio. 𝅗𝅥 = 80.
cor, ch'io vi-va an-cor, ch'io vi-va an - cor
spare me, oh let me, let me live.
Pie-tà!
Have pi - ty!
ca - - - di, giù, ca - - - di, pro-sti - tu - ta!
down with thee, ha! down with thee thou strum - pet!
tutta forza
pp

89
D.
Ch'io vi - va que-sta not - te... U - n'o - ra... Un i -
Let me but live to - night... An hour But one
O.
Muo - ri!! No! No!
No! No! No!
92
D.
stan - te. Sol ch'io di - ca u - n'A - ve.
mo - ment. While I say my pray - er.
O.
No! È
No! Too
cre - scen - do poco a poco
95
(la soffoca)
(he stifles her)
O.
tar - di!
late
f

DESDEMONA: (grido)
Ah! (shriek)
Ah!
8va
97
fff
(dal di fuori, bussa alla porta)
(knocking at the door)
100
EMILIA
E.
dim.
103
sempre decresc.
morendo
sempre più piano
p
(picchio di nuovo)
(another knock)
107
EMILIA (outside)
senza misura
A - pri - te! a - pri - te!
With-in there, oh op - en!
OTELLO (contemplando il corpo inerte di Desdemona)
(looking on the motionless form of Desdemona)
O.
pp
Cal - ma co - me la tom - ba.
Calm, calm as the grave.
ppp
senza misura

(picchia ancora)
(another knock)
(111)
Presto
E.
Si - gnor mio… ven pre - go, la - scia - te ch'io vi par - li… A -
Good my - lord, do hear me, I would but speak a word,— do
(trabalzando)
(faltering)
O.
Chi è là! Chi bat - te!
Who's there? Who knocks there?
FF a tempo
112
(entrando)
(entering)
pri - te!
o - pen!
Un gran de - lit - to!
It is foul mur - der.
(aprendo)
(opening the door)
E - mi - lia! che av - ven - ne?
È - mi - lia! What is it?
FF a tempo
legato
pp
ppp
116
Cas - sio uc - ci - se Ro - dri - go.
Cas - sio's killed Ro - de - ri - go.
Vi - ve.
Lives.
E Cas - sio?
And Cas - sio?
Cas - sio
Cas - sio

(dal letto)
(from the bed)
119
DESDEMONA pp stentate
sempre pp
D.
In-giu-sta-men - te... uc-ci-sa in-giu-stamen - te...
I die here guilt - less... I have been slain un-just - ly...
(accorrendo al letto)
(running to the bed)
Presto
E.
Chi ge-me là? Or-
What cry is that? Great
senza misura
O.
vi - ve!!
lives!
ff
senza misura
ppp
122
senza misura
D.
Muo - io in - no - cen - te...
I die here guilt - less...
Nes-
Oh,
E.
ror!
God!
Gran Dio... Chi fu? chi fu?
Oh Heav'n! who did this deed?
ff
senza misura
pp
123
D.
su - no... io stes-sa...
no one... my - self
Al mio Si - gnor
Un - to my lord
pp legato

127
D.
(muore.)
(she dies.)
Allegro
mi rac - co - man - da...
pray you com - mend me...
Muo-io in-no - cen - te...
I die here guilt - less...
Ad - di - o...
fare - well!
OTELLO
O.
O men-ti-
She dies a
Allegro
133
EMILIA
E.
As- sas - si - no!
Vile as- sas - sin.
tri - ce! io l'uc - ci - si.
li - ar! I have killed her.
Fu di Cas - sio la dru - da.
Strum-pet she was to Cas - sio.
A Ja - go il
Your hus - band
137
a tempo prestissimo
senza appoggiature
A Ja - go?!
My hus-band?
Stol - to!! e tu il cre - de - sti?
Fool thou! and didst be - lieve him?
Non ti
Thee I
(fa per avventarsi contro Emilia)
(threatening Emilia)
chie-di.
told me.
A Ja - go.
Your hus-band.
Ne - gar-lo ar-dis - ci?!
Dare you de - ny it?

(si svincola e corre verso la porta, gridando disperatamente)
(frees herself and runs to the door crying loudly)

140

E. te - mo. O - là! Soc-cor-so! A - iu - to! O - tel - lo uc-ci - se De-
fear not. Oh help! bring res-cue, As - sis-tance! The Moor hath mur - dered my

(la afferra)
(takes hold of her)

O. Ba-da!
Tar-ry!

GG **Come prima.** 𝅗𝅥 = 80.

144

E. sde - mo-na!
mis - tree!

GG
Come prima. 𝅗𝅥 = 80.

f

Nationalism and Virtuosity
Franz Liszt

157

Franz Liszt
Hungarian Rhapsody No. 15 (*Rákóczy March*) (1853)

Franz Liszt's nineteen Hungarian Rhapsodies for piano are artistic arrangements of traditional Hungarian and Gypsy music. Liszt chose the term "rhapsody" for their title to suggest a specifically national character. The word itself originally designated a recitation of epic poetry, and Liszt thought of his own rhapsodies in this same sense, as declamations of a Hungarian national epic, stated in music rather than words.

The Hungarian Rhapsody No. 15 is a virtuosic arrangement of the rousing "Rákóczy March," named in honor of the early Hungarian patriot Francis II Rákóczy. The march is in ternary form (march-trio-march) with each section cast in rounded binary form. However, instead of simply writing in repeat signs, Liszt often recomposes the repetitions. His arrangement evokes the sound of a Gypsy band, with an introduction based on the so-called "Gypsy scale" (a minor scale with two augmented seconds), and an imitation of the sound of the cimbalom (a Hungarian dulcimer) toward the end.

Intro.	March				Trio					
	A	A	B	A	C	C	D	C	D	C
1	15	23	31	~~42~~ 43	~~59~~ 61	~~69~~ 71	~~79~~ 81 or 82	~~91~~ 94	~~101~~ 104	~~113~~ 117

Cadenza	March				Coda
	A	A	B	A	A
~~127~~ 131	~~147~~ 152	~~155~~ 161	~~163~~ 169	~~177~~ 184	~~193~~ 200

Numbering of the measures is incorrect, #'s refer ~~#~~ to the uncorrected measure numbers.

Franz Liszt
Hungarian Rhapsody No. 15 (*Rákóczy March*) (1853)
CD 10/2

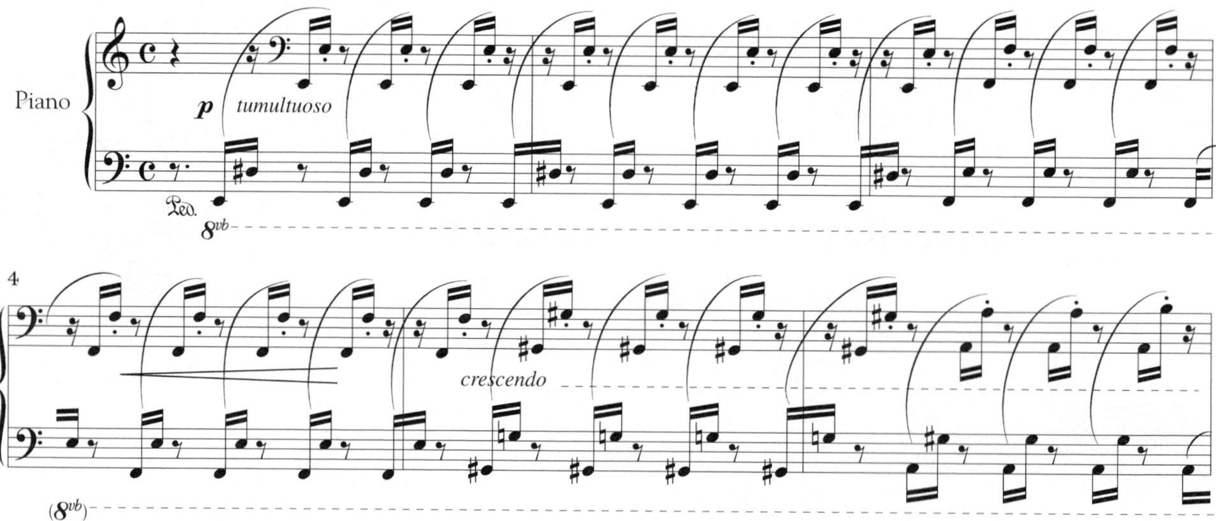

7
(8vb)
10
8va
strepitoso molto rinforzando
(8va)
13
loco
Tempo di Marcia animato
15
marcatissimo
17
21
3
sempre ff
3
8va
(8va)
26

(8va)
30
loco
ff
Ossia
cresc.
p non legato
cresc.
f
f
ff
8va
(8va)

(8va)
51
8va
8va
loco
55
rinforz.
8va
Un poco meno Allegro
marcato con grazia
60
dolce
8va
(8va)
66
loco
8va
(8va)
70
sempre piano
8va
(8va)
loco
74
8va
loco

8va
78
p
loco
83
87
8va
(8va)
90
(8va)
92
loco
8va
5
p brillante
5

(8va)
94
(8va)
97
loco
8va
loco
8va
(8va)
100
(8va)
103
ff
8va
109

(8va)
113
loco
8va
116
5
p
brillante
5
(8va)
119
loco
8va
(8va)
122
loco
8va
più piano
(8va)
125
pp
(8va)
128
3
3
3
3
3
3
3
3
3
3

legeramente
8va
131
Cadenza ad libitum
Kürzer zum Zeichen 𝄋 Seite 12.
loco
133
135
p sotto voce
8vb
137
(8vb)
139
p
(8vb)
141
crescendo
(8vb)

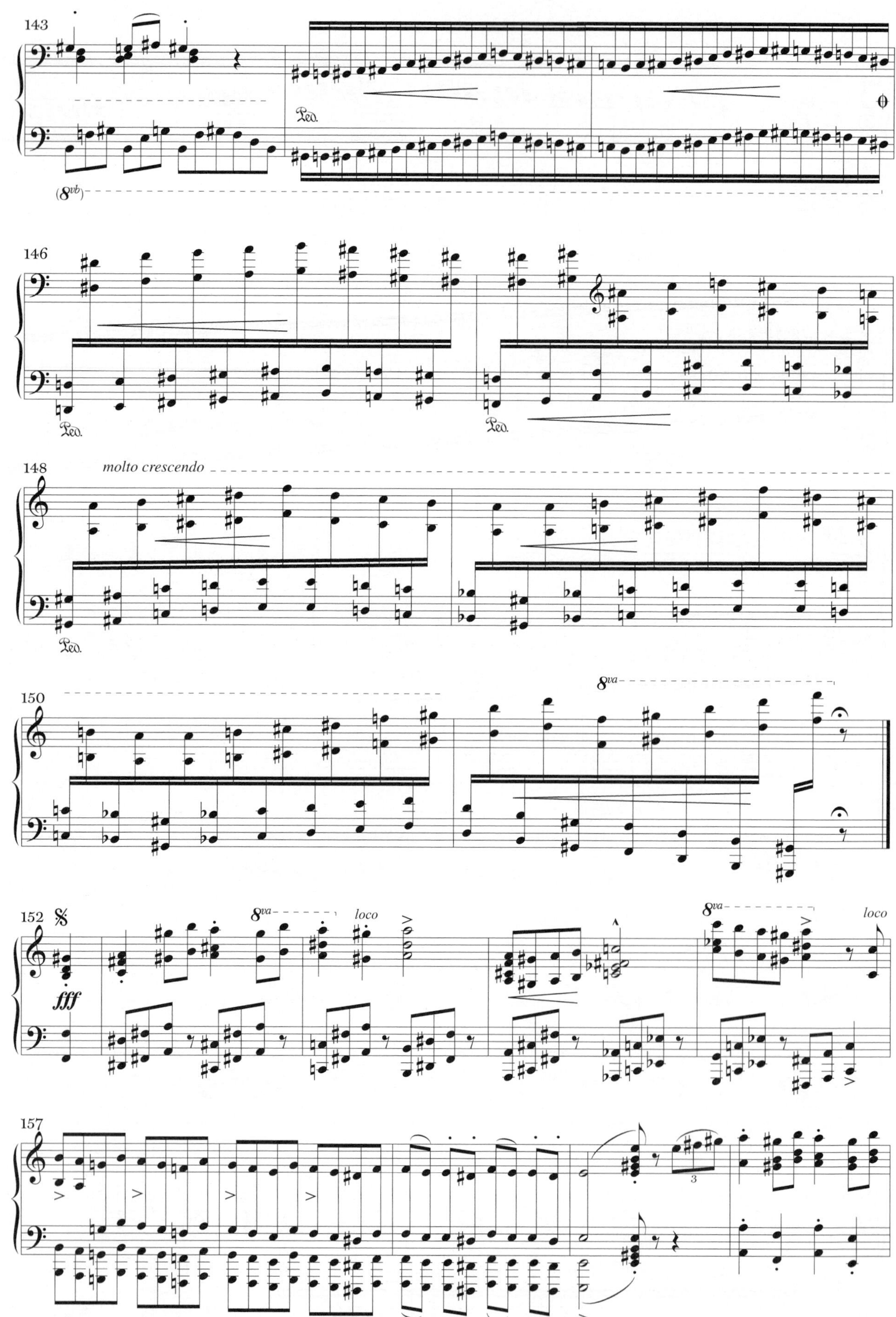
143
(8vb)
Ped.
146
Ped.
Ped.
148
molto crescendo
Ped.
150
8va
152
fff
8va
loco
8va
loco
157
3

162
8va
166
(8va)
ff
Facile
8va
loco
glissando
172
sf
Ossia
f con bravura
176
(8va)

178
loco
8va
180
f
crescendo
183
loco
ff
187
(8va)

(8va)
loco
8va
loco
192
8va
rfz
loco
197
più rinforz
8va
loco
8va
fff
(8va)
201
loco
8va
loco
8va
(8va)
205
sempre ff
(8va)
209

213
(8va)
loco
217
8va
221
loco
8va
225
(8va)
8va

Vienna in the Late Nineteenth Century
Brahms and Bruckner

158

Johannes Brahms
Symphony No. 3 (1883)
First movement, *Allegro con brio*

The four symphonies of Johannes Brahms bring the styles and forms of Beethoven's middle-period symphonies into the late nineteenth century. Outwardly, Brahms's Symphony No. 3 is a work in the mold of Beethoven. It avoids the overt programmatic tendencies found in the orchestral music of composers such as Hector Berlioz and Franz Liszt, and it adheres instead to the "absolute," or purely musical, content that reigned in symphonies of the Classical period. Brahms calls for an orchestra of moderate size, one with roughly the same makeup as the orchestra of Beethoven's Ninth Symphony. The symphony also adheres to the classical sequence of four movements, and it is moderate in length. The first movement conforms to the generally established conventions of sonata form—including an exposition that is repeated—and it ends with a long coda. Also evident is Brahms's use of contrapuntal devices such as inversion and diminution as well as such rhythmic techniques as hemiola and metric displacement.

At the same time, the F-Major Symphony shows that Brahms is a thoroughly "progressive" composer. The work has a warm and intense expressivity more characteristic of the late Romantic period than the Classical, and its harmonic language, irregularity of phrases, metric flexibility, and tonal plan suggest the thinking of a modern composer of the 1880s.

Exposition				Development				
Theme I	Transition	Theme II	Closing	Cl.	Th. II	Cl.	false recap.	Th. I
F	mod.	A		mod.	c♯	mod.	E♭	
1	15	36	49	71	77	90	101	112

Recapitulation				Coda
Theme I	Trans.	Theme II	Closing	Theme I
F		D	d	F
120	137	149	158	181

Johannes Brahms
Symphony No. 3 (1883)
First movement, *Allegro con brio*
CD 10/3

Flöten.
Hoboen.
Clarinetten in B.
Fagotte.
Contrafagott.
Hörner in C.
Hörner in F.
Trompeten in F.
Posaunen.
Pauken in F. C.
Violine I.
f passionato
Violine II.
f passionato
Bratsche.
Violoncell.
Bass.

Allegro con brio.

6

10

15
A
p
cresc.
f
A p

19

B
23
p
p dolce
p
p dolce
p
p
p
p dolce
p
p
fp
dolce
fp
dolce
fp
dolce
p
p dolce
pizz.
p
p dolce
B

28
p
p
p
pizz.
pizz.

31
Fl.
più p
Hb.
Cl.
più p
mutano in A.
Fag.
più p
Hr.
Viol.
arco
Fl.
p
pp
Cl.
grazioso
p m.r.
pp
Fag.
m.r.
p
pp
Viol.
p
pp
pizz.
p
pizz.
pp
p
pp

40
Fl.
dolce
Hb.
p grazioso
m.r.
pp
Cl.
p
pp
Fag.
p
pp
Hr. in F.
p
pp
Viol.
p
pp
p
pp
p m.r.
p grazioso
pp
p
pp
p
pp
C
p
p
p
pizz.
p
pizz.
p
a 2.
p
p
C p

46
Fl.
Hb.
Cl.
mutano in B.
Fag.
arco
mp espress.
dim.
Viol.
pizz.
p
Fl.
p legg.
Hb.
dolce
Cl.
Fag.
Hr. in F.
pp
pdolce
a 2.

53
p legg.
p
arco
arco
arco
p

56
cresc.
cresc.
cresc.
cresc.
cresc.
arco
cresc.
arco
cresc.
cresc.
cresc.
cresc.

59
D
p legg.
f
p
p legg.
cresc.
D f

63
a 2.
a 2.
a 2.
a 2.
cresc.

66

69
1.

2.
74
più f
ff

77
E
f agitato
divisi
f
f agitato
f agitato
E f

81
Fag.
Viol.
ben marc.
ben marc.
ben marc.
ben marc.
Fl.
f
Hb.
f
Cl.
f
Fag.
f
Viol.
f agitato
cresc.
cresc.
cresc.
cresc.
cresc.

89
Fl.
Hb.
Cl.
Fag.
Viol.
f
f
F
Fl.
Hb.
f
Cl.
f
Fag.
f
dim.
dim.
f
Hr.
f
mf
Viol.
mf
mf
dim.
mf
dim.
mf
F

96
Fl.
Hb.
Cl.
Fag.
Hrn. in C.
Viol.
p
dim.
f

103
G
Cl.
Fag.
p
Ctrf.
p
p
p
Hrn.
in C.
espress.
f
p
Viol.
p
p
p
p
espress.
f
Hb.
Ctrf.
Hrn.
in C.
cresc.
f
p
Viol.
G

111
poco rit.
H Un poco sostenuto
pp sempre
pp sempre
pp sempre
pp sempre
dim.
p dim.
p dim.
p dim.
p dim.
pp sempre
p dim.
H pp sempre
poco rit.
Un poco sostenuto

116
rit.
pp sempre
cresc.
cresc.
cresc.
cresc.
pp
pp
pp
tr
pp cresc.
pp sempre
cresc.
pp sempre
cresc.
pp sempre
cresc.
cresc.
cresc.
rit.

121
Tempo I.
Tempo I.

127
sf
sf
f
f
f
f
sf
sf
sf

132
f
marc.
f
marc.
marc.
f marc.
cresc.
f
cresc.
f
cresc.
f
cresc.
f
cresc.
f

136
I p
p
p
p
p
p
espress.
sf
sf
sf
p
p
p
p
I p

141
p
p
p dol.
legg.
p
legg.
legg.
p
legg.
pizz.
p

145
mutano in A
più p

151
Fl.
Hb.
Cl. in A.
Fag.
p grazioso
Hr. in F.
Viol.
pizz.
pp dol.
Cl.
pizz
a 2

158
p legg.
dol.
in B
p
p legg.
p
p
arco
mp espress.
dim.
pp
pizz.
p
arco
mp espress.
dim.
pp
pizz.
p
arco
mp espress.
dim.
pp
pizz.
p
arco
mp espress.
dim.
pp
p dol.

163
cresc.
p
cresc.
cresc.
p
cresc.
cresc.
cresc.
cresc.
arco
p
cresc.

167
K
a 2.
cresc.
p cresc.
p cresc.
f
arco
arco
arco
K f

171
p
f
cresc.
p legg.
fp

175
a 2.
ff
a 2.
ff
ff
a 2.
ff
f
f
sf
f
sf
sf
f
sf
sf
f
sf
f
sf
sf
f
sf
sf
f
sf
sf
f
sf
sf

178
f
f
f
f
sf
sf
ff
ff
ff
ff
sf
ff

181
sf
f

186
L
sf
f marc.
a 2.
L

191
più f
più f
più f
più f
sf
sf
3
1
cresc.
cresc.
cresc.
cresc.
f
cresc.

195
sf
f
tr
più f

199
C muta in B.

203
M
rf
p
f
a 2.

208

214
pp
p cresc.
p
cresc.
p

221
p
f
p
fp
p
fp
p
fp
p
f
fp
p
f
p
f
p
f
p
f
p
tr
pizz.
arco
fp
dim.
pizz.
arco
fp
dim.
pizz.
arco
f
p dim.
pizz.
arco
f
p dim.
pizz.
arco
f
p dim.

159

Johannes Brahms

"Feldeinsamkeit," Opus 86, No. 2 (c1879)

The artless folk song was the ideal model for the *Lieder* composer of the Romantic period. Brahms's celebrated song "Feldeinsamkeit" ("Alone in the Country") is based on a poem by Hermann Allmers that praises the most unsophisticated of activities and moods. Brahms's setting is laid out in a varied strophic form, with the burden of expression placed squarely in the singer's melodic line. (Brahms sent a copy of the *Lied* to the poet, but the author did not care for the setting—he felt it was too complex and artful for the simple mood.)

Johannes Brahms
"Feldeinsamkeit," Opus 86, No. 2 (c1879)
CD 10/4

Langsam (slowly)

Singstimme

Ich ru - he still im

Pianoforte

p

4

ho - hen grü - nen Gras und sen - de lan - ge mei - nen Blick nach —

7
o - ben, nach o - ben, von
10
Gril - len rings um-schwirrt ohn' Un - ter - lass, von Him - mels-bläu - e
13
wun - der-sam um-wo - ben, von Him - mels - bläu - e wun - der - sam um -
16
- wo - - - - - ben. Die
p

19
schö - nen wei - ssen Wol - ken ziehn da - hin durchs tie - fe Blau, wie
dim.
22
schö - ne stil - le Träu - me, wie schö - ne stil - le
25
Träu - me; mir ist, als ob ich längst ge - stor - ben
dolce
p
28
bin und zie - he se - lig mit durch ew' - ge Räu - me, und

Ich ruhe still im hohen grünen Gras
und sende lange meinen Blick nach oben,
von Grillen rings umschwirrt ohn' Unterlaß,
von Himmelsbläue wundersam umwoben.

Die schönen weißen Wolken ziehn dahin
durchs tiefe Blau, wie schöne stille
Träume;—
mir ist, als ob ich längst gestorben bin
und ziehe selig mit durch ew'ge Räume.

—Hermann Allmers

I rest quietly in the tall green grass
and cast my gaze upward,
while crickets around me chirp ceaselessly,
with the blue of heaven woven around me.

The beautiful white clouds move on
through the deep blue, like beautiful quiet
dreams;
it's as though I have long been dead
and drift blissfully with them through
eternal space.

160

Anton Bruckner

Christus factus est (1884)

Anton Bruckner was the most original composer of Catholic liturgical music of the late Romantic period. An example of his broad outlook on the art of composing for the church is found in his exquisite motet *Christus factus est.* The piece is performable either as a concert work or as the Gradual in the celebration of Mass on Maundy Thursday.

The music of *Christus factus est* suggests a fusion of the motet tradition harking back to Palestrina and the Renaissance with the most advanced harmonic language in existence in the 1880s. On the surface of the piece, the antiquarian features are obvious. Like a Renaissance motet, *Christus factus est* is sung *a cappella.* Its smooth rhythmic profile and succession of short phrases that freely alternate between homophonic and polyphonic settings create a work that exhibits the Cecilian ideal of serenity. Yet Bruckner does not ignore the implications inherent in the text. He subtly uses gesture and vocal color to paint the meaning of various words, such as the descent into the lower vocal ranges for "mortem" ("death").

Existing side by side with Bruckner's glances toward the past is a thoroughly modern harmonic and tonal idiom. The consonant harmony is nevertheless quite chromatic. It begins in D minor but then moves far afield, and no central tonality controls the work until the final D major cadence. In its free chromatic motions and its bypassing of primary triads in the central key, the motet reminds us of the most progressive works from the 1880s.

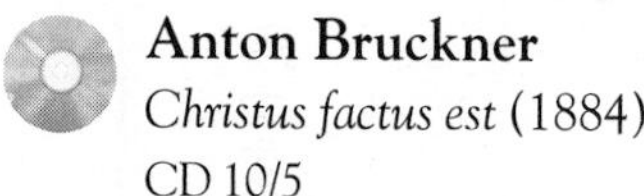

Anton Bruckner
Christus factus est (1884)
CD 10/5

Moderato misterioso

Soprano: Chri - stus fac - tus est pro no - bis - o be - di-ens, o-
Alto: Chri - stus fac - tus est pro no - bis o - be - di-ens o - be - di - ens o-
Tenor: Chri - stus fac - tus est pro no - bis o - be - di - ens o - be - di-ens
Bass: Chri - stus fac - tus est pro no - bis o - be - di-ens o-

7

Soprano: be - di - ens o - be - di - ens o - be - - - di - ens us - que ad
Alto: be - - - - - - - di - ens us - que ad
Tenor: o - be - di-ens o - be - di-ens o - be - - - di - ens us - que ad -
Bass: be - - - - - - - - - di - ens us - que ad

12

Soprano: mor - tem, - mor tem au - tem cru - - -
Alto: mor - tem, - mor tem au - tem cru - - -
Tenor: mor - tem, - mor tem au - tem cru - - -
Bass: mor - tem, mor - tem au - tem cru - - - - - - -

19
A
poco a poco cresc.
cis. Prop - ter quod et De - us ex - al - ta - vit il - lum
cis. Prop - ter quod et De - us ex - al - ta - vit il - lum
cis. Prop - ter quod et De - us ex - al - ta - vit il - lum prop - ter
cis. Prop - ter quod et De - us ex - al - ta - vit il - lum
25
B
prop-ter quod et De - us ex - al - ta - vit il - lum et de - dit il - li no - men et
prop-ter quod et De - us ex - al - ta - vit il - lum et de - dit il - li no - men et
quod et De - us ex - al - ta - vit il - lum et de - dit il - li no - men et
prop - ter quod et De - us ex - al - ta - vit il - lum et de - dit il - li no - men et
cresc.
31
C
de - dit il - li no - men quod est su per su - per
de - dit il - li no - men quod est su per su - per
de - dit il - li no - men quod est su - per
de - dit il - li no - men, quod est su - per su - per
37
su - per om - ne no - men quod est su per om - ne no - men
su - per om - ne no - men quod est su per om - ne om - ne
su - per om - ne no - men quod est su per om - ne om - ne
su - per om - ne no - men quod est su - per om - ne no - men

D
mf
su - per su - per quod est su - - - - -
no - men
quod est su - per su - per
mf
no - men quod est su - - per su - - - - per
mf
quod est su - - - per su - - - - - per
E p poco a poco cresc.
f cresc.
- per om - ne no - men su - - - per su - per om - ne
cresc.
om - ne no - men quod est su - per om - ne
p poco a poco cresc.
cresc.
om - ne no - men su - - per - su - per om - ne
cresc.
p poco a poco cresc.
om - ne no - men su - - - per su - per om - ne
ff
fff
F
no - men - quod est su per om - - - ne
no - men - quod est su per om - - - ne
no - men - quod est su per om - - - ne
no - men - quod est su per om - - - ne
dim.
p
G
pp
no - men - om ne no - men
no - men - om ne no - men quod est
no - men - om ne no - men
no - men - om ne no - men quod est

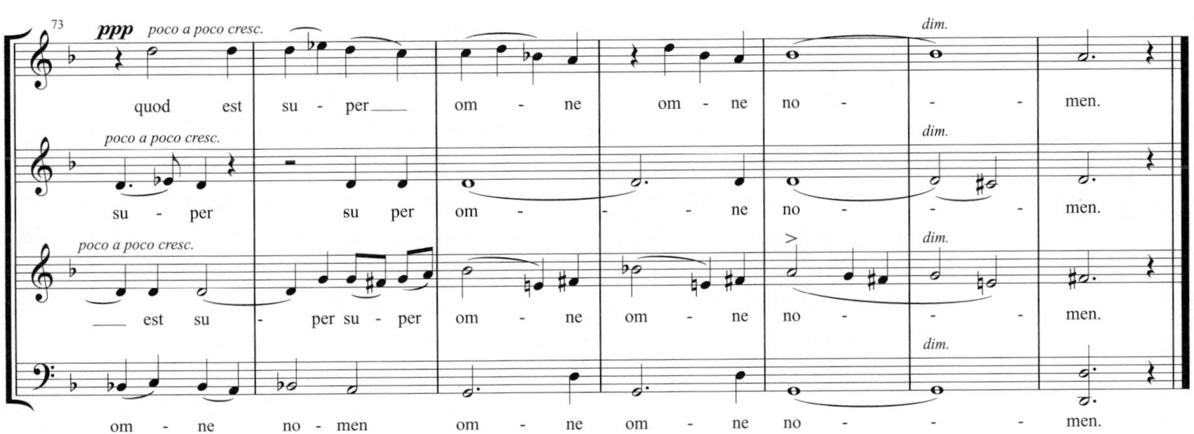

Christus factus est pro nobis obediens usque ad mortem, mortem autem crucis.	Christ was for us obedient unto death, unto death on the cross.
[verse] Propter quod et Deus exaltavit illum, et dedit illi nomen, quod est super omne nomen.	Therefore God exalted him, and gave him a name that is above every other name.

Chapter 59 Music and Ballet in Nineteenth-Century Russia *Mussorgsky and Tchaikovsky*

161

Modest Mussorgsky
Sunless, "Within Four Walls" (1874)

Mussorgsky composed *Sunless*, a cycle of six songs, in the spring and summer of 1874, at virtually the same time that his opera *Boris Gudonov* was being heard at St. Petersburg's Mariinsky Theater. The reception of the opera—even among musicians within his circle—was unsympathetic. César Cui, reviewing the work for a St. Petersburg newspaper, concluded, "There is little music in it and its recitatives are not melodic."

Such criticism could only have increased Mussorgsky's depressive state of mind, which is grimly evident in *Sunless*. The texts, by Mussorgsky's friend Arseny Golenishchev-Kutuzov, consist of poems that are spoken in the first person by a narrator who is trapped by life, bereft of love, and filled with resentment. These sentiments are apparent in the first song, "Within Four Walls," in which the speaker's world is lighted only by the faintest glimmer of a distant happiness.

Mussorgsky's setting realistically interprets the words of the poem and their depressive sentiments. While it is true that the music lacks the flowing lyricism we would expect from a nineteenth-century composer, these are precisely the qualities that give the song its great originality. Mussorgsky was a believer in musical realism, both in an unvarnished depiction of true-to-life feelings and also in a melodic and harmonic style that allows the words to stand as though spoken. Notice the contrast in textures between the closely spaced harmonies of measures 3 to 4 and the spare openness of the following bars. The song's harmonic progression gradually increases in tension as the bass and treble chords become more widely separated (mm. 9–12), then collide in biting dissonance (mm. 13–14). Tranquility—born of despair perhaps—returns in the final bars as the vision of distant happiness is shut out by impenetrable shadows, leaving the poet isolated within four walls.

My room is small, quiet, pleasant;
the shadows are impenetrable and unanswering.
My thoughts are deep, my song melancholy,
yet in my beating heart hope lies hidden.

The moments fly swiftly by, one by one,
while my eyes are fixed on distant happiness,
full of doubts, I wait patiently,
thus it is, this night, my night of loneliness.

—Arseny Golenishchev-Kutuzov

Modest Mussorgsky

Sunless, "Within Four Walls" (1874)

CD 10/6

Andante tranquillo

p

Ком-нат-ка тес-на-я, ти-ха-я, ми-ла-я;

Kom-nat-ka tes-na-ya, ti-kha-ya, mi-la-ya;

pp

тень не про-гляд-на-я, тень без от-вет-на-я; ду-ма глу-бо-ка-я,

ten' ne pro-glyad-na-ya, ten' bez ot-vet-na-ya; du-ma glu-bo-ka-ya,

пес-ня у-ны-ла-я; в бью-щем-ся серд-це на-деж-да за-вет-на-я,

pes-nya u-nï-la-ya; v b'yu-shchem-sya serd-tse na-dezh-da za-vet-na-ya,

быст - рый по - лёт за мгно - ве - ньем мгно - ве - ни - я; взор не - под - виж - ный на
bïst - rïy po - lyot za mgno - ve - n'yem mgno - ve - ni - ya; vzor ne - pod - vizh - nïy na
poco accelerando e cresc.
сча - стье да - лё - ко - е; мно - го сом - не - ни - я, мно - го тер - пе - ни - я.
shcha - st'ye da - lyo - ko - ye; mno - go som - ne - ni - ye, mno - go ter - pe - ni - ya.
Meno mosso e tranquillo
Вот о - на ночь мо - я, ночь о - ди - но - ка - я.
Vot o - na noch' mo - ya, moch' o - di - no - ka - ya.
pp

162

Peter Ilyich Tchaikovsky
The Nutcracker (1892)
Act 1, scene 8

Tchaikovsky wrote his ballet *The Nutcracker* for the 1892 Christmas season of St. Petersburg's Mariinsky Theater, and, ever since, the work has brought joy and delight to audiences the world over at Christmastime. The ballet is loosely based on a children's bedtime story, "Nutcracker and Mouse King," by E.T.A. Hoffmann. At a family party before Christmas, Clara is given a toy nutcracker. Late that night she steals back to see her toys by the Christmas tree, and to her amazement the nutcracker comes to life and leads his army of toy soldiers in battle against a ruthless horde of mice. With Clara's help, the nutcracker vanquishes its foe, whereupon it is magically transformed into a handsome prince. In gratitude for her assistance, the prince takes Clara to visit his home in the Land of Sweets.

The music to which Clara and the Prince sail off through the snow-laden trees is some of the most inspiring and memorable of the whole ballet. Here we find the composer's unmatched ability to write a stirring melody. In the present day, the passage is choreographed in differing ways. Sometimes, as envisioned by Tchaikovsky and Marius Petipa (the work's original choreographer), Clara and the prince sail through the air in a sleigh; in other productions they dance a romantic *pas de deux*.

Although this dance is in ternary form, the return of the **A** section in measure 39 is perceived as the climax of the scene rather than a repetition of the beginning. This is due to the fact that the **B** section does not modulate away from the tonic key of C major and its theme is not strikingly different (as it is in the "Dance of the Reed Pipes"). At the moment where the **A** section returns, Tchaikovsky creates a climactic high point for the dancers. He accomplishes this by bringing in the tutti orchestra (omitting the two harps) and, a few bars later, intensifying the rhythm with a swirling countermelody played by the strings. This musical energy dissipates rapidly in the coda as the dance concludes.

A	B	A	Coda
1	19	39	58

Peter Ilyich Tchaikovsky
The Nutcracker (1892)
Act 1, scene 8
CD 10/7

3
cantabile
p cantabile
p
p
cantabile
p cantabile
p
3
p
p
p

6
poco cresc.
poco cresc.
poco cresc.
mf
mf
poco cresc.
poco cresc.
mf
mf
poco cresc.
poco cresc.
poco cresc.
poco cresc.
poco cresc.
poco cresc.
poco cresc.

9
f
dim.
mp
mf
p

12
cresc.
cresc.
cresc.
cresc.
cresc.
cresc.
cresc.
cresc.
cresc.
cresc.
cresc.
cresc.
cresc.

15

18
A
Sul G
espr.
Sul G
espr.
divisi
espr.

21
3
3

24
cresc.
ff
cre - scen - do

27
unis.
arco
arco

31
fff
ff
largamente
div.

37
B
Timp.
Piatti
unis.
unis.
B

40
ff

43
3
3
3
3
3
3

46
C
a 2
marcatissimo
Piatti.

50
con tutta forza
sempre ff
pp
f
fff

56
mf
(Muta E in D.)
pizz.
pizz.

60
mp
mp
mp
mp
mp
dim.
mp
dim.
dim.
mp
dim.
pizz.
mf
pizz.
mf
pizz.
mf
mp
mp
mp
mp
mp

63
D
p
cresc.
f
crescendo
D

66
ff
dim.
dim.
di
mi
nu
f
mf

69
p
en
do
en
do
p
mp
pp

Vienna at the Turn of the Twentieth Century *Gustav and Alma Mahler*

163

Gustav Mahler
"Um Mitternacht" (1901)

The turn of the twentieth century initiated for Gustav Mahler a new phase in his career as a song composer. In his earlier songs, he favored texts drawn from *Des knaben Wunderhorn (The Youth's Magic Horn)*, a multivolume anthology of old German folk verse. But in 1901 he turned to the more sophisticated and artful poetry of Friedrich Rückert (1788–1866), on whose verse he then composed a series of independent songs and the cycle *Kindertotenlieder*. "Um Mitternacht" is one of the former group.

The through-composed setting is tied together by three important motives, all present in the first two measures: the rocking or "ticking" gesture in the clarinets and flutes, and the descending Phrygian scale in the French horns. The second through fourth stanzas are all based on variants and paraphrases of the first (mm. 1–16). In these stanzas, the poet stands at the brink of the abyss, pondering, struggling to understand the darkness of eternity, symbolized by the stroke of midnight. In the fourth stanza, he gives up the battle for enlightenment and places himself in the hands of God. The setting turns to the major mode, and the full brass section and the "heavenly" harp, held back until this moment, move with grandiose majesty to the final cadence. The orchestral accompaniment is highly unusual, as Mahler omits the strings, retaining only instruments from the brass, woodwinds, and percussion sessions, to which he adds the harp and piano.

Um Mitternacht hab' ich gewacht und aufgeblickt zum Himmel! Kein Stern vom Sterngewimmel hat mir gelacht um Mitternacht!	At midnight I awakened and gazed up to heaven! Not a star from the starry host smiled back at me, at midnight!
Um Mitternacht hab' ich gedacht hinaus in dunkle Schranke! Es hat kein Lichtgedanke mir Trost gebracht um Mitternacht.	At midnight I pondered to the dark limits! No enlightenment brought me peace, at midnight.
Um Mitternacht hab' ich in Acht die Schläge meines Herzens! Ein einz'ger Puls des Schmerzens war angefacht um Mitternacht.	At midnight I noticed the beating of my heart! A single throb of pain flared up, at midnight.
Um Mitternacht kämpft' ich die Schlacht, O Menschheit, deiner Leiden. Nicht konnt' ich sie entscheiden mit meiner Macht um Mitternacht.	At midnight I fought the battle, O mankind, of thy suffering. But I could not prevail with my frail powers, at midnight.

Um Mitternacht hab' ich die Macht in deine Hand gegeben! Herr! Herr über Tod und Leben. Du hältst die Wacht! Um Mitternacht!	At midnight I fought the battle, O mankind, of thy suffering. But I could not prevail with my frail powers, at midnight.

—Friedrich Rückert

Gustav Mahler
"Um Mitternacht" (1901)
CD 10/8

Ruhig, gleichmäßig
Tranquillo, con moto equale

Flauti
Oboe d'amore
Clarinetti in [A La
Fagotti
Contrafagotto
Corni in [Es Mib
Trombe in [Es Mib
Tromboni
Tuba basso
Timpani
Voce
Arpe e Pianoforte

Ruhig, gleichmäßig

Um Mit - ter-nacht
The mid - night hour

5

1
Fg.
Cfg.
Cor. (Es)
Voce
hab' ich ge-wacht und auf-ge-blickt zum Him-mel;
boomed from the tower; tho' bright the heavens were gleam-ing,
10
Fl.
Ob. d'am.
Fg.
Cfg.
Cor. (Es)
Voce
kein Stern vom Stern-ge-wim-mel
no star in a-zure beam-ing,
hat mir ge-lacht um Mit-ter-
smiled on my bower, at mid-night
15
a tempo
rit.
herunterziehen
strisciando in giù
2
Ob. d'am.
Cl. (A)
Fg.
Cfg.
Cor. (Es)
Voce
molto
herunterziehen
espr.
nacht.
hour.
20
Um Mit-ter-
At mid-night

3 Fließend
Sciolatamente
Cl. (A)
Fg.
Cfg.
Cor. (Es)
Voce
a 2
espr.
zart¹⁾
nacht hab' ich ge - dacht hin-aus in dunk - le Schran - ken.
hour, with all its power, my soul a - spired to heav - en.
25
4
Zart, aber sehr ausdrucksvoll
Tenero, ma molto espress.
Nicht schleppen
Non stentare
Ob. d'am.
Um Mit - ter-nacht.
At mid - night hour.
30
Es hat kein
O'er me no
rit.
5 Tempo I.
Licht - ge-dan-ken mir Trost ge - bracht um Mit - ter - nacht.
light from heav - en did sol - ace pour at mid-night hour.

1) tenero

Cl. (A)
Fg.
Cfg.
Cor. (Es)
Voce
2.4. a 2
pp
2.
pp
pp
35
Um Mit - ter - nacht
At mid - night hour,
nahm ich in acht die
throb-bing with power, my
Ob. d'am.
Cl. (A)
Fg.
Cfg.
Cor. (Es)
Voce
f
p
2.
p
espr. string.
Schlä - ge mei - nes Her - zens;
heart de-sired the mor - row,
40
ein einz'- ger
one con-stant
Puls_ des Schmerzens war
thought of sor - row would
Nicht schleppen
6
Non stentare
Fl.
Ob. d'am.
Cl. (A)
Fg.
Cor. (Es)
Voce
a 2
f
p
pp
2.
molto espr.
3.4. a 2
p
pp
an - ge-facht um Mit-ter-nacht.
haunt my bower at mid-night hour.
45
Um Mit-ter-
At mid-night

molto espr.
Ob. d'am.
Cl. (A)
Fg.
Cfg.
Cor. (Es)
Voce
nacht kämpft' ich die Schlacht, o Mensch-heit, dei-ner Lei-den;
hour, fled from my bower, I fought the fight of an-guish;
50
55
7 Fließend
Scioltamente
a 2
1. espr.
espr.
Fließend
2. espr.
4. espr.
mit großem Ausdruck
con grande espress.
nicht konnt' ich sie ent-schei-den
de-feat-ed, now I lan-guish;
60

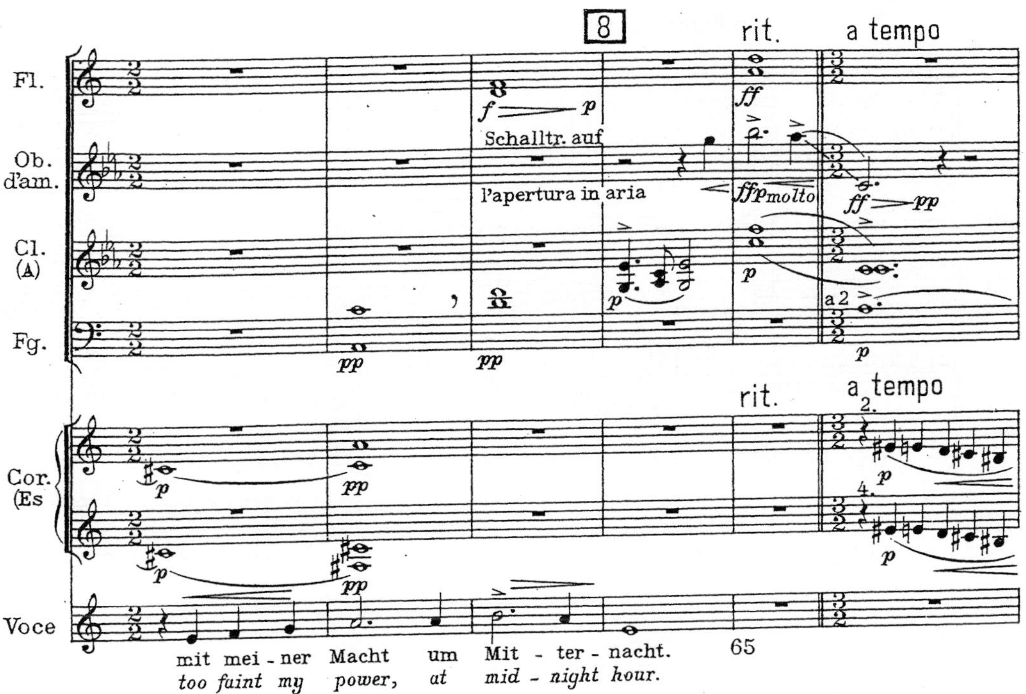
8
rit.
a tempo
Fl.
Ob. d'am.
Cl. (A)
Fg.
Schalltr. auf
l'apertura in aria
ffp molto
a 2
Cor. (Es)
Voce
mit mei - ner Macht um Mit - ter - nacht.
too faint my power, at mid - night hour.
65

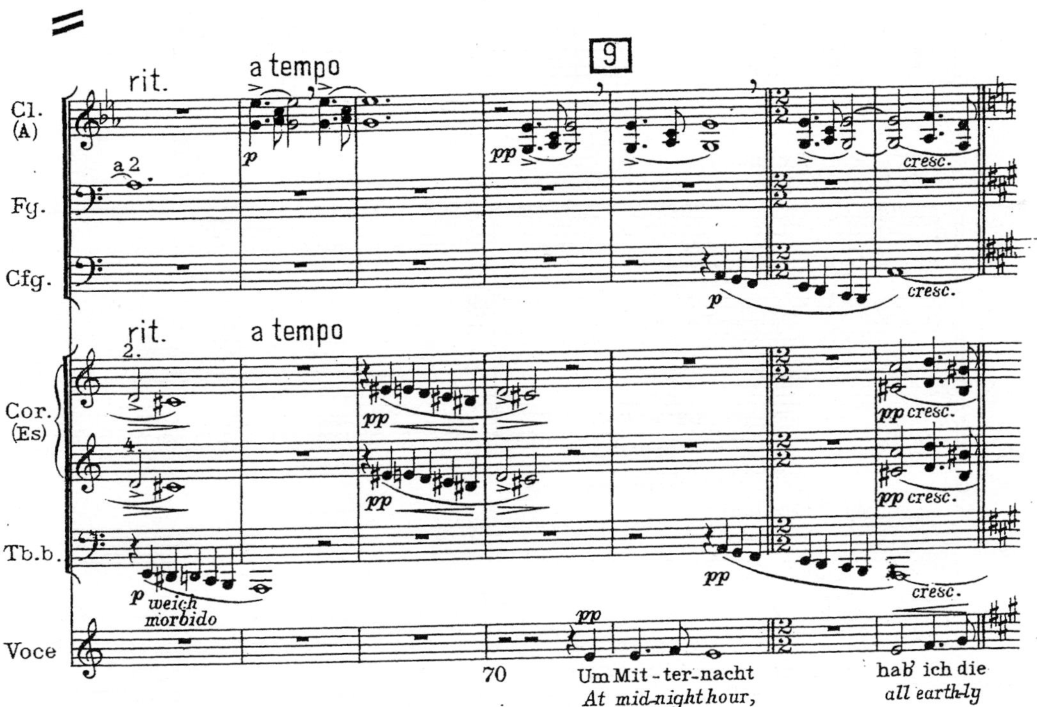
9
rit.
a tempo
Cl. (A)
Fg.
Cfg.
Cor. (Es)
Tb.b.
Voce
a 2
cresc.
pp cresc.
weich
morbido
70
Um Mit - ter-nacht
At mid-night hour,
hab' ich die
all earth-ly

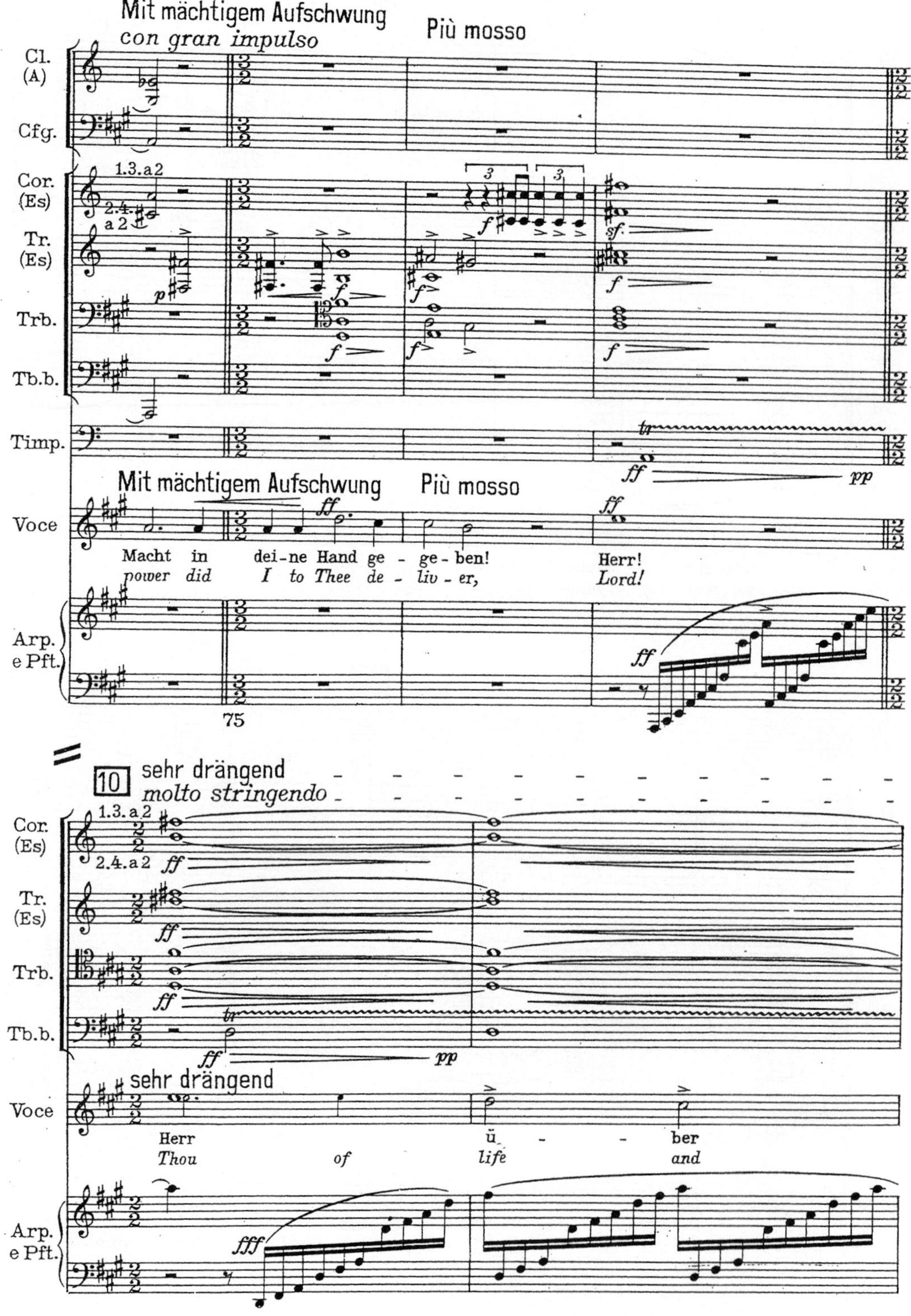
Mit mächtigem Aufschwung
con gran impulso
Più mosso
Cl. (A)
Cfg.
Cor. (Es)
Tr. (Es)
Trb.
Tb.b.
Timp.
Voce
Macht in dei-ne Hand ge- ge-ben! Herr!
power did I to Thee de- liv-er, Lord!
Arp. e Pft.
75
10 sehr drängend
molto stringendo
Herr ü - - ber
Thou of life and

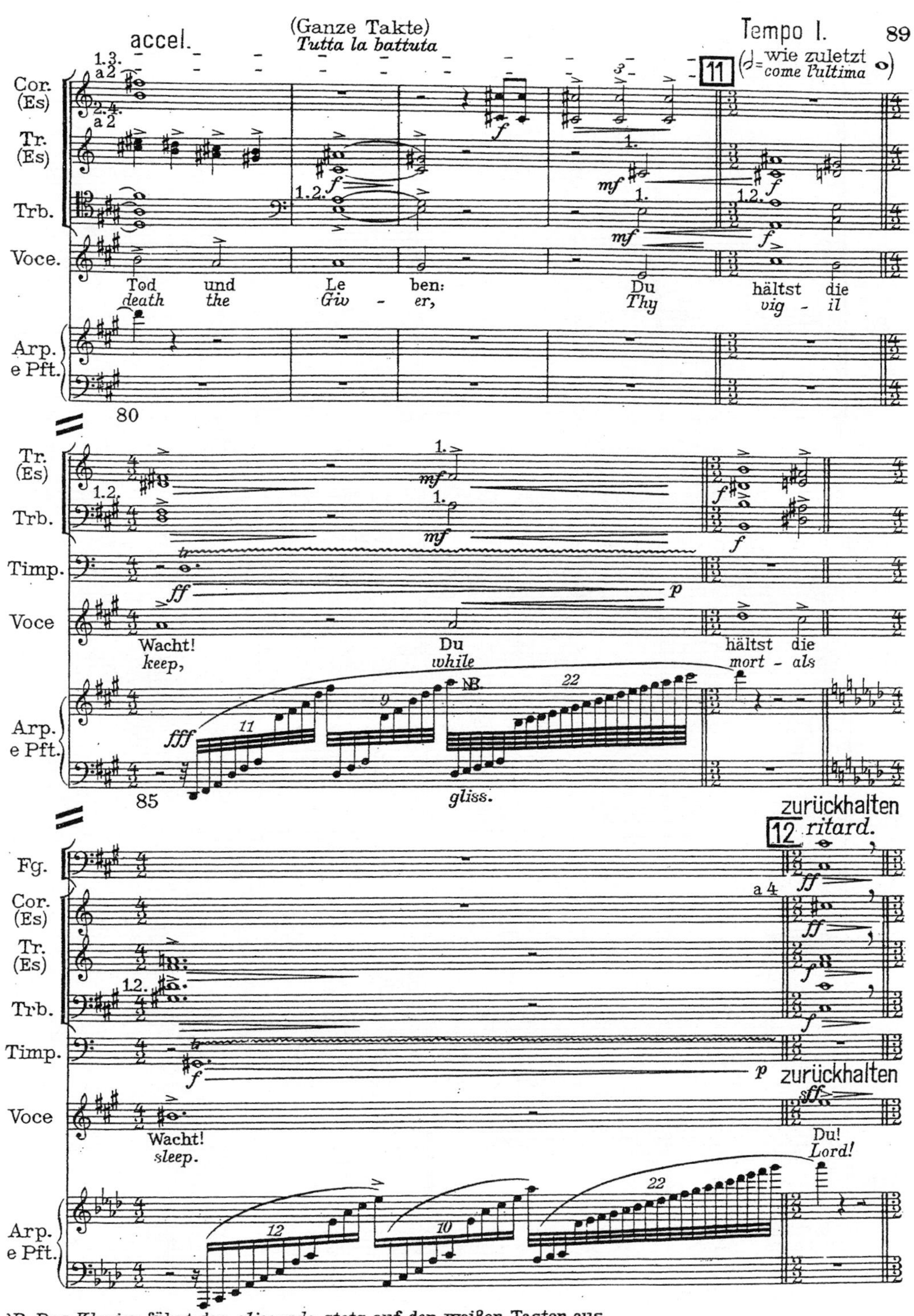

NB. Das Klavier führt das *glissando* stets auf den weißen Tasten aus.
Pianoforte *glissando* sulla tastiera bianca.

Breit
Largo
rit.
Fl.
Ob. d'am.
Cl. (A)
Fg.
Cfg.
Cor. (Es)
Tr. (Es)
Trb.
Tb.b.
Timp.
Voce
Arp. e Pft.
Du hältst die Wacht um Mit - - ter -
Lord! guard my bower at mid - - night
90

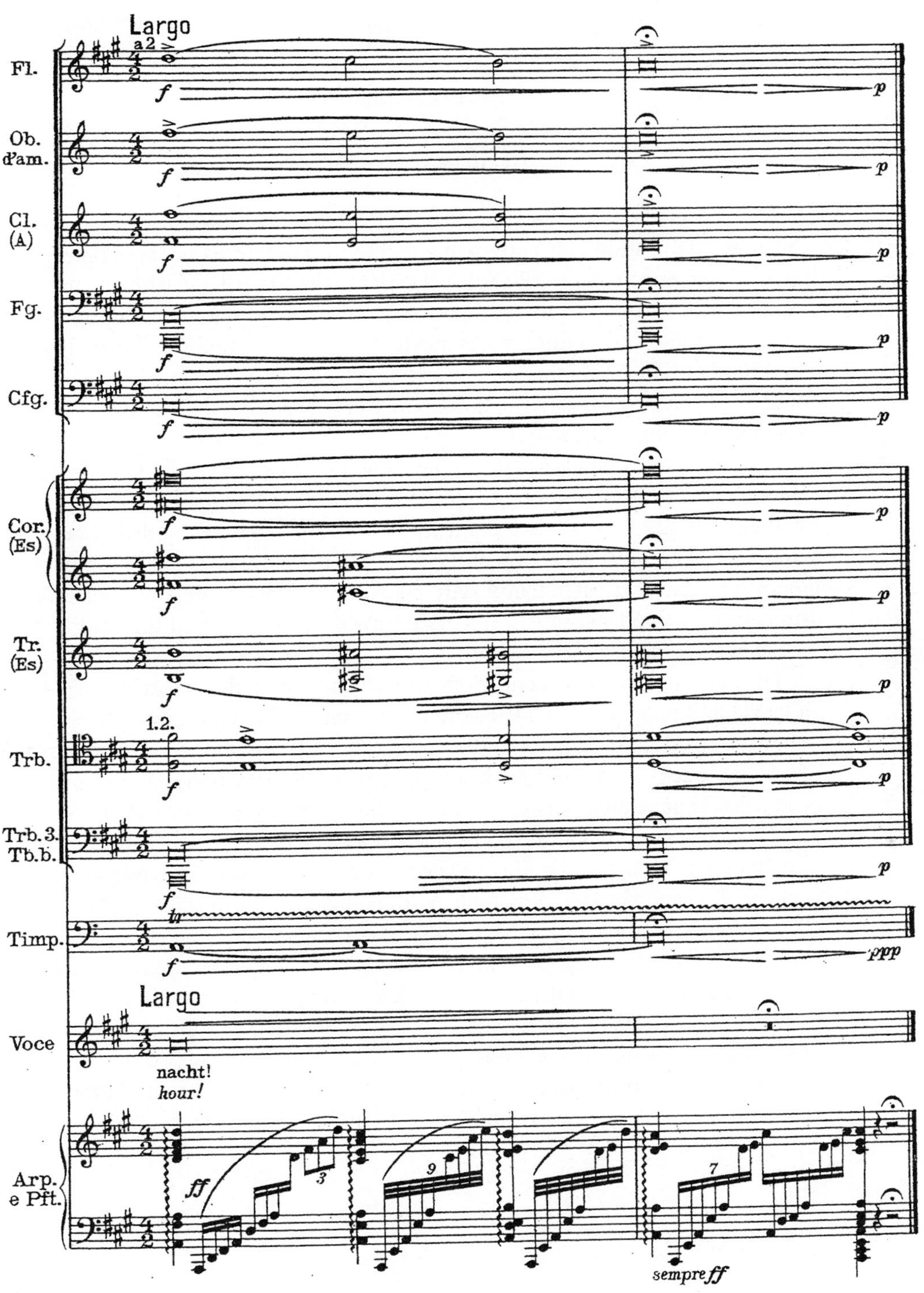
Largo
a 2
Fl.
Ob. d'am.
Cl. (A)
Fg.
Cfg.
Cor. (Es)
Tr. (Es)
1.2.
Trb.
Trb. 3. Tb.b.
Timp.
Largo
Voce
nacht!
hour!
Arp. e Pft.
sempre ff

164

Gustav Mahler
Symphony No. 5 (1902)
Fourth movement, *Adagietto*

Just as 1901 marked the beginning of a new direction in Mahler's songs, the year also saw him strike out on new paths as a symphonist. His four earlier symphonies were decidedly programmatic works. All deal with Mahler himself and with his struggle to understand the world and his own fate. In the first two symphonies (1888 and 1894), the hero-protagonist confronts the inevitability of death and the prospects for an afterlife. The Third Symphony (1896) returns to earth to explore nature in all of its dimensions and grandeur. Symphony No. 4 (1900) transports the soul to heaven, where many delights are found.

In his Symphony No. 5, Mahler dispenses with any such overt displays of programmatic meaning. "Nothing in any of my conversations with Mahler," recalled Bruno Walter, "and not a single note point to the influence of extra-musical thoughts or emotions upon the composition of the *Fifth*." In the place of Mahler's earlier philosophical musings, Walter found only pure music. This is, he wrote, "a work of strength and sound self-reliance, its face turned squarely toward life, and its basic mood one of optimism."

The fourth of five movements in the Fifth Symphony is the famous *Adagietto*. It is a lyrical and tranquil interlude before the boisterous finale. Mahler composed this slow movement in ternary form; the outer sections are in F major while the middle **B** section opens in the distant key of G♭ major. In section **A**, the theme moves through several related phrases, reaches its climax in measure 30, and then subsides to the cadence eight bars later. A brief transitional passage (mm. 39–46) introduces the **B** section (mm. 47–71). This middle section of the movement is primarily developmental, using melodic ideas from **A** to modulate through different tonal areas. When **A** returns, the theme is very much abbreviated.

This movement, for good or ill, has often been excised from the rest of the symphony and played as an independent movement. It was featured in the soundtrack to the 1971 film *Death in Venice*, but perhaps the most moving instance occurred in 1968. Leonard Bernstein—a musician whose career closely matched that of Mahler (composer and controversial conductor)—conducted this movement during the funeral Mass for Robert Kennedy in New York City's St. Patrick's Cathedral.

Gustav Mahler
Symphony No. 5 (1902)
Fourth movement, *Adagietto*
CD 10/9

12
1
Harfe
Vln. I
Vln. II
Vla.
Vcl.
Bs.
geteilt
breiter strich
unis.
p espress.
geteilt
arco
20
Rit.
Wieder äusserst langsam
pp mit emfindung
pp morendo
morendo
espress.
sempre pp
1. arco
2. pizz.
unis.
pizz.
poco a poco

Etwas drängend
Fliessend
Zurückhaltend
Harfe
Vln. I
Vln. II
Vla.
Vcl.
Bs.
cresc.
cresc. molto
molto
viel Bogen wechseln
geteilt
arco
dim.
Griffbrett
espress.
2 Fliessender
Mit wärme
(G-saite)
grosser Ton
pizz.

41
Harfe
Vln. I
Vln. II
Vla.
Vcl.
Bs.
D-Saite
(G-Saite)
espress.
nicht geteilt
molto
sempre cresc.
cresc.
48
pp subito
geteilt
unis.
pizz.
arco

56
Harfe
Fliessend
Vln. I
Vln. II
Vla.
Vcl.
Bs.
geteilt
pizz.
arco
cresc.
subito
63
Zurückhaltend
Molto rit.
(A-saite)
espress.
sempre dim.
morendo
dim.
geteilt
arco

3
72
Tempo I (molto adagio)
Harfe
pp
cresc.
p
(D-saite)
gliss.
Vln. I
ppp
morendo
pp
Vln. II
ppp
p molto espress.
pp
Vla.
ppp
get.
pp espress.
Vcl.
pp
pizz.
Bs.
80
4 Rit.
Zögernd
pp vibrato
mitinnigster empfindung
morendo
ppp
arco
morendo
pizz.

Noch langsamer
87
Harfe
Vln. I
Vln. II
Vla.
Vcl.
Bs.
p
poco a poco cresc.
pizz.
pp
geteilt
arco
pizz.
94
viel Ton!
Drängend
Lang
viel Bogen wechseln
f
ff breit
sempre
ff
morendo
pppp
mf
ff viel Bogen wechseln
ff vial Ton!
molto

165

Alma Mahler

"Die stille Stadt" (c1901)

Alma Schindler was a composition student of Alexander Zemlinsky when she met her future husband, Gustav Mahler, in 1901. She shared Zemlinsky's admiration for writings by the German poet Richard Dehmel (1863–1920), whose richly romantic verse was an inspiration to many German and Austrian progressive musicians—Richard Strauss and Arnold Schoenberg, in addition to Zemlinsky. In 1898 Zemlinsky completed a set of four piano "Fantasies" reflecting on poems by Dehmel, and at about the same time Schoenberg was at work on a programmatic string sextet, *Verklärte Nacht,* also based on a Dehmel poem. So it is no surprise that Alma would compose songs to Dehmel's poetry during this period of musical apprenticeship. One of these is the beautiful "Die stille Stadt" ("The Quiet City").

Her budding career in music was cut short when she married Mahler in 1902. Mahler insisted that she give up composing, and she complied. In 1910 she returned to her earlier songs, then with her husband's blessings, and collected five of them for publication. "Die stille Stadt" was placed first in this striking though belated compositional debut.

After the brief but ominous prelude (see MWC, p. 564), we hear—as if from a Tyrolean village—the piano echoing parts of the vocal line. Yet the echo is somehow "wrong"; the scales are close, but never quite the same. In the passage where the fog closes in, hiding everything from view (mm. 18–19), the music gropes around the tonic, but never quite finds it. As if lighting the way, the F-major chord in measure 26 leads the poet out of this harmonic and textual fog ("aus dem Rauch"; m. 28) and comes to a solid D-minor triad. Finally, when we hear the "hymn of praise from a child's lips" (mm. 31–32), we arrive in D major.

Alma Mahler
"Die stille Stadt" (c1901)
CD 10/10

rit.
a tempo
blas - ser Tag ver - geht,
es wird nicht lang mehr
sf
pp
f warm
dau - ern,
bis we - der Mond noch Ster - ne, nur
cresc.
dim.
p
Nacht am Him - mel steht.
m.s.
Von al - len Ber - gen drük - ken
Ne - bel auf die Stadt,
sehr drängend
es dringt kein Dach noch Hof noch Haus, kein

19
Laut aus ih - rem Rauch her-aus, kaum Tür - me nach und Brük-ken
cresc.
f
Wieder zurückkehrend zu Tempo I.
doch als der Wan - - - drer
p subito
dim.
cresc.
ppp
grau - te,
da ging ein
Tempo I.
Licht - - - lein
f
dim.
pp
steigernd
auf im Grund und aus dem Rauch und Ne - - - bel be -
appassionato

Die stille Stadt

Liegt eine Stadt im Tale,
ein blasser Tag vergeht;
es wird nicht lang mehr dauern,
bis weder Mond noch Sterne,
nur Nacht am Himmel steht.

Von allen Bergen drükken
Nebel auf die Stadt;
es dringt kein Dach, noch Hof noch Haus,
kein Laut aus Ihrem Rauch heraus,
kaum Türme nach [noch] und Brükken.

Doch als der [den] Wandrer
graute,
da ging ein Lichtlein auf im Grund;
und aus dem Rauch und Nebel
begann ein Lobgesang,
aus Kindermund.

—Richard Dehmel, from *Aber die Liebe* (1896)

The Quiet City

A city lies in the valley;
the pale day slips by;
it won't be long now
until moon and stars are gone
and only night remains in the sky.

Down from all the mountains
come mists upon the town;
no roof, no courtyard nor house is seen,
no sound gets through their smoke—
the spires and bridges just barely so.

But just when the travelers were feeling by
fear,
a little light came on down below;
and out of the smoke and fog
arose a hymn of praise
from a child's lips.

England at the End of the Romantic Period *Elgar and Vaughan Williams*

166

Edward Elgar
"Enigma" Variations (1899)
a. Theme
b. Ninth Variation ("Nimrod")

Edward Elgar's orchestral Variations on an Original Theme ("Enigma") was his first work to achieve an international success and the one that launched him into a celebrated compositional career. Part of its attraction—beyond its great romantic warmth—is the subtitle "Enigma," which Elgar used to describe the work's opening theme. But the composer was tantalizingly silent about what this enigma was. "The Enigma I will not explain," he insisted, "Its 'dark saying' must be left unguessed."

Elgar was not averse to dropping hints about his musical riddle. "Through and over the whole set [of variations]," he wrote, "another and larger theme 'goes,' but is not played. . . . So the principal Theme never appears." What is this missing theme? Many answers have been proposed, such as the traditional melody to "Auld lang syne," although Elgar assured his friends that this was not the correct solution. Regardless of its enigmas, Elgar's Variations has stirred generations of listeners.

The theme, unusual for its short, fragmented phrases, is cast in a ternary form. The **a** phrases (mm. 1–6, 11–17) are in G minor, while the middle **b** portion (mm. 7–10) is in the parallel key of G major. Elgar left the statement of the theme plain: It is the work of the variations to show what can be done with it. The remainder of the composition is a set of fourteen variations. Each of these (except for the thirteenth variation) is labeled with the name or initials of an acquaintance of the composer.

The longest and most famous of the variations is the ninth, titled "Nimrod," the name of a hunter mentioned in the Bible (Genesis 10:9). This is a playful reference to Elgar's friend and publisher, August Johannes Jaeger—*Jaeger* means hunter in German. This noble variation not only turns the short phrases of the theme into long, majestic lines, but also changes the key from G minor to E♭ major. Part of its spacious quality derives from Elgar's expansion of the theme from a three-part to a four-part **aaba** form in which the original six-bar **a** phrase is progressively lengthened to eight, eleven, and twelve measures. The climax is reserved for the final statement of **a**, and the full orchestra swells to a regal splendor, which recedes only in the coda. This variation has since transcended its initial model and—like Elgar's *Pomp and Circumstance* March No. 1—come to represent all of England. In recent times it was used for just such a purpose in the soundtrack for the film *Elizabeth*.

Edward Elgar
"Enigma" Variations (1899)
a. Theme
CD 10/11

Andante. ♩ = 63.

I Flauti II (e picc.)
Oboi I. II.
Clarinetti I. II in B♭
Fagotti I. II.
Contra Fagotto.
I. II Corni in F III. IV.
Trombe I. II. III in F.
I. II Tromboni III e Tuba.
Timpani.
Tamburo piccolo e Triangolo.
Gran Cassa e Piatti.

Organo, *ad lib.*
Man.
Ped.

Andante.
legato e sostenuto
ten.
p molto espress.
ten.
dim.
cresc.
pp
div.
unis.
simile

I Violini II.
Viole.
Violoncelli.
Bassi.

Andante.

ten.
p
cresc.
dim. molto
1
(Flauto.)
pp
ten.
dim. molto
p
pp
ten.
div.
sul G.
sostenuto
cresc.
pp cresc.

rit.
a 2.
p
mf dim.
allargando
pp
I.
dim.
pp
p dim.
p
ten.
div.
sempre p
IV
mf dim.
rit.
mesto
unis.
pp dim.
dim.
p
f
allargando
pp
mf dim.
rit.

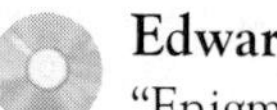

Edward Elgar

"Enigma" Variations (1899)

b. Ninth Variation ("Nimrod")

CD 10/12

33 Adagio. (♩ = 52.)

Flauti I e II.

Fl.

Ob.

Cl.

Fg.

C. Fg.

Cor.

Tr.

Tromb. e Tuba.

Timp. (in E♭, B♭, F.)

Tamb. picc. e Triang.

G. C. e Piatti.

33 Adagio.

sul D

sul A

sul D

Viol. I. II. *ppp*

cresc. *dim.* *pp*

div.

ppp *cresc.* *dim.* *pp*

Viole. div.

ppp *cresc.* *mf* *dim.* *pp*

mf

ppp *cresc.* *p* *dim.* *pp*

Vcl. e Bassi.

ppp *cresc.* *p* *dim.* *pp*

Adagio.

34
pp
cresc.
mf
p
a 2
34
div.
unis

35
dim.
espress.
cresc.
a 2
p cresc. molto
mf cresc.
p cresc.
pizz.
arco
div.
cresc. molto

36
legatissimo
mf
f
legatissimo
ff
a 2.
legatissimo
legato
legato
III.
legato
p
mp
sonore
dim.
legatissimo
largamente
sempre f
div.
unis.
sf

37
rit.
cresc.
ff
pp
dim.
p
f marcato
rf
sf
I. e III.
II.
I.
III.
IV.
molto cresc.
(E♭ in D,–F in G)
largamente
ffz
div.

Opera in Milan after Verdi
Puccini, Toscanini, and Verismo

167

Giacomo Puccini
Madama Butterfly (1904)
Aria, "Dovunque al mondo"

On a visit to London in 1900, Giacomo Puccini saw a performance of the play *Madame Butterfly*, by the American writer David Belasco, and he immediately recognized a story that could be made into a successful opera. The composer and his librettists, Luigi Ilica and Giuseppe Giacosa, set about to reshape the play so that it would fit into the operatic mold that Puccini had created in his earlier opera *La Bohème*. Like Mimi in *Bohème*, the central character in *Madama Butterfly* is a fragile and innocent woman who lives—and is fated to die—for love.

As the opera begins, on a hill near Nagasaki, an American naval officer, Benjamin Franklin Pinkerton, is preparing to marry the Japanese girl known as Madame Butterfly. She is unaware that Pinkerton plans to abandon her as soon as his ship departs. In his aria "Dovunque al mondo" ("Wherever in the World"), he explains his philosophy of life. He describes himself as a Yankee vagabond, sampling the world's delights with no long-term commitments. The American consul, Sharpless, disapproves of this outlook, but they can readily agree on a toast: "America forever!"

The aria begins with a short introduction based on the opening phrase of "The Star-Spangled Banner," a phrase that does not return until the end of the aria. However, the phrase that concludes the introduction (mm. 7–8) is heard throughout the aria's accompaniment. The two stanzas of "Dovunque al mondo" are treated in a strophic style, but Pinkerton never gets very far into his brash declaration of self-centered philosophy before breaking off to talk about something else. During these digressions, a *parlando* (speechlike) setting predominates. There is a bit of text painting in measures 34 to 39, when he likens personal problems to a sudden squall upsetting a ship—a metaphor for life that appeals to this Yankee vagabond. Here the harmony releases its solid hold on G♭ major and becomes chromatically unstable.

Pinkerton is one of the great cads of the operatic stage (the Duke in Verdi's *Rigoletto* is another), and "Dovunque al mondo" exposes his bankrupt morality. The drama poses the question: Can this scoundrel find redemption through love? Butterfly believes so, and marries him, but in the end we see her hopes dashed. Pinkerton rejects her devotion—after all, she was just part of the deal when he leased the house in Nagasaki—and takes their beloved child to be raised by his new American bride. Crushed by the loss, she commits one of the most horrifying suicides in operatic literature. When he rushes on stage as the curtain falls, he registers shock, but not one word of regret. There is no redemption, just tragic loss.

Giacomo Puccini
Madama Butterfly (1904)
Aria, "Dovunque al mondo"
CD 10/13

(21) **Allegro sostenuto con spirito.** ♩=112.

cantando

f *p* *pp*

Pinkerton

(frankly)

The whole world o-ver, on bu-siness and pleasure,
Do - vun-que al mondo lo Yankee va-ga - bon-do

p

Pinkerton

the Yankee tra - vels all dan - ger scorn - ing. His
si go-de e traffi-ca sprezzan - do ri - schi. Af-

(22) *cantando*

sentito

p

Pinkerton

an - chor bold - ly he casts at ran-dom....
-fon - da l'ân-co-ra al - la ven - tu-ra....

f *p*

Pinkerton
(breaking off to offer Sharpless a drink)
Milk-Punch, or Whis-ky?
Milk-Punch, o Wis-ky?
23
sentito
p
f
Pinkerton
(resuming)
His an-chor bold-ly he casts at ran-dom,
Af-fon-da l'àn-co-ra al-la ven-tu-ra
f
allarg. poco a poco
Pinkerton
un-til a sud-den squall up-sets his ship, then
fin-chè u-na raf-fi-ca scom-pi-gli na-ve e or-
p cresc.
cresc.
allarg. poco a poco
Pinkerton
a tempo
up go sails and rig-ging.
And life is not worth
-meg-gi, al-be-ra-tu-ra.....
La vi-ta ei non ap-
poco allarg.
a tempo sentito
24
f
p
Ped.
*
Ped.

Pinkerton
poco rall.
liv - ing if he can't win the best and fair - est of each
-pa - ga se non fa suo te - sor i fio - ri d'o - gni
pp
poco rall.
Pinkerton
a tempo
(continuing)
poco rall.
coun - try,..
pla - ga,..
and the heart of each
d'o - gni bel - la gli a-
Sharpless
That's an eas - y - go - ing gos - pel...
E un fa - ci - le van - ge - lo...
a tempo
p
poco rall.
Pinkerton
a tempo
maid.
-mor.
Sharpless
sostenendo
A ve - ry ea - sy gos - pel which makes life ve - ry
è un fa - ci - le van - ge - lo che fa la vi - ta
dolce
p
a tempo
p sostenendo
Sharpless
pleas - ant, but is fa - tal in the end.
va - ga ma che in - tri - sti - sce il cor.
p cresc. e allarg.

57
Pinkerton
Iº Tempo. sostenendo
Fate can-not crush him, he tries a-gain un - daunted.
Vin - to si tuf - fa, la sor - te rac - ciuf - fa.
25
Pinkerton
No one and no - thing breaks his pluck - y spi - rit. And so I'm
Il suo ta - len - to fa in o - gni do - ve. Co - sì mi
Pinkerton
mar - ry - ing in Ja - pa - nese fashion, tied for nine hun - dred and nine - ty
spo - so all'u - so giap - po - ne - se per no - ve - cen - to - no - van - ta - no - ve
Pinkerton
nine years! Free, though, to an - nul the marriage monthly!
an - ni. Sal - vo a pro-sciogliermi ogni me - se.
Sharpless
An ea - sy go - ing
È un fa - ci - le van-
dolce
rit.
a tempo

73 Pinkerton

"A - me - ri - ca for e - ver!"
„A - me - ri - ca for e - ver!"

Sharpless gos - pel.
-ge - lo.

"A-
„A-

Sharpless. - me - ri - ca for e - ver!"
- me - ri - ca for e - ver!"

Paris in the *Belle Époque*
Debussy, Fauré, and Lili Boulanger

168

Claude Debussy
Fêtes galantes I (1891)
"En sourdine"

As we have seen, French musical traditions have often taken an independent path rather than adopt the traditions of foreign cultures. From *La Guerre des Bouffons* during the Enlightenment to combating the influence of Wagner in the late nineteenth century, French composers have desired above all to be "French." This independent spirit can also be observed in the genre of song. Unlike German *Lieder*, in which introspection often becomes pathological (for example, in Schubert's *Winterreise* and Schumann's *Dichterliebe*), French song tended toward lightness and wit, even when considering such intense and weighty topics as love and death. "En sourdine" touches upon both themes. In this poem, two lovers are at one in a quiet wood, where nothing matters but the pleasure of the moment. There is no memory of the past, no plans for future happiness, and even the shadow of death is not enough to disturb the precious present.

Debussy had a particular affinity for setting the poetry of Paul Verlaine. Fully one-third of his songs are settings of Verlaine's lyrics, works that Debussy had known for years. In fact, the poet's mother-in-law had been Debussy's piano teacher when he was a boy and helped prepare him for the entrance examinations required by the Paris Conservatory. After an early infatuation with Wagner's music in the 1880s (he once won a bet that he could play the entire score of *Tristan* by memory), Debussy rejected Germanic influences and moved to a simpler style more in keeping with French tradition. The ambiguous harmonic progressions he developed enabled his songs to evoke the text with sensitive delicacy. Text painting is rarely overt and frequently becomes apparent only in hindsight. In "En sourdine" we can observe Debussy's penchant for a syllabic vocal line, expanded harmony, and motivic economy that conveys the meaning of the text with great subtlety.

Claude Debussy
Fêtes galantes I (1891)
"En sourdine"
CD 10/14

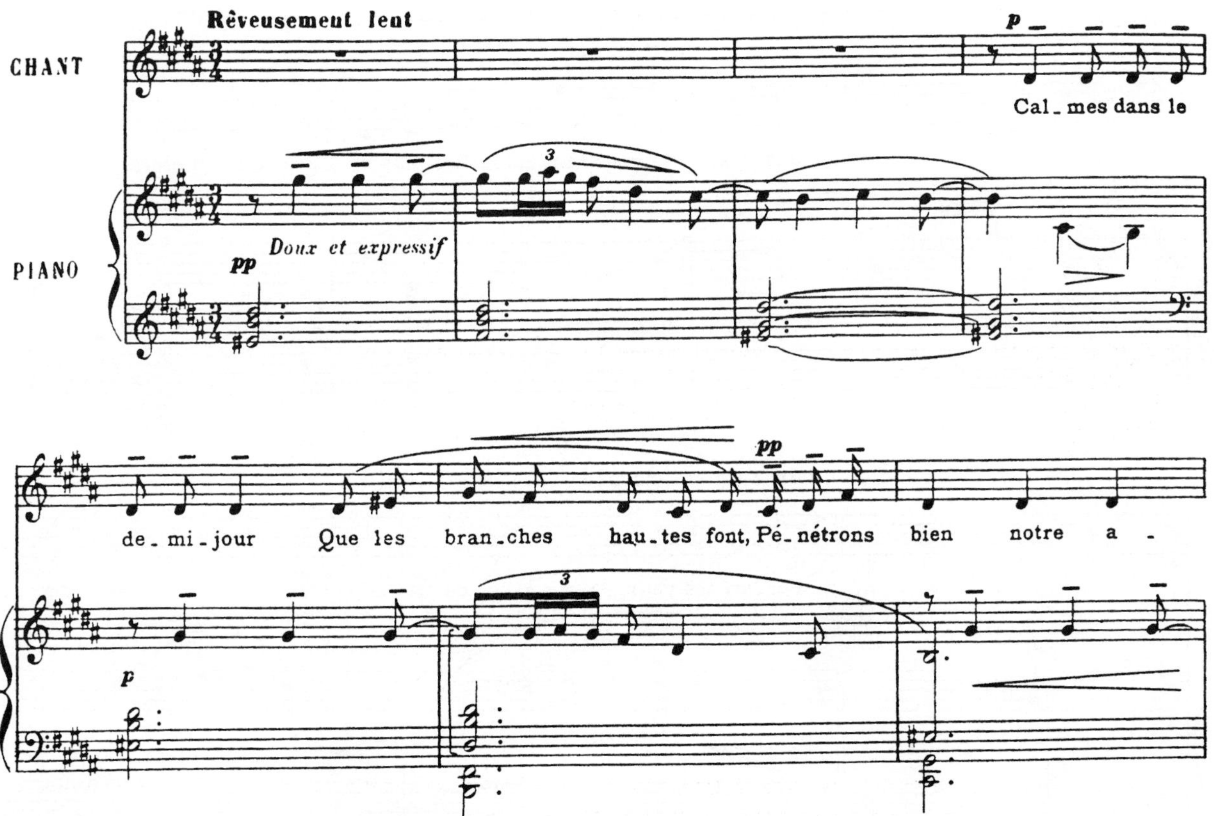

8
-mour De ce si - len-ce pro-fond
Toujours très doux
Peu à peu animé
Fon - dons nos â - mes, nos cœurs Et nos sens ex - ta -
-siés, Par - mis les va-gues langueurs Des pins et des ar-bou-siers.
Rit.
1er Mouvt
più p
pp
En animant un peu
Fer-me tes yeux à de - mi, Croi-se tes
Délicatement

20
bras sur ton sein, Et de ton cœur en - dor -
poco cresc.
-mi Chasse à ja - mais tout des - sein.
Molto dim.
pp
Intimement doux
Lais - sons - nous per - su - a - der Au
souf - fle ber - ceur et doux
Poco cresc.
Qui vient à tes pieds ri -
Poco cresc.

30
Un peu plus lent
-der Les on-des de ga-zon roux.
mf Dim.
p
Et quand so-len-nel, le soir. Des chê-nes
più p
Lent
Doux et expressif
noirs tom-be-ra
Voix de no-tre dé-ses-
pp
-poir, Le ros-si-gnol chan-te-ra.
più pp

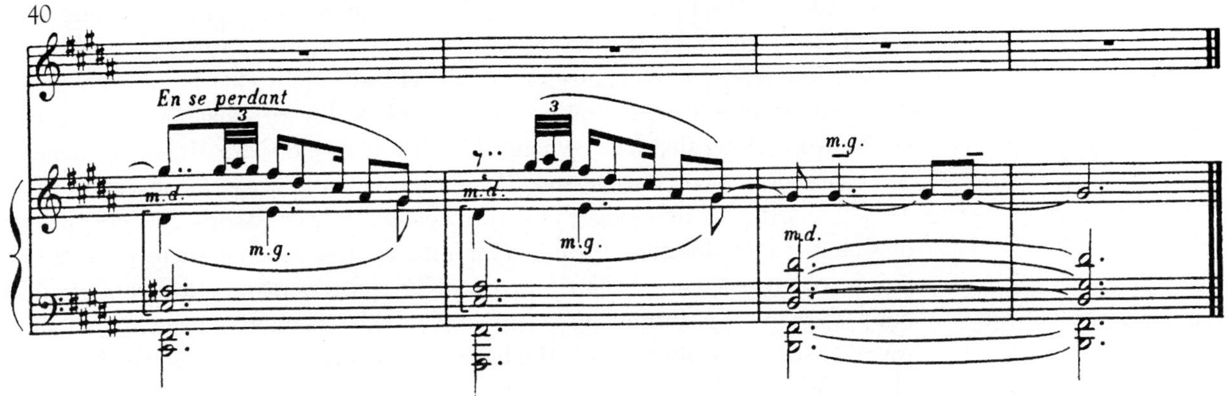

Calmes dans le demi-jour
Que les branches hautes font,
Pénétrons bien notre amour
De ce silence profond.

Fondons nos âmes, nos cœurs
Et nos sens extasiés,
Parmis les vagues langueurs
Des pins et des arbousiers.

Ferme tes yeux à demi,
Croise tes bras sur ton sein,
Et de ton cœur endormi
Chasse à jamais tout dessein.

Laissons-nous persuader
Au souffle berceur et doux
Qui vient à tes pieds rider
Les ondes de gazon roux.

Et quand, solennel, le soir
Des chênes noirs tombera,
Voix de notre désespoir,
Le rossignol chantera.

In the twilight calm
made by the high branches,
let us imbue our love
with a deep silence.

Let us merge our souls, our hearts,
and our ecstatic senses
amid the vague languishments
of the pines and strawberry trees.

Close your eyes halfway,
cross your arms on your chest,
and from your sleeping heart
banish forever all intentions.

Let us make believe,
as the sweet and lulling breeze
which ripples by your feet
makes waves in the russet grass.

And when, solemnly, evening
falls from the dark oaks—
voice of our despair—
the nightingale will sing.

169

Claude Debussy

Images I (1905)

"Reflets dans l'eau"

In contrast to the sonata tradition established by Haydn, Mozart, and Beethoven, in which clearly defined musical form, driving energy, and drama predominate, "Reflets dans l'eau" is better characterized by terms such as ambiguity and tranquillity. Yet while it lacks the monumental nature of the sonata, this composition is no less a masterpiece and demonstrates as much perfection and originality of conception as Beethoven's "Pathétique." Debussy—always a perceptive observer—once described the stylistic character of *Images* as falling between the works of Robert Schumann and Frédéric Chopin. If "Reflets dans l'eau" is more overtly programmatic than Chopin's compositions, it is not as idiosyncratic in expression or style as those by Schumann. While it is a characteristic of Debussy's music that form is ambiguous and open to multiple interpretations, it is possible to discern a *soupçon* of sonata form in this work. After the development of a three-note motive as the main theme, a subsidiary idea emerges in measure 25, while the quasi-development section (mm. 44–71) successively reformulates the two "themes" to a constantly changing palette of scale patterns. Instead of a full recapitulation (m. 72–end) there is more of a reprise, one that merely recalls the opening. The programmatic title certainly guides our perception. It is entrancing to contemplate the reflection of reality in a body of water, to see how it shimmers in the light and is distorted by ripples, but there is no climax. We do not sit and wait for the reflection to become most perfect before turning away with a sigh of satisfaction; we enjoy the moment for what it is. So this work captures beauty without the necessity of attaining a point of arrival.

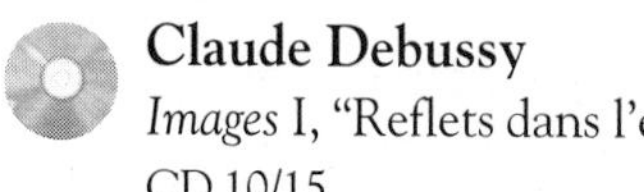

Claude Debussy
Images I, "Reflets dans l'eau"
CD 10/15

Andantino molto
(Tempo rubato)

PIANO

pp

12
Rit.
più p
a Tempo
pp
pp
pp
p
p
pp
Quasi cadenza
pp poco a poco cresc. e stringendo

Mesuré
25
ppp
pp doux et expressif
ppp
mf
f
pp
Rit.
p
più p
pp

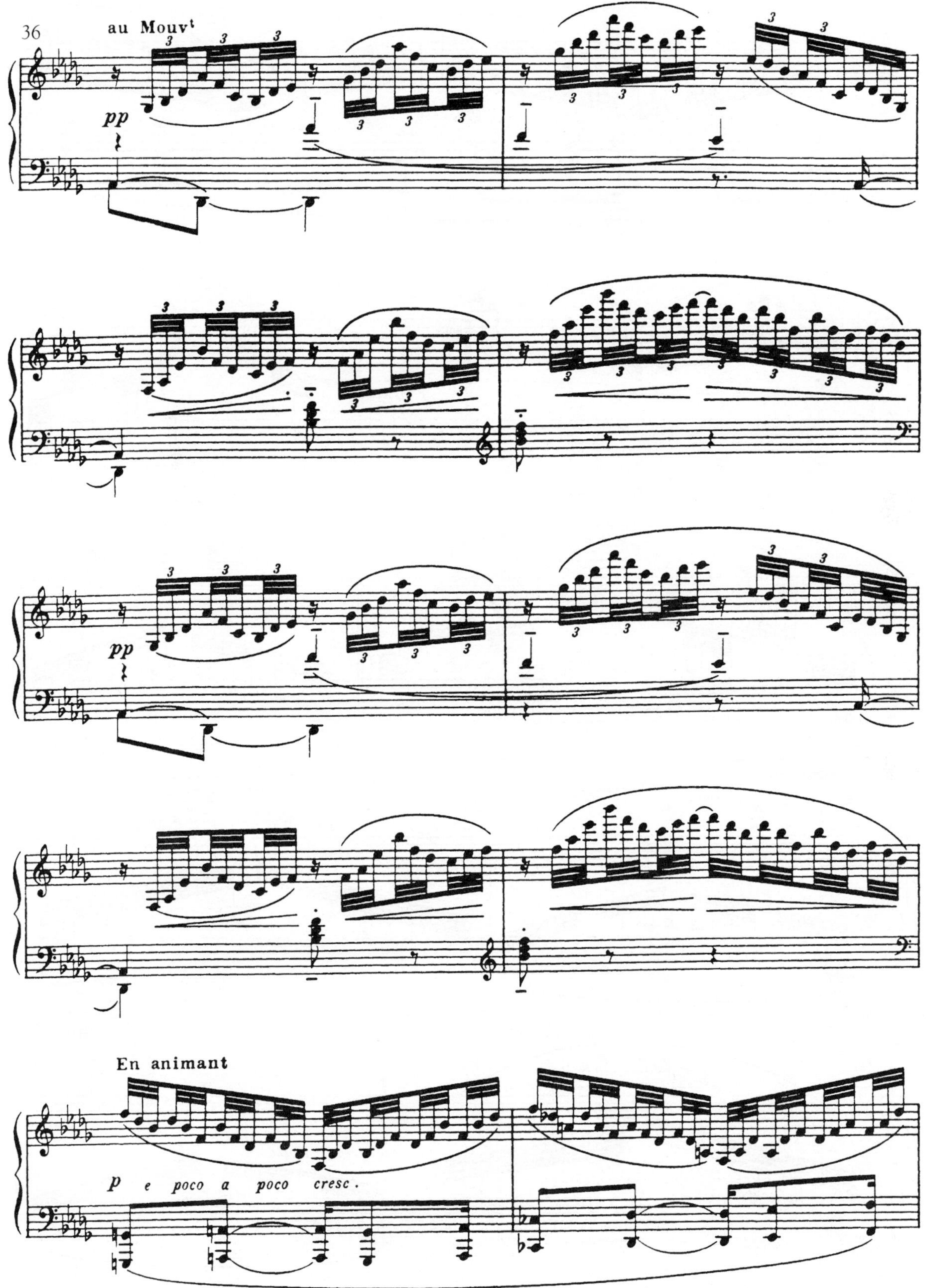
36
au Mouv^t
pp
pp
En animant
p e poco a poco cresc.

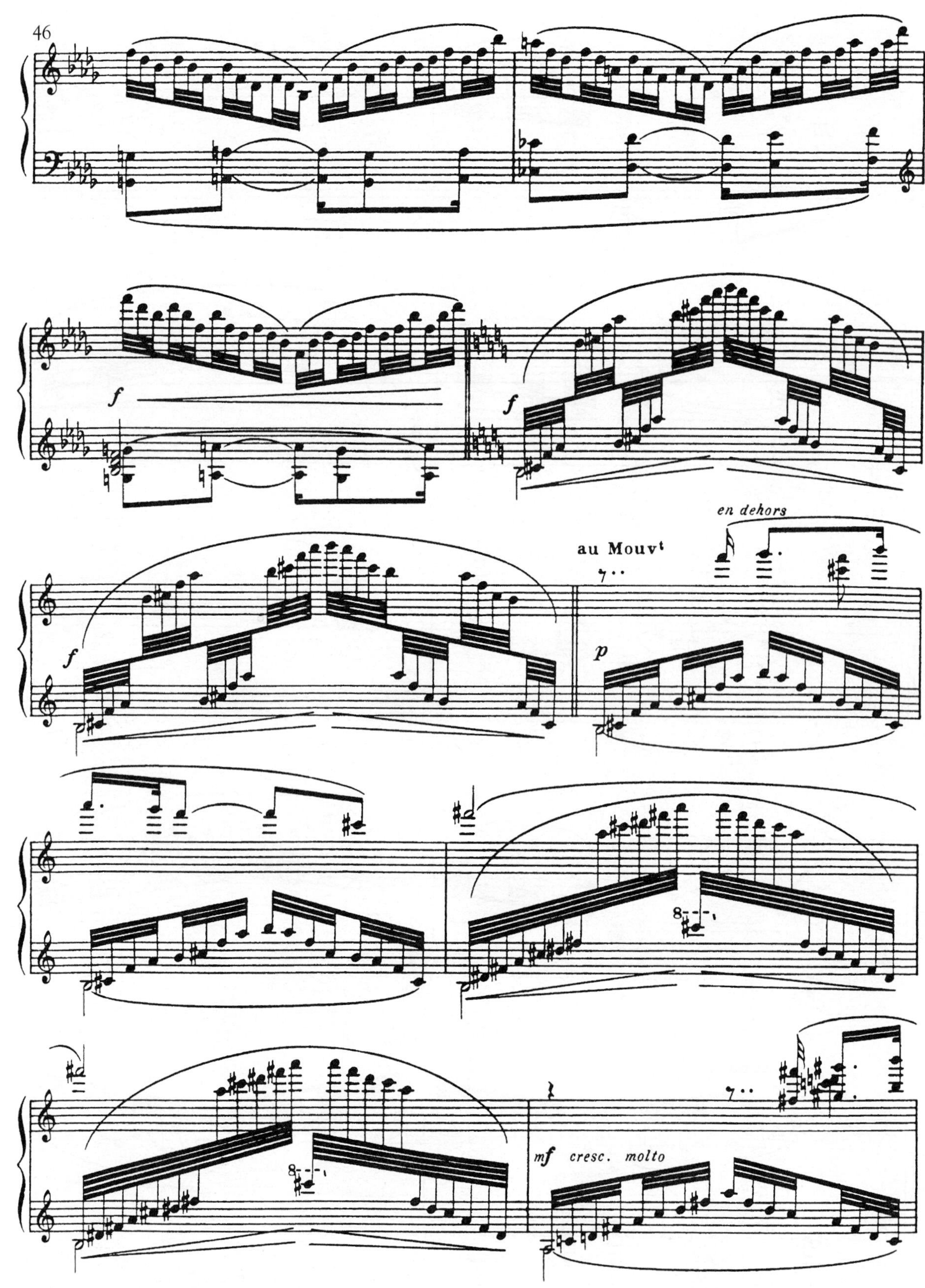

46
f
f
f
au Mouvᵗ
en dehors
p
8
8
mf cresc. molto

56
f
ff
Rit.
dim
p
Molto rit.
più p
au Mouvt
(plus lent)
pp

68
ppp
18
8
3
pp
sempre pp
3
1º Tempo (en retenant jusqu'à la fin)
pp 3
3
3
3
3
3
3
3
3
Rit.
3
pp
ppp
Lent (dans une sonorité harmonieuse et lointaine)
p un peu en dehors
3
3
8
3
3
8

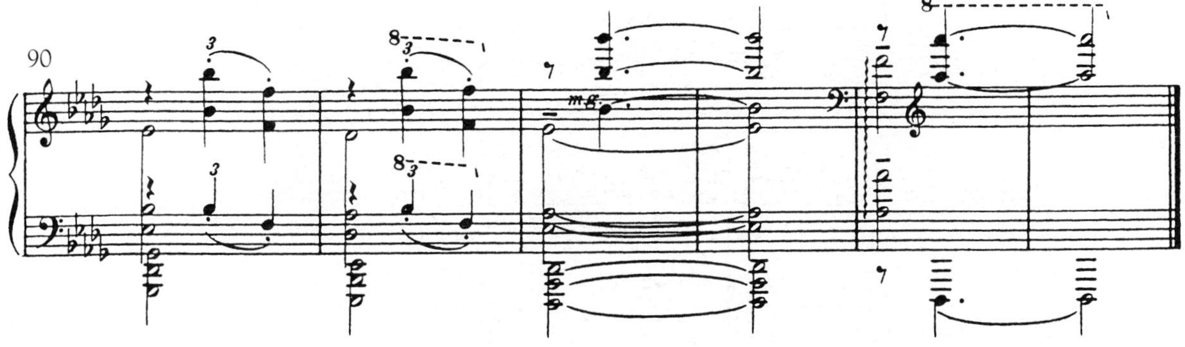

170

Claude Debussy
Nocturnes (1900)
"Nuages"

In 1871 the American artist James McNeill Whistler (1834–1903) painted the first of a series of canvases, each to be entitled *Nocturne*. They became some of his most important contributions to the history of art. These paintings display great variety: from quiet scenes in the half-light of twilight and dawn to dark, dramatic images of fireworks or a wheel of flame blazing across the midnight sky. The important aspect of these paintings is not the image, but the interplay and emotion of color. The two most noticeable features of one painting, *Nocturne: Blue and Silver—Chelsea*, are the lack of motion and the severely limited color palette. Debussy, who shared many of the same aesthetic principles as Whistler, admired these paintings, and they may have been the source for the title of his second orchestral masterpiece, *Nocturnes*. His first great orchestral composition, Prelude to *The Afternoon of a Faun*, was completed in 1894. Six years separate that work from the completion of *Nocturnes*, yet the stylistic change was significant. In "Nuages," the first movement of *Nocturnes*, the most apparent change occurs in the orchestral ensemble: It uses a limited orchestral timbre, while *Faun* is far more varied and colorful. Another important contrast between the two compositions is the sense of motion. Whereas *Faun* moves toward climaxes and important cadences, "Nuages" carefully controls the rhythm, melody, and harmony to dispel any sense of musical momentum. Change tends to be slow and subtle, often nothing more than repeating a phrase, but switching parts between different instruments. (Although the effect is much different, another Parisian musician, Perotinus, utilized much the same technique in his four-voice organum *Viderunt omnes* [see no. 21].) It is characteristic that Debussy, even while providing his audience with a descriptive title, leaves the meaning of the work vague. At one point he wrote that "Nuages" suggested gray clouds, flecked with white; another time he was quoted as saying it was just a nighttime reflection of clouds in the Seine. Either way, there is no story, just the effortless and timeless movement of ethereal objects.

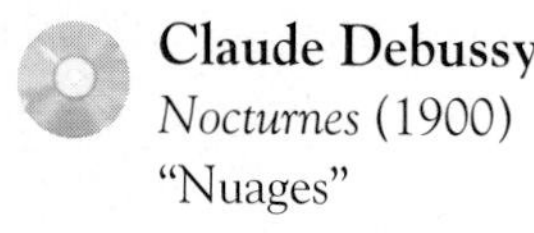

Claude Debussy
Nocturnes (1900)
"Nuages"
CD 11/1

Modéré

2 Flûtes

2 Hautbois

1°

pp

Cor Anglais

pp très espressif

più pp

Clarinettes En B♭

pp très espressif

pp

1
2
Bassons

3

pp

più pp

1
2
Cors

3
4

Timbales

Harpe

Modéré

Div. Sourdines

Violons I

Div. Sourdines

Violons II

Div. Sourdines

Altos

Div. Sourdines

Violoncelles

Sourdines

Contrabasses

1
Fl.
espressif
Cor. Ang.
Cl.
Bsn. 1 2
Cors 1 2 3 4
Timb.
Vln. I
Div. en 6
Vln. II
Div. en 6
Alt.
Vcl.
Cb.

11
Vln. I
Vln. II
Alt.
Vcl.
Cb.
a3
a2
pp
pizz.
16
Cor. Ang.
2
Très espressif
Div.

22
Cor. Ang.
p
1
2
Cors
3
4
1
p
3
p
Vln. I
Vln. II
Alt.
Vcl.
pp
pp
Cb.
pp

27
3
Cor. Ang.
Cors
1
2
3
4
Vln. I
Vln. II
Alt.
Vcl.
Cb.
p
pp
f

32
Hb.
1°
Cl.
1
2
Bsn.
3
1
2
Cors
3
4
Vln. I
Vln. II
Alt.
Vcl.
p
pp

37
Hb.
Cl.
Bsn.
Vln. I
Vln. II
Alt.
Vcl.
Cb.
a2
p
cre
scen
do

4
42
Hb.
Cor. Ang.
Cl.
1
2
Bsn.
3
1°
1
2
Cors
3°
3
4
4
Vln. I
Vln. II
pizz.
pizz.
Alt.
pizz.
Vcl.
pizz.
Div.
Cb.
f
pp

46
5
Cor. Ang.
1° Sourdines
Cors 1 2
p
5
pizz.
Vln. I
pizz.
arco
Vln. II
Alt.
pizz.
Vcl.
arco
Cb.

Cor. Ang.
Bsn. 1 2
Cors 1 2
1°
Vln. I
Vln. II
Alt.
Vcl.
Cb.
pp
p
più p
6
Hb.
p expressif
Alt. Solo
sans sourdines
ppp

59
Hb.
Cl.
Bsn.
Vln. I
Vln. II
Alt. Solo
Alt.
Vcl.
Cb.
pp
più p

7
Un peu animé
1°
très espressif
Fl.
Cl.
pp
Bsn. 1 2
Hrp.
(Sol♭, Re♭, La♭, Mi♭, Si♭)
Vln. I
Vln. II
Alt.
Vcl.
Cb.

69
Fl.
Cl.
pp
1° sourdines
Cors
1
2
3
4
pp
3° sourdines
Hrp.
Vln. I Solo
sans sourdines
p
très exptressif et très sontenn
Vln. I
Vln. II
Alt. Solo
très exptressif et très sontenn
Alt.
Vcl. Solo
sans sourdines
très exptressif et très sontenn
Vcl.
Cb.
pizz.
arco

74
8
Fl.
p
Cl.
pp
Bsn. 1 2
pp
1°
Cors 1 2
pp
3°
3 4
pp
Hrp.
Vln. I Solo
pp
ppp
Vln. I
Vln. II
Alt. Solo
Alt.
Vcl. Solo
Vcl.
Cb.

79
1° tempo
Fl.
più p molto dim.
pp
Cor. Ang.
sfz p
p
p
Cl.
sfz p
pp
p
Bsn. 1 2
sfz p
pp
1 2 Cors 3 4
p
più p pp
3°
Hrp.
1° tempo
Vln. I
Vln. II
Alt.
sur la touche
pp
Vcl.
sur la touche
pp
Cb.

9
85
Hb.
1°
p
più p > pp
Cor. Ang.
p molto dim.
Cl.
1
2
Cors
3
4
3°
p
più p > pp
Timb.
tr
ppp
9
Vln. I
pp
Vln. II
Alt.
Vcl.
Cb.
à 4 sur la touche

91
Plus lent
10
Cor. Ang.
pp
Bsn. 1 2
pp
1°
pp
Timb.
tr
ppp
pp
Plus lent
10
Vcl.
pp
pp
pp
à 8
Cb.
pp
à 4
ppp
97
Encore plus lent
Fl.
Cors 1 2 3 4
Sourdines
pp
ppp
pp
ppp
Timb.
tr
pp
pp
Vln. I
pizz.
pp
pizz.
pp
ppp
Vln. II
pizz.
pp
pp
pizz.
pp
pp
Alt.
pizz.
pp
pp
ppp
pizz.
pp
pp
ppp
Vcl.
più pp
pizz.
pp
ppp
3 3 3
pizz.
pp
ppp
Cb.
pizz.
pizz.
pp
ppp

171

Gabriel Fauré

"Dans la forêt de septembre," Opus 85, No. 1 (1902)

Today, Fauré's Requiem and Pavane (Op. 50) are his most famous compositions. However, he is one of the greatest composers of French song. The sensuous lyricism of these intimate vocal works embodies the same timeless beauty as Impressionist paintings. These songs were composed during the *Belle époque* for intimate concerts in the salons of elite Parisian society, where, as the composer himself stated, amateur singers would give works such as this a most appropriate and sympathetic performance. Such an environment was a perfect venue for his refined lyrical expression and subtle harmonies. "Dans la forêt de septembre" was written as the 60-year-old Fauré entered the autumn of life, a period when the poem's imagery—a traveler comparing his own physical decay and mortality with that of the ancient forest—would resonate powerfully. It is characteristic of Fauré's style that the song does not convey detailed examples of text painting, but instead evokes its mood through tender lyricism, enriched tonal harmony, and subtle contrasts in texture.

Gabriel Fauré
"Dans la forêt de septembre," Opus 85, No. 1 (1902)
CD 11/2

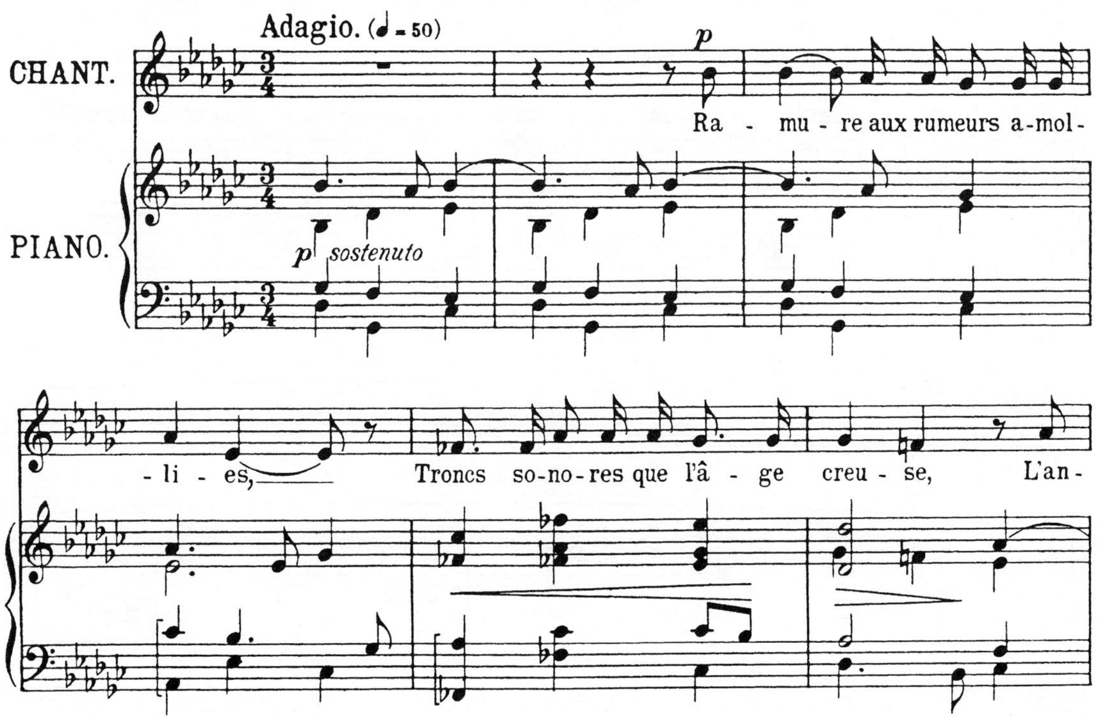

7
-ti-que fo-rêt dou-lou - reu - se S'ac - cor - de à nos mé-lan-co-
-li - es. O sapins agrif-fés au gouf - - fre,
p
Nids dé-serts aux bran-ches bri - sé - - es, Hal-liers brû-
mf
-lés, fleurs sans ro - sé - - - - es,
mf

17
p
dolce
Vous savez bien com-me l'on souf - - fre! Et lors-que
p
pp
l'homme, pas-sant blê-me, Pleu-re dans le bois so-li-tai-re, Des
plain-tes d'om-bre et de mys-tè-re L'ac-cueil-lent en pleu-rant de
mê - me. Bon-ne fo-rêt! pro-mes-se ou-
p
dolce

30
-ver - te de l'e-xil que la vi-e im-plo - re, Je
viens d'un pas a-ler-te en - co - re Dans ta pro-fon -
3 poco cresc.
3
-deur en-cor ver - - te. Mais d'un fin bou -
dolce
p dolce
-leau de la sen - - te, U-ne feuil-le,un peu rous-se, frô - le Ma

39
tê - te et trem - ble à mon é - pau - le;
espressivo
cresc.
f
C'est que la fo-rêt vieil-lis - san-te, Sa -
p
p dolce
- chant l'hi-ver, où tout a - vor - te, Dé-jà pro-che en moi comme en
el - - le, Me fait l'au-mô - ne fra-ter -
f

Dans la forêt de septembre	**In September's forest**
Ramure aux rumeurs amollies,	Weakened, murmuring branches,
Troncs sonores que l'âge creuse,	sonorous tree trunks, hollowed by age,
L'antique forêt douloureuse	the ancient, aching forest
S'accorde à nos mélancolies.	is in tune with our melancholy.
O sapins agriffés au gouffre,	O fir trees clinging to the gorge,
Nids déserts aux branches brisées,	dry nests in broken boughs,
Halliers brûlés, fleurs sans rosées,	burnt thickets, flowers without dew,
Vous savez bien comme l'on souffre!	you know of suffering!
Et lorsque l'homme, passant blême,	And when man, entering palely,
Pleure dans le bois solitaire,	cries in your solitary woods,
Des plaintes d'ombre et de mystère	shadowy and mysterious plaints
L'accueillent en pleurant de même.	greet him with sympathetic tears.
Bonne forêt! promesse ouverte	Good forest! Open promise
de l'exil que la vie implore,	of the exile that life implores,
Je viens d'un pas alerte encore	I come with footsteps still quick
Dans ta profondeur encor verte.	into your depths still green.
Mais d'un fin bouleau de la sente,	But from a slender birch on the path,
Une feuille, un peu rousse, frôle	a russet leaf grazes
Ma tête et tremble à mon épaule;	my head and lights trembling on my shoulder.
C'est que la forêt vieillissante,	The aging forest—
Sachant l'hiver où tout avorte,	knowing that winter, where all miscarries,
Déjà proche en moi comme en elle,	is now at hand in me as in it—
Me fait l'aumône fraternelle	presents me with a fraternal tribute
De sa première feuille morte!	of its first dead leaf!

—Catulle Mendès

172

Lili Boulanger
Clairières dans le ciel (1914)
"Elle est gravement gaie"

In 1913, the 19-year-old Lili Boulanger made international headlines when she became the first woman to win the coveted Prix de Rome. This famous prize was presented to musicians (awards were also made to artists, sculptors, and architects) beginning in 1803, and was offered annually until 1968, when student uprisings led to its dissolution. While most of the winners have been forgotten, a significant group became major figures in the history of French music: Berlioz, Gounod, Bizet, and Massenet. For Lili Boulanger, it was a matter of great familial pride. Her father had won the prize in 1835, five years after Berlioz, and her sister Nadia, eventually to become one of the most famous composition teachers in the twentieth century, had tried repeatedly but without success. As the award stipulated, Lili went to Rome, a requirement that some recipients thought more akin to exile than honor. An unexpected boon came in the form of a contract with the publishing house of Ricordi, a well-established Italian firm that had printed the operas of Verdi and Puccini. Ricordi offered to pay her an annual fee in order to have the right of publishing her compositions before anyone else. Soon after arriving in Rome, she began composing a song cycle to a collection of poems by Francis Jammes, entitled *Clairières dans le ciel.* According to her biographer, Léonie Rosenstiel, Boulanger felt a strong personal identification with the poetry of this cycle (Rosenstiel, 173). The poet writes of the young girl he loves, but who for some unknown reason disappears from his life. (In real life, the girl's parents refused to allow Jammes to marry their daughter.) Due to the exigencies of the First World War, the cycle was not published until 1919, a year after the composer's untimely death from intestinal tuberculosis.

Lili Boulanger
Clairières dans le ciel (1914)
"Elle est gravement gaie"
CD 11/3

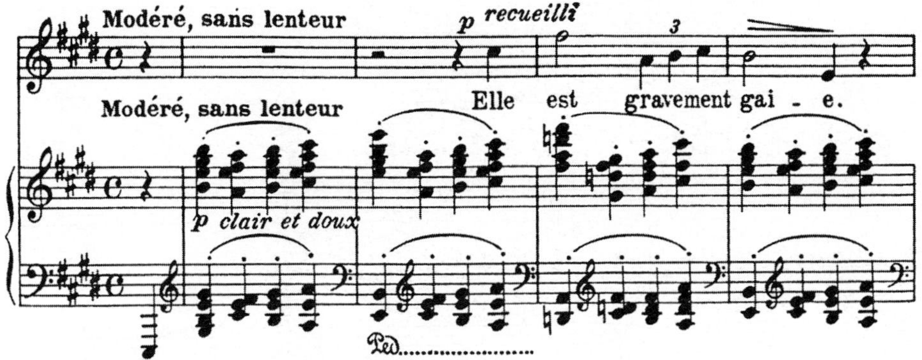

Ped.
Par mo-ments son re-gard se le-vait com-
poco più f
cresc.
rit.
a tempo
pp subito
-me pour sur-pren-dre ma pen-sé-e.
pp sub.
expressif en dehors
pp
Elle é-tait douce a-
p
m.d.
expressif et très fondu
-lors
contenu
cresc., ma sempre poco
Com-me quand il est tard
poco accel.

Elle est gravement gaie. Par moments son regard
se levait comme pour surprendre ma pensée.

Elle était douce alors comme quand il est tard
le velours jaune et bleu d'une allée de pensées.

—Francis Jammes

She is solemnly cheerful. Sometimes she looks up,
as though to interrupt my thoughts.

She was sweet then, as is—when it is late—
the yellow and blue velvet path of pansies.

Part VII
THE EARLY TWENTIETH CENTURY

Chapter 64
Richard Strauss in Berlin

173

Richard Strauss
Salome (1905), concluding scene

Richard Strauss composed his controversial opera *Salome* while he was music director of the Royal Opera in Berlin. After seeing a production of Oscar Wilde's spoken play *Salome* in 1902, Strauss was determined to make the drama into an opera. He created the libretto by radically abbreviating Hedwig Lachmann's German translation of Wilde's play, carefully preserving the shock value, lurid atmosphere, and trenchant parody contained in the original. Even a century after its premiere, the concluding scene is still revolting.

Wilde's play is a fantasy of forbidden love. Its central theme concerns the imprisonment and beheading of John the Baptist (Wilde uses his Hebrew name, Jochanaan) at the hands of King Herod, his wife, Herodias, and her daughter, Salome. Salome, whose lust for Jochanaan has only been inflamed by his disdain, performs the famous "Dance of the Seven Veils" for her lecherous stepfather, Herod. Aroused by her sensuality, he offers her any reward she desires. Coached by her mother, Salome demands the head of Jochanaan. Just prior to the excerpt given below, the black arm of the executioner lifts the decapitated head out of the pit. In her climactic final monologue, Salome's thoughts shift between expressions of triumph, hatred, and love before she finally kisses the dead lips of John. Aghast, Herod orders her death, and the curtain falls as the soldiers crush her beneath their shields.

Although Wilde's characters are based on comic types, the music of this scene is anything but laughable. Instead it conveys Salome's madness and passionate sensuality. Strauss organized this through-composed scene by a developmental web of leitmotifs, including those sometimes labeled "Ecstasy"—heard when she describes her attraction to the prophet's body (Rehearsal 335–337)—or "Kiss" (Rehearsal 343–348) and "Lust" (Rehearsal 347, 355–357). Like Wagner, Strauss generally kept these leitmotifs in the orchestra, above which the melodic line flows freely.

Strauss used all of the tools of the modern composer of 1905 to bring the story alive. The music slips between tonality and atonality, just as Salome wavers between lucidity and insanity. There are passages where clear tonal areas are established, such as C♯ major just prior to Rehearsal 333 and at 359. But even the tonal sections are handled in a nontraditional manner: At the conclusion of the opera, the harmony suddenly veers away from C♯ major to Cminor as Salome is crushed to death. There are also examples of bitonal chords. In measure 269, a stark juxtaposition of A♭ major and C-minor triads accompanies Herod's command to kill his stepdaughter. Strauss starkly juxtaposes G♭ major and C-minor triads. He also alternates tonal and atonal chords. We hear this when Salome kisses the lips of John the Baptist (Rehearsal 355): The tonal setting for the "Lust" leitmotif alternates with a chord consisting of atonal cluster notes, giving the scene a sense of bizarre magic. In *Salome*, the restrictions on dissonance and tonality have been removed, the final vestiges stripped away. It is no wonder that Arnold Schoenberg and other younger modernists were profoundly influenced by the opera.

Richard Strauss
Salome (1905), concluding scene
CD 11/4

etwas fliessender
M. ♩=72
323
Sal.
A - ber wa - rum siehst du mich nicht
But where - fore dost thou not look at
un poco più mosso
pp
4
an, Jo - cha - na - an? Dei - ne Au -
me, Jo - ka - na - an? Thine eyes
324
6
gen, die so schreck - lich wa - ren so vol - ler Wut und Ve - rach - tung,
that were so ter - ri - ble, so full of rage and con - tempt,
f
p
sfz

smorzando
rit.
sind jetzt ge - schlos - sen.
they are now closed
Wa - rum sind sie ge - schlos - sen?
Where-fore then are they clo - sed?
pp
espr.
smorz.
p marc.
mf
sfz
a tempo
Off - ne doch die Au - gen, so he - be dei - ne Li - der, Jo - cha -
O - pen thou thine eyes, lift up a - gain thine eye - lids, Jo - ka -
pp
325
na - an! Wa - rum siehst du mich nicht an? Hast du
na - an! Why dost thou not look at me? Art thou a -
molto espr.
dim.
f
Angst vor mir, Jo - cha - na - an, dass du mich nicht an -
fraid of me? Jo - ka - na - an that thou wilt not look
p espr.
cresc.

calando
326
M. ♩= 72
a tempo
se - - - hen willst?
at me?
Und dei - ne Zun - ge, sie
And thy red tongue doth
(kurz und hart)
dim.
espr. cantabile
p
pp
spricht kein Wort, Jo - cha - - - - na-an, die - se Schar - lach - nat - ter, die ih - ren
speak no word, Jo - ka - - - - na-an, that scar - let vi - per spat - ting its
(sotto)
327
Gei - - - fer ge - gen mich spie. Es ist selt - sam, nicht?
poi - - - son, it stirs no more. It is stran - ge, aye?
cresc.
pp
Wie kommt es, dass die - se ro - te Nat - ter sich
How is it that this small scar - let vi - per doth
cresc.

328
nicht mehr rührt?
stir no more?
dim.
p
espr.
Du sprachst böse Worte gegen mich, gegen
Thou didst use evil language against me, against
cresc.
mich, Salome, die Tochter der Herodias, Prinzessin von Ju-
me, Salomé, the daughter of Herodias, Princess of Ju-
fp cresc.
marc.
fp cresc.
8va
329
accelerando
dä- a.
dae- a.
f
più mosso
ziemlich lebhaft
Nun wohl!
Well then!
M. ♩=96

330
Ich le - be noch, a - ber du bist tot, und dein Kopf,
I'm li - ving still, but thou art dead, and thy head,
immer bewegter
sempre più mosso
dein Kopf ge - hört mir! Ich kann mit ihm tun,
thy head be - longs to me! I'm free to do with
was ich will. Ich kann ihn den Hun - - den vor - wer - fen
it what I will I may give it the dogs to feed on,
331
und den Vö - geln der Luft. Was die Hun - de
and the birds in the air. What is left by
ff
f
sfz
p
mf
dim.

50
üb - rig las - sen, sol - len die Vö - - - - - gel der Luft
the dogs may be de - voured by the birds
8va
52
ver - zeh - - - ren . . .
of the air.
332
cresc.
accelerando molto
54
Ah! Ah! Jo - cha - - - na -
Ah! Ah! Jo - ka - - - na -
f p molto cresc.
ff
57
poco ritardando
an, Jo - cha - - - na - an, du warst
an, Jo - ka - - - na - an, thou wert
dim. espr.

un poco mosso
zart bewegt
333
schön. Dein Leib war ei - ne El -
fair! Thy bo - dy was a co -
M. = 52
(sehr singend)
p
pp
pp
Ped. tenuto
334
fen - bein - säu - le auf sil - ber - nen Füs - sen. Er war ein
lumn of i - vo - ry set on a sil - ver sock - et. It was a
pp
Gar - ten vol-ler Tau - ben in der Sil - ber - li - lien
gar - den full of do - vès, full of sil - ver li - lies
cresc.
dim.
sempre più mosso
immer fliessender im Zeitmass
335
molto appassionato
Glanz. Nichts in der Welt war so weiss wie dein
shine. No thing on earth was so white as thy
pp
cresc.
f espr.
dim.

336
Leib. Nichts in der Welt war so schwarz wie dein
skin. No thing on earth was so black as thy
Haar. In der gan - zen Welt war nichts
hair. And in all the world was no -
so rot wie dein Mund.
thing so red as thy mouth.
337
Un poco più tranquillo
(ma sempre alla breve)
etwas ruhiger (aber stets ¢)
M. 𝅗𝅥 = 44
Dei - ne Stim - me war ein Wei -
But thy voice was a cen -
p
f
fp
dim.
pp
cresc.
espr.
ritard.
marc.

90
accelerando
rauch - ge - fäss
ser of sweet scents,
und wenn ich dich
and when I looked
marc.
pp
marc.
tr
94
ritard.
più ritard.
lento (sempre ¢)
langsam (stets ¢)
an - sah, hör - te ich
on thee I could hear
ge - heim - nis - vol - le Mu - sik. . .
a mu - sic of strange sounds
8va
dim.
pp
espr.
339
cresc.
dim.
(Lost in thought as she gazes upon Jokanaan's head)
(In den Anblick von Jochanaans Haupt versunken)
105
340
Ah!
Ah!
Wa - rum
Where - fore
l.h.
pp
mf espr.
111
ritard.
a tempo
hast du mich nicht an - ge - sehn,
didst thou ne - ver look at me,
Jo - cha -
Jo - ka -
pp

allmählich fliessender
poco accelerando
un poco più mosso
etwas bewegter
M. 𝅗𝅥 = 60
na - an? Du leg - test ü - ber dei - ne Au - gen die
na - an? Thou didst put u - pon thine eyes the
p
espr.
341
sempre più vivo
immer lebhafter
Bin - de ei - - - - - - nes, der sei - nen Gott schau - en woll -
cov - 'ring of him who seek - eth God in all His glo -
p espr.
te. Wohl! Du hast dei-nen Gott ge-sehn, Jo - cha - - - - - na - an,
ry. Well! Thou may'st have seen thy God, Jo - ka - - - - - na - an,
fp
pp
342
accelerando
a - ber mich, mich, mich
but me, me, me,
cresc.
f

132
sempre più mosso
immer bewegter
hast du nie ge - sehn. Hät - test du
thou didst ne - - - - - - - ver see If thou hadst
molto espr.
espr.
p
espr.
136
343
mich ge - sehn, du hät - test mich ge - - - liebt!
looked at me, thou wouldst have loved
cresc.
f
appassionato
139
molto mosso
sehr bewegt M. 𝅗𝅥 = 80
me.
Ich dür - ste nach dei - ner
I'm thir - sting for all thy
ff
p
143
344
Schön - - - heit. Ich hung - - - re nach dei - nem
beau - - - ty I'm hun - - - gry for thy bo - - - -
f

147
Leib.
dy.
Nicht Wein noch Äp - fel kön - - - - nen mein Ver - lan - gen
Neith - er wine nor app - les can ap - pease all my de -
cresc.
dim.
espr.
345
152
stringendo
mit grosser Steigerung
stil - len...
sire
Was soll ich jetzt tun, Jo - cha - - -
What shall I do now, Jo - ka - - -
espr.
cresc.
157
na - an?
na - an?
Nicht die Flu - - - ten,
Not by floods
346
noch die gro - ssen
nor by the great
cresc.
161
Was - - ser
wa - - ters
kön - nen die - ses brün - - - - - - - - - sti - ge Be -
can e - ver the heat of my strong
cresc.

347
molto allegro
sehr lebhaft
geh - ren lö - schen...
passion be quen - ched
Oh!
Oh!
Wa - rum
Where - fore
ff
più accelerando
sahst du mich nicht an?
didst thou not look at me?
Hät - test du
If thou hadst
cresc.
f
sfz
ff
348
lento
mehr als dopplet so
mich an - ge - sehn
look - ed at me
du
thou
hät - test mich ge - liebt.
wouldst have lov - ed me.
M. ♩= 63
mf
cresc.
ff
p
espr.
langsam
Ich weiss es wohl, du hät - test mich ge -
I know it well, thou wouldst have lov - ed
cresc.
molto
ff

349
molto ritenuto
liebt.
me,
Und das Ge - heim - nis der Lie -
and the great mys - te - ry of love
dim.
p
dim.
pp
350
be ist grö - - - sser als das Ge - heim - - - nis des
is grea - - - ter than the mys - te - ry
dim.
ppp
pp
moderato
mässig bewegt
To - - - - - des...
of death...
M. ♩= 80
ppp
Herod (with lowered voice to Herodias)
Herodes (leise zu Herodias)
351
Sie ist ein Un - ge - heu - er, dei - ne Toch - ter. Ich sa - ge dir, sie ist ein
She is a hi - deous mons - ter, thy daugh - ter. I tell it thee, she's al - to
pp

199
Herodias (stark)
Mei - ne Toch - ter hat recht ge - tan.
I ap - prove of my daugh - ter's deed.
Ich möch - te jetzt hier blei - ben.
And I will now stay here.
Un - ge - he - uer!
geth - er mons - trous!
Ah!
Ah!
ff
dim.
ff sfz
trem.
201
Da spricht mei - nes Bru - ders Weib.
There speaks my broth - er's wife.
(weaker)
(schwächer)
Komm, ich will nicht an die - sem Or - te blei - ben.
Come, I will no long - er stay in this place.
8va
dim.
p
352
203
(vehemently)
(heftig)
Komm, sag ich dir!
Come, I tell thee!
Si - cher, es wird
Sure - ly, some-thing
ff p
ff
205
Schreck - li - ches ge - schehn.
ter - ri - ble will hap - pen.
Wir wol - len uns im Pa - last ver - ber - gen,
Let us hide our - selves in the pa - lace,
He - ro - di - as, ich fan - ge
He - ro - di - as, I am be -
mf

(the moon disappears)
353
(der Mond verschwindet)
an zu er - zit - tern...
gin - ning to trem - ble...
doppelt so schnell
(auffahrend)
molto allegro (doppio movimente)
(rising suddenly)
Man - nas - sah, Is - sa - char, O - zi - as, löscht die
Ma - nas - seh, I - sa - char, O - zi - as, put out the
Fa - ckeln aus. Ver - bergt den Mond, ver - bergt die Ster - - - - ne!
tor - ches. Hide the moon, hide the stars
(es wird
becomes very dark)
ganz dunkel)
Es wird Schreck - li - ches ge - - schehn.
Some-thing ter - ri - ble will come.
marc.
dim.
lento
doppelt so langsam
355
poco f

(faintly)
Salome (matt.) sehr gedehnt M. ♩= 58
226
Ah! Ich ha - be dei-nen Mund ge-küsst. Jo - cha -
Ah! I have kissed thy mouth, Jo - ka -
pp
230
356
- na - an. Ah! Ich ha - be ihn ge - küsst, dei - nen
- na - an. Ah! I have kissed thy
p
pp
233
Mund, es war ein bit - te - rer Ge - schmack auf dei - nen Lip - pen
mouth, there was a bit - ter, bit - ter taste on thy red lips.
p
236
357
Hat es nach Blut ge - schmeckt? Nein! Doch es schmeck - te viel - leicht nach
Was it the taste of blood? Nay! But per - chance this is the taste of
pp
mf
espr.

240
Lie - be...
love...
molto espr.
mf
p
245
Sie sa - gen, dass die Lie - - be bit - ter schmecke...
They say that love hath a bit - ter taste...
mf
249
Al - lein was tut's
But what of that?
molto espr.
mf
Was tut's?
What of that?
p
253
359
M. ♩= 60
ff
Ich ha - be dei - nen Mund ge -
I have now kissed thy

360
küsst, Jo - cha - na - an. Ich ha - be ihn ge - küsst
mouth, Jo - ka - na - an. I have now kissed
dim.
molto espr.
ritard.
molto largo
sehr breit
361
(A moonbeam falls
(Der Mond bricht
dei - - - - nen Mund.
thy mouth.
ff
sfz
on Salomé, covering her with light.)
wieder hervor und beleuchtet Salome.)
Herod (turning round)
Herodes (sich umwendend)
schneller
frei
Man tö - - - - - te die - ses
Go, kill at once that
ritard.
più mosso
dim.
sfz
ff
molto allegro
sehr schnell
(Die soldaten stürzen sich auf Salome
und begraben sie unter ihren Schilden.)
362
Weib!
wench!
(The soldiers rush forward and
crush Salomé under their shields.)
M. 𝅗𝅥 = 80
ff

Music in Russia During the Silver Age
Igor Stravinsky

174

Igor Stravinsky
The Rite of Spring (1913)
a. Procession of the Sage
b. The Sage
c. Dance of the Earth

Igor Stravinsky's score for the ballet *Le sacre du printemps* (*The Rite of Spring*), completed and premiered in Paris in 1913, proved to be a turning point in the history of twentieth-century music. The work's rawboned power and elemental excitement were imitated for the remainder of the century by composers throughout the world. Such diverse works as Prokofiev's *Scythian* Suite, Silvestre Revueltas's *Sensemayá*, and the "Rumble" in Leonard Bernstein's *West Side Story* could not have been composed without it. Stravinsky's music showed that the language of atonality—when joined to a brilliant orchestration and liberated rhythm—could produce an enduring masterpiece.

Although *The Rite of Spring* is far better known as an orchestral tone poem than as a ballet score, its music closely follows the original choreography, which evokes springtime rituals as practiced by ancient Russian tribes. In Part 1 of the ballet, tribes gather at the foot of a sacred mountain to honor and invoke the gods of springtime. After a series of dances, some of which mimic athletic competition, an ancient and revered Sage approaches the scene of celebration. His solemn procession is represented by four tubas, who state a hypnotically repetitive and largely octatonic melody that begins almost imperceptibly at Rehearsal 64 (the score and recording begin at this point) in the midst of a passage in which rival tribes are engaged in relaxed and graceful dancing. By Rehearsal 66 the octatonic march has pushed aside the graceful diatonic melodies of the earlier dancing, and the music begins to accumulate a mass of sound and energy that is suddenly broken off at Rehearsal 71, when the Sage arrives at center stage (page 1474). All stand in silent awe as the elder then lies on the earth and gives it his blessing in the form of a kiss. This action unleashes the Dance of the Earth, the final section of Part 1 of the ballet (page 1474). "Dance" is perhaps too conservative a term to describe the action. The assembled tribes erupt in pure pandemonium and run amok until the curtain falls. The music for this dance moves like the wind and has irregularly placed accents within the $\frac{3}{4}$ meter. The three-note ostinato figure (F♯–G♯–A♯) eventually grows into a full whole-tone scale as the music masses to a great climax. This section ends Part 1 of the ballet.

Igor Stravinsky
The Rite of Spring (1913)
a. Procession of the Sage
b. The Sage
c. Dance of the Earth
CD 11/5, 11/6, and 11/7

64
65
Picc.
Fl. gr.
Fl. alto
Ob
C. ing.
Cl. picc. in Re
Cl. in Sib
Cl. bas. in Sib
Fag.
C. Fag.
Cor. in Fa
mf cantabile
Tr. picc. in Re
Tr. in Do
Trbn.
Tbe. Ten. in Sib
a2
mf molto pesante
Tbe. Bas.
mf molto pesante
Timp.
G. C.
secco
Tam-t.
Guero
Vln. I
arco
non divisi
Vln. II
arco
Violen
arco
non divisi
Vcl.
Cb.

66
Picc.
Fl. gr.
Fl. alto
Ob
C. ing.
Cl. picc. in Re
Cl. in Si♭
Fag.
C. Fag.
Cor. in Fa
Tr. picc. in Re
Tr. in Do
Trbn.
Tbe. Ten. in Si♭
Tbe. Bas.
G. C.
Vln. I
Vln. II
Violen
Vcl.
Cb.
Fltlzg.
flttzg.
Fl. picc. 2 muta in Fl. gr. 3
f ma non tanto
a2 sempre sim.
gliss.

67
Procession of the Sage
Cotège du Sage
68
Picc.
Fl. gr.
Fl. alto
Ob
sempre poco sf
C. ing.
Cl. in Sib
Cl. bas. in Sib
Fag.
mf
C. Fag.
Cor. in Fa
mf
Tr. in Do
Trbn.
Tbe. Ten. in Sib
a2
Tbe. Bas.
Timp.
bacch. dura, sempre stacc.
G. C.
Tam-t.
Vln. I
Vln. II
Violen
div.
Vel.
3 soli
Tutti, div.
Cb.

20
69
Picc. 1 2
Fl. gr. 1 2
Ob 1 2
C. ing.
Cl. in Si♭ 1 2
Cl. bas. in Si♭ 1 2
Fag. 1 2 3
C. Fag. 1 2
2.
1.
mf
2.
f
f
Cor. in Fa 1 2 3 4 5 6
Tr. in Do 1 2 3 4
Trbn. 1 2
Tbe. Ten. 1 2 in Si♭
a2
Tbe. Bas. 1 2
a2
Timp.
G. C.
Tam-t.
69
Vln. I
Vln. II
Violen
Vcl.
Cb.

25
70
Fl. gr.
Fl. alto
Ob
C. ing.
Cl. picc. in Re
Cl. in Sib
Cl. bas. in Sib
Fag.
C. Fag.
Cor. in Fa
Tr. picc. in Re
Tr. in Do
Trbn.
Tbe. Ten. in Sib
Tbe. Bas.
Timp.
G. C.
Tam-t.
Guero
Vln. I
Vln. II
Violen
Vcl.
Cb.
ff (non legato)
stacc.
(non legato)
sempre sf
ff maestoso
fff sul pont. sino al segno
unis.

29
Picc.
Fl. gr.
Fl. alto
Ob
C. ing.
Cl. picc. in Re
Cl. in Sib
Cl. bas. in Sib
Fag.
C. Fag.
Cor. in Fa
Tr. picc. in Re
Tr. in Do
Trbn.
Tbe. Ten. in Sib
Tbe. Bas.
Timp.
G. C.
Tam-t.
Guero
Vln. I
Vln. II
Violen
Vcl.
Cb.
fff
trem.
ff
a2
div.
sul pont. sino al segno
sul pont. sino al segno

32
71 Lunga
Picc. 1 2
Fl. gr. 1 2 3
Fl.gr.3 muta in Fl.picc.2
Fl. alto
Ob 1 2 3 4
C. ing.
Cl. picc. in Re
Cl. in Sib 1 2
Cl. bas. in Sib 1 2
Fag. 1 2 3
C. Fag. 1 2
Lunga
Cor. in Fa 1 2 3 4 5 6
Tr. picc. in Re
Tr. in Do 1 2 3 4
Trbn. 1 2 3
Tba. 2 muta in Cor. 8
a2
Tbe. Ten. in Sib 1 2
a2
Tbe. Bas. 1 2
Lunga
Timp.
G. C.
Tam-t.
Guero
71 Lunga
Vln. I
Vln. II
Violen
Vcl.
Cb.

The Sage
Le Sage
36
Lento ♩ = 42
72
Dance of the Earth
Danse de la Terre
Prestissimo ♩ = 168
Picc.
Fl. gr.
Fl. alto
Ob
C. ing.
Cl. picc. in Re
Cl. in Sib
Cl. bas. in Sib
Fag.
C. Fag.
non ma marc.
Solo
Cor. in Fa
Tr. in Do
Trbn.
Timp.
G. C.
Tam-t.
a2
gliss.
sf sempre
p sub.
molto
The Sage
Le Sage
Lento ♩ = 42
72
Dance of the Earth
Danse de la Terre
Prestissimo ♩ = 168
Vln I Tutti, unis.
2 Vln. Soli
Vln. II Tutti, unis.
Vla. Sola
Vle. Tutti, unis.
Tutti, unis.
5 Vcl. Soli
con sord.
senza sord.
2 Cb. Soli
sul Re

44
73
Picc. 1 2
Fl. gr. 1 2
Fl. alto
Ob 1 2 3 4
C. ing.
Cl. picc. in Re
Cl. in Sib 1 2
a2
Cl. bas. in Sib 1 2
Fag. 1 2 3
C. Fag. 1 2
Cor. in Fa 1 2 3 4 5 6 8
marcatiss.
Tr. picc. in Re
sf marc.
Tr. in Do 1 2 3 4
marc.
Trbn. 1 2 3
Timp.
G. C.
molto
p sub.
sf p
Tam-t.
Vln. I
gliss.
sff
Vln. II
Violen
Vcl.
Cb.

50
Picc. 1 2
Fl. gr. 1 2
Fl. alto
Ob 1 2 3 4
C. ing.
Cl. picc. in Re
Cl. in Sib 1 2
Cl. bas. in Sib 1 2
Fag. 1 2 3
C. Fag. 1 2
a2
Cor. in Fa 1 2 3 4 5 6 8
Solo (cuivrez)
f assai
Tr. picc. in Re
Tr. in Do 1 2 3 4
Trbn. 1 2 3
Timp.
G. C.
Tam-t.
tr
p sub.
Vln. I
gliss.
f
Vln. II
Violen
Vcl.
Cb.

56
74
Picc.
a2
Fl. gr.
Fl. alto
Ob
C. ing.
Cl. picc. in Re
Cl. in Sib
Cl. bas. in Sib
Fag.
C. Fag.
Cor. in Fa
Solo (cuivrez)
f assai
Tr. picc. in Re
Tr. in Do
Trbn.
Timp.
G. C.
p sub.
sf p
Tam-t.
Vln. I
gliss.
Vln. II
Violen
Vcl.
Cb.

(75)

62

Picc. 1 2 — a2

Fl. gr. 1 2 — a2

Fl. alto

Ob 1 2 / 3 4

C. ing.

Cl. picc. in Re

Cl. in Sib 1 2 — a2

Cl. bas. in Sib 1 2 — a2 — 1. *p* — *p*

Fag. 1 2 / 3 — a2

C. Fag. 1 2 — a2 — C. Fag. 2 muta in Fag. 4

Cor. in Fa 1 2 / 3 / 5 / 6 8 — a2 — *p sub.*

Tr. in Do 1 2

Trbn. 1 2 / 3

Timp.

G. C.

(75)

Vln. I

Vln. II

Violen — *p sub. détaché*

Vcl. — *p sub.*

Cb.

68
Picc. 1 2
Fl. gr. 1 2
Cl. in Sib 1 2
Cl. bas. in Sib 1 2
1.
Fag. 1 2
Cor. in Fa
1
2
3
4
5
6 8
mf
solo
Tr. in Do 4
Timp.
G. C.
Vln. I
Vln. II
detaché
Violen
poco cresc.
Vcl.
Cb.

76
74
a2
Cl. in Sib 1 2
Cl. bas. in Sib 1 2
Fag. 1 2
Cor. in Fa
Tr. in Do 3 4
Timp.
G. C.
Vln. I
Vln. II
Violen
Vcl.
Cb.
mf
f
p

77
80
a2
Cl. in Sib 1 2
a2
Cl. bas. in Sib 1 2
Fag. 1 2
Cor. in Fa
1
2
3
4
5
6 8
2.
mf
Tr. in Do
1 2
3 4
Timp.
G. C.
77
tr
mf
Vln. I
Vln. II
Violen
Vcl.
Cb.

85
a2
Cl. in Sib 1 2
Cl. bas. in Sib 1 2
Fag. 1 2
Cor. in Fa
Tr. in Do
Timp.
G. C.
Vln. I
Vln. II
Violen
Vcl.
Cb.
cresc.
f

90
78
Picc.
Fl. gr.
Fl. alto
Ob
C. ing.
Cl. picc. in Re
Cl. in Sib
Cl. bas. in Sib
Fag.
Cor. in Fa
Tr. picc. in Re
Tr. in Do
Trbn.
Tbe. Bas.
Timp.
G. C.
Vln. I
Vln. II
Violen
Vcl.
Cb.
fff
sfff
a2
div.
cresc.
mf
f
tr

95
Picc.
Fl. gr.
a2
Fl. alto
Ob
C. ing.
Cl. picc. in Re
Cl. in Sib
Cl. bas. in Sib
Fag.
Cor. in Fa
Tr. picc. in Re
Tr. in Do
Trbn.
Tbe. Ten. in Sib
Tbe. Bas.
Timp.
G. C.
Vln. I
Vln. II
Violen
Vel.
Cb.
cresc.
unis.
fff
ff

Atonality
Schoenberg and Scriabin

175

Arnold Schoenberg
Piano Piece, Opus 11, No. 1 (1909)

When Schoenberg first began composing, he wrote tonal music in a style consistent with late Romanticism, but around 1908 he rejected its harmonic language and turned instead to atonality. The word "atonal"—of which Schoenberg himself never approved—suggests music that has no large-scale functional harmonic progressions. It draws tones from the chromatic scale as though they were all structurally equal, and uses chords (emphasizing dissonances) of any size and intervalic makeup. The reasons for Schoenberg's dramatic change from Romanticism to atonality are not entirely known. Certainly, an important factor was his wish to find an original and distinctive voice as a composer, and atonality also conformed to certain states of mind that he wished his music to express. The Three Piano Pieces, Opus 11, are among Schoenberg's earliest essays in the atonal style.

Piano Piece No. 1 reveals the intense and highly concentrated expressivity that characterizes Schoenberg's atonal language. The work has many familiar features, such as its pervasive development of the motives heard at the opening, but the high degree of abbreviation, sudden mood swings, and novel harmonic language were found daunting by most early audiences. Even today, many listeners find it necessary to hear the piece numerous times before beginning to understand it.

While the harmony is complex and the melody highly fragmented, the formal structure is based on a simple ternary plan that is easy to perceive, even upon a first hearing. The **A** section (mm. 1–11) consists of a melody that is itself a smaller ternary form (**aba'**). The substantial **B** section (mm. 12–52) develops motives derived from the first five bars. For example, see how many times the theme's head motive is embedded in the passage beginning at measure 34. The return to **A** that begins in measure 53 is not an exact repetition, but is extensively recomposed to give it a greatly expanded texture, new harmonies, and further development of the melody.

Arnold Schoenberg
Piano Piece, Opus 11, No. 1 (1909)
CD 11/8

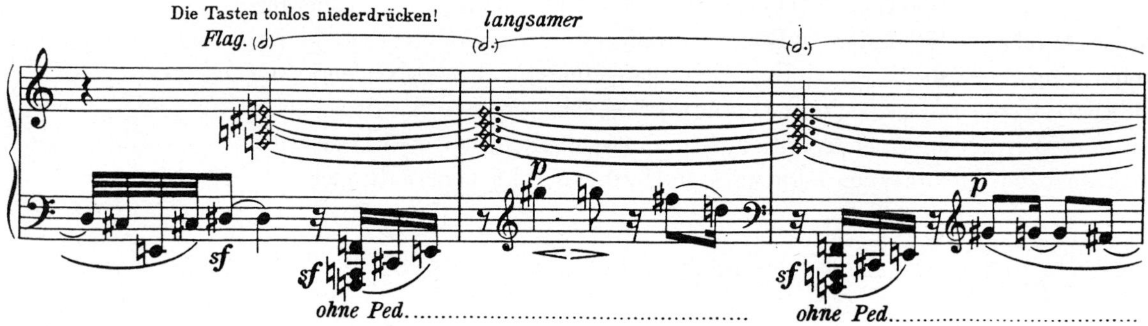

17
sehr langsam
f
p
f
p
f
rit.
Mäßig.
p
p
rascher
p
langsam
f
f
pp
pp
fließender
pp
ppp

37
p cresc.
ppp
pp
sf
pp
sf
f
pp
f
pp
pp
pp

49
accel.
f
ff
martellato
ohne Pedal
pp
p
gebunden
cresc.
f
p
sf dim.
pp
4′

176

Arnold Schoenberg
Pierrot lunaire (1912)
No. 8, "Nacht (Passacaglia)"

While many aspects of *Pierrot lunaire* are revolutionary, its genre, melodrama, has a long history. Melodrama—spoken text over an instrumental accompaniment—dates back to Rousseau and eighteenth-century France. Perhaps two of the most famous examples of this type of composition occur in the second act of Beethoven's *Fidelio* and in the "Wolf's Glen Scene" from *Die Freischütz* (no. 153). Schoenberg's composition sounds dramatically different from these earlier works, and, unlike Stravinsky's *Rite of Spring,* it still sounds revolutionary nearly a century after its premiere in 1912. This shocking freshness results in part from the atonal harmony, the lack of traditional melody, and *Sprechgesang,* Schoenberg's term for the recitational style in which rhythms are strictly notated, but pitches are only approximated. (Schoenberg called the reciter the *Sprechstimme*, a word often used as a synonym for *Sprechgesang.*)

The artist who commissioned this work, Albertine Zehme, was a champion of melodrama during the early years of the twentieth century. She had been a respected stage actress and a pupil of Cosima Wagner before retiring after her marriage to a successful lawyer in Leipzig. (Her husband's family was aghast that he would ruin his reputation by marrying a theatrical woman.) His money and Frau Zehme's artistic sensibility supported the creation of one of the great masterpieces of modern music. She eventually returned to the stage in 1904 and often performed melodramas, including a setting of Albert Giraud's *Pierrot* poetry by a young composer, Otto Vrieslander (1880–1950), whose Lieder were highly regarded at the time. Having established a reputation for her performances of melodrama, she desired a better musical setting for *Pierrot,* and commissioned Schoenberg to write one. After some initial work in March, he began composing the work in earnest on 17 April 1912 (two days after the *Titanic* disaster), and completed *Pierrot lunaire* in mid-July. The premiere performance received a mixed reception. The audience gave the composition such an ovation that Schoenberg and Zehme repeated the entire work. However, the print reviews were hostile, suggesting that some concertgoers could not leave the hall fast enough.

In spite of its avant-garde character, *Pierrot lunaire* makes use of historical techniques like the *passacaglia* in "Nacht." The basic motive of the movement, presented most clearly by the voice in measure 10, infuses every measure of "Nacht." While the work may sound baffling at first hearing, Schoenberg's setting is exceptionally attuned to the suffocating atmosphere and sense of despair conveyed by Giraud's poem.

Arnold Schoenberg
Pierrot lunaire (1912)
No. 8, "Nacht (Passacaglia)"
CD 11/9

Flatterzunge
B-Kl. (B)
Vcl.
am Steg
pp
cresc.
pp dim.
ppp
f
Tie - fen steigt ein Duft, Erinnrung mordend! Fin - stre, schwar - ze
stacc.
ohne Ped.
I. Tempo
am Griffbrett
dim.
ff
fff
Rie - senfal - ter tö - te - ten der Sonne Glanz.
15
Ped.
espress.
Flag.
molto legato
Und vom Him - mel er - denwärts sen - ken sich mit schwe - ren Schwin - gen

sehr große Pause, aber quasi im Takt, dann folgt:

Gebet an Pierrot.

Klavier, Klarinette in A.

Finstre, schwarze Riesenfalter Töteten der Sonne Glanz. Ein geschlossnes Zauberbuch, Ruht der Horizont—verschwiegen.	Dark, black, giant butterflies killed the sunshine. Like a closed magic book, the horizon rests—hidden.
Aus dem Qualm verlorner Tiefen Steigt ein Duft, Errinrung mordend! Finstre, schwarze Riesenfalter Töteten der Sonne Glanz.	From the smoke of forgotten depths wafts a fragrance, killing the memory! Dark, black, giant butterflies killed the sunshine.
Und vom Himmel erdenwärts Senken sich mit schweren Schwingen Unsichtbar die Ungetüme Auf die Menschenherzen nieder . . . Finstre, schwarze Riesenfalter.	And from heaven toward earth sink with heavy swinging the invisible monsters down upon the hearts of mankind . . . Dark, black, giant butterflies.

—Albert Giraud

177

Alexander Scriabin

Piano Prelude, Opus 74, No. 5 (1914)

Alexander Scriabin, like Arnold Schoenberg, moved to an atonal harmonic style around 1908, after he had established a career as a composer of Romantic music. Scriabin's Five Preludes for piano, Opus 74, are among his final compositions before his untimely death from blood poisoning in 1915 at the age of forty-four. These short preludes are highly expressive and seemingly improvisatory in their spontaneous rhythms. They are stylistically very unlike Schoenberg's Opus 11 from the same period.

The last of the Opus 74 preludes, No. 5, reveals Scriabin's use of two related collections of tones: the octatonic scale and the so-called "mystic" chord. An octatonic scale—long a favorite resource for Russian composers—proceeds by an alternation of half and whole steps. The six tones of the "mystic" chord—for example, B♭ C♭ D♭ E♭ F and G, the notes that occur on the first half-note beat of measure 2—are close to a whole-tone scale, since only one note (B♭ in this example) deviates from a fully whole-tone arrangement. Scriabin uses these two collections of notes in lines and chords, in transpositions and symmetric inversions, and in incomplete forms.

A	B	A	B
mystic chord	octatonic scale	mystic chord	octatonic scale
mm. 1–4	5–8	9–12	13–17

Alexander Scriabin

Piano Prelude, Opus 74, No. 5 (1914)

CD 11/10

Fier, belliqueux.

Piano.

p

f

p

f

p

impérieux

cresc.

f
p
p
cresc.
f

French Music at the Time of World War I
Ravel and Satie

178

Maurice Ravel
Le tombeau de Couperin (1914–1917)
Rigaudon

Maurice Ravel's interest in early music is repeatedly manifest in his original compositions for piano. One of his earliest works is a "Minuet antique" (1895) that revives the form and atmosphere of the minuets from harpsichord suites by the Baroque composer Jean-Philippe Rameau. His *Sonatine* for piano (1905) draws its form and substance from Haydn's piano sonatas. In 1909 Ravel returned to the old minuet style in his *Menuet sur le nom d'Haydn* (*Minuet on the Name HAYDN*).

So it was no surprise when Ravel turned in 1914 to the music of the great French harpsichordists to find inspiration for his piano suite *Le tombeau de Couperin* (*Couperin's Monument*). Ravel's suite is closely related to the four Royal Concerts that Couperin published in 1722, and which Ravel evidently studied prior to composing his *Tombeau*. Couperin's Concerts, which could be played by harpsichord alone or with the addition of a few instruments, are suites of dances. One of the dances appearing in the Fourth Royal Concert is a spirited "rigaudon." This was a favorite social and theatrical dance at the court of Versailles during the reign of Louis XIV; its lively duple meter and high spirits were often featured in the operas and instrumental suites of French Baroque composers.

In the Rigaudon for his *Tombeau*, Ravel copied elements of the style and form of his Baroque model, but he ultimately produced a work that is thoroughly modern in harmony and tonal organization. The **A** section (mm. 1–36) of this movement is organized in asymmetrical binary form (**aabb**). Notice in particular the close hand positions in the first eight measures, where the right hand has to play beneath the left. The style changes dramatically in the **B** section (mm. 37–92), where the long-held notes recall the drones that Baroque composers used to suggest pastoral images. When the vigorous **A** section returns (m. 93), it is played without repeats.

Maurice Ravel

Le tombeau de Couperin (1914–1917)

Rigaudon

CD 11/11

Assez vif

PIANO

16

più f

31
f
ff
Moins vif
pp
Ped.
51
soutenu

69

pp

Sourdine

p

84

pp

Tempo I°

ff

mp

99
ff
ff
mf
f
più f
114
pp
f
ff

179

Erik Satie

Sarabande No. 2 for Piano (1887)

By the time the twenty-two-year-old Parisian composer Erik Satie completed his three Sarabandes for piano in 1887, his prospects for a career in music seemed bleak. He had recently dropped out of the Paris Conservatory—his professors considered him the laziest student in the school—and enlisted in the French infantry. He didn't care much for that, either. Satie soon turned instead to the life of a popular musician—a pianist and accompanist in the rising world of French cabarets, located in the Montmarte district of Paris. For a long time, his serious piano pieces attracted no attention. They seemed very thin in musical substance beside the flashy and evocative character pieces for piano that were being composed in the 1880s by such established figures as Emmanuel Chabrier, Vincent d'Indy, and André Messager.

In 1911 Satie's fortunes as a composer of serious music picked up, thanks to the attention of his friend Maurice Ravel, who performed the Sarabande No. 2 in a concert in Paris. (When Satie republished the composition later that year, he dedicated it to Ravel.) By then French audiences were tiring of Romanticism, and Satie's musical eccentricities seemed refreshing. The Second Sarabande shows Satie's contrarian spirit in music. There is very little melody or harmonic direction in the piece, no counterpoint or memorable rhythm, and the form is based on simple repetition. Gradually, Satie's style was accepted and recognized as a forerunner of the anti-Romantic music of the 1920s.

Sarabande No. 2 may best be considered a work in free ternary form. The **A** section (mm. 1–44) consists of two statements of the same phrase, made without any alteration. The phrase begins on the tonic triad (D♯ minor) and ends on the minor dominant chord, but, other than that, the chords rarely convey the functions of tonal harmony. In the **B** section (mm. 45–68), the theme is based on ideas derived from **A**, and the harmony suggests a contrasting tonality of E major and minor. The final section combines elements of **A** and **B** in alternation.

Eric Satie
Sarabande No. 2 for Piano (1887)
Thomson-Schirmer Website

diminuer
ralentir
29
diminuer

ralentir
61

p
p
f
p
f
p
p

New Music in Paris After World War I

Stravinsky and The Six

180

Igor Stravinsky
Octet (1923)
First movement, "Sinfonia"

Igor Stravinsky's Octet is an example of a new musical style that critics in the 1920s dubbed Neoclassicism. Works of this type have two faces—one that looks backward toward music of the Baroque and Classical periods, and another that gazes toward the future of music. Most of all, early Neoclassical music like the Octet takes on an identity by rejecting the musical ethos of Romanticism. The Octet is brief and life-sized, not exaggerated or larger than life like much music prior to World War I. It is not an expressive or pictorial composition, but one that is objective and concerned mainly with purely musical elements and structures. Its sound is lean and hard, without the Romantic emphasis on a blended euphony.

Stravinsky's glances toward the past in his Octet are easy to see. The work is cast in a chamber genre that has antecedents in Mozart's wind serenades. The first movement reveals a design close to the Classical sonata form, and its rhythms have the driving, mechanical quality that is typical of the Baroque period. At the same time, the Octet is a thoroughly modern composition in its liberated dissonances, novel harmonic language, and changing meters. In this work Stravinsky positions himself neither in the past nor in the future, but in his own present day. His references to older music have the flavor of a witty parody far more than any naive revival of a musical language from the eighteenth century.

The first movement opens with a slow introduction that develops the rhythms and intervals presented in the first four bars. Notice the musical humor in measures 36 to 37: The woodwinds race up the scale, but it is the trumpet that jumps in with the resolution! This section concludes on a dominant-seventh chord in the key of E♭ major, which serves as the tonic key when the exposition begins at measure 42. We hear the first theme three times in succession, but each statement is slightly different. The lyrical second theme is introduced by the trumpet at measure 71, and again the theme is immediately spun into new shapes. Unlike most sonatas from the Classical period, this has no clear boundary marking the beginning of the development section. When the second theme returns at measure 128, it is initiated by the clarinet and trombone, and the movement concludes with three statements of the first theme.

Igor Stravinsky
Octet (1923)
First movement, "Sinfonia"
CD 11/12

Lento (♪ = 76)

1

Flauto
Clarinetto in Sib
Fagotti I
Fagotti II
Trombe I in Do
Trombe II in La
Tromboni I Tenore
Tromboni II Basso

p *sfp* *poco sfp* *mf* *p*

Fl.
Cl. in Sib
Fag. I
Fag. II

p

13
2
Fl.
Cl. in Sib
I
Fag.
II
3
4
mf
5
I in Do
Tr.
II in La
p
poco sfp
Trb.
sfp

6 Allegro moderato (𝅗𝅥 = 104)
Fl.
Cl. in Sib
I
Fag.
II
I in Do
Tr.
II in La
I
Trb.
II
p
f
sim.
7
mf
stacc.
sempre stacc.
p subito

55
8
Fl.
Cl. in Sib
I
Fag.
II
poco sfp
sim.
sfp
subito meno f
sfp
stacc.
sfp
I in Do
Tr.
II in La
poco sfp
sim.
p subito
sim.
I
Trb.
II
p subito
stacc.
9
ff
sfp
ff
sim.
mf marc.
mf marc.
stacc.
poco
mf
stacc.

10
Fl.
Cl. in Sib
I
Fag.
II
stacc. leggiero
p stacc. accompagnando
Sola
I in Do
Tr.
II in La
cant. tranquillo
p
I
Trb.
II
subito
11
Cl. in Sib
marcato
sim.
I
Fag.
II
secco
secco
I in Do
Tr.
II in La
sub.
sub.
p leggiero
12
Fl.
p
sim.
Cl. in Sib
I
Fag.
II
sempre p e stacc.
sempre pp
I in Do
Tr.
II in La
mp
subito pp
Trb. I
p

13
Fl.
Cl. in Sib
I
Fag.
II
cresc. e stacc.
I in Do
Tr.
II in La
poco sf
p
poco meno f
molto
pp
p leggierissimo
mf
Trb. I
14
tres court
mf
ben marcato
I
Trb.
II
poco sf

103
15
Fl.
Cl. in Sib
I
Fag.
II
I in Do
Tr.
II in La
I
Trb.
II
poco sf
poco sf
un poco sf (secco)
leggiero
mf
16
marc.
stacc.
mf leggiero
p
Trb. II

114
17
Fl.
Cl. in Sib
I
Fag.
II
I in Do
Tr.
I in La
leggierissimo
Fl.
Cl. in Sib
I
Fag.
II
I in Do
Tr.
II in La
sub. pp
Trb. II

125
18
Fl.
sff
Cl. in Sib
sim.
ff
pp
fp
sf
I
Fag.
II
sf
ff
pp
mf
stacc.
I in Do
Tr.
II in La
sf
con sord.
Solo cantabile
I
Trb.
II
fp
sim.
f
pp
Cl. in Sib
I
Fag.
II
p
fp
sf
ff
sim.
Trb. I
138
19
Cl. in Sib
ff
Fag. I
marcato
stacc.
Tr. in La
mf stacc. marcato
senza sord.
Trb. I

20
Fl.
Cl. in Sib
f p f p
sim.
I
Fag.
II
leggiero
I in Do
Tr.
II in La
21
ff
cresc.
f
stacc.
Trb. I
22
subito

184
23
Fl.
Cl. in Sib
I
Fag.
II
I in Do
Tr.
II in La
I
Trb.
II
ff
subito meno f e sempre stacc.
f
stacc.
p
fp
f
sempre stacc.
stacc.
Fl.
Cl. in Sib
I
Fag.
II
I in Do
Tr.
II in La
I
Trb.
II
stacc.
stacc.
sf
stacc.
sf

181

Darius Milhaud

Saudades do Brazil (1920)
"Botafogo"

During World War I, Darius Milhaud was employed by the French diplomatic corps. Much to his delight, he was stationed in Rio de Janeiro, where his musical inquisitiveness led him to seek out and study the local popular dance music—the sambas, tangos, and maxixes that were heard in bars and restaurants throughout Rio. Milhaud developed a great fondness for the musical subtleties and tone of these dances, which range from the sultry to the exuberant.

When he returned to Paris in 1918, he imitated the lazy syncopations of Brazilian dances in a collection of short piano pieces that he appropriately titled *Saudades do Brazil—Longing for Brazil.* This particular movement, "Botafogo," is a samba. While there are various versions of this dance, they typically share two musical characteristics: a marchlike bass line (Ex. a) and a melody that incorporates a syncopated pattern (Ex. b).

In addition to their evocation of Brazilian dances, Milhaud's pieces are also studies in polytonality—the simultaneous statement of two keys in different strata of the texture. Polytonal chords, Milhaud declared, were "more subtly sweet and more violently potent" than normal ones. In "Botafogo" from *Saudades do Brazil,* the hands quickly pull apart into different keys, the left playing in F minor, the right giving the melody in F♯ minor. The resulting sound has just the sweetness and potency that the composer sought.

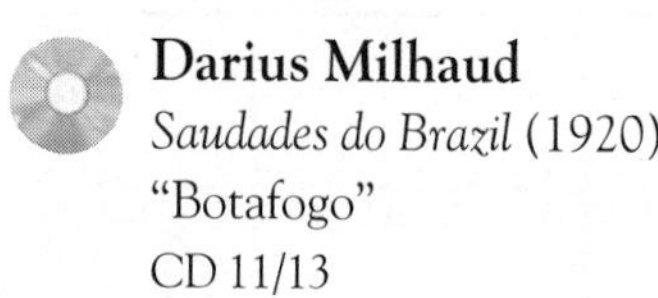

Darius Milhaud
Saudades do Brazil (1920)
"Botafogo"
CD 11/13

f
mp
f
p
Ani - mez un peu
p clair

mf
p
Ral.
Mouvt du début
mp
f
mp
f
Sans ralentir
pp

Vienna in the Aftermath of War
Twelve-Tone Methods

182

Arnold Schoenberg
String Quartet No. 4 (1936)
First movement, *Allegro molto, energico*

Schoenberg's Fourth String Quartet is one of the major chamber compositions of the twentieth century. It is a work in which the composer demonstrated that the twelve-tone method could result in music of powerful emotion, color, and diversity—in addition to a deep and multifaceted structure.

On the surface, the quartet reminds us of its Classical ancestors, going back as far as the string quartets of Haydn and Beethoven. It has four concise movements in the sequence fast/scherzo/slow/fast. The design of the first movement has much in common with the Classical sonata form, although Schoenberg was himself hesitant to describe it by this term, no doubt due to the absence of a Classical tonal plan. Despite the lack of modulations, which can differentiate one section of a work from another, Schoenberg finds other musical features—some residing within his twelve-tone method itself—to create contrasts. The first theme, for example, is bold and decisive, while the second theme (beginning at m. 66) is tranquil. The first theme uses the basic row (D C♯ A B♭ F E♭ E C A♭ G F♯ B), while the second theme is shaped from this row transposed up a fifth. The listener will also wish to focus on the constant development of the work's themes and motives, which Schoenberg leads through the most probing of developments.

The movement loosely conforms to a thematic plan inherited from Classical sonata form. It opens with a main theme and is followed by transitional materials that mix new motives with an intense development of earlier ones. As is typical with traditional sonata form, the second theme is in a contrasting style that is more serene in character than the first. The development section begins at measure 95, opening with a statement of the main theme. Shortly thereafter, a new theme enters (III in the chart below), one which Schoenberg described as part of an episode—that is to say, a passage that stands apart from its surroundings. An unusual feature of this quartet is that it has two recapitulations. In the first, the main and subsidiary themes return, although reordered and transformed in shape when compared to their presentation in the exposition. The second recapitulation is far more succinct than the first and contains only the two central themes of the sonata. A short coda, based on motives from the main theme, completes the movement.

Exposition		Development		Recapitulation I		Recapitulation II		Coda
I	II	I	III	I	II	I	II	I
1	66	95	116	165	190	239	259	274

Arnold Schoenberg
String Quartet No. 4 (1936)
First movement, *Allegro molto, energico*
CD 11/14

12
13
14
15
16
17
18
19
20
21
22
pp dolce
p dolce

p dolce
pizz
arco
cresc

32
33
34
35
36
37
38
39
40
p dolce

41
42
43
44
45
46
47
48
49
impetuoso
pizz
pizz

50
51
52
ff
pizz
arco
pizz
arco
ff
fp
f
ff
fp
f
arco
53
54
55
fp
p
fp
p
fp
p
f
p
f
p
f
p
f
56
57
58
f
ff
f
ff
f
ff
ff

PESANTE
RIT
sf
sf
ff
ff

POCO MENO MOSSO
MOLTO RIT
p
sfpp
pizz
arco
sul ponticello
p
sfpp
pizz
arco
sul ponticello
p
sfpp
pizz
arco
sfpp
sul ponticello

A TEMPO, MA POCO TRANQUILLO

(presto)
ppp
arpeggio
sul pont
pp
pp
dolce
p
f
fp
pp

68
69
70
mf
pp
71
72
73
74
75
76
pp dolce
pizz
ppp
arco
sempre pp

77
78
79
80
81
82
83
84
(D)
(G)
(D)
pizz
arco
arco
pizz
arco
arco
pp
p
f
ff

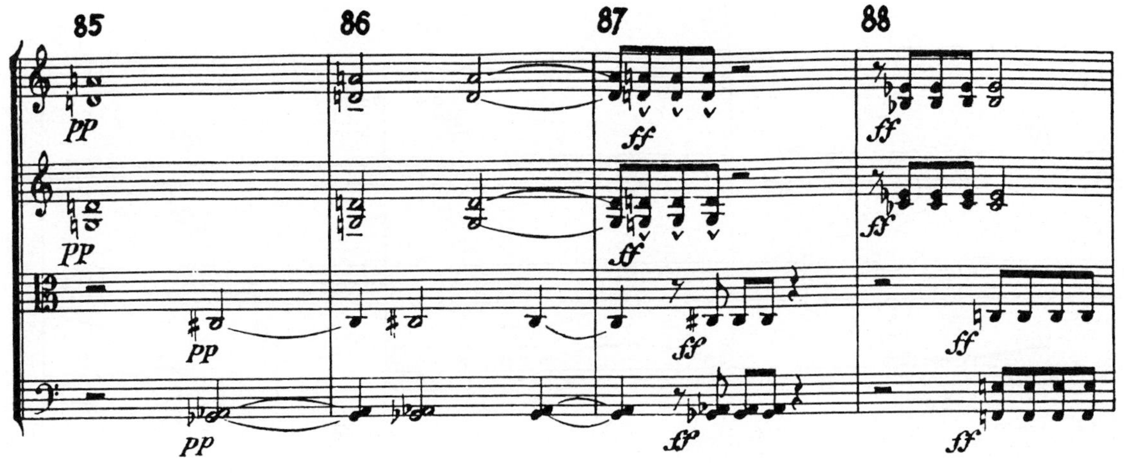
85
86
87
88
pp
ff

89
90
91
92
sul ponticello
(trem)
ff
p
pp
f
fp
sul ponticello

TEMPO I^mo

93
94
95
96
ff
f

97
98
99
100
101
102
103
104
105

106
107
108
ponticello
(trem)
fpp
ponticello
(D)
(G)
109
110
111
112
113
114

115
116
117
mf
f
f
f
impetuoso
118
119
120
121
122
123
mf
f
mf
impetuoso
mf

124
125
126
p
127
128
mf
129
f
impetuoso
130
131
132

133
134
135
f impetuoso
136
f martellato
137
138
139
140
141

142
143
144
145
146
147
148
149
150
151
dolce

POCO A POCO ACCELERANDO
152
153
154
155
156
157
158
159
160

161
162
163
TEMPO I^MO
164
RIT
165
166
(G)
ff
pizz
167
168
169
fp
f

170
171
172
arco
173
174
175
RIT
PESANTE
POCO MOSSO
176
177
178

179
180
181
182
183
184
185
186

UN POCO TRANQUILLO
187
188
189
p dolce
pp
mf
p
190
191
192
193
194
195
pp

196
197
198
199
200
201
202
203
204

205
206
207
208
209
210
211
212
213

214
215
216
217
218
219
sempre ff
sempre ff
sempre ff
sempre ff
220
221
222
mf
pizz
f
f
pizz
f
mf
pizz
f

223
224
225
arco
arco
arco
mf
f
226
227
p
228
229

230
231
232
pizz
pizz

233
234
235
arco
arco
p
p
p
pizz
f

RIT.
236
237
238
sf
sf
sf
ff
ff
arco
ff

POCO MENO MOSSO
♩= 108
239
240
mf
mf
mf
ff
241
242
ff
mf
mf
mf
243
244
245
f
f
f
f
ff

246
247
248
ff
249
250
f
mf
251
252
253
p

POCO A POCO CALANDO
254
255
256
RIT
POCO MENO MOSSO
257
258
259
260
261
262
pizz
arco

263
264
265
p
pizz
pp
pp
pp

266
267
268
pp
p
pp
pp
p
pp
pp
p
pp
pp
p
pp

CALANDO
269
270
271
p
pp
arco
pp
arco
pp
arco
pp

TEMPO I^MO
PESANTE
272
273
274
275
276
277
278
279
280
281
282
283
284
ff
f
fff

183

Anton Webern

Symphony, Opus 21 (1928)
Second movement, *Sehr ruhig*

The symphony waned in interest for young progressive composers in Europe around the turn of the twentieth century. Richard Strauss, for example, gave up the genre after composing two youthful symphonies in the 1880s, turning instead to the form of the tone poem. No symphonies were completed by Claude Debussy, Maurice Ravel, Arnold Schoenberg, or Alban Berg. But in the 1920s, 1930s, and 1940s, the genre made a comeback under the influence of Neoclassicism. Stravinsky led the way with his Symphonies of Wind Instruments, Symphony in C, and Symphony in Three Movements, and these works seemed to unleash a torrent of new symphonic compositions by composers worldwide.

Although Anton Webern, like his teacher, Arnold Schoenberg, had only derision for Neoclassicism, he could not remain entirely isolated from the larger artistic and musical trends of his time. In a letter to Schoenberg in November 1927, Webern remarked that he was just then writing a "little symphony." Originally envisioning a compact three-movement work, Webern by the summer of 1928 had completed a movement using strict theme-and-variations form. A slow movement was added, after which Webern determined that the symphony was complete in two movements, with the variations placed second. The new composition received its premiere performance in New York in 1929.

The second movement consists of a theme, seven variations, and coda, each spanning exactly eleven measures. The work adheres strictly to Webern's interpretation of the twelve-tone method of composition, and the basic row (heard in the clarinet at the outset) has the tones F A♭ G F♯ B♭ A E♭ E C C♯ D B. The use of this and related rows becomes ever more complex as the variations proceed.

One of the most fascinating analytical aspects of this movement is the use of palindromes and canons. Each section is written as a palindrome. This is easiest to observe in the presentation of the theme (mm. 1–11). Halfway through measure 6, the theme and accompaniment reverse their rhythmic pattern and the intervalic distance between notes. Further, the order in which instruments play their notes in the accompaniment is a mirror image of the first half. The deployment of rows and canonic imitations creates a palindrome that arches over the entire movement. For example, the theme and coda are for the same number of instruments and use the same rows. The first and seventh variations are paired together, as are the second and sixth, and the third and fifth. Only the fourth variation, the central section in the movement, stands alone. This symmetrical arrangement makes the entire movement into one large palindrome. Yet each variation has its own distinctive character and tempo, which gives it a unique personality and provides the movement with momentum and purpose.

Anton Webern

Symphony, Opus 21 (1928)
Second movement, *Sehr ruhig*
CD 11/15

Thema
Sehr ruhig (𝅗𝅥 = ca 54)

I. Variation
lebhafter (𝅗𝅥 = ca 66)

II.Var.
sehr lebhaft (𝅗𝅥 = ca 84)
Kl.
Bkl.
ohne Dämpfer
1. Hrn. 2.
Hrf.
1.Gg.
2.Gg.
Br.
Vlc.
pizz.
arco
rit.

III. Var.
wieder mäßiger (𝅗𝅥 = ca 66)
Kl.
Bkl.
(o. Dpf.)
(m. Dpf.)
1.
Hrn.
2.
Hrf.
pizz.
arco
1. Gg.
2. Gg.
Br.
Vlc.
rit.
tempo
gedämpft
offen
Dämpfer auf

IV. Var.
molto rit.
äußerst ruhig (𝅗𝅥 = ca 40)
molto rit.
Kl.
Bkl.
1. Hrn. 2.
m. Dpf.
(m. Dpf.)
Hrf.
Solo arco
(Solo)
Solo
1. Gg.
2. Gg.
Br.
Vlc.
(Solo)
V. Var.
rit.
sehr lebhaft (𝅗𝅥 = ca 84)
Dämpfer ab
arco Alle (geteilt)
Alle (geteilt)

57
58
59
60
Kl.
Bkl.
1.
Hrn.
2.
Hrf.
1.Gg.
2.Gg.
Br.
Vlc.
pp
p
cresc.
61
62
63
64
mf
p cresc.
mp cresc.
p

VI. Var.
rit. marschmäßig (♩= ca 66), nicht eilen
Kl.
Bkl.
o. Dpf.
1. Hrn. 2.
Hrf.
1. Gg.
2. Gg.
Br.
Vlc.
mf cresc.
gedämpft
offen
dim.
cresc.

Kl.
Bkl.
1.
Hrn.
2.
Hrf.
1.Gg.
2.Gg.
Br.
Vlc.
VII.Var.
etwas breiter
(𝅗𝅥 = ca 54)
rit.
tempo
rit.
tempo rit.
(o.Dpf.)
(m.Dpf.)
pizz.
arco

tempo
rit.
tempo
Coda
rit.
tempo
rit.
tempo
rit.
tempo
Kl.
Bkl.
Hrn.
Hrf.
1. Gg.
2. Gg.
Br.
Vlc.
(m. Dpf.)
(o. Dpf.)
(pizz.)
arco
pizz.
Solo
(Solo)
Solo pizz.
(pizz.)
f dim.
1928

Musical Theater in Germany in the 1920s *Berg and Weill*

184

Alban Berg
Wozzeck (1914–1922), Act 3, scene 2

Alban Berg found the text for his opera *Wozzeck* (1914–22) in a spoken play, *Woyzeck*, by Georg Büchner (1813–37). Büchner based his drama, which was left in an incomplete and fragmentary state, on reports from a sensational murder trial in Leipzig in 1821. In that year, Johann Christian Woyzeck, an impoverished soldier, was found guilty of murdering his lover, a widow named Mrs. Woost. Despite legal arguments that Woyzeck was insane, he was executed by a public beheading in Leipzig in 1824.

In Büchner's play and Berg's adaptation of the libretto, Wozzeck (the name of the title character in early editions of the play) represents the common man, a simple creature at the mercy of a society that is both cruel and indifferent to the powerless. The ghoulish doctor, who represents the dehumanizing element of science, subjects him to medical experiments. Wozzeck's dignity is further assailed by the captain of his regiment, who symbolizes the hypocrisy of people in positions of authority. All that Wozzeck has in the world are his common-law wife, Marie, and their child. Finally, even Marie's love is snatched away from him by the drum major of his regiment, who represents the brutish element of society. In the end, Wozzeck, crazed and demented, brutally murders Marie and commits suicide, leaving their young son an orphan.

The climax of the opera is reached in scene 2 of Act 3. As in other scenes in this act, Berg achieves musical coherence by dwelling on an ever-present musical element—here the tone B♮—that provides unity at the same time that it represents the murderous obsession that grips Wozzeck. Other symbolic motives are heard in the largely through-composed scene, especially at the moment of Marie's death, when the principal motives symbolizing her life rush by in a mad jumble. The singing in this scene is primarily in *Sprechmelodie* ("speech melody"), a style of melodious narration devised by Arnold Schoenberg (Berg's teacher) for his melodrama *Pierrot lunaire* (see no. 176).

The music of the scene is divided into two parts, the first ending after measure 96 and marked there by a long, foreboding silence. The only significant leitmotif of the first part—the descending chromatic figure at the end of measure 77—is associated with Wozzeck's knife. In the second part of the scene (mm. 97–108), an ascending line in the trombones and trumpets is heard as a blood-red moon rises above the marsh. When Wozzeck plunges his knife into Marie's neck, the rhythms become frantic and chaotic; then the music gradually dies away and the scene concludes in silence. During the scene change (mm. 109–121), the music replays the B♮ that was central to the previous passage and also forecasts the central element of the next scene (the rhythms heard in mm. 114–115). The ferocity of the crescendo can be fully experienced only in a live performance; any other medium—CD, video, radio broadcast—can impart only a pale shadow of the effect.

Alban Berg
Wozzeck (1914–1922)
Act 3, scene 2
CD 11/16

Neue 𝅗𝅥 = voriges ♩
(𝅗𝅥 = somit 42-40)
Marie kommt mit **Wozzeck** von rechts

Dort links — geht's in die Stadt. 's ist noch weit. Komm schneller.

Hr gestopft — Es Kl — Gg — flüchtig — non legato — Fag — Pos

Zwei-händig

75

zögernd — Etwas langsamer (♩= 70) aber poco acc. — wieder rit.

Marie: A-ber ich muß fort.

sie setzen sich

Wozzeck: Du sollst da-blei-ben, Ma-rie. Komm, setz' Dich, komm. Bist

Fl — 1 Gg — Hr — Hr — Br — Str allein — Bs Kl — Fag — K Bs — molto — poco — molto

Noch langsameres Tempo (♩= 60)

Wozz: weit ge-gan-gen, Ma-rie. Sollst Dir die

cantabile — lang gezogen — poco cresc — (Str) — Vcl — (Fag)

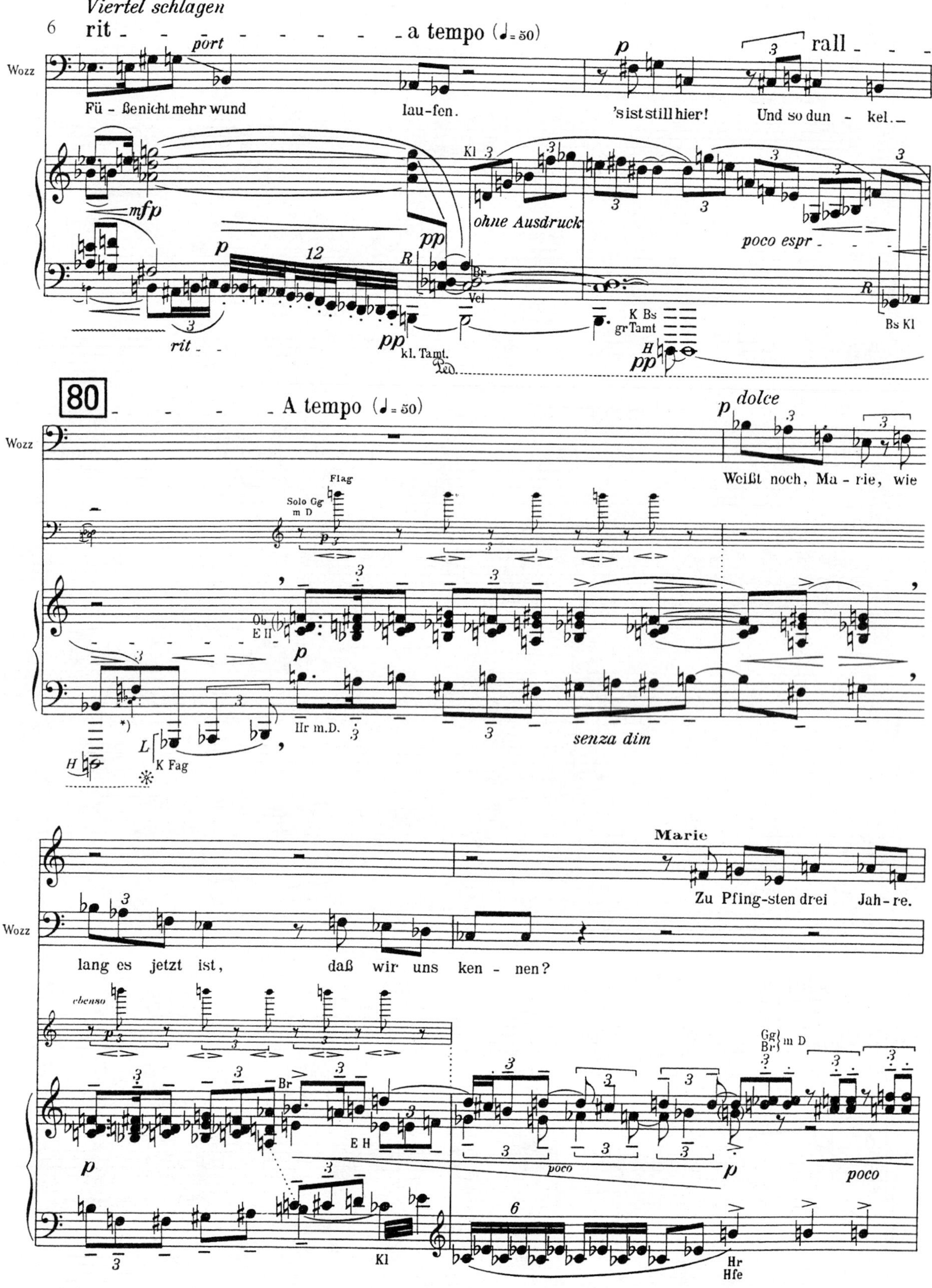

*) *Hier sind die durch Pedal gehaltenen Töne c und des wieder aufzunehmen.*
The notes C and D♭ held by the pedal are to be repeated.

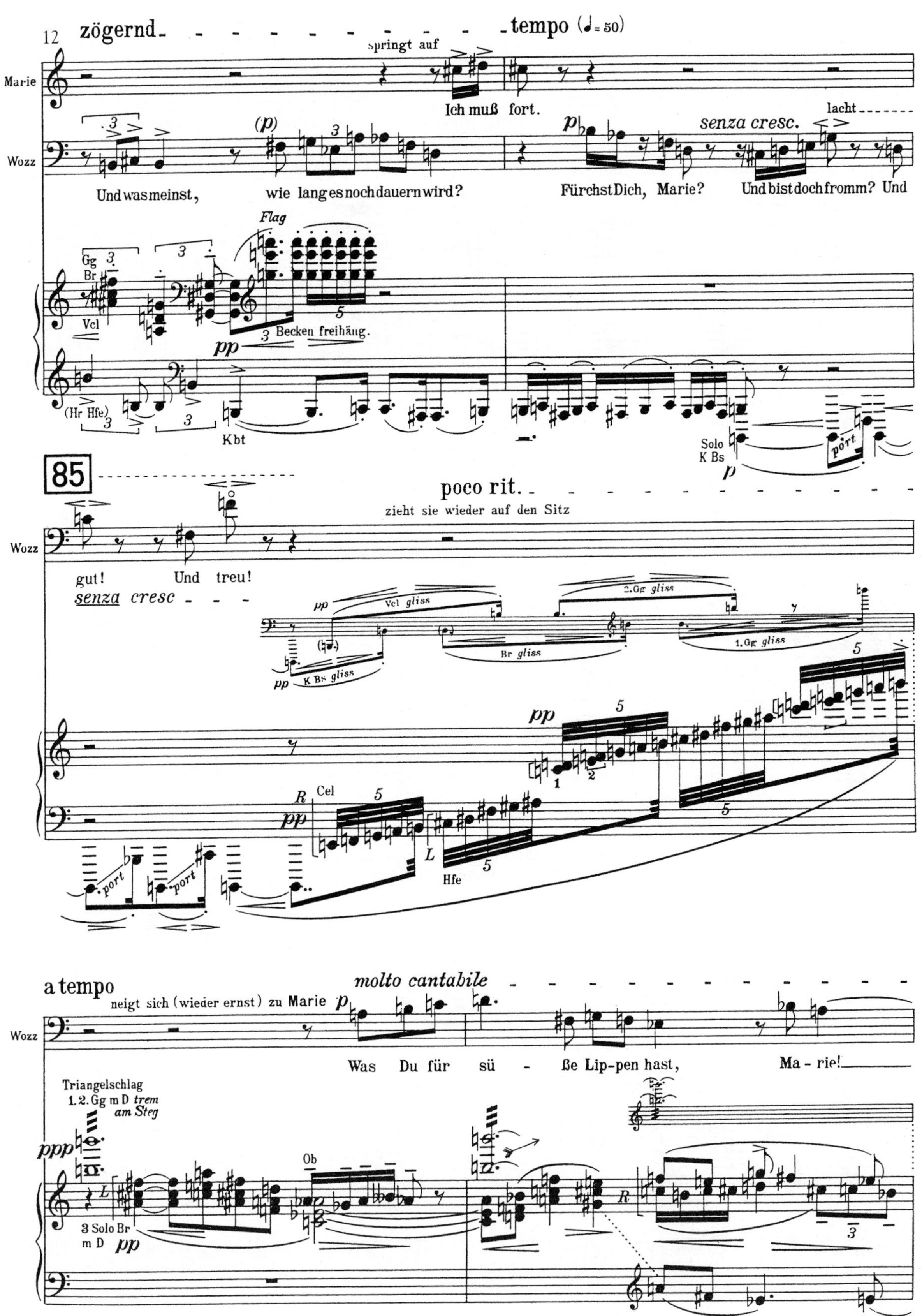
12
zögernd
tempo (♩= 50)
springt auf
Marie
Ich muß fort.
Wozz
(p)
Und was meinst, wie lang es noch dauern wird?
p
senza cresc.
lacht
Fürchst Dich, Marie? Und bist doch fromm? Und
Flag
Gg
Br
Vcl
pp
Becken freihäng.
(Hr Hfe)
Kbt
Solo
K Bs
p
port
85
poco rit.
zieht sie wieder auf den Sitz
gut! Und treu!
senza cresc
pp
Vcl gliss
2.Gg gliss
Br gliss
1.Gg gliss
K Bs gliss
pp
R
Cel
L
Hfe
a tempo
molto cantabile
neigt sich (wieder ernst) zu Marie
Was Du für sü - ße Lip-pen hast, Ma - rie!
Triangelschlag
1.2.Gg m D trem
am Steg
ppp
Ob
3 Solo Br
m D pp

*) Diese 16tel Figur der Hörner immer „etwas hastig."
This 16th figure in the horns is always "somewhat hurried."

95
24
(♩= 60)
Marie
Wozz
Was sagst Du da?
den friert nicht mehr! Dich wird beim Mor - - gen - tau nicht frie - ren.
p
Kl
dim - - ppp
tr
Bs Kl
pp
ppp
Bs Kl
♩=♩ (= 50)
lang
die Bs Klar fortsetzend
pp
langes Schweigen
Nix.
p
Wie der
Der Mond geht auf.
Str
(Str)
ppp
1.Trp m D
2.Trp m D
1.Pos m D
2.Pos m D
3.Pos m D
4.Pos m D
Str
(Tamtam)

29
100
Marie
Mond rot auf - geht!
Wozz
p
Wie ein blu - tig Ei - sen!
(Hfe Gg)
4 Trp (Fltz)
sempre pp
3.Trp m D
(trem)
4.Trp m D
(Str)
ppp
ppp
Ped.
4 Hr gest
Kbt m D
p
pp
Str Hfe
Marie
springt auf
Was zitterst?
Was willst?
mf molto cresc.
zieht ein Messer
Wozz
Ich nicht, Marie! und kein
(Hfe)
Ich nicht, Marie! und kein
8 Pik
Kl
Singstimme fortsetzend
fp
Br col leg
mf
Xyl
Gg pizz
Ob
f
ff
mf
Vcl pizz
Pos dazu
cresc
R
Br col leg
pp
Pke
poco a poco cresc
Kl

33
Marie
Wozz
Hil - - - - - - - - - - fe!
packt sie an und stößt ihr das Messer in den Hals
An-drer auch nicht!
An-drer auch nicht!
4 Trp u 4 Ob
Hfe
Ob dazu
alle Str
pizz
u Hfe
Str Stimme richtig
2 Pkn

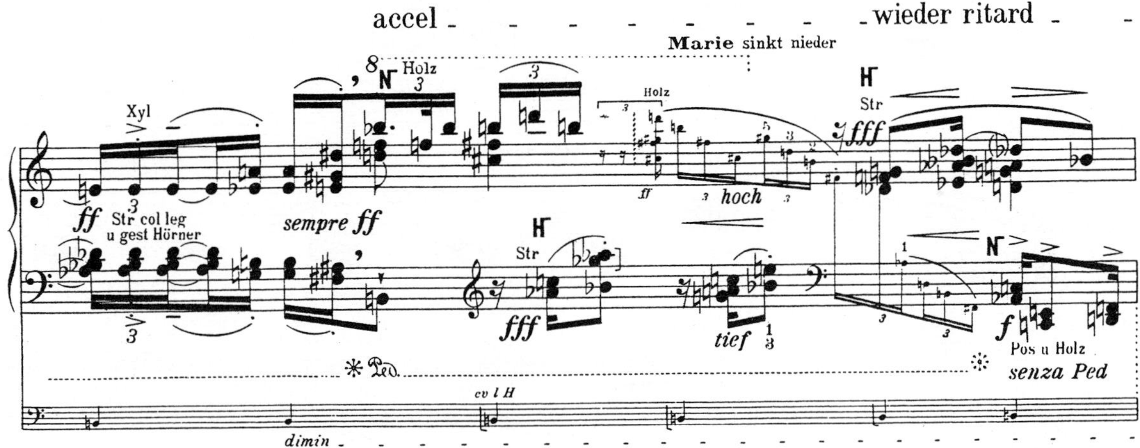
accel - - - - - - - - - - wieder ritard - -
Marie sinkt nieder
Xyl
Holz
Str
Str col leg
u gest Hörner
sempre ff
hoch
tief
Pos u Holz
senza Ped
cv l H
dimin

Str
dim
(senza Ped)
1 Pke allein

105

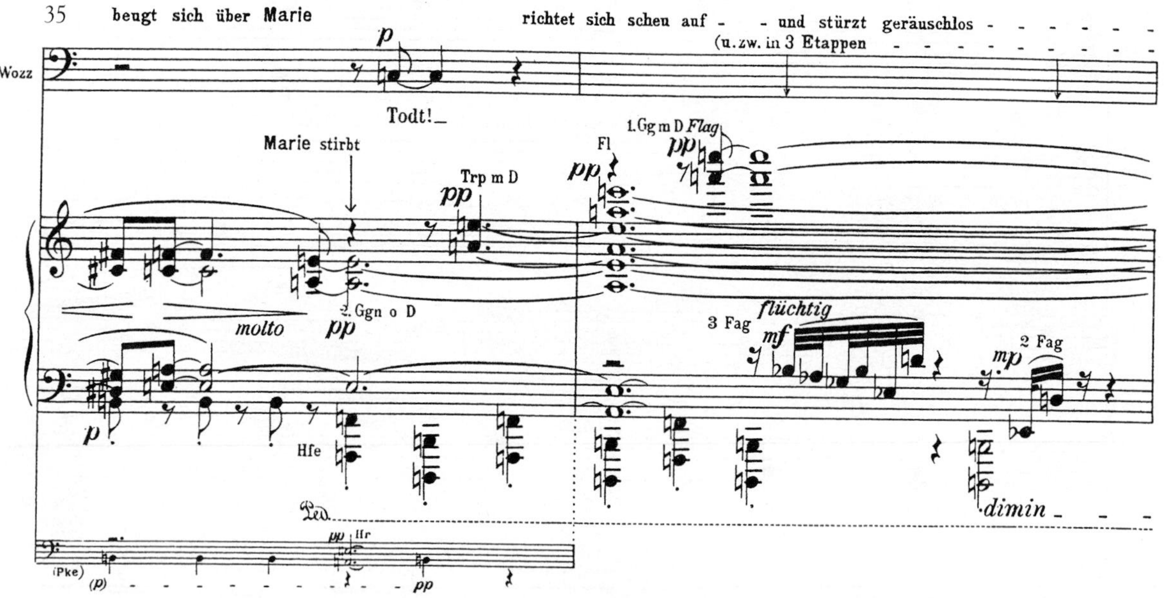
quasi Tempo I (♩ = 40)
35
beugt sich über Marie
richtet sich scheu auf - - und stürzt geräuschlos
(u. zw. in 3 Etappen
Wozz
Todt!
Marie stirbt
Trp m D
Fl
1. Gg m D Flag
2. Ggn o D
molto
3 Fag
flüchtig
2 Fag
Hfe
dimin
Hr
(Pke)

davon
Vorhang zu
Verwandlung
Mäßige 𝅗𝅥 (= ca 80)
Der neue ganze Takt = letztes ♩
(also ca 40)
110
verlöschen
K Fag
Bs Kl
1 Hr m D
1. Ggn
4 Kl
3 Hr o D
Solo Vcl
4 Ob
Tub, Fag
2. Ggn
4 Trp 4 Pos
Solo Gg (m D)
Solo Br
Br
KBs
nach und nach ppp = Einsätze und cresc aller Instrumente mit Ausnahme des Schlagwerks

Tempo, aber etwas schwerer
115
Tutti
GP
sehr rhythmisch
(quasi gr. Trommel)

Marie Dort links geht's in die Stadt. 's ist noch weit. Komm schneller.	Here to the left goes back to town. It's a long way. Come quicker.
Wozzeck Du solst dableiben, Marie. Kom, setz' Dich, komm.	You should stay here, Marie. Come, sit down, come on.
Marie Aber ich muß fort.	But I've got to be going. (*She sits down.*)
Wozzeck Bist weit gegangen, Marie. Sollst Dir die Füße nicht mehr wund laufen. 's ist still hier! Und so dunkel. Weißt noch, Marie, wie lang es jutzt ist, daß wir uns kennen?	You've gone far enough, Marie. You shouldn't hurt your feet any more. It's quiet here! And so dark. Do you remember, Marie, how long it's been since we've known each other?
Marie Zu Pfingsten drei Jahre.	Three years on Whitsunday.
Wozzeck Und was meinst, wie lang es noch dauern wird?	And what do you think? How long will it go on?
Marie Ich muß fort.	(*Leaping up*) I've got to go!
Wozzeck Fürchst Dich, Marie? Und bist doch fromm? Und gut! Und treu! Was Du für süße Lippen hast, Marie! Den Himmel gäb' ich drum und die Seligkeit, wenn ich Dich noch oft so küssen dürft. Aber ich darf nicht! Was zitterst?	Are you afraid, Marie? After all, you're devout, and good, and faithful! (*He draws her down again and leans toward her seriously.*) What sweet lips you have, Marie! (*He kisses her.*) I'd give heaven and salvation if I could keep on kissing them. But I must not! What is this trembling?
Marie Der Nachttau fällt.	The night dew is falling.
Wozzeck Wer kalt ist, den friert nicht mehr! Dich wird beim Morgentau nicht frieren.	(*Whispers to himself*) Whoever is cold will freeze no more! When the morning dew comes, you won't be freezing.
Marie Was sagst Du da?	What are you saying?
Wozzeck Nix.	Nothing.
Marie Wie der Mond roth aufgeht!	See how the moon rises red!
Wozzeck Wie ein blutig Eisen!	Like a bloody knife!
Marie Was zitterst? Was willst?	What is this trembling? (*Wozzeck draws a knife.*) What do you want? (*She leaps up.*)
Wozzeck Ich nicht, Marie! und kein Andrer auch nicht!	If not I, Marie, then no one else!
Marie Hülfe!	Help! (*He grabs her and drives the knife into her neck. She sinks down; he bends over her.*)
Wozzeck Todt!	Dead! (*He straightens up and rushes quietly off.*)

185

Kurt Weill
The Threepenny Opera (1928)
"Ballad of Mac the Knife"

In the year 1928 the Berlin dramatist Bertolt Brecht and his assistant Elisabeth Hauptmann were preparing a revival of John Gay's famous ballad opera *The Beggar's Opera* (1728) (see no. 119). Brecht's idea was to update Gay's biting satire of society and politics in eighteenth-century London so that it would apply to those of Germany during the Weimar Republic—the post–World War I government that preceded Adolf Hitler and the Nazi party. In Brecht's vision, as in Gay's, hypocrisy reigns everywhere. The police are corrupt, criminals run free, churches are filled with hypocrites, and people generally don't care. Brecht also wanted to update the music for his revival, so he turned to Kurt Weill, who composed songs and choruses in a light style. The result was *Die Dreigroschenoper* (*The Threepenny Opera*), which premiered in Berlin in 1928 and immediately became one of the greatest successes in musical theater of the entire twentieth century.

Brecht's conception of theater was different from that of operas or musical comedies of the time. He did not want the drama to create an illusion that could transport the audience to some remote time or place or to absorb it in any imaginary story. Those who attended early performances of *The Threepenny Opera* knew that they were in Berlin in the 1920s. The singers did not impersonate characters in the story so much as interrupt the narrative to comment on the proceedings. This is the effect of the first song in the show. A balladeer stands and speaks to the audience: "First, you'll hear a ballad about the robber Macheath, known as 'Mac the Knife.'" He then sings his ballad, a strophic pop song, to the accompaniment of a small pit band. The German title for this song, "Moritat von Mackie Messer" (Messer is the German word for "knife"), has a double meaning. "Moritat" can be translated as "street ballad" or as "murderous deed"; both translations are appropriate because it is a song about murder, robbery, and rape. The song has a simple strophic form, although the accompaniment becomes thicker and more animated as it proceeds. Originally, three additional stanzas were present, but these were eliminated in the first edition of the music. Weill's desire to bridge the gulf between serious and popular music was completely successful. His *Threepenny Opera* is now performed in both opera houses and Broadway theaters, and the "Ballad of Mac the Knife" quickly became a popular jazz standard.

Kurt Weill
The Threepenny Opera (1928)
"Ballad of Mac the Knife"
CD 11/17

Blues-Tempo (𝅗𝅥 = 66)
Ausrufer

Und der Hai-fisch, der hat Zäh-ne, und die trägt er im Ge-
schö-nen blau-en Sonn-tag liegt ein to-ter Mann am

(In der Art eines Leierkastens)

mf

Arf.

-sicht, und Mac-heath der hat ein Mes-ser, doch das Mes-ser
Strand und ein Mensch geht um die Ek-ke, den man Mak-kie

14

Arf.

1. 2. A

sieht man nicht. An 'nem
Mes-ser nennt. Und Schmul Mei-er bleibt ver-

p

Arf.

-schwun-den, und so man-cher rei-che Mann, und sein

26
Arf.
Geld hat Mak-kie Mes - ser, dem man nichts be - - wei - sen
kann. Jen - ny Tow - ler ward ge - fun - den mit 'nem
Mes - ser in der Brust, und am Kai geht Mak - kie
44
Mes - ser, der von al - lem nichts ge - wußt. Und das
gro - ße Feu-er in So - ho, sie - ben Kin - der und ein
B
C
mf
p

56
Arf.
Greis, in der Men - ge Mak - kie Messer, den man nichts fragt und
der nichts weiß.
D
Und die min - der - - - jähr'ge Wit - we,
mf
de - ren Na - men je - der weiß,
f
wach - te auf und war ge -
76
-schän - det, Mak - kie, wel - ches war dein Preis,
E
p subito
wach - te auf und
(espr.)
war ge - schän - det, Mak - kie, wel - ches war dein Preis?
pp

Und der Haifisch, der hat Zähne,
und die trägt er im Gesicht,
und Macheath der hat ein Messer,
doch das Messer sieht man nicht.

An 'nem schönen blauen Sonntag
liegt ein toter Mann am Strand,
und ein Mensch geht um die Ekke,
den man Makkie Messer nennt.

Und Schmul Meier bleibt verschwunden,
und so mancher reiche Mann,
und sein Geld hat Makkie Messer,
dem man nichts beweisen kann.

Jenny Towler ward gefunden
mit 'nem Messer in der Brust,
und am Kai geht Makkie Messer,
der von allem nichts gewußt

Und das große Feuer in Soho,
sieben Kinder und ein Greis,
in der Menge Makkie Messer,
den man nichts fragt und der nichts weiß.

Und die minderjähr'ge Witwe,
deren Namen jeder weiß,
wachte auf und war geschändet,
Makkie, welches war dein Preis?

And the shark, he's got teeth,
and he packs them in his face,
and Macheath, he's got a knife,
but no one sees that knife.

On one fine Sunday
there lies a dead man on the bank,
and a man goes round the corner,
a man whose name is Mac the Knife.

And Schmul Meier is still missing,
like many a rich man,
and Mac the Knife has his money,
but no one can prove it.

Jenny Towler was found
with a knife in her chest,
and on the waterfront walks Mac the Knife,
who knows nothing about it.

And the great fire in Soho—
seven children and an old man lost.
Mac the Knife's in the crowd
but no one questions him or knows a thing.

And the underage widow
whose name everyone knows,
woke up and was raped.
Mac, what was your price?

Béla Bartók and Hungarian Folk Music

186

Béla Bartók
Eight Hungarian Folksongs
"Fekete főd" (c1907)

The artistic folk song arrangement rose to great importance among twentieth-century composers. Arrangements of folk songs had been made by leading musicians since the time of Beethoven and Haydn, but in the hands of modern composers, including Maurice Ravel, Benjamin Britten, and Béla Bartók, such music became a major vehicle for expressing original ideas. Bartók arranged Hungarian folk music in numerous collections for solo voice and chorus as well as for piano. The folkish text is omitted in these latter compositions.

His *Eight Hungarian Folksongs*, published in 1922, is an arrangement of peasant tunes that Bartók had noted down during his trips to Transylvania (in modern-day Romania) in 1906–1907. On these excursions, he would set up one of Thomas Edison's early phonographs and ask peasants to sing into a cone, recording their singing onto wax disks. Later, Bartók would listen to these songs over and over again, transcribing every nuance. Ethnomusicologists still engage in the same activity today, but fortunately have much better equipment. In Transylvania, Bartók found a pocket of isolated Hungarian culture among the Székely people, who, he found, preserved ancient Hungarian music in an unusually pure form.

The tune of "Fekete főd" has the starkly simple musical materials that appealed to Bartók. Its tones are drawn entirely from a single pentatonic scale, and it uses the flexible "parlando-rubato" rhythm characteristic of Hungarian ballad tunes. It differs from the typical Hungarian peasant song only in that its two stanzas are each shortened from the normal four to two lines each. Bartók's harmonization is a masterpiece of originality in an unassuming guise. The composer at first restricts the accompaniment to the pentatonic tones of the melody, but he then gradually adds pitches from outside the scale. The billowing arpeggios at the opening of each stanza evoke the sound of the cimbalom, a Hungarian dulcimer.

Béla Bartók
Eight Hungarian Folksongs
"Fekete főd" (c1907)
CD 11/18

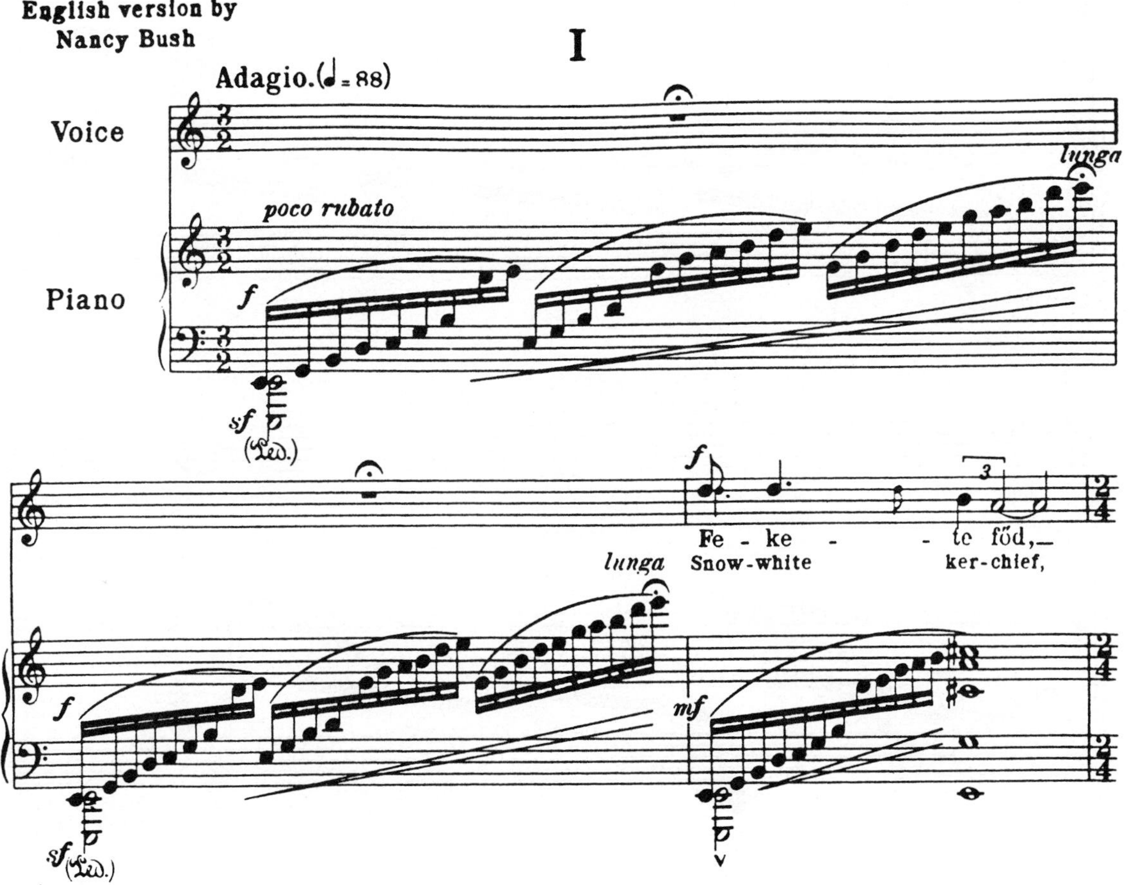

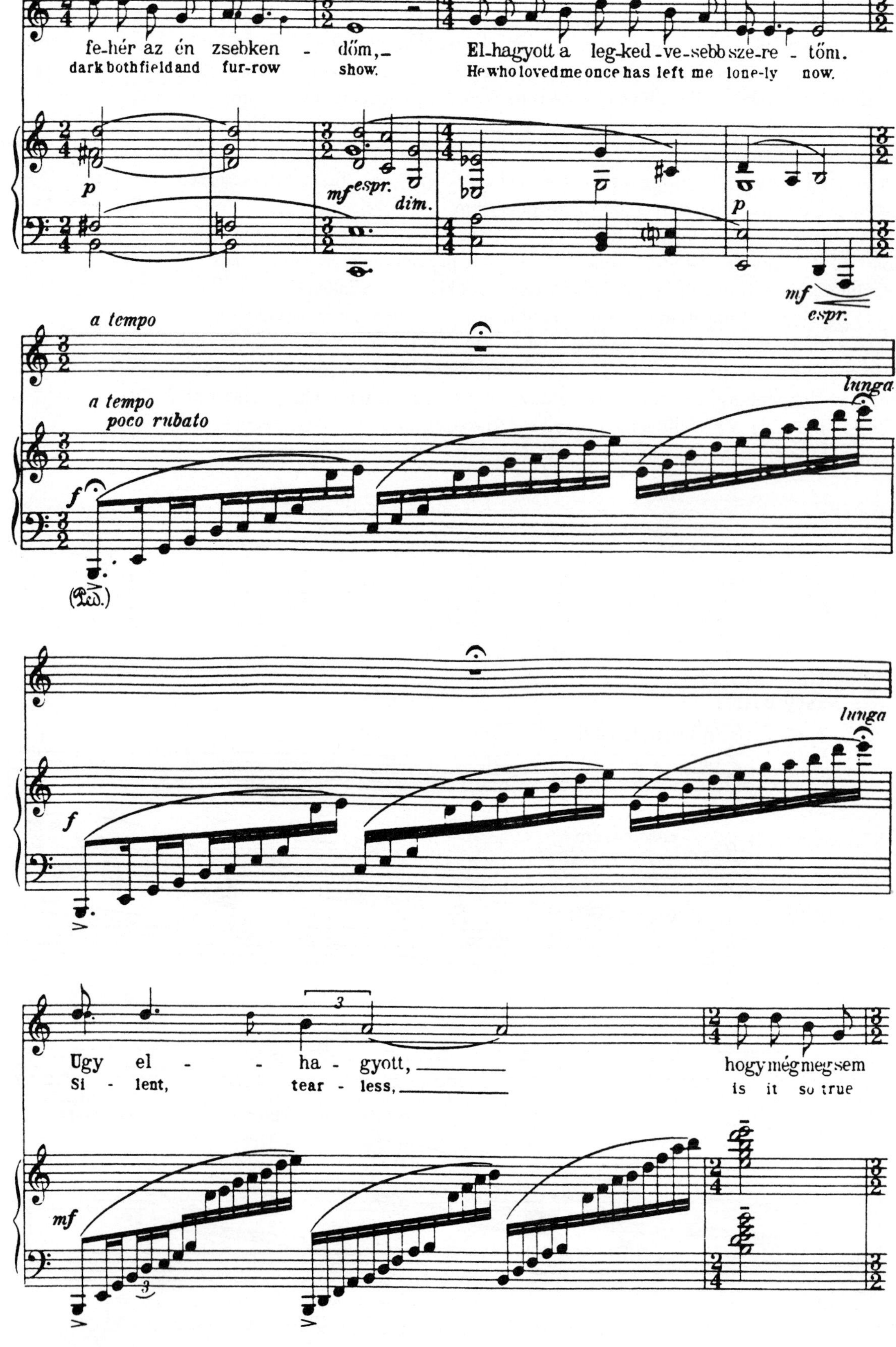
fe-hér az én zsebken - dőm,
dark both field and fur-row show.
El-hagyott a leg-ked-ve-sebb sze-re - tőm.
He who loved me once has left me lone-ly now.
p
mf espr.
dim.
p
mf
espr.
a tempo
a tempo
poco rubato
f
lunga
f
lunga
Ugy el - - ha - gyott,
Si - lent, tear - less,
hogy még meg sem
is it so true
mf

187

Béla Bartók

Concerto for Orchestra (1943)

First movement, *Andante non troppo; Allegro vivace*

In 1943 Bartók was hospitalized in New York City, undergoing tests to diagnose the cause of his lingering—and ultimately fatal—illness. The composer, irritated by physicians he considered incompetent, received a welcome visit from the conductor of the Boston Symphony Orchestra, Serge Koussevitsky, who offered a commission to write a work for orchestra. It was just the tonic Bartók needed. He began to compose the Concerto for Orchestra on 15 August, while residing at a cottage in the Adirondack Mountains. It was completed three months later to the day, 15 October, and the premiere took place a year later on 1 December 1944. Koussevitsky was delighted with the composition and told Bartók, who was present for the rehearsals as well as the performance, that it was the best piece of orchestral music to appear since the end of World War I. It was warmly received by the audience and most of the critics gave it a favorable review. Since then it has become one of the most frequently performed pieces of twentieth-century orchestral music. The reasons for its popularity are plain enough: It makes brilliant use of the coloristic resources of the orchestra, and its musical materials are original while always appealing directly to the audience.

Bartók's title, "Concerto," refers to the soloistic and virtuosic treatment of the orchestra's instruments—for example, the flute and trumpets near the beginning of the first movement—although the form of the work is generally closer to that of the symphony than to the Classical concerto. Bartók wrote the word *Introduzione* at the beginning of the first movement, although it is not clear whether this word applies to the entire movement or to its slow opening passage. As in many comparable introductions in the symphonic works of Beethoven or Haydn, the opening section of the Concerto for Orchestra is free in form and presents motives that will subsequently be spun into main themes. A decidedly Classical symphonic logic arises in the movement in Bartók's adaptation of sonata form and his intensely organic interconnecting of themes and motives. At the same time, echoes of Hungarian folk music are heard in the pentatonic scales of the opening and the folklike rhythmic ideas.

Introduction	Exposition		Development	Recapitulation	
(I)	Theme I	Theme II	see below	Theme II	Theme I
1	76	154	231	396	488

The development brings back all the major themes and spins them into new shapes. Imitative processes such as stretto, canon, and fugue play a prominent role in developing these ideas. Canonic passages are differentiated from fugatos in that canonic entries all come in on the same pitch sequence, while fugato entries use the subject-and-answer method found in the Baroque fugue (see Bach's Fugue in C Minor, no. 114).

Development							
Theme I	stretto	canon	Theme II	Theme I	fugato	canon	Theme I
231	242	248	272	313	342	363	386

Béla Bartók
Concerto for Orchestra (1943)
First movement, *Andante non troppo; Allegro vivace*
CD 11/19

12
Flts. I,II
pp
Vlns.I
(sim.)
Vlns.II
(sim.)
(sim.)
Vls.
Vcs.
D.Bs.
stringendo - - - tornando - - - - - - al Tempo I. (♩= 64)
22
30
p
ord.
unis.
p
pp
pp

35
Fl. I
pp
Timp.
p
Vlns. I
Vlns. II
Vls.
pp
Vcs. (div.)
pp
D.Bs.
1' 38''
pp
Hn. I in F
p
I, III
Trpts. in C
II
pp
Timp.
Vls.
Vcs. (div.)
D.Bs.

44
Hn.I in F
dim.
I, III
Trpts. in C
II
dim.
Trb. I
p
dim.
Timp.
44
Vls.
Vcs.
(div.)
D.Bs.
1'
51
♩ = 73
Flts. I, II
f
Obs. I, II
f
Clts. I, II
in B♭
Hns. I, II
in F
51
senza
sord.
div.
Vlns. I
f
senza sord.
div.
Vlns. II
f
Vls.
f
unis.
Vcs.
f
D.Bs.
f

58
Flts. I, II
Obs. I, II
Clts. I, II in B♭
Hns. I, II in F
Timp.
58
unis.
Vlns. I
cresc.
Vlns. II
cresc.
unis.
Vls.
più f
Vcs.
più f
D.Bs.
più f
poco a poco accelerando
66
Obs. I, II
mf, cresc.
a 2
Clts. I, II in B♭
cresc.
Bsns. I, II
mf
cresc.
a 2
Hns. I, II in F
mf, cresc.
Trpts. I, II in C
mf, ma marcato
Timp.
p, cresc.
IV
poco a poco accelerando
66
Vlns. I
Vlns. II
Vls.
mf, cresc.
Vcs.
mf, cresc.
D.Bs.
mf, cresc.

♩. = 76
Flts. I, II
cresc.
ff
a 2
Obs. I, II
Clts. I, II in B♭
a 2
Bsns. I, II
Hns. I, II in F
f
Trpts. I, II in C
Timp.
Vls.
Vcs.
D. Bs.
50"
76
Allegro vivace, ♩. = 83
Obs. I, II
Clts. I, II in B♭
Bsns. I, II
I, III
Hns. in F
II, IV
a 2
Vlns. I
Vlns. II
Vls.
Vcs.
D. Bs.

86
molto ritenuto
a tempo
95
Flts. I, II
Obs. I, II
Clts. I, II in B♭
Bsns. I, II
I, III
Hns. in F
II, IV
Trbs. I, II
Tuba
Timp.
Vlns. I
Vlns. II
Vls.
Vcs.
D.Bs.
a 2
cresc.
IV
102

110
a 2
Obs. I, II
a 2
Clts. I, II in B♭
div.
unis.
Vlns. I
Vlns. II
Vls.
Vcs.
D. Bs.
mf
122
a 2
p, cresc.
f
Obs. I, II
Clts. I, II in B♭
Bsns. I, II
Hn. I in F
122
cresc.
mf, cresc.
Vlns. I
Vlns. II
Vls.
Vcs.
D. Bs.

135
Flts. I, II
Obs. I, II
Clts. I, II in B♭
Bsns. I, II
Hn. I in F
Trb. I
a 2
f
mf
135
Vlns. I
Vlns. II
Vls.
Vcs.
D. Bs.
mf
142
Fl. I
Ob. I
Cl. I in B♭
Trb. I
f
dim.
pp
142
Vlns. I
Vlns. II
Vls.
Vcs.
dim.
p
1'

149
poco a poco più
155
Tranquillo, ♩. = 70
Fl. I
Ob. I
p, dolce
simile
con sord.
Hns. I, II in F
pp
Harp I
p, distinto
div.
Vlns. I
p
non div.
IV III
sim.
div.
Vcs.
p
165
Ob. I
Hns. I, II in F
Harp I
p
gliss.
Vlns. I
Vcs.
175
181
Ob. I
p
Clts. I, II in A
p, dolce
p
simile
senza sord.
Hns. I, II in F
p
Harp I
p
p
unis.
Vlns. I
p
Vlns. II
p
non div.
Vcs.
p

192
Flts. I, II
Ob. I
Clts. I, II in A
dim.
B. Cl. in B♭
I. II
Hns. in F
III
Harp I
con sord.
punta d'arco div. 2 Vlns. in each group
Vlns. I
Vlns. II
Vls.
Vcs.
198
Cl. I in A

1591

*always use a soft (cardboard) mute.

231
Tempo I. (♩. = 83)
237
Flts. I, II
a 2
ff
Obs. I, II, III
a 3
Clts. I, II, III in B♭
Bsns. I, II
Bsns. III
senza sord.
Hns. in F I, III
Hns. in F II, IV
(senza sord.)
f
Trpts. I, II in C
Trbs. I, II
Tuba
Timp.
Tutti unis.
Vlns. I
Vlns. II
Vls.
Vcs.
D. Bs.
f sub.
1'25"

242
Picc.
Flts. I, II
I, II
Obs.
III
Clts. I, II, III in B♭
Bsns. I, II, III
I, III
Hns. in F
II, IV
Trpts. I, II in C
Trbs. I, II
Tuba
Timp.
Vlns. I
Vlns. II
Vls.
Vcs.
a 2
a 3
ff
f
p
mf
cresc.

248
254
Picc.
a 2
Flts. I, II
ff
I, II
Obs.
III
f, ben marc.
Clts. I, II, III in B♭
a 3
Bsns. I, II, III
I, II
f
f, ben marc.
I, III
Hns. in F
II, IV
Trpts. I, II in C
Timp.
Vlns. I
Vlns. II
f, ben marc.
Vls.
Vcs.
Obs. I, II
Clts. I, II in B♭
Bsns. I, II
D. Bs.
[f]

pochiss. allarg.
265
I
Flts.
II, III
a 2
Obs. I, II
Clts. I, II in B♭
Bsns. I, II, III
a 3
[f]
ff
I, III
Hns. in F
II, IV
p
cresc.
f
Trbs. I, II
Timp.
Vlns. I
Vlns. II
Vls.
Vcs.
D. Bs.
f cresc.
gliss.
30''
272
Tranquillo, ♩. = 76-70
pochiss. rall.
Cl. I in B♭
p, dolce
pp

288
a tempo
Fl. I
C.A.
p, dolce
Cl. I in B♭
288
Vlns. I
Vlns. II
Vls.
Vcs.
300
306
rit.
Picc.
Fl. I
C.A.
Cl. I in B♭
B. Cl. in B♭
p, dolce
300
306
rit.
Vlns. I
Vls.
pizz.
Vcs.
D. Bs.
43"

313
Tempo I., ♩. = 83-90
323
Flts. I, II
Obs. I, II
Clts. I, II in B♭
Bsns. I, II
a 2
Hns. I, II in F
ossia
I
Trbs.
II
f, ben marc.
Timp.
313
Tempo I., ♩. = 83-90
323
Vlns. I
Vlns. II
Vls.
Vcs.
arco
D. Bs.
329
335
I
Trpts. in C
II
Trpts. in C
III
f, ben marc.
I
Trbs.
II

342
349
Flts. I,II,III
Obs. I,II,III
Clts.I,II,III in B♭
I
Bsns.
II,III
I,III
Hns. in F
II,IV
a 2
f, ben marc.
ossia
I,II
Trpts.in C
III
f ben marc.
mf
I,II
Trbs.
III
Timp.
Vlns. I
Vlns. II
Vls.
Vcs.
D.Bs.
354
359
364
Hns. I,III in F
Trpts.in C
f, ben marc.
marc.
Trbs.

376
I
Trpts. in C
II
Trpts. in C
III
marc.
I
Trbs.
II
Trbs.
III
f, marc.
marc.
f, marc.
380
386
Flts. I, II
a 2
ff
Obs. I, II, III
a 3
Clts. I, II, III in B♭
Bsns. I, II, III
I, III
Hns. in F
II, IV
cresc.
f cresc.
I, II
Trpts. in C
III
Trbs. I, II
Trb. III Tuba
f
380
386
Vlns. I
Vlns. II
non div.
p, cresc.
Vls.
mf, cresc.
Vcs.
non div.
p, cresc.
D.Bs.
f
ff

396
pochiss.allarg. Tranquillo, ♩. = 70
402
Picc.
Flts.I,II
Obs. I,II,III
Clts.I,II,III in B♭
Bsns. I,II,III
Hns.in F I,III
II,IV
con sord.
Trpts.in C I,II
III
Trbs.I,II
Trb.III Tuba
Timp.
with the thick end of the Side Drum stick.
Cym.
Harp I
p, espr.
Vlns.I
Vlns.II
Vls.
Vcs.
D.Bs
pizz.
55"

413
Cl. I in B♭
Hns.II,IV in F
Harp I
Vlns. I
Vlns. II
D.Bs.
424
Flts.I,II
p, espr.
Ob.I
p, espr.
Cl.I in B♭
Hns.II,IV in F
gliss.
Harp I
p
4
424
con sord.
5
Vlns.I
mf
p
p
Vlns.II
mf
p
pizz.
arco
Vls.
p
con sord.
5
Vcs.
mf
p
p
div.
arco
arco
pizz.
D.Bs.
mf
p

Flts.I,II
Ob.I
Cl. I in B♭
p, espr.
Harp I
Vlns.I
Vls.
Vcs.
D.Bs.
438
Flts.I,II
Ob.I
Cl. I in B♭
Harp I
f
near the sound-board with an appropriately shaped wooden (if possible metal) stick
Harp II
f
438
Vlns.I
Vlns.II
mf
Vls.
mf
Vcs.
mf
[unis.]
D.Bs.
mf

447
Fl.I
Ob.I
Cl.I in B♭
più p
più p
più p
Vlns.II
Vls.
Vcs.
D.Bs.
pizz.
senza sord.
arco
456
Fl.I
Obs.I,II
C.A.
Cl.I in B♭
B.Cl. in B♭
Trpts. I,II,III in C
con sord.
Harp I
456
4 soli con sord.
2 soli
Vlns.I (div.)
4 soli div. in 2 con sord.
2 soli
4 soli div. in 2 con sord.
Tutti div. in 3
Vlns.II
sul ponticello
Vls.
Vcs.
D.Bs.

467
sempre più tranquillo
Flts. I,II,III
I. II. a 2
p
più p
C.A.
Clts.I,II in B♭
B.Cl. in B♭
con sord.
Hn.I in F
mf, ma marc.
mf
Trpts. I,II,III in C
Harp I
f
4 soli div. in 2
Vlns.I
Vlns.II
Vls.
Vcs.
mf, ma marc.
D.Bs.
476
482
♩ = 60
accelerando
Flts. I,II,III
pp
a 3
Ob.I
Clts.I,II in B♭
Bsns.I,II
f, cresc.
Hns.I,III in F
senza sord.
a 2 (senza sord.)
cresc.
Tutti senza sord.
Vlns.I
Vls.
Vcs.
D.Bs.

488
al
Tempo I. (♩. = 83)
a 2
ff
a 2
f
ff
a 2
f
ff
a 2
Flts. I, II
Obs. I, II
Clts. I, II in B♭
I, II
Bsns.
III
ff
f, cresc.
ff
Hns. I, III in F
a 2
ff
I, II
Trbs.
III
f
f
Tuba
f
Timp.
488
al
Tempo I. (♩. = 83)
Vlns. I
cresc.
ff
ordinario
senza sord.
Vlns. II
f, cresc.
ff
Vls.
cresc.
ff
Vcs.
cresc.
ff
D. Bs.
cresc.
ff
1' 27"

494
500
Flts. I,II
a 2
ff
Obs.
I,II
III
Clts.in B♭
Bsns.I,II
Hns. in F
I,III
II,IV
senza sord.
f
Trpt.I in C
Trbs.
Tuba
Vlns.I
Vlns.II
Vls.
Vcs.
D.Bs.

509
Obs. I
II
Obs.
III
I
Clts.in B♭
II
Clts.in B♭
III
a 2
I, II
Bsns.
III
f
cresc.
I, III
Hns. in F
II, IV
a 2
Timp.
p, cresc.
Vlns. I
f, cresc.
Vlns. II
Vls.
Vcs.
f, cresc.
D.Bs.
ff

514
521
Picc.
I
Flts.
II
I
Obs.
II
Obs.
III
I
Cltsin B♭
II
Cltsin B♭
III
I, II
Bsns.
III
I, III
Hns. in F
II, IV
Trpts I, II, III in C
Trbs. I, II
Trb. III Tuba
Timp.
Vlns. I
Vlns. II
Vls.
Vcs.
D. Bs.
f, cresc.
f cresc.
ff
a 2
a 3
senza sord.
ossia
gliss.
22"

Early Jazz

188

Scott Joplin
"Maple Leaf Rag" (1899)

"Maple Leaf Rag" is perhaps the most famous example of a style of American popular music called ragtime. In works of this type, an accompaniment in a regular rhythm is placed beneath a syncopated, or "ragged," melody. Although ragtime rhythms were encountered at the turn of the twentieth century in many types of songs and dances, especially the genre known as the "Cakewalk," the idiom gradually became associated with a marchlike piano character piece called a "rag."

Rags were among the few types of jazz or pre-jazz that were composed and published as sheet music. Initially, improvisation played little if any role in how they were performed. Sales of this particular rag earned Scott Joplin a tidy sum of money during his lifetime. In an age when most publishers paid the composer a flat fee for each rag, Joplin retained a lawyer who prepared a contract that entitled him to a penny per copy. If the composition flopped, Joplin would earn virtually nothing. However, "Maple Leaf Rag" was a spectacularly successful hit, and within ten years, close to 500,000 copies had been sold. It has been estimated that a decade after its publication Joplin was earning about $600 per year off the royalties—about the same as the annual wage of a typical industrial laborer. While it may not seem like much today, it covered his basic living expenses and allowed him to spend more time composing.

Joplin's "Maple Leaf Rag" shows the main features of the ragtime style. The music has the duple meter, moderate tempo, and form of a band march. The piano is treated percussively, and our attention is primarily drawn to the infectious syncopated rhythms of the pianist's right hand. "Maple Leaf Rag" uses the classic rag format: **AABBACCDD**. Each theme consists of sixteen bars and the last two (**C** and **D**) form the trio section. The **A** theme, characterized by an ascending motive, is balanced by **B**, which is based on a descending chromatic line. It is not until the trio that the composition modulates away from A♭ major. The **C** theme is placed in the subdominant key of D♭ major, but the harmony returns to A♭ for the final strain (**D**), which is in a strutting, marchlike style.

Note: Because most early jazz and blues recordings were improvisatory, scores are not provided for CD 12/2–12/5.

Scott Joplin
"Maple Leaf Rag" (1899)
CD 12/1

Tempo di marcia.

f

p

r. h.

l. h.

l. h.

r. h.

mf

1.

2.

17
f stacc.
1.
2.
33
f
p
r. h.
l. h.
mf

49
TRIO.
1.
2.
65
1.
2.

Paul Hindemith and Music in Nazi Germany

189

Paul Hindemith
Mathis der Maler (1935)
Scene 6, entrance 3

Paul Hindemith composed his opera *Mathis der Maler* (*Mathis the Painter*) between 1933 and 1935, just when the Nazis had taken control of the German government and had begun to transform every aspect of German intellectual life. Hindemith, who wrote the libretto himself, based his opera on the life of the Renaissance painter Matthias Grünewald, who, like Hindemith, lived at a time of social turmoil so intense that it forced artists to reassess the meaning of their work.

In Hindemith's libretto, Mathis questions the relevance of his career as a painter. In a complex dream, the painter sees himself as St. Anthony, who, in the desert seeking seclusion, was tempted by the devil. As the dream unfolds, Mathis sees St. Anthony seek the advice of another hermit, St. Paul of the Desert, reproducing a meeting that was depicted in one of Grünewald's most famous paintings.

In the climactic third entrance of scene 6, St. Anthony and St. Paul examine the dilemma, and the hermit commands St. Anthony (Mathis) to serve God and humanity by fulfilling his calling as an artist. This part of the scene (Rehearsal F to G) is set in rondo form. Subsequently, Paul elaborates upon this advice in an aria that concludes with the exhortation: "Go forth and create!" Hindemith set this aria in the form of strophic variations, the third being the freest in style. Anthony sees the wisdom of this advice, and the two saints conclude the scene by singing an ecstatic duet. After an introduction, the duet is subdivided into three sections (six bars after Rehearsal 97, Rehearsal 99, and Rehearsal 101) and a coda on "Alleluia."

Paul Hindemith
Mathis der Maler (1935)
Scene 6, entrance 3
CD 12/6

Slow, free in measure
Langsam, frei im Zeitmaß
Paulus (Kardinal Albrecht)

St Anthony lies prostrate on the ground. St. Paul (Cardinal Albrecht), clad in a garment made of bulrushes, helps him rise.
Antonius liegt am Boden. Paulus (Kardinal Albrecht), in geflochtenem Schilfkleid, hebt ihn auf.

(F) *mf* freely frei

Mein Bru - der, ent - rei - ße dich der höl - len-tie-fen Qual.
My Broth - er, a - rise and flee the hell of your de - spair.

81

Antonius (Mathis)

p Laß_ mich im Pfuh - le un - ter - ge - hen, ich bin nicht wert, daß du aus-streckst dei - ne Hand.
Un - to the deep — I must sur - rend - er, with - draw your hand from one so de - praved and worth - less!

Slow, free in measure
Langsam, frei im Zeitmaß

mf *f*

livelier
Lebhafter
Paulus (Albrecht)

Dei - nes Un - werts Be - wußt - sein er - höht dich,
Your hu - mi - li - ty speaks in your fav - or,

82

calm again
Wieder ruhig

mf

all dein töd - li - cher Krampf wird ge - löst,
ease your mind and un - burd - en your-self.

f *p*

Pls (A)
nimmst du mich als dei-nen Beich-ti-ger.
If you wish, you may con-fess to me!
Antonius (Mathis)
mf
Die heil-gen Män-ner
Our hon-ored Saints have
Slow, in firm tempo
Langsam, festes Zeitmaß (♩ 54)
pp
mf
Ant (A)
83
fand der Tod wie al-le Men-schen. Gleichwohl le-ben sie. Ich, der ich le-be, bin ge-
had to die, just like all oth-er men, yet they stay a-live. I am a-live, yet live no
Paulus (Albrecht)
Und wie starbst du?
How did you die?
Ant (M)
mf
storben. Ich tö-te-te mich selbst und weiß nicht wie. Was ich auch
long-er. I killed myself, and yet I know not how. If to the
mf

84
freely
p frei
Pls (A)
Du warst zu
You were too
Ant (M)
trieb, ob es in Got - tes Au - ge gut, ob ü - bel ist, mir erschien es recht.
Lord some of my deeds seemed sin - ful, I have al-ways done what I thought was right.
eilig, hast nicht gut be - dacht. Set - ze dich hier, bis ich dir klär - te, was trü - be scheint.
hast - y, did not stop to think. Sit by my side so I may show you where you went wrong.
Moderately moved
Mäßig bewegt (♩ bis 104)
They sit facing each other, approximating the scene shown on the altar piece.
Sie sitzen sich gegenüber. Das ist ungefähr die Szene des Altarbildes.
85
In der Hut deiner Ar - beit leb-test du. Geborgen warst du. Mei-sterschaft trug dich, der Vä - ter Kenntnis.
All ab - sorbed by your work, you lived in peace, had found a shel - ter. Braced by the past, you be-came a master.
Du warst, da du tie-fer schaust als an-dre, den Kreis bald ab - ge-schrit-
And so, to see far-ther yet than oth-ers, you stepped out-side the nar-row

Pls (A)
ten, der dir nach Ü-ber-lie-fe-rung und Standesbrauch ge-steckt__ war. Weil du all-zu
fold, in which some long e-stab-lished rules would gent-ly have con-fined__ you. Yet, who stands a -
86
leading
einleiten
fest standst, wank - test du__ Dich - berühr-
- lone will start to sway.__ Wand' - ring in
Slower
Langsamer - The same crotchets
Dieselben Viertel
87
te in Welsch-land frem - der, süßer Kunst neue Ver-kün - dung. Stür - me durch-to - sten unsre
foreign lands, you found in their art a new, glit-ter-ing pro - mise. Storm - winds were howling through the
hei - li-ge Kir-che, dich rissen sie fast aus dem Boden. Du__ flohst zur Armut, Zwei-
Church where we wor-ship. They narrowly failed to up-root you. You__ fled to mis-ery, torn__

88
89
Pls (A)
-fel quäl - ten dich. In E - lend und Krankheit hau-stest du. Stär-ker bekämpften sich in dir
___ by bit - ter doubt. You wanted to share in the grief you found, fight-ing an in - ner batt - le be -
Wankelmut und Treu - e. Wo nur für Kampf und Blut Platz ist, ge-deiht nicht die Kunst.
tween your faith and conscience. Where blood and war are all that counts, your art could not thrive.
Der Zeit Ge - bre-chen mahnten dich, du fühl-test dich mitschul-dig und warfst dich selbst in den
You felt - mis - for-tune point at you, as though you were found want-ing, and so at last went to
Streit.___
war.
Antonius (Mathis)
Ja, meinem Gott mich dar-zu-bie-ten, meinem Vol-ke Blut und Geist zu op-fern.
Yes, to do right by God and coun-try, I was glad to risk my life in batt - le.
Slow, free in measure
Langsam, frei im Zeitmaß

90
Pls (A)
Ant (M)
Und war-um war ich nicht würdig der Gna-de?
And yet it was I whose gift was re-ject-ed?
Du bist zum Bil-den ü-ber-menschlich be-gabt. Un-
You have been lent a rare and won-der-ful skill: Why
dank-bar warst du, un-treu, als du dreist gött-li-che Ga-ben verleugnetest.
did you flout it, wanton and un-grate-ful, what our father had giv-en you?
as before
Wie vorher (♩ 104)
91
Dem Volke ent-zogst du
By joining the ones you would
dich, als du zu ihm gingst, deiner Sendung ent-sag-test.
help, you be-trayed them both, your task and your peo-ple.
Keh-re zu-rück zu bei-dem:
Wise-ly re-sume your du-ty:
92
Al-les, was du schaffst, sei Opfer dem Herrn,
Work, and seek the Grace of Heaven a-bove,
so wird in je-dem Wer-ke er wirk-sam
and find your high-est aim in the Glo-ry of

G
Vivid, with vigor
Lebhaft, mit Kraft
Pls (A)
sein.
God!
Wenn du de - mü - - - - - - tig dem
When in self - less love you have
Bru - der dich bogst, ihm selbst - los dein Hei - lig -
humb - led your - self, have giv - en un - to the
93
stes zu bie-ten wag - test mit ei - gen-stem Kön - nen, wirst du ge - bun - - -
world with op-en heart, what to you must be sac - red, you will be tied
- den und frei ein star - - - - - - ker Baum im Mut - - -
and yet be free, a migh - - - - ty tree, a gi - - -

Pls (A)
mf
- - - - - - - ter - - bo - den ste - hen.
- - - - - - - ant strong - ly root - ed,
Stumm,
lone,
p
94
groß, ein Teil des Vol - - - kes, Volk selbst.
great, a part of man - - - kind, one and all.
cresc.
Wenn man dir al - les nahm und dich dar - ob ver - gaß:
And though the world may not re - mem - ber who you are:
ff
Der Baum weiß nicht um
The tree knows not of the
ff
f

95
Pls (A)
sei- - ne Frucht. Und wenn sie dich gleich er-
fruit it bears. And were they at last to
schlü- gen: Das Schöp- - fer- tum mit sei- nem Lei- - be zah- - -
kill you: a life like yours so full of grace, is worth
- - len, ist das schwer? Was
the high - est price. What
du ge- sucht, ge- - lit- - - - - - - ten,
you have won by suff' - - - - - ring
f
mf
f

96
Pls (A)
dei-nem Wir - - ken ge - - be es den Se - - - - gen der Un - -
will be - stow on you the last - ing grace of im - mor - -
mf
broadening
verbreitern-
sterb - - - - - - - lich - - keit.
ta - - - - - - - li - - ty.
f
broad
Breit
97
free
frei
The landscape changes again, this time to a sun-
Die Landschaft verwandelt sich abermals.
Geh hin und bil - - - - - - - - de.
Go forth and fash - - - - - - - - ion!
Antonius (Mathis)
Mich hat in dir Gott selbst be-
The word of God came from your
broad
Breit
free
frei
f
f

drenched view of the town of Mainz and the Rhine river.
Man sieht in hellstem Morgenlichte die Stadt Mainz und den Rhein.
Ant (M)
rührt, der Mund des Vol - kes sprach durch dich.
lips. I hear my peo - ple's voice in yours.
ff
Pls (A)
f
Dem Kreis, der uns ge - bo - - - - - -
The cir - - - - cle whence your life
Ant (M)
f
Dem Kreis, der uns ge - bo - - - - - -
The cir - - - cle whence your life
f
98
Pls (A)
ren hat, kön - nen wir nicht ent -
sprang forth has for - ev - - er con -
Ant (M)
ren hat, kön - nen wir nicht ent -
sprang forth has for - ev - - - - - er con -
mf

Pls (A)
rin- - - - - nen, auf al- - - - - - - - len
fined us. Wher - ev - - - - - - er we
Ant (M)
rin- - - - - nen, auf al- - - len
fined us. Wher - e'er we
f
Pls (A)
We- - - gen schrei - ten wir stets in
wan - - - der, we can nev - - - - er step
Ant (M)
We- - - gen schrei- - - - ten
wan - - - der, we can't step
99
Pls (A)
ihm hin- ein. Ü- - - - ber
out of it. Yet be
Ant (M)
wir hin - ein.
out of it.
mf

Pls (A)
uns zeigt sich ein wei - te - rer Kreis:
yond we see a high - er do - main:
Ant (M)
Ü - - ber uns zeigt sich ein
Yet be - - yond we see a
f
Pls (A)
Die Kraft, die uns
A realm whence we
Ant (M)
wei - te - rer Kreis:
high - er do - main.
Die
A
mf
100
Pls (A)
auf - recht er - hält.
draw ou - r strength,
mf
Was
what
Ant (M)
Kraft, die uns auf - recht er - hält.
realm whence we draw ou - r strength,
mf
Was
what
p

Pls (A)
cresc.
f
wir auch be - - gin - - - nen: Sol - len
ev - - - er may blind us, if we
Ant (M)
cresc.
f
wir auch be - - gin - - - nen: Sol - len
ev - - - er may blind us: if we
f
Pls (A)
wir uns echt be - wäh - - - ren, muß
are to do our du - - - ty, our
Ant (M)
wir uns echt be - wäh - - - ren, muß
are to do our du - - - ty, our
Pls (A)
un - - - - - - - ser Tun nach bei - den
de - - - - - - - sti - niy calls for a
Ant (M)
un - - - - - - - ser Tun nach bei - den
de - - - - - - - sti - niy calls for a
mf

A little livelier
101 Etwas lebhafter
Pls (A)
Mit- - - - - - - - ten wei-sen.
two - - - fold en - deav-or:
Laßt uns dem
Grate - ful to
Ant (M)
Mit- - - - - - - - ten wei-sen.
two - - - fold en - deav-or:
A little livelier
Etwas lebhafter
f
f
Pls (A)
Bo- - den dan-ken. Laßt uns den Him- - - mel - prei- - - - -
soil and peop-le, let us praise God, for ev - - - -
Ant (M)
Laßt uns dem Bo- - den dan-ken. Laßt uns den Him-mel prei- - - -
grate - ful to soil and peo-ple, let us praise God for ev - - - -

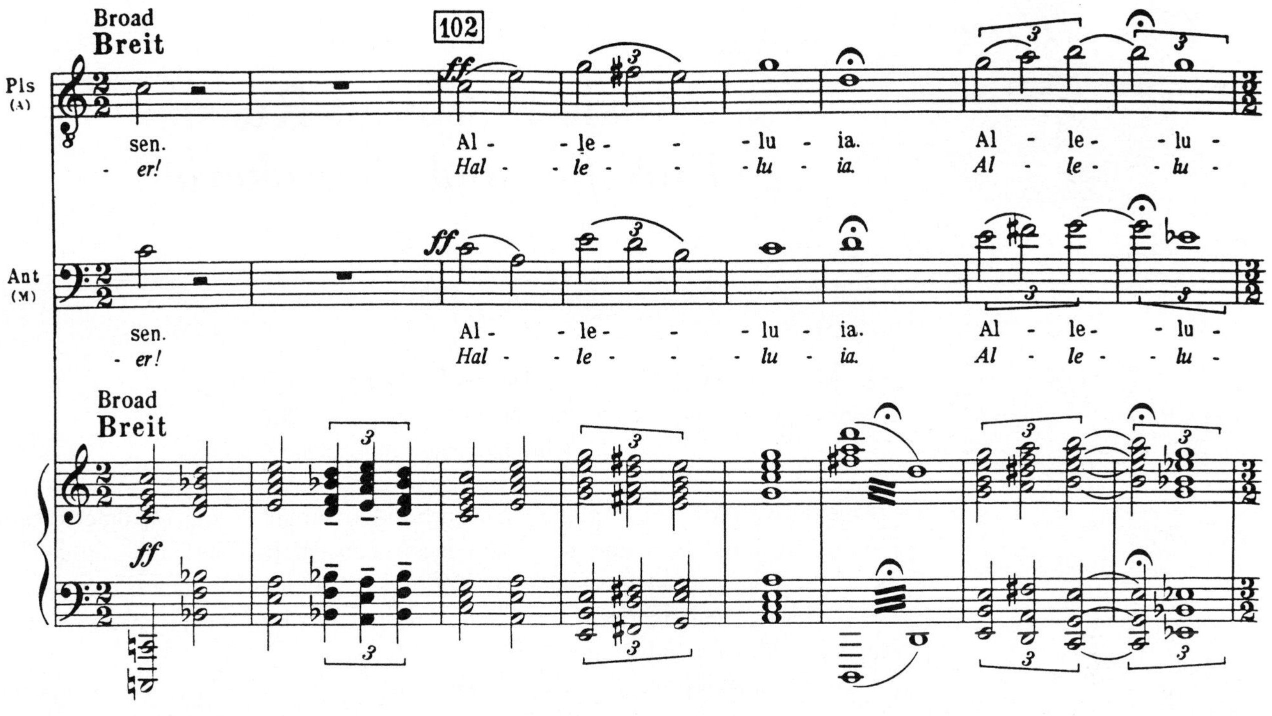
Broad
Breit
102
Pls (A)
sen. Al - le - - - lu - ia. Al - le - - lu -
- er! Hal - - le - - - lu - ia. Al - le - - lu -
Ant (M)
sen. Al - - le - - - lu - ia. Al - le - - lu -
- er! Hal - - le - - - lu - ia. Al - le - - lu -
Broad
Breit
ff
ff
ff

103
Curtain
Vorhang
Pls (A)
ia. Al - le - - - - - - - - lu - ia.
- ia. Al - - le - - - lu - ia! Hal - le - lu - ia.
Ant (M)
ia. Al - le - - - - - - - - lu - ia.
- ia. Al - le - - - lu - ia! Hal - le - lu - ia.

Chapter 74 Music in Soviet Russia *Prokofiev and Shostakovich*

190

Sergei Prokofiev
Piano Sonata No. 7 (1939–1942)
Third movement, *Precipitato*

Sergei Prokofiev began to plan his Seventh Piano Sonata during a summer vacation in the Caucasus (the region in southern Russia between the Black and Caspian Seas) in 1939, shortly before the beginning of World War II. The sonata was completed by 1942, during the height of the war, and it received its highly acclaimed first performance in Moscow in January 1943.

The sonata has proved to be one of Prokofiev's most often played works, especially known for its impetuous finale. Prokofiev described this type of movement as relating to the traditional toccata, in which a motoric rhythm—like that heard in measures 50 to 65—outweighs any lyric impulse. The listener is, in fact, swept along by a rhythmic whirlwind. Here, driving eighth-notes are spread asymmetrically over a $\frac{7}{8}$ meter. A cool and witty tone lurks behind the precipitous rhythms and cascades of notes, as jazzy blue notes appear in the pianist's left-hand ostinato.

The movement may be analyzed as a ternary **ABA'** form, even though there is no strongly contrasting middle part. The **A** section (mm. 1–44) is characterized by its asymmetrical rhythm and the ostinato figure of the opening, which undergoes a continual process of growth. After a brief reference to the opening motive, a succession of new figures is heard in the **B** section (mm. 45–127). Some of these develop small fragments from **A**, and the tonal focus moves away from B♭. With the return of **A** (mm. 127–171), the opening materials are brought back in a more complex state, leading to a brief but climactic coda at measure 171.

Sergei Prokofiev
Piano Sonata No. 7 (1939–1942)
Third movement, *Precipitato*
CD 12/7

III

5
9
mf
13
cresc.
17
f
mf
22
26

30
34
38
f
42
cresc.
ff
46
p
50
mf
f marcato
54

58
f marcato
62
66
f
f marcato
70
74
78
p
f
mf non legato

82
mf espress.
86
p
90
p
mp
94
cresc.
f
non legato
98
8va
102
8va
détaché

106
f marcato
110
114
f
f marcato
118
122
126
ff
mp
130
cresc.

134
mf
138
142
f
146
m.d.
150
8va
154
8va

157
161
165
168
171
ff détaché
8va
174
ff
8va

191

Dmitri Shostakovich
Piano Concerto No. 1 (1933)
First movement, *Allegro moderato*

Dmitri Shostakovich, like other important Soviet composers in the twentieth century, was attracted to traditional instrumental genres of music—especially the symphony, string quartet, and concerto. His Piano Concerto No. 1 exemplifies the composer's renovation of Classical genres and forms into a modern idiom. Among the surprising alterations is the elimination of the huge nineteenth-century orchestra in favor of an ensemble consisting solely of strings and a trumpet. Needless to say, with the addition of the solo trumpet, the work has at least two soloists. The piano banters with the trumpet, and occasionally the first cellist also chimes in. The spirit of the work is satirical and humorous. Shostakovich once wrote that he was happy if listeners laughed aloud during a performance of his music. Humor, he concluded, was an appropriate emotion to be explored by the classical composer, and he didn't waste any time in introducing it here. The key signature (and presumably the concert program) tells us to expect C minor; instead the pianist rips down a C-major scale, but lands on the wrong note—D♭! As if to correct the mistake, the performer runs back up a D♭-major scale and then moves chromatically to G before finally coming to rest on C. The orchestra then plucks a soft tonic chord—in C minor—reminding the pianist that the key of the concerto is in the minor mode. If Victor Borge or Peter Schickle (aka P.D.Q. Bach) were playing, the audience would be snorting in delight.

The first movement is in sonata form. The first theme begins in measure 6, following the soloist's whimsical opening and two additional bars of preparation by the left hand. Just prior to the arrival of the second theme in measure 46, a figure in the strings leads us to expect a melody filled with tender lyricism and beauty. Instead, we hear something more akin to a comic march. The beginning of the development is uncertain; perhaps it starts in measure 86, when the first theme enters in the wrong key. In measure 113 the pianist tries to begin the recapitulation, but starts the first theme in F♯, only to be corrected two bars later by the first violins. As the recapitulation progresses, the themes become more abbreviated. The movement concludes with a short twelve-bar coda.

Dmitri Shostakovich
Piano Concerto No. 1 (1933)
First movement, *Allegro moderato*
CD 12/8

8
Piano
Viol. I
Viol. II
Viola
Vc.
Bass
pizz.
p
pizz.
p
2
♩= 108
Piano
Viol. I
p espr.
arco
Viol. II
p
Viola
Vc.
Bass
Piano
Viol. I
cresc.
Viol. II
cresc.
Viola
arco
Vc.
cresc.
arco
Bass
cresc.

19
3
♩= 132
Piano
Viol. I
Viol. II
Viola
Vc.
Bass
dim.
p
cresc.
pizz.
f
ff
4
arco div.
unis.
arco

28
Piano
Viol. I
Viol. II
Viola
Vc.
Bass
ff
f
sul G
sul D
sul A

35
5
Piano
Viol. I
Viol. II
Viola
Vc.
Bass
p
ff
cresc
fff
dim.
f

43
6
Allegro vivace ♩= 160
Piano
f marcatissimo
Viol. I
Viol. II
Viola
Vc.
Bass
p
mf
marc.
7
f
p marc.

56
8
senza sord.
SOLO
cresc.
Trpt.
Piano
pizz.
p
Viol. I
Viol. II
Viola
Vc.
Bass
giocoso
div. pizz.
pp
pizz.

62
9
Trpt.
Piano
Viol. I
Viol. II
Viola
Vc.
Bass
unis. arco
unis. arco
unis. arco
arco
arco
espres.
f espr.
div.
mf

68
Trpt.
Piano
dim.
Viol. I
div.
unis.
Viol. II (Div.)
Viola
div.
unis.
Vc.
dim.
Bass
dim.
10
SOLO
p marc.
p
unis.
pp
pp
pp
unis.
mf dim.
pp
unis.
pp

74
Trpt.
Piano
Viol. I
unis.
Viol. II
Viola
Vc.
Bass
11
cresc.
ff dim.
pp
dim.
div.

80
Trpt.
Piano
Viol. I
Viol. II
Viola
Vc.
Bass
f marc.
f espr.
mp
mp

86
Trpt.
Piano
Viol. I
Viol. II
Viola
Vc.
Bass
cresc.
marc.
12
f
f marc.
f marc.

93
Piano
Viol. I
Viol. II
Viola
Vc.
Bass
cresc.
fff
ff
dim.
13
ff marc
f marc
f marc.
Piano.

102
Piano
14
Piano
pizz.
Viol. I
mf
cresc.
pizz.
Viol. II
mf
cresc.
pizz.
Viola
mf
cresc.
pizz.
Vc.
mf
cresc.
pizz.
Bass
mf
cresc.
SOLO
Trpt.
ff
cresc.
Piano
Viol. I
ff
Viol. II
ff
Viola
ff
Vc.
ff
Bass
ff

15
112
Trpt.
Piano
fff
arco
Viol. I
Viol. II
Viola
Vc.
Bass
16
dim.
p
Allegretto. ♩= 132
pizz.

120
Trpt.
Piano
p
espr.
Viol. I
Viol. II
Viola
arco
Vc.
arco
Bass
17
Trpt.
Piano
Viol. I
pp
Viol. II
pp
Viola
pp
Vc.
dim.
pp
Bass
dim.
pp

127
18
rit.
p espres.
Allegro ♩=144
Trpt.
Piano
Viol. I
Viol. II
Viola
Vc.
Bass
19
div.
p
div.pizz.
mp
pizz.
mp
pizz.
p
mp
pizz.
p
mp

139
Trpt.
Piano
Viol. I
Viol. II
Viola
Vc.
Bass
20
Trpt.
Piano
Viol. I
Viol. II
Viola
Vc.
Bass

145
Piano
Viol. I
Viol. II
Viola
Vc.
Bass
21
espr. f

152
Piano
Viol. I
Viol. II
Viola
Vc.
Bass
arco
unis.
div.
22
passion.
espr.
pizz.

160
23
Moderato. 𝅗𝅥 = 84
Piano
Viol. I
Viol. II
Viola
Vc.
Bass
pizz.
div.
unis.
cresc.
dim.
Trpt.
p espr.
Attacca

Self-Reliance in American Music
Ives, Seeger, Nancarrow

192

Charles Ives
"Feldeinsamkeit" (1897)

In 1922 Charles Ives collected 114 songs that he had composed since the 1890s and published them at his own expense. In a note placed at the end of the anthology, he commented in a self-deprecating tone on his intentions in bringing out the pieces: "I have merely cleaned house," he remarked. "All that is left is out on the clothes line,—but it's good for a man's vanity to have the neighbors see him—on the clothes line."

Ives then pointed to the astonishing diversity of styles represented in his collection. While a few are composed in a traditional manner, others are decidedly experimental. "Some of the songs in this book," Ives wrote concerning the more experimental pieces, "particularly among the later ones, cannot be sung." Why should they exist? "A song has a *few* rights, the same as other ordinary citizens," he answered puckishly.

The diversity in style of Ives's songs is seen by comparing "Feldeinsamkeit" and "Charlie Rutlage" (no. 193). The first, written in 1897 as a composition assignment for Horatio Parker, Ives's composition teacher at Yale, conforms to the norm for songwriting in the late nineteenth century. Here Ives used the same poetic text by Hermann Allmers, "Feldeinsamkeit" ("Alone in the Fields"), that had been set to music by Johannes Brahms (no. 159) some twenty years before.

Songs such as this, as well as his famous *Variations on America,* prove that Ives was not a rich, eccentric dilettante writing without regard to musical tradition. He was well aware of what other composers had accomplished and was not shy about adapting what he liked to his own robust musical idiom.

Charles Ives
"Feldeinsamkeit" (1897)
CD 12/9

pp
Ich
Quite
ru - he still im ho - hen, grü - nen Gras und
still I lie where green the grass and tall and
sen - de lan - ge mei - nen Blick nach o - ben, nach
gaze a-bove me in - to depths un - bound - ed, un -
o - ben von Gril - len rings um - schwirrt ohn'
bound - ed, by voi - ces of the wood - land a

Un - ter-lass, ohn' Un - ter-lass, von Him - mels bläu - e
con - stant call, a con - stant call, and by the won - drous
wun - der-sam um - wo - ben, um - wo - -
blue of Heav'n sur - round - ed, sur - round - -
ben. Die
ed. The
p
shö - nen, weis - sen Wol - ken ziehn da-hin durch's tie - fe Blau wie
love - ly snow white clouds drift far and wide, like si - lent dreams through
p

schö - ne stil - le Träu - me, schö - ne, stil - le Träu - me,
deeps of a - zure wend - ing, like si - lent dreams,
Meno mosso
schö - ne stil - le Träu - me; mir ist als ob ich längst ge -
through the a - zure wend - ing; I feel as though I long a -
pp
stor - ben bin, mir ist, als ob ich längst ge - stor - ben bin und
go had died, I feel as though I long a - go had died, to
mf
zie - he se - lig mit durch ew' - ge Räu - me, zie - he se - lig
drift with them through realms of bliss un - end - ing, to drift through

193

Charles Ives
"Charlie Rutlage" (c1920)

"Charlie Rutlage" shows the more experimental side of Ives's creative coin. The text, taken from a collection of homespun cowboy ballads by D.J. O'Malley, tells the story of a good cowpuncher, Charlie Rutlage, who is killed in an accident during a round-up. The story plainly attracted Ives in a way that Allmers's romantic verse in

"Feldeinsamkeit" did not. The poem speaks about a moment of spiritual destiny intruding into everyday life. This was what art could do, thought Ives. Every morning, a glorious sunrise can bring the same level of transcendent spirituality into our lives as art does in a more sophisticated setting. For Ives, art was for everyone.

In "Charlie Rutlage" Ives creates a musical environment in which a folksy tune accompanying Charlie's everyday world alternates with experimental materials—tone clusters, recitation, free dissonance—that depict Charlie's death.

Decades were to pass before Ives's music began to be performed with any frequency and his reputation as a prominent American composer was established. However, even though his songs were not readily available, "Charlie Rutlage" did occasionally appear on concert programs. As early as 1924 it was sung at Tulane University in Louisiana. Within ten years, Aaron Copland had become aware of it, and the song was included in a festival of American music held in upstate New York in 1932. The audience enjoyed "Charlie Rutlage" so much that it had to be repeated before the concert could continue.

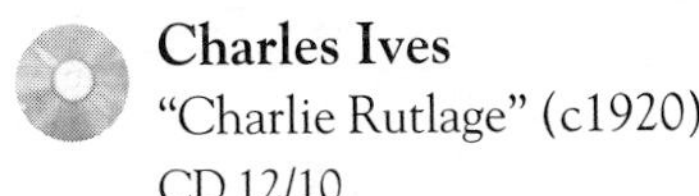

Charles Ives
"Charlie Rutlage" (c1920)
CD 12/10

oth - er place is va-cant on the ranch of the X I T, 'Twill be hard to find an-oth-er that's
mf
f
liked as well as he. The first that died was Kid White, a man both tough and
p
brave, While Charlie Rutlage makes the third to be sent to his grave, Caused
faster (half spoken)
recite -- following the piano
by a cow-horse falling, While run-ning af-ter stock; 'Twas on the spring round up, A
faster
(octs. ad lib.)

(hold back)
ff
fast
place where death men mock, He went for-ward one morn-ing on a
(hold back here)
fast
(Whoopee ti yi yo, git a-long lit-tle dogies,
ff
circle through the hills, He was gay and full of glee, and
Whoopee ti yi yo, etc.)
free from earth-ly ills; But when it came to fin-ish up the
(a little slower)
(fast again)
work on which he went, Noth-ing came back from him; his time on earth was spent. 'Twas
(fast again)
(a little slower)

*In these measures, the notes are indicated only approximately; the time, of course, is the main point.

mf
pp
— e-ternity, I hope he'll meet his parents, will meet them face to face, And that they'll
grasp him by the right hand at the shining throne, the shin - ing throne, the shining throne of grace.

194

Charles Ives

The Unanswered Question (1906)

Ives first composed his tone poem *The Unanswered Question* in 1906, and revised it in the early 1930s. It is this revision that is included here. A small group of graduate students at Juilliard gave the first performance of the revised version in 1946 (the original was not played until 1984). In this work Ives uses music to explore the meaning of life through a metaphysical drama that is compressed into a brief instrumental composition.

There are three layers of music, each representative of a specific idea, and these three strata float together without strict coordination in time. The strings symbolize Existence itself; Ives called them "silent druids." Their tones—continuous, serene, and moving with all the speed of a glacier—seem to be oblivious of what happens around them, and the pitches are so widely spaced that passing dissonances lose their harshness. The solo trumpet provides the second layer, a repeated phrase that Ives associated with the enigmatic question concerning the meaning or purpose of existence—a question that has always confronted mankind. The trumpet's query is polite, but insistent; it never gets louder as if demanding an answer. It is just there, repeatedly asking the same question but not receiving a satisfactory answer. As if resigned to the silence of the druids, the final statement is softer than the others. The final layer is played by the woodwinds. Each time the trumpet poses this question, the woodwinds—who represent mankind—try to find an answer. But they cannot do so, at least not to everyone's satisfaction, and their frustrations become increasingly clear as they bicker furiously and finally fall sullenly silent.

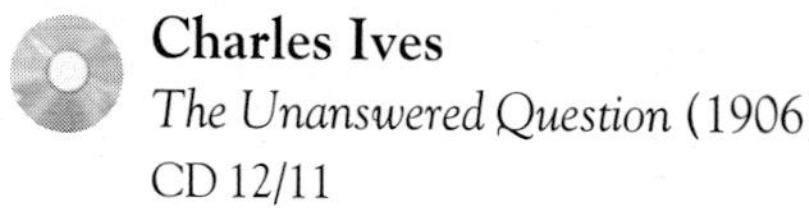

Charles Ives
The Unanswered Question (1906)
CD 12/11

I
II
Flutes
(or Oboe) III
(or Clarinet) IV
Largo molto sempre (for strings & trumpet) (about 50=♩)
Trumpet (or English Horn, or Oboe, or Clarinet)
Violin I
ppp con sordini
Violin II
ppp con sordini
Viola
ppp con sordini
Violoncello (8va Contrabass)
ppp con sordini

I
II
Flutes
(or Oboe) III
(or Clarinet) IV
Trumpet (or English Horn, or Oboe, or Clarinet)
actual notes
p
Violin I
Violin II
Viola
Violoncello (8va Contrabass)

Adagio
Andante
Flutes
(or Oboe) III
(or Clarinet) IV
Trumpet
(or English Horn, or Oboe or Clarinet)
Violin I
Violin II
Viola
Violoncello
(8va Contrabass)

Allegretto
I
II
Flutes
(or Oboe III
(or Clarinet IV
Allegretto
Trumpet
(or English Horn,
or Oboe,
or Clarinet)
Violin I
Violin II
Viola
Violoncello
(8va Contrabass)
Allegro
I
II
Flutes
(or Oboe) III
(or Clarinet) IV
Allegro
Trumpet
(or English Horn,
or Oboe,
or Clarinet)
Violin I
Violin II
Viola
Violoncello
(8va Contrabass)

Allegro molto
Flutes
I
II
(or Oboe) III
(or Clarinet) IV
Allegro molto
Trumpet (or English Horn, or Oboe, or Clarinet)
Violin I
Violin II
Viola
Violoncello (8va Contrabass)
Allegro-accel. to Presto
Trumpet holds here until Flutes start.

Molto agitando
Con fuoco
Con fuoco
Con fuoco
Con fuoco
Molto agitando Con fuoco
Con fuoco
Flutes
(or Oboe) III
(or Clarinet) IV
Trumpet
(or English Horn, or Oboe or Clarinet)
Violin I
Violin II
Viola
Violoncello
(8va Contrabass)
If played by Oboe and Clarinet, last measure ends
Oboe
Clarinet
actual notes

195

Ruth Crawford Seeger
String Quartet (1931)
Third movement, *Andante*

The String Quartet by Ruth Crawford Seeger is an example of the originality and independence of the creative mind that characterizes American music of the twentieth century. Of all the traditional genres of music, the string quartet demands the greatest degree of strictness and adherence to Classical models. But in the hands of Seeger, this music becomes a laboratory for new ideas.

The slow third movement of the quartet is an example of her independent thinking. The notes of the movement enter one by one to create a single line, and these tones are sustained to form densely chromatic clusters of sound. The most remarkable element of the music is its manipulation of dynamic levels, as each instrument follows its own pattern of crescendos and decrescendos to create a counterpoint.

When the composition was first performed in New York in 1933, in a concert of works by American composers, Seeger's quartet was considered a great success; the third movement was especially well received. The American avant-garde composer Henry Cowell was quite enthusiastic about this movement and convinced Charles Ives to underwrite a recording of it. It was one of the few recordings made of contemporary American art music before World War II.

Ruth Crawford Seeger
String Quartet (1931)
Third movement, *Andante*
CD 12/12

The dotted ties indicate that the first tone of each new bow is not to be attacked; the bowing should be as little audible as possible throughout.
The crescendi and decrescendi should be equally gradual.

10
sempre simile
sempre simile
15
sempre legatissimo
pp mp pp mp
20
sempre legatissimo
pp mp pp mp mf p mf p
sempre simile
mf p
25
decrescendo to meas. 29
30
pp mp pp

crescendo to meas. 43
35
40
45
decrescendo
50
crescendo to meas. 66

55
60
mf
ff
mf
65
f
fff
70
75
sempre fff
sempre fff
sempre fff
sempre fff
3
ffz

*The half-notes in measures 85 to 88 should be faster than the quarter-notes in measure 77.

American Composers Return from Europe
Copland and Barber

196

Aaron Copland
Piano Variations (1930)

Aaron Copland composed music alternately in two styles: one difficult and modernistic, the other traditional and often filled with Americana. The Piano Variations is one of his greatest works of the first category. The piece begins with an eleven-measure theme, which is followed by twenty variations (each marked in the score by a circled number). The work ends with a climactic coda. With its abstraction and rawboned percussiveness, the Piano Variations forms a complex challenge for performer and listener alike.

The variations move through strongly contrasting moods, from the pensive early variations to the whirlwind virtuosity of the final ones. Like all of Copland's music, the work is intensely unified, and here he freely adapts Schoenberg's serial technique in the recurring use of the opening row of tones: E C D♯ C♯. Like Schoenberg in his serial pieces composed between 1920 and 1923, Copland uses a row that contains fewer than all twelve notes of the chromatic scale, and, also like Schoenberg, he brings back the row in transposed, inverted, and retrograde forms. Although Schoenberg's musical language is very different from Copland's, Schoenberg's serial method forced Copland to rethink his process of composition.

The theme itself is divided into five phrases, each of which contains a different permutation of the opening tone row. Extra notes can be added, as is the A♮ in measure 3 or the G♯ in measure 8; this latter note results in a prominent E-major chord. The composer stated that the twenty variations were divided into two equal sections and that all twenty were to be performed as a single unit without any breaks or pauses between them. The first variation, which is seamlessly elided with the fifth phrase of the theme, is a canon where the second voice is rhythmically elongated. (The treatment is reminiscent of the opening *Kyrie* in Johannes Ockeghem's permutation canon *Missa Prolationum*, no. 47.) Halfway through this variation, the permutation canon changes to a series of inverted entries in a freer imitative style. Each variation increases in tempo and complexity until the eighth; variations nine through twelve have a more relaxed pace and a more expressive character. Variation thirteen begins a steady increase in speed, and the sections soon run together in a fast, driving tempo that is one of the hallmarks of Neoclassical music. The coda completes the composition with slow, bell-like tones.

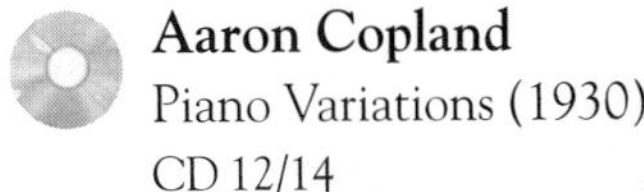

Aaron Copland
Piano Variations (1930)
CD 12/14

THEME

Grave (♩ = 48)

(strike each note sharply)

Piano

f non legato, deliberamente *sff*

sff *sff* *sff* *p* *sff* *sff* *f*

11

1

(♩ = 54)

p molto espress.

p *p*

p *pp* Più *mf* poco

*◇ = press down silently

The metronomic markings are to be taken only as approximate indications of correct tempi.

2 mosso (𝅗𝅥 = 72)
p
l.h.
l.h.
l.h.
marc.
legato
3 Più mosso (𝅗𝅥 = 100)
27
p
simply, naively
poco accell.
39
rit.
a tempo
4 Meno mosso (𝅗𝅥 = 80)
mf
p
f
molto legato
sff

5
54
6 Piu mosso (♩ = 112)
sempre marc.
f clangorous
mark the melody
62
7
boldly
sff
Ped.

72
8
sff
sff
8
Più mosso ancora (♩ = 132)
blurred
sub. mf
sim.
sim.
sim.
83
sub. p
sf
sff
9
warmly
mf
cantabile
f
mf
f

10 Più largamente (♩ = 76)
marc. e legato
ff
ff
107
f
f
mf
mf
Lento (♩ = 66)
11 molto espress. e liberamente
p
pp
pp
116
l. h.
3
ppp
12 Subito allegretto (♩ = 126)
mp . scherzando
senza Ped.
pp

129
13
Poco più mosso (𝅗𝅥 = 188)
p
mp threatening
14 Allegro con brio (𝅗𝅥 = 176)
f
l.h.
l.h.
142
meno f ma marc.
f
l.h.
meno f ma marc.

153
l.h.
f
l.h.
15
heavy stacc.
l.h.
mf
simile
164
mark the melody
f
ff
mf
176
f
mf
ff

183
meno f
p
pp
sub. f
mf
f
ff
16
non legato
mf
sf secco
ff secco
203

216
very sharply
17
f
ff
sempre ff
226
very sharply
sub. p
sub. ff
238

18
sub. pp scherzando
p
pp
p
248
pp
p
mf l.h.
p
mf
l.h.
pp
259
p
pp
mf rit.
19 Molto meno mosso (♩=104)
Subito allegro (♩=152)
p
mf
poco sf
più f secco

274
f
ff
20 not too fast, well articulated
secco ff
285
sub. p
sf
f
f
295
sub. p
sf
sf

300
p
f
f
309
poco accell. e cresc.
Allegro vivo (♩=184)
8
fff brillante
sff
(♩=208)
Poco accell. ancora
317
Ped.
*

327
1
1
CODA
Subito lento moderato (♩ = 72)
f pesante
339
348
Poco largamente (♩ = 66)
r. h. molto marcato
fff
l. h. molto marcato

354

Più largamente ancora (♩ = 58)

sf sf sf sf mf ff

Ped. * Ped. *

362

r. h. simile

l. h. simile

sff sff sff sff sff sff

Sust Ped.

r. h.

*)

l. h.

sff sff sff sff sff

Ped.

*for pianos without Sustaining Pedal

197

Aaron Copland

Appalachian Spring (Suite 1945)
Variations on a Shaker Hymn

Aaron Copland was invited to compose music for the ballet *Appalachian Spring* by the American choreographer and dancer Martha Graham. Graham devised a scenario, but did not inform Copland of the title, *Appalachian Spring,* until the night before its premiere. In its final form, the story concerns a pioneer couple—Husband and Bride—who are building their future home in rural Pennsylvania in the early nineteenth century. They are visited by a revivalist minister and his followers (four rather dour young women), and the couple takes heart and looks optimistically to the future.

For a scene depicting everyday work on the farm, Graham suggested that Copland write variations upon an appropriate melody, and the music that Copland supplied for the scene—the Shaker hymn "Simple Gifts" (c1840)—has become the most famous of the entire score. The melody is heard first on the clarinet and, in the four variations that follow, it passes around to other sections of the orchestra.

In 1945, the year after the ballet received its premiere performance in Washington, D.C., Copland was awarded a Pulitzer Prize for the work. The *New York Times* ran the story on its front page, right under the banner headline that proclaimed the unconditional surrender of Germany. That year Copland also created a suite from the ballet, which he scored for full orchestra. (The original was written for chamber orchestra.) In creating the 1945 suite, Copland made certain changes in the form of the various numbers to give them a greater symphonic continuity. This 1945 orchestral suite represents the music of *Appalachian Spring* as it is now best known.

Aaron Copland
Appalachian Spring (Suite 1945)
Variations on a Shaker Hymn
CD 12/15

12
Picc.
Fl. 1
Ob.
B♭ Cl. 1
B♭ Cl. 2
Bsn.
B♭ Tpt.
Hp.
Pno.
p
mf
II.
I. Solo
mp
Solo
II. Solo
con sord.
21
Ob.
Bsn.
B♭ Tpt.

58
29
Fl. 1
fsf
mf
Fl. 2
fsf
mf
a2
Ob.
fsf
I. Solo
mf
B♭ Cl. 1
fsf
mf
B♭ Cl. 2
fsf
mf
a2
Bsn.
fsf
II. Solo
mf
(Open)
Hn.
fsf
mf
Trgl.
sf
Glk.
p
8va
Hp.
p
Pno.
p
senza Ped.
div.
pizz.
Vln. II
p

59
38
Fl. 1
Fl. 2
Ob.
B♭ Cl. 1
B♭ Cl. 2
Bsn.
p leggiero
Hn.
con sord.
senza sord.
a2
f cant.
B♭ Tpt.
Tbn.
I. Solo
mf cant. dolce
Glk.
Hp.
(8va)
Pno.
Vln. I
cant. sonore
div.
f
Vln. II
Vla.
cant. dolce
mf

60
48
Fl. 1
Fl. 2
Ob.
B♭ Cl. 1
B♭ Cl. 2
Bsn.
Hn.
B♭ Tpt.
Tbn.
Glk.
(8va)
Hp.
Pno.
Vln. I
Vln. II
Vla.
Vc.
f
sonore
D.B.

56
Fl. 1
Fl. 2
Ob.
B♭ Cl. 1
B♭ Cl. 2
Bsn.
Hn.
B♭ Tpt.
Tbn.
Glk.
(8va)
Hp.
Pno.
Vln. I
Vln. II
Vla.
Vc.
D.B.
p

61
62
Fl. 1
Solo
Ob.
I. Solo
B♭ Cl. 1
B♭ Cl. 2
Bsn.
cresc.
Hn.
non legato
cresc.
vigoroso e marc.
a2
B♭ Tpt.
Tbn.
II.
Vln. I
Vln. II
arco
sostenuto
Vla.
Vc.
pizz.
D.B.
unis.

86
a2
Ob.
vigoroso e marc.
B♭ Cl. 1
vigoroso e marc.
B♭ Cl. 2
vigoroso e marc.
Hn.
B♭ Tpt.
vigoroso e marc.
Tbn.
Vln. I
Vla.
93
64
A trifle slower (𝅗𝅥 = 66)
Ob.
B♭ Cl. 1
B♭ Cl. 2
Hn.
B♭ Tpt.
Tbn.
Vln. I
Vla.

101
Ob.
I. Solo
mf
B♭ Cl. 1
Solo
mf
B♭ Cl. 2
mf
Bsn.
I. Solo
mf
B♭ Tpt.
p
Tbn.
p
101
Vln. I
Vla.
Vc.
arco
p
D.B.
arco
p
109
Fl. 1
mf
Fl. 2
mf
Ob.
B♭ Cl. 1
B♭ Cl. 2
Bsn.
Vc.
D.B.

65
Broadly (in 2)
118
Fl. 1
Fl. 2
Ob.
B♭ Cl. 1
B♭ Cl. 2
Bsn.
Hn.
B♭ Tpt.
Tbn.
Timp.
Hp.
Pno.
Vln. I
Vln. II
Vla.
Vc.
D.B.
legato e marc.
marc.
a2
unis.
fff
8vb

66
127
Fl. 1
Fl. 2
Ob.
B♭ Cl. 1
B♭ Cl. 2
Bsn.
Hn.
B♭ Tpt.
Tbn.
Timp.
Hp.
Pno.
Vln. I
Vln. II
Vla.
Vc.
D.B.
sf
p
(8vb)
8vb

198

Samuel Barber
Hermit Songs (1953)
"Sea-Snatch"

Samuel Barber composed his *Hermit Songs* in 1952 following a visit to Ireland. The spirit of the Emerald Isle seems to pervade the entire composition, from its evocative music to the Celtic verses, written by medieval monks, that Barber selected for it. Celtic literature is written in several different languages, including Old Irish, Welsh, and Gaelic, but Barber used modern English translations for his musical texts. Many of the ancient poems are brief because they were set down in the narrow margins of a manuscript that the monk-author was copying.

"Sea-Snatch," a fragmentary poem that tells of a ship trapped in a storm, is the sixth song of Barber's cycle. It dates to the ninth century, the same period as the poetic developments of Tuotilo of St. Gall and Notker Balbulus that resulted in the trope and sequence (see *MWC*, Chapter 5; also nos. 10–11). With great economy, Barber creates a gripping musical portrait of the storm, whose waves boil within the piano part. The voice seems to hang on for dear life to the piano's surging rhythms, finally calling out to God for mercy.

The American soprano, Leontyne Price (b. 1927), sang these songs, with the composer accompanying, at the premiere performance in October 1953. Barber was so taken with her rendition that they performed them together many times over the years. He wrote a number of other significant works for her, including the role of Cleopatra in his last opera. The *Hermit Songs* have been described one of the greatest song cycles from the twentieth century and, along with his *Adagio for Strings*, are among the composer's most frequently performed compositions.

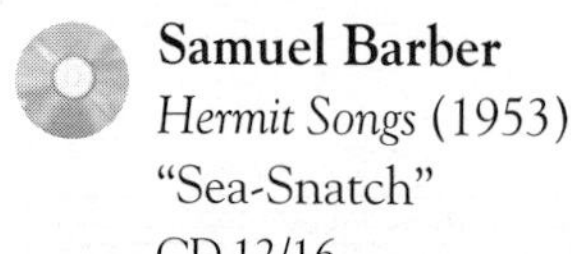

Samuel Barber
Hermit Songs (1953)
"Sea-Snatch"
CD 12/16

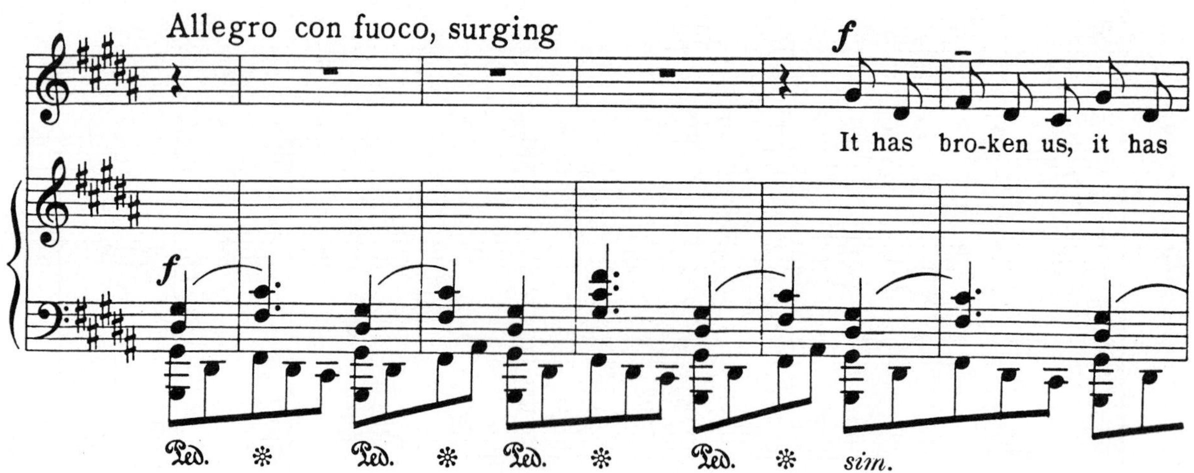

crushed us, it has drowned us, O
King of the star-bright King-dom of Heav-en;
sf
mf
f
the wind has con-
sf
sumed us, swal-lowed us, as tim-ber is de-voured by crim-son fire from Heav-en.

più f
marcato
mf
p
cresc. molto
It has bro-ken us, it has crushed us, it has drowned us, O
sf
p
sf
cresc. molto
Ped.
ff
King of the star-bright King-dom of Heav-en!
ff
* Ped. *

Tin Pan Alley and the Broadway Musical

199

George Gershwin
"The Man I Love" (1924)

George Gershwin's song "The Man I Love" is a classic example of the Tin Pan Alley song of the 1920s. Its lyrics—written by Gershwin's brother, Ira—speak of wistfully reaching out for a happiness that seems just beyond grasp. The romantic idealism of the song reflects an attitude far more characteristic of American society of the 1920s than of the present day.

The musical form of "The Man I Love" is typical of American popular songs of the time. Following an introduction, the voice sings a "verse" consisting of two short stanzas with the same music in each. Both text and music here have a tentative, almost introductory, quality. The verse is followed by the "refrain" (often called the "chorus"). This part of the song contains the main tune and the central thought. It extends over thirty-two measures, with four musical phrases laid out in the form **AABA**. The chorus is sung twice in succession.

"The Man I Love" was composed by Gershwin for the show *Lady, Be Good,* but was cut (along with nine other songs) to speed up the plot of the first act. Because the lyrics were general enough to fit into almost any show from the "Roaring Twenties," it was later included in *Strike Up the Band* (1927). While that show was not especially successful, the song was performed and recorded as a single, and it soon took on a life of its own.

George Gershwin
"The Man I Love" (1924)
CD 12/17

5
When the mel - low moon be-gins to beam, Ev - 'ry night I
p molto semplice
8
dream a lit - tle dream, And of course Prince Charm - ing is the theme The
11
he for me. Al - though I re - al - ize as well as you,
15
It is sel - dom that a dream comes true, To me it's

18
clear
That he'll ap - pear.
dim.
poco rall.
Refrain (slow)
21
p
Some-day he'll come a-long,
The man I love;
And he'll be big and strong,
p molto semplice e dolce
24
The man I love;
And when he comes my way,
I'll do my best to
27
make him stay.
He'll look at me and smile,
p

30
I'll un - der-stand;
And in a lit - tle while
He'll take my hand;
33
And though it seems ab-surd,
I know we both won't say a
36
word.
May - be I shall meet him Sun - day, May - be Mon - day, may - be
mp
poco espr.
40
not;
Still I'm sure to meet him one day, May - be Tues - day Will be
poco rit.

200

Richard Rodgers and Oscar Hammerstein II

Oklahoma! (1943)

"I Cain't Say No!"

The show *Oklahoma!* is a classic of the American musical theater and the first in a series of unprecedented successes created for Broadway by the team of Rodgers and Hammerstein. The story is set in Oklahoma near the turn of the twentieth century, and, like comedies past and present, it concerns young love winning out despite great odds. The librettist, Oscar Hammerstein II, adapted an existing play by Lynn

Riggs, creating several subsidiary characters to add humor and local color. One of them is Ado Annie, a purely comic character who is boy crazy. While her official boyfriend, Will, is away in Kansas City, she has taken up with a fast-talking peddler named Ali Hakim. In the song "I Cain't Say No!" she confesses to her friend Laurey that she simply can't say "No" to any man.

Her song has an irrepressible wit, and Rodgers's music makes her helplessness around men seem touchingly believable. In terms of form, the song rests upon the familiar verse-and-refrain pattern that dominated American popular songs throughout the twentieth century. Rodgers takes certain liberties with the form to make the song dramatically plausible. Just as Ado Annie does not fall in with the social proprieties of the other girls, the phrases of her song do not hew to the standard eight-bar norm. Each phrase in the verse is reduced to only seven bars, and the latter half of each is reduced even further as Ado Annie sings the notes twice as fast (quarter-notes becoming eighths). In the chorus, the character still cannot conform to the norm. The **B** phrases of the **AABA** refrain have sixteen bars, and the final **A** is twenty-four. Rodgers also adds a contrasting section, or "trio," between the two statements of the song's refrain.

Richard Rodgers and Oscar Hammerstein II
Oklahoma! (1943)
"I Cain't Say No!"
CD 12/18

Cue: Ado Annie "Yeow, they told me."

8
heared a lot of sto - ries and I reck - on they are true A -
+Stgs.
Hp.
12
'bout how girls 're put up - on by men. I
Br.
Stgs.
Hns.
Stgs.
15
know I mus - n't fall in - to the pit, But when I'm with a fel - ler I fer -
Hp.
Stgs.
W.W.
18
git!
Br. Stgs.
f
dim.

22
Refrain (brightly)
I'm jist a girl who cain't say no, I'm in a
I'm jist a girl who cain't say no, Cain't seem to
Stgs.
Hn
Hp.
Perc.
mp
27
tur - ri - ble fix
say it at all
I al - ways say "come
I hate to dis - ser -
32
on, le's go," Jist when I or - ta say "nix!"
point a beau When he is pay - in' a call.
37
38
When a per - son tries to kiss a girl, I
Fer a while I ack re - fined and cool, A -

42
know she or - ta give his face a smack. But as soon as some - one
set - tin' on the vel - ve - teen set - tee 'Nen I think of thet ol'
W.W. Stgs.
+Hns.
Hp.
48
kiss - es me, I some - how sor - ta want - a kiss him back!
gold - en rule, And do fer him whut he would do fer me!
W.W. Stgs.
Xyl.
W.W.
Gliss.
54
I'm jist a fool when lights are low I cain't be pris - sy and
I cain't re - sist a Ro - me - o, In a som - bre - ro and
Tutti
W.W.
Hp.
Perc.
60
quaint I ain't the type that c'n faint
chaps Soon as I sit on their laps
W.W. Stgs.
Tutti
Hns.
cresc.
+Br.

66
70
How c'n I be whut I ain't? I cain't say
Sump-'n in-side o' me snaps! I cain't say
Tutti
73
To Trio
Final Ending
no!
no!
cresc.
fp
sfz
80 Trio
Whut you goin' to do when a fel-ler gits flirt-y and starts to talk purt-y, Whut you goin' to do?
Stgs. Guit.
p
Cls.
84
S'pos-in' 'at he says 'at yer lip's 're like cher-ries, er ros-es er ber-ries, Whut you goin' to do?

201

Leonard Bernstein
West Side Story (1957), "Cool"

The Broadway musical *West Side Story* (1957) retells Shakespeare's tragic play *Romeo and Juliet*. The librettist, Arthur Laurents, updates the feuding Montague and Capulet families to rival gangs that inhabit Manhattan's Upper West Side during the 1950s. A Puerto Rican gang—the Sharks—is led by Bernardo; their adversaries, the Jets, are led by Riff. Tony (Romeo in disguise) has lost interest in the Jets, his gang of old, but he agrees to attend the dance that evening, despite the presence of the hated Sharks. At the dance, Tony sees Maria, Bernardo's sister, and the two are suddenly transfixed with love. Tony rushes to the alley behind Maria's apartment, climbs the fire escape, and they embrace.

In the number "Cool," the Jets wait nervously inside Doc's drugstore for the arrival of the Sharks, with whom they will set the ground rules for a rumble to work out their animosities. Despite Riff's admonition to keep cool, members of the Jets erupt into wild dancing.

Leonard Bernstein's music for "Cool" reveals the remarkable musical sophistication, complexity, and raw excitement that this composer brought to the genre of the Broadway musical. The number is framed by a verse-and-refrain song ("Boy, boy, crazy boy"), but in its middle lies a fully developed fugue, which accompanies fierce dancing by the Jets.

Introduction	Refrain	Dance		Refrain	Coda
ostinato	**A B A B**	Fugue	Development	**A B**	**A'**
1	9	45	96	147	163

Leonard Bernstein
West Side Story (1957)
"Cool"
CD 12/19

Cue: **RIFF: ... a red hot umbrella and open it. Wide.**

RIFF: You wanna live? You play it cool.
ACTION: I wanna get even!
RIFF: Get cool.
A–RAB: I wanna bust!

Solid and boppy 𝅗𝅥 = 90

Fl., Alto Sax, Vibr., El. Gtr.
Piano
pp jazz feel
Pno., Traps
Bar. Sax, Cb.
3
+Tpt. I
fz

RIFF: Bust cool.
BABY JOHN: I wanna go!
RIFF: Go cool!

4
–Tpt. I
+Tpt. I
fz
–Tpt. I
+Tpt. I
fz
Bs. Cl.
3
3

7
RIFF *(almost whispered)*
p
Boy, _ boy, _ cra-zy boy, ___ Get cool, boy! _
Vibr., El. Gtr.
+Pno.
p Traps (cont.)
Pno., Vcs., Cb. (pizz.)
+Bar. Sax
+Bar. Sax

11
Riff
Got a rock-et in your pock - et, Keep cool - ly cool, boy!
–Pno.
+Pno.
Fl., Tpt. III
+Bar. Sax
+Bar. Sax
–Vcs.
15
Riff
Don't get hot, 'Cause, man, you got Some high times a - head.
3
Vibr., El. Gtr.,
Pno., Bs. Cl.
+Bsn.
19
Riff
Take it slow and, Dad - dy - o, You can live it up and die in bed!
+Bsn.
–Bsn.
–Bsn.
+Strs. (arco)

23
Riff
Boy, boy, cra-zy boy, Stay loose, boy!
Vibr., El. Gtr.
+Pno.
p –Vlns.
Pno., Vcs.,
Cb. (pizz.)
+Bar. Sax
+Bar. Sax
27
Riff
Breeze it, buzz it, eas-y does-it. Turn off the juice, boy!
–Pno.
+Pno.
Fl., Sop. Sax
+Bar. Sax
+Bar. Sax
–Vcs.
31
Riff
dim. molto
Go, man, go, But not like a yo-yo school-boy. Just play it
Fl., Vibr., El. Gtr.,
Pno.
Vibr., El. Gtr.
Pno., Bs. Cl.
mp
+Br. (cup mutes)
dim. molto

pp sub.
35
37
Riff
cool, boy, Real cool!
pp
Vcs., Cb. (pizz.)
+Bsn., Pno.
39
Poco più mosso
Vibr., El. Gtr.
Pno.
Traps Hi-hat
Pno., Cb.
43 [FUGUE]
Tpt. I (cup mute)
+Tpts. II & III (open)
Vibr., El. Gtr.
pp cresc.
molto
sfz
pp
(Traps continue)
Traps HH
(Traps cont.)
Tpt. I
–Pno.
SD rim shot
–Cb.
49
cresc.
molto
sfz
pp
+Pno.
(Traps continue)
SD rs
Cb.

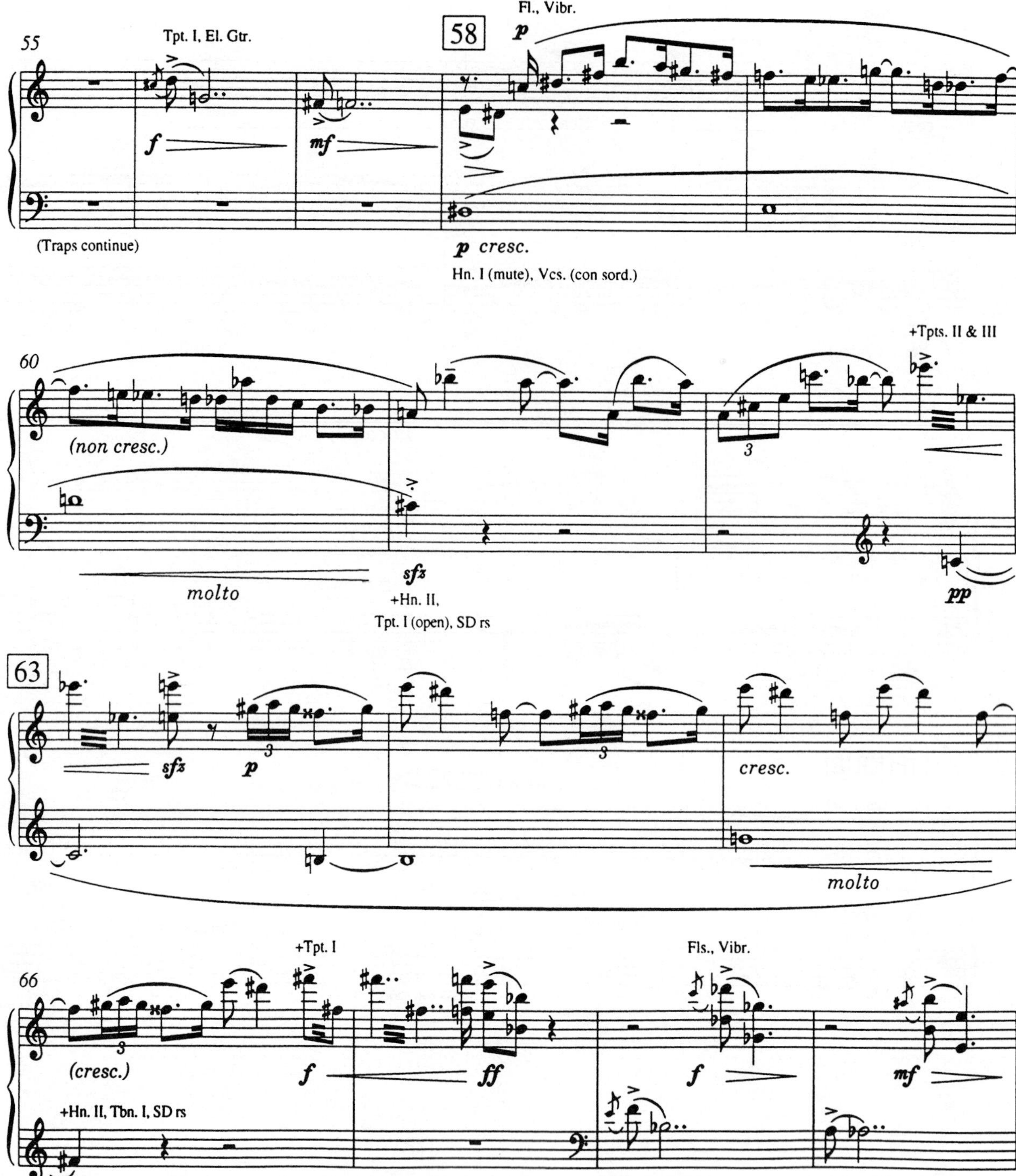
55
Tpt. I, El. Gtr.
f
mf
58
Fl., Vibr.
p
(Traps continue)
p cresc.
Hn. I (mute), Vcs. (con sord.)
60
(non cresc.)
molto
sfz
+Hn. II,
Tpt. I (open), SD rs
+Tpts. II & III
3
pp
63
sfz
p
3
3
cresc.
molto
66
(cresc.)
3
+Tpt. I
f
ff
Fls., Vibr.
f
mf
+Hn. II, Tbn. I, SD rs
sfz
f
mf
+El. Gtr.

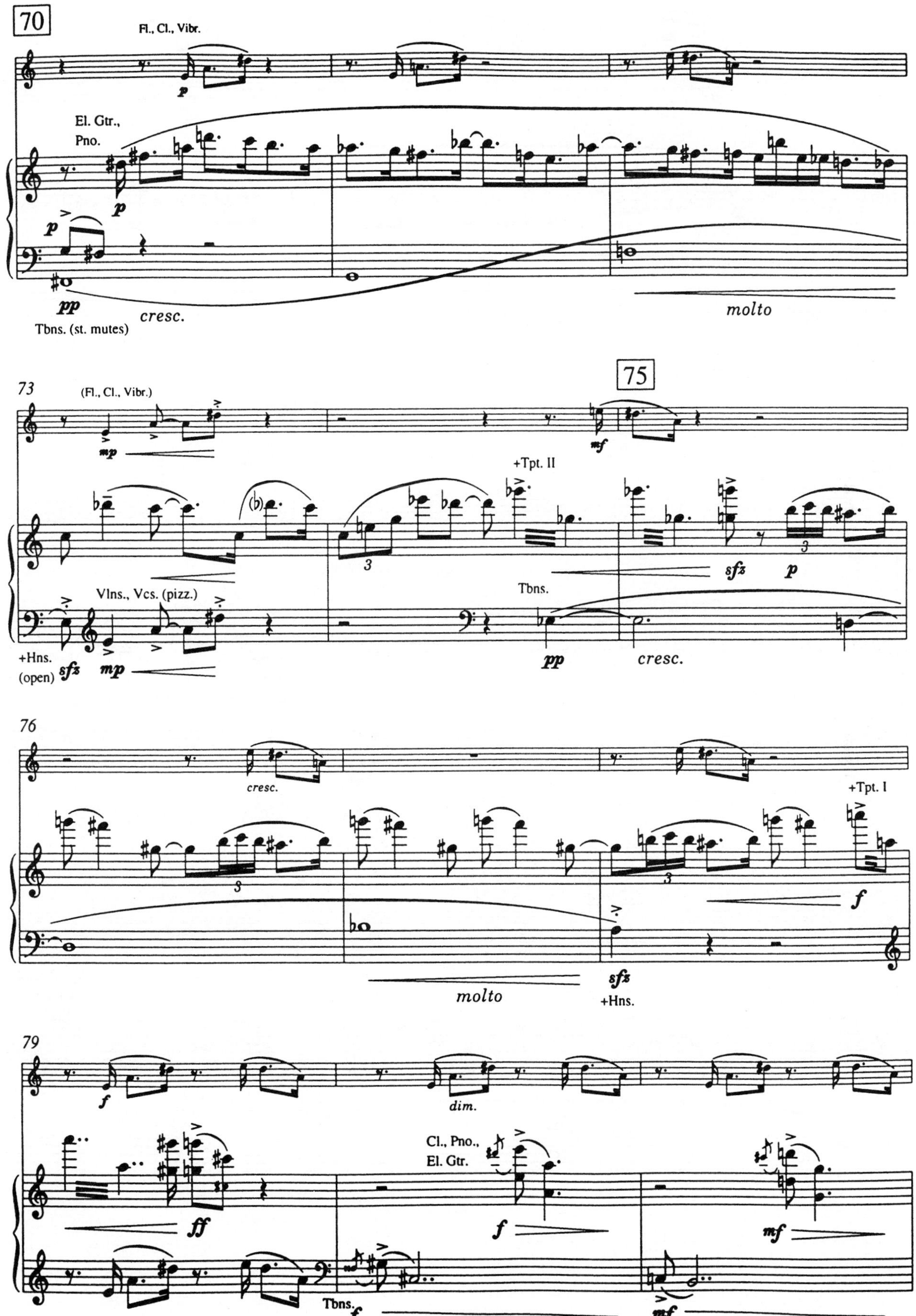

70
Fl., Cl., Vibr.
El. Gtr.,
Pno.
p
pp
cresc.
Tbns. (st. mutes)
molto
73
(Fl., Cl., Vibr.)
mp
75
mf
+Tpt. II
(♭)
3
sfz
p
Tbns.
Vlns., Vcs. (pizz.)
+Hns.
(open)
sfz
mp
pp
cresc.
76
cresc.
+Tpt. I
f
molto
sfz
+Hns.
79
f
dim.
Cl., Pno.,
El. Gtr.
ff
f
mf
Tbns.

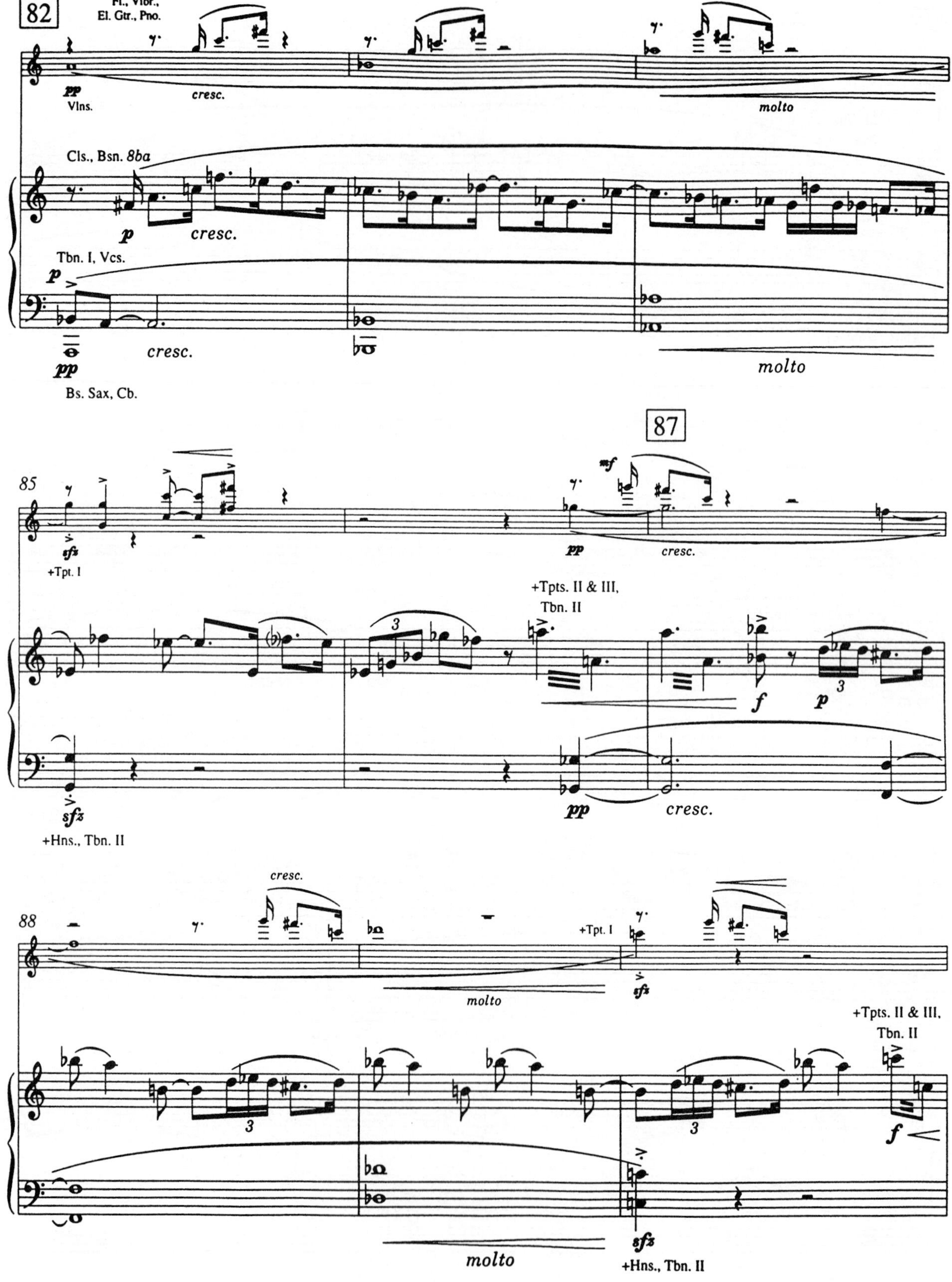
82
Fl., Vibr., El. Gtr., Pno.
pp
cresc.
Vlns.
molto
Cls., Bsn. 8ba
p
cresc.
Tbn. I, Vcs.
p
cresc.
pp
molto
Bs. Sax, Cb.
87
85
sfz
+Tpt. I
mf
pp
cresc.
+Tpts. II & III, Tbn. II
f
p
sfz
+Hns., Tbn. II
pp
cresc.
88
cresc.
molto
+Tpt. I
sfz
+Tpts. II & III, Tbn. II
f
molto
sfz
+Hns., Tbn. II

91
f
cresc. sempre
f cresc. sempre
+Tpts. II & III
ff
f cresc. sempre
+Tbn. II
94
Fl., Cl., Tpt. I, El. Gtr.
f
Tpts.
Br.
+Pno.,
Vlns.
f
sfz
sfz
sfz
sfz
Bs. Sax, Bsn.,
Vcs., Cb.
97
99
3
8va
-Pno., Vlns.
+Pno.,
Vlns.
sfz
sfz
sfz
3
3

100
sfz
sfz
sfz
sfz
sfz
fp
cresc.
103
104
Tutti
ff
106
109
Traps solo (ad lib.)
mf
ff
mf
ff
ff
(Traps cont.)
110
8va
Traps solo (ad lib.)
mf
ff
mf
ff

114
JETS
Cool!
Go!
Cra-zy!
Cool!
Go!
ff
118
119
Cra-zy!
Br.
+E♭ Cl.,
El. Gtr.
–Hns.
+Pno.,
Xylo.,
Vlns.
(pizz.)
Bs. Sax, Bsn.,
Vcs., Cb.
122
(shout ad lib.)
+Pno.,
Xylo.,
Vlns.
+Pno.,
Xylo.,
Vlns.
+Pno.,
Xylo.,
Vlns.
+Hns.
fz
125
Tpts. shake
WW., Br.
ff
WW., Hns,
Tbns.
Pno.,
Vcs.,
Cb.

128
WW., Vibr.,
El. Gtr., Pno.
ff
130
Tpts. (shake)
WW., Hns, Tbns.
Pno., Vcs., Cb.
131
WW., Br.
WW., Vibr.,
El. Gtr.,
Pno.
134
WW., Br.
ff
3
Cb.
+Vcs.
137
WW., Vibr.,
El. Gtr., Pno.
ff
138
WW., Br.
140
WW., Vibr., El. Gtr.
Pno., Vcs.
ff
dim. molto

143
145
JETS
Boy, boy,
–E♭ Cl.
–Alto Sax
Vibr., El. Gtr.
–Bsn.
–Bar. Sax, Pno., Vcs.
Pno., Vcs., Cb. (pizz.)
146
Jets
cra - zy boy,
Stay loose, boy!
+Pno.
+WW., Br.
ff sub.
+Bar. Sax
149
Jets
cresc. molto
Breeze it, buzz it, eas-y does it. Turn off the juice, boy.
+Pno.
+WW., Br.
–WW., Br., Pno. (r.h.)
pp sub.
153
Jets
dim. molto
RIFF solo
Go, man, go, But not like a yo - yo school - boy. Just play it
WW., Br.
shake
Vibr., El. Gtr.
Pno.
dim. molto
Pno., Cb.

Applause Segue

Part VIII
CONTEMPORARY MUSIC

Chapter 78
Reflections on War
Britten, Penderecki, and Others

202

Benjamin Britten
War Requiem (1961)
Agnus dei

When we think of the early 1960s, we cannot avoid iconic images of John F. Kennedy, "Leave it to Beaver," Elvis, and Beatlemania. Yet when the decade began, the conclusion of World War II, with its slaughter of 20,000,000 lives, was distant by only fifteen years, and few wartime leaders remained on the world stage. Eisenhower, the Supreme Allied Commander, had just finished his second term as president; Charles de Gaulle, the leader of the French resistance, was president of France; and Winston Churchill was England's Grand Old Man.

In 1961, as the painful memories of war were slipping away, Benjamin Britten introduced his *War Requiem*, a monumental composition that reflects upon the destruction brought by World War II and, by implication, of all warfare. It is a nonliturgical requiem (like the *German Requiem* by Brahms), because its words are not limited to those prescribed for the Catholic Requiem Mass. Britten uses English-language poetry by Wilfred Owen, which he mingles with Latin words from both the regular Mass and the Requiem Mass. By assembling such mixed resources, the composer creates a work of powerful emotion and stark opposites.

The "Agnus dei" movement is the shortest of six major sections in the *War Requiem*. Here a tenor soloist sings Owen's poem "At a Calvary Near the Ancre." Britten alternates its lines with those from the *Agnus dei* text, sung by the chorus, as it occurs in the Catholic Requiem Mass. In this section of the Mass, the liturgy requires three statements of the phrase beginning "Agnus dei," but Britten's tripartite organization for the movement does not conform to their symmetry. Close to two-thirds of the music—covering eight of the twelve lines of Owen's poem and two of the three iterations of the *Agnus dei* text—is devoted to the first **A** section (mm. 1–35). This unbalanced division is not by chance. The opening eight lines of the poem focus on the image of the crucified Christ. Owen's next two lines begin the **B** section (mm. 36–42), and here the poet castigates those who monger war under the guise of patriotism. In the last two lines, Owen states that there is a greater love—a love for humanity—that trumps nationalism, and these thoughts begin the concluding **A** section (mm. 42–52). Britten withholds the final benediction, "dona eis requiem sempiternam" ("grant them eternal rest"), until the concluding moment, and its sentiments are reinforced in the coda (mm. 53–55) by the soloist's "Dona nobis pacem" ("Grant us peace").

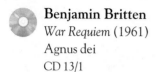

Benjamin Britten
War Requiem (1961)
Agnus dei
CD 13/1

16
97
pp
T. Solo
And now the Sol - diers bear with Him.
ppp smooth
S. A.
A - gnus De - i, qui tol - lis pec - ca - ta mun - di,
CHORUS (seated)
T.
B.
97 FULL ORCHESTRA
Str., W.W.
Cham. Orch.
more marked and cresc.
Near Gol - go - tha strolls ma - ny a priest,
do - na e - is re - qui - em.
CHORUS
CHAMBER ORCHESTRA
p
Bsn.
Str.
Full Orch.
cresc.

26
T. Solo
And in their fa-ces there is pride That they were flesh-marked by the Beast By whom the gen - tle
S. A.
CHORUS
T.
B.
Cl.
p
Ob.
mf
dim.
Cham. Orch.
98
pp
Christ's de - nied.
ppp
A-gnus De-i, qui tol-lis pec-ca-ta mun - di, do - na e - is re-qui - em.
98 FULL ORCHESTRA
Str., W.W.
ppp

36
f animated
T. Solo
The scribes on all the peo - - ple shove And bawl al - le - giance to the
S. A.
CHORUS
T.
B.
CHAMBER ORCHESTRA
Str.
Harp
S.D.
mf
Str.
99
p quietly
state, But they who love the grea - ter
ppp
A-gnus De-i, qui tol-lis pec-ca-ta mun - di,
99 FULL ORCHESTRA
CHAMBER ORCHESTRA
Ob. Cl. Bsn.
express.
ppp Str., W.W.
pp Str.

45
100
T. Solo
love
Lay down their life;
they do not hate.
CHORUS
S.
A.
T.
B.
Do-na e - is
100 FULL ORCH.
Cham. Orch.
Str. W.W.
dim.
Do-na no-bis pa - cem.
re - qui-em sem-pi-ter - nam. (m)
Full Orch.

Agnus Dei, qui tollis peccata mundi, dona eis requiem.	Lamb of God, who takes away the sins of the world, grant them rest.
Agnus Dei, qui tollis peccata mundi, dona eis requiem.	Lamb of God, who takes away the sins of the world, grant them rest.
Agnus Dei, qui tollis peccata mundi, dona eis requiem sempiternam.	Lamb of God, who takes away the sins of the world, grant them eternal rest.
Dona nobis pacem.	Give us peace.

203

Krzysztof Penderecki

Threnody for the Victims of Hiroshima (1960)

Threnody for the Victims of Hiroshima (1960), by the Polish composer Krzysztof Penderecki, embodies new ideas concerning musical texture. In the place of such traditional textures as homophony and polyphony, made from lines and chords, *Threnody* uses sound masses as basic elements. These masses are the raw material that the composer shapes into musical and expressive form. When listening to the work, we do not hear the lines of any of the fifty-two strings. They are instead merged into a succession of masses distinguished by their volume, density, and timbre. Penderecki's novel approach to the orchestra was influenced by experiments with electronic music by European composers in the 1950s.

To instruct the players in realizing sound masses, Penderecki uses "graphic notation"—shapes and symbols that are not part of conventional musical notation and that instruct the performers to play the instruments in unusual ways. For example, in measures 6 to 9 the strings are called upon to play physically uncoordinated figures that demand a whole new technique of string playing. They must play on both sides of the bridge, create percussive effects with their instruments, and negotiate rapid-fire arpeggios and quarter-tone tunings.

The listener hears six different sections within Penderecki's evolving sound patterns. In the first (mm. 1–6), strident high tones gradually dissolve into vibrato patterns. The crackling articulations of the second section (mm. 6–9) have been noted above. Tone clusters (mm. 10–25) give way to the pointillistic textures of the fourth section (mm. 26–62), but return in measure 62, and the work fades away with a final diminuendo in the coda (m. 70). Penderecki specified the duration of each measure by timings entered at the bottom of the score. However, conductors often have their own ideas, and different recordings will vary in length. The resulting music, as always with Penderecki, is highly expressive.

Krzysztof Penderecki
Threnody for the Victims of Hiroshima (1960)
CD 13/2

Abbreviations and symbols

sharpen a quarter-tone

sharpen three quarter-tones

flatten a quarter-tone

flatten three quarter-tones

highest note of the instrument (no definite pitch)

play between bridge and tailpiece

arpeggio on 4 strings behind the bridge

play on the tailpiece (arco) by bowing the tailpiece at an angle of 90° to its longer axis

play on the bridge by bowing the wood of the bridge at a right angle at its right side

Percussion effect: strike the upper sounding board of the violin with the nut or the finger-tips

several irregular changes of bow

molto vibrato

very slow vibrato with a 1/4 tone frequency difference produced by sliding the finger

very rapid non rhythmisized tremolo

ordinario	ord.
sul ponticello	s. p.
sul tasto	s. t.
col legno	c. l.
legno battuto	l. batt.

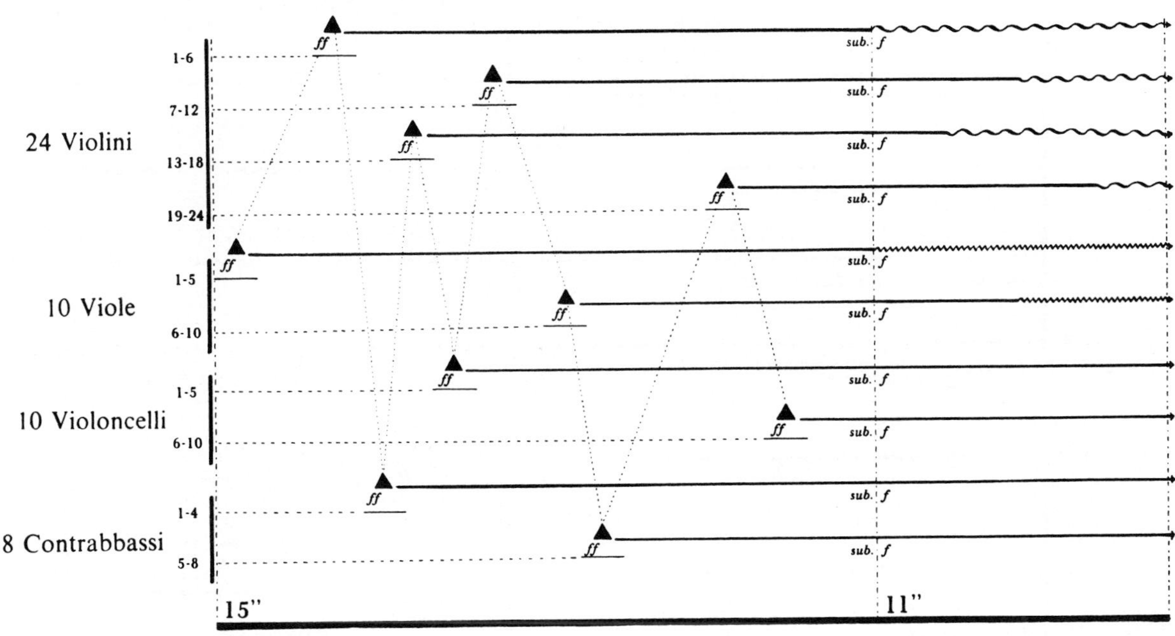
24 Violini
1-6
7-12
13-18
19-24
10 Viole
1-5
6-10
10 Violoncelli
1-5
6-10
8 Contrabbassi
1-4
5-8
ff
sub. f
15"
11"

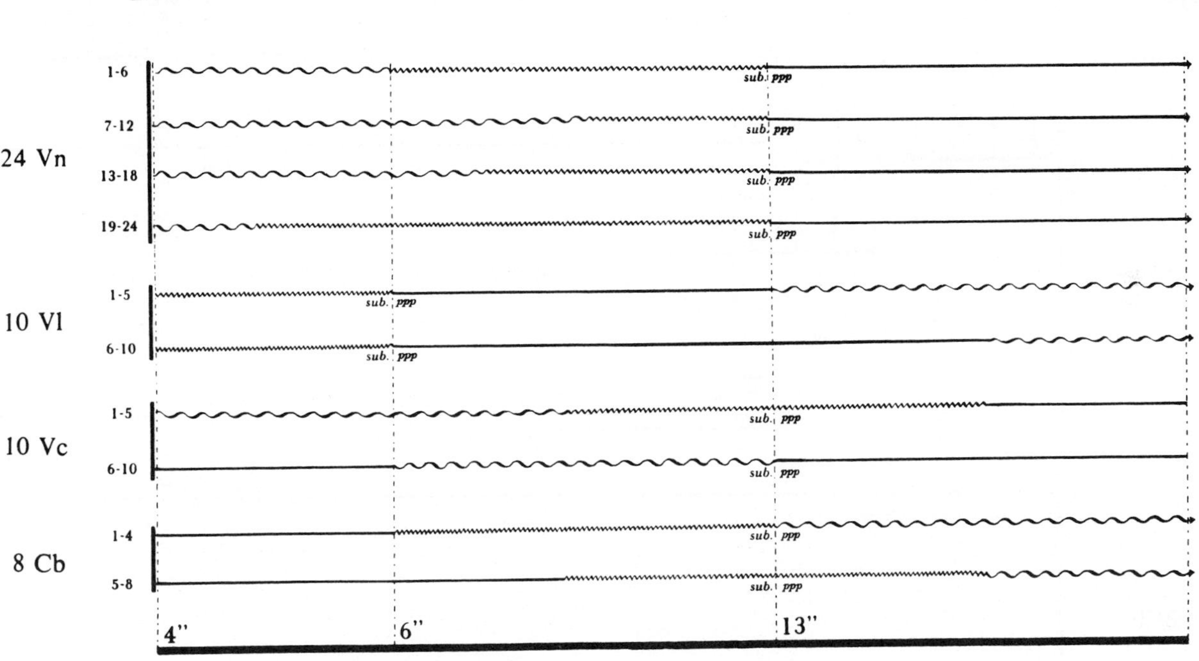
24 Vn
1-6
7-12
13-18
19-24
10 Vl
1-5
6-10
10 Vc
1-5
6-10
8 Cb
1-4
5-8
sub. ppp
4"
6"
13"

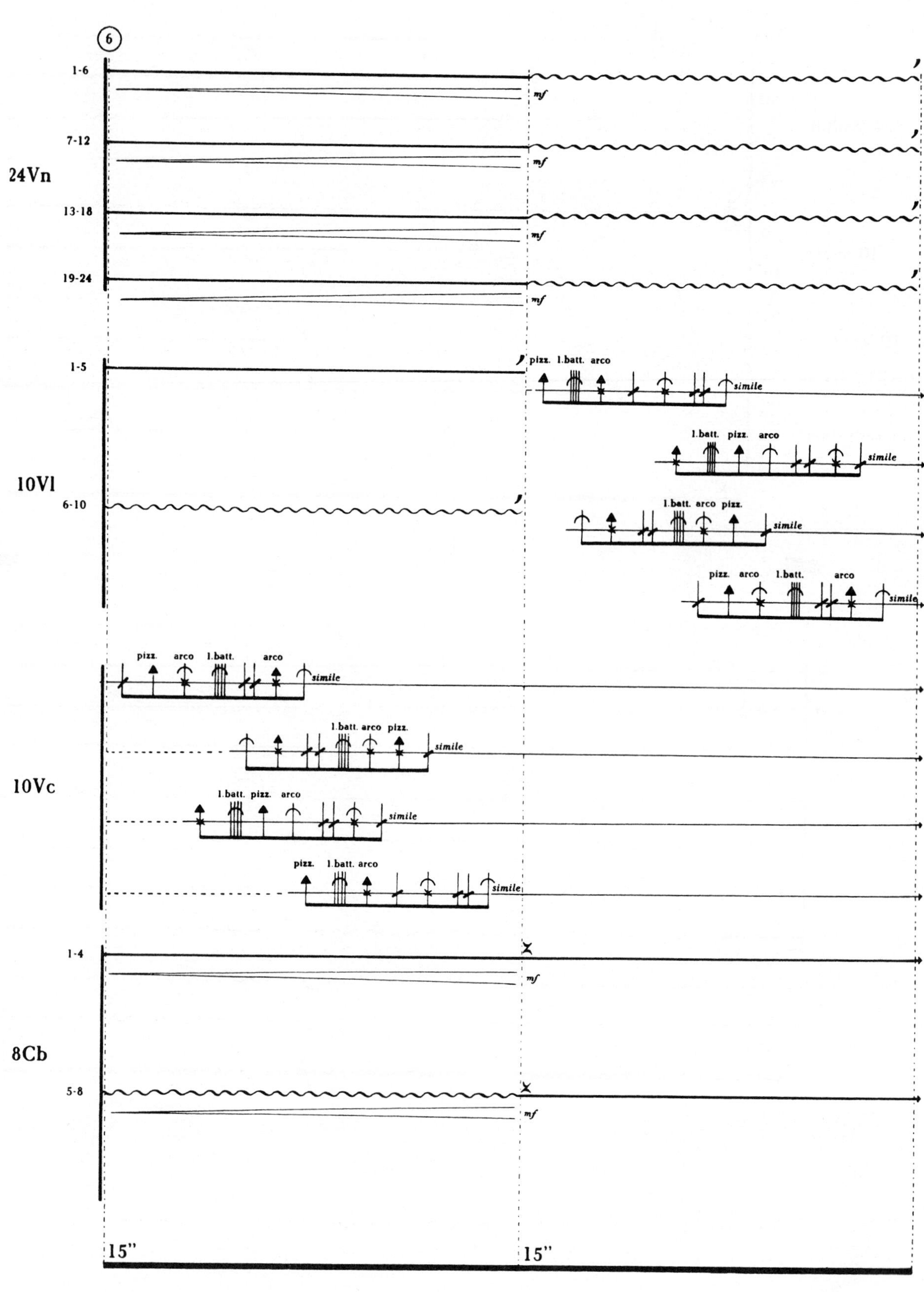

6
1-6
7-12
24Vn
13-18
19-24
mf
1-5
10Vl
6-10
pizz. l.batt. arco
l.batt. pizz. arco
l.batt. arco pizz.
pizz. arco l.batt. arco
simile
10Vc
1-4
8Cb
5-8
15"
15"

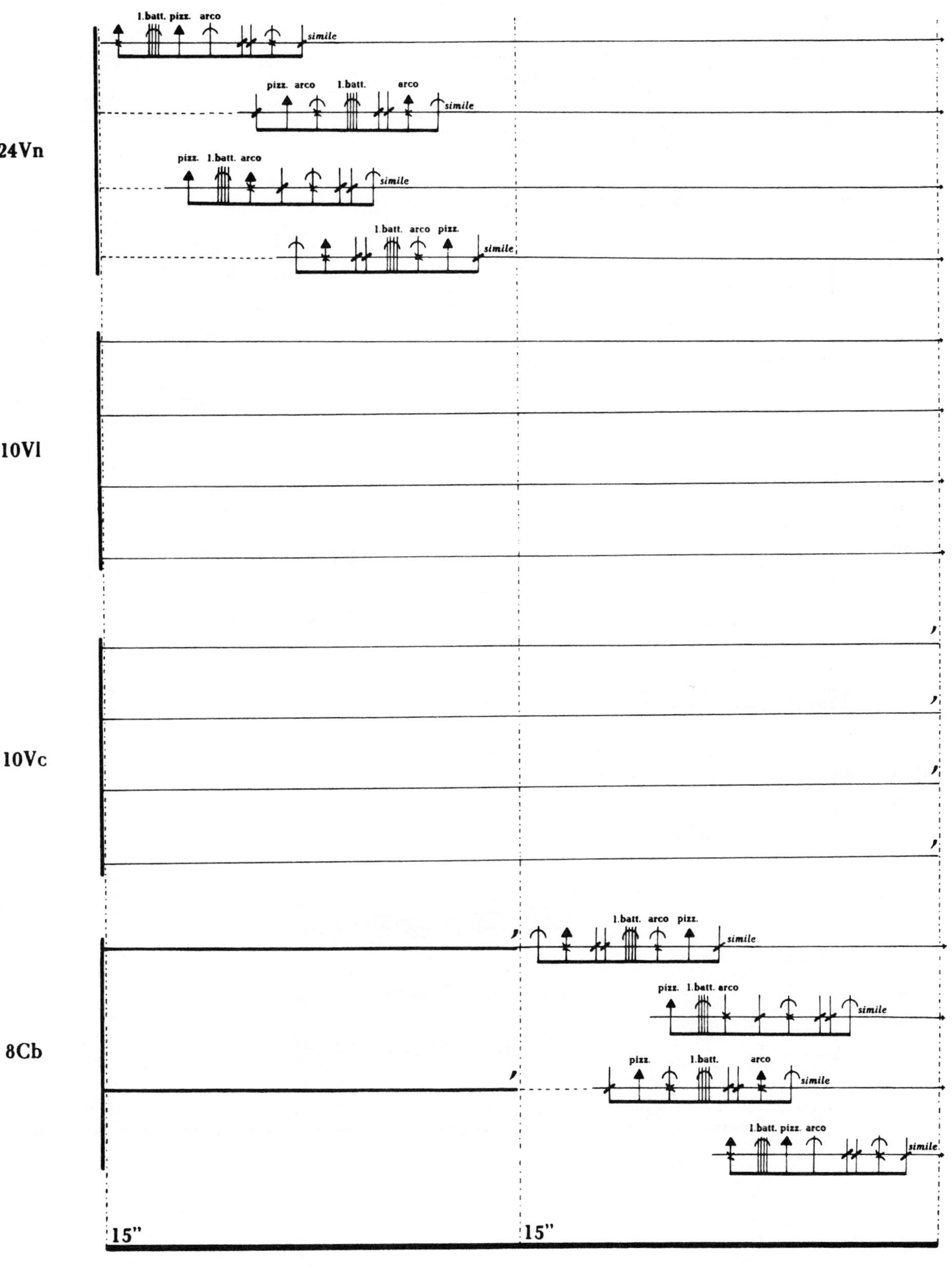
1.batt. pizz. arco
simile
pizz. arco 1.batt. arco
simile
24Vn
pizz. 1.batt. arco
simile
1.batt. arco pizz.
simile
10Vl
10Vc
1.batt. arco pizz.
simile
pizz. 1.batt. arco
simile
8Cb
pizz. 1.batt. arco
simile
1.batt. pizz. arco
simile
15"
15"

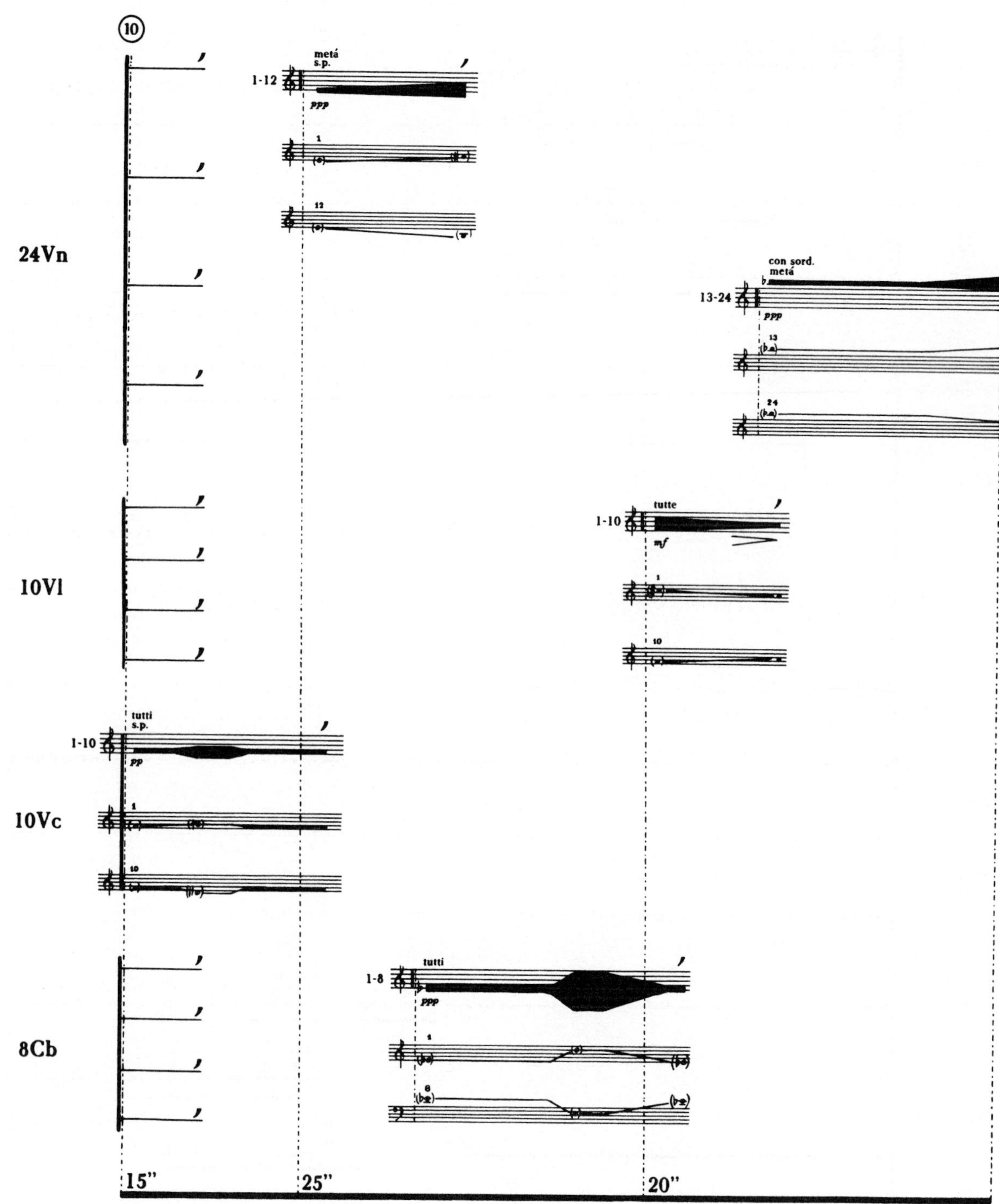
10
24Vn
1-12
metá
s.p.
ppp
13-24
con sord.
metá
ppp
10Vl
1-10
tutte
mf
10Vc
1-10
tutti
s.p.
pp
8Cb
1-8
tutti
ppp
15"
25"
20"

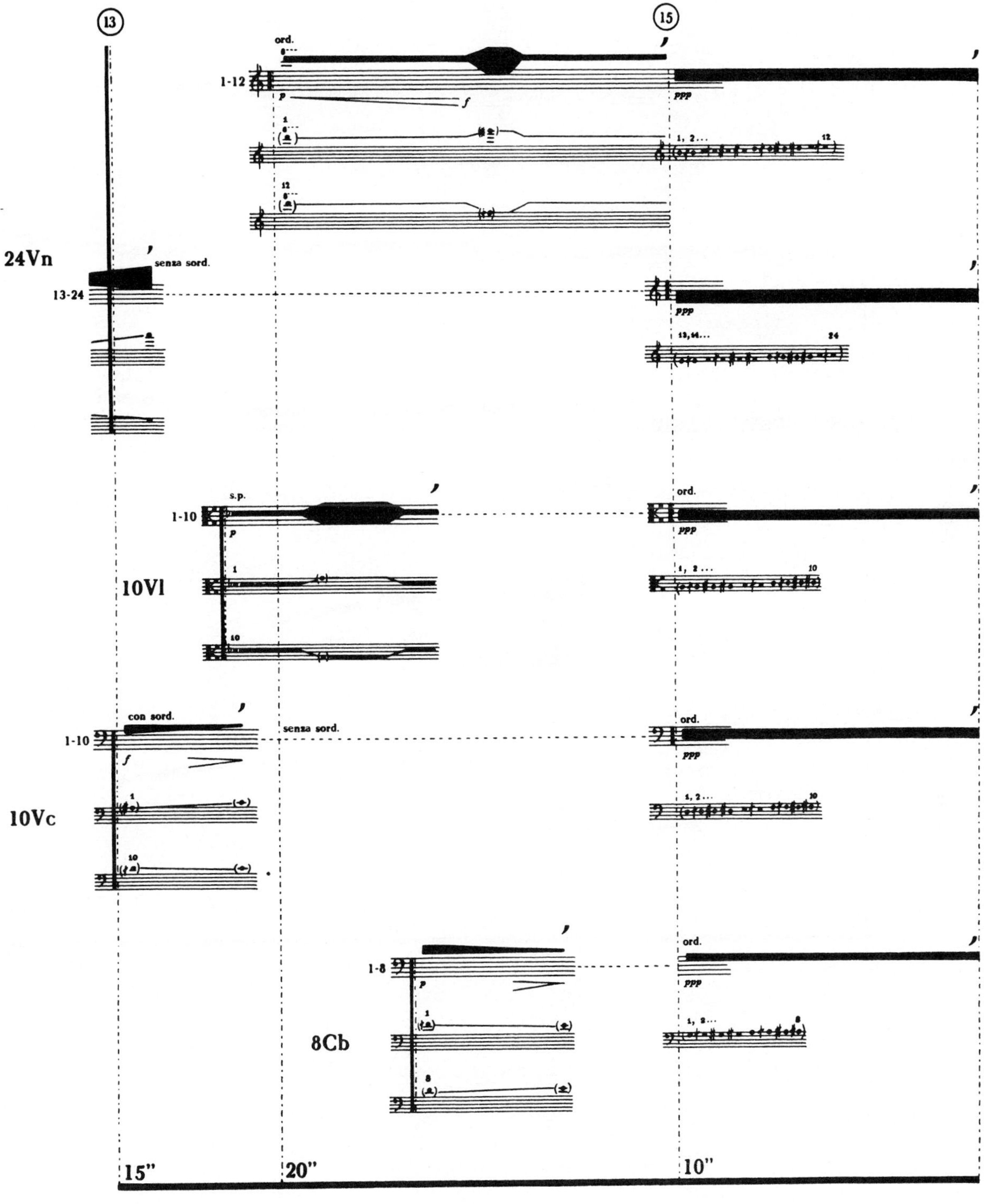
13
15
ord.
1-12
p
f
ppp
24Vn
senza sord.
13-24
s.p.
1-10
10Vl
ord.
con sord.
senza sord.
10Vc
1-8
8Cb
15"
20"
10"

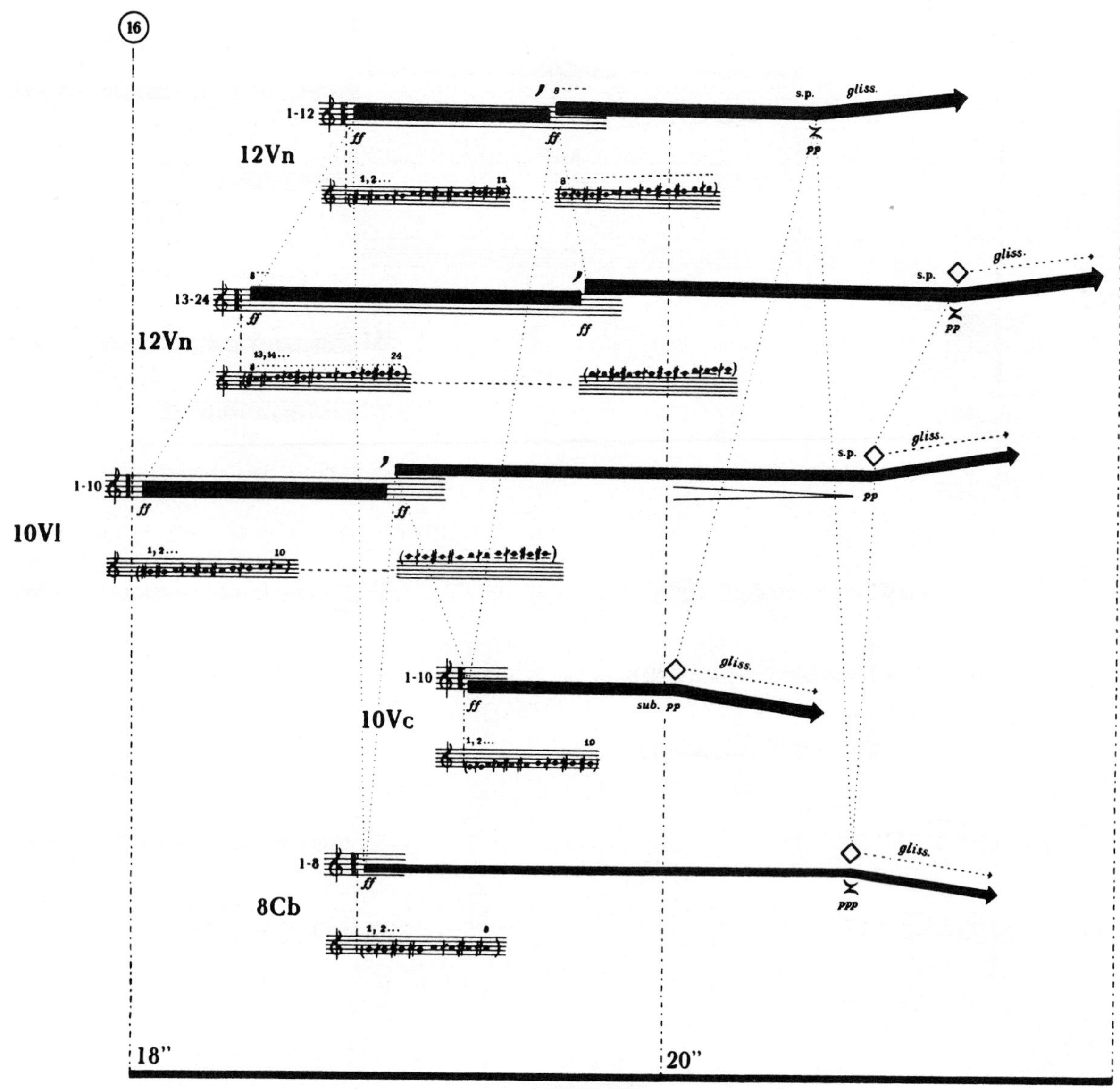
16
1-12
12Vn
ff
ff
s.p.
gliss.
pp
13-24
12Vn
ff
ff
s.p.
gliss.
pp
1-10
10Vl
ff
ff
s.p.
gliss.
pp
1-10
10Vc
ff
sub. pp
gliss.
1-8
8Cb
ff
gliss.
ppp
18"
20"

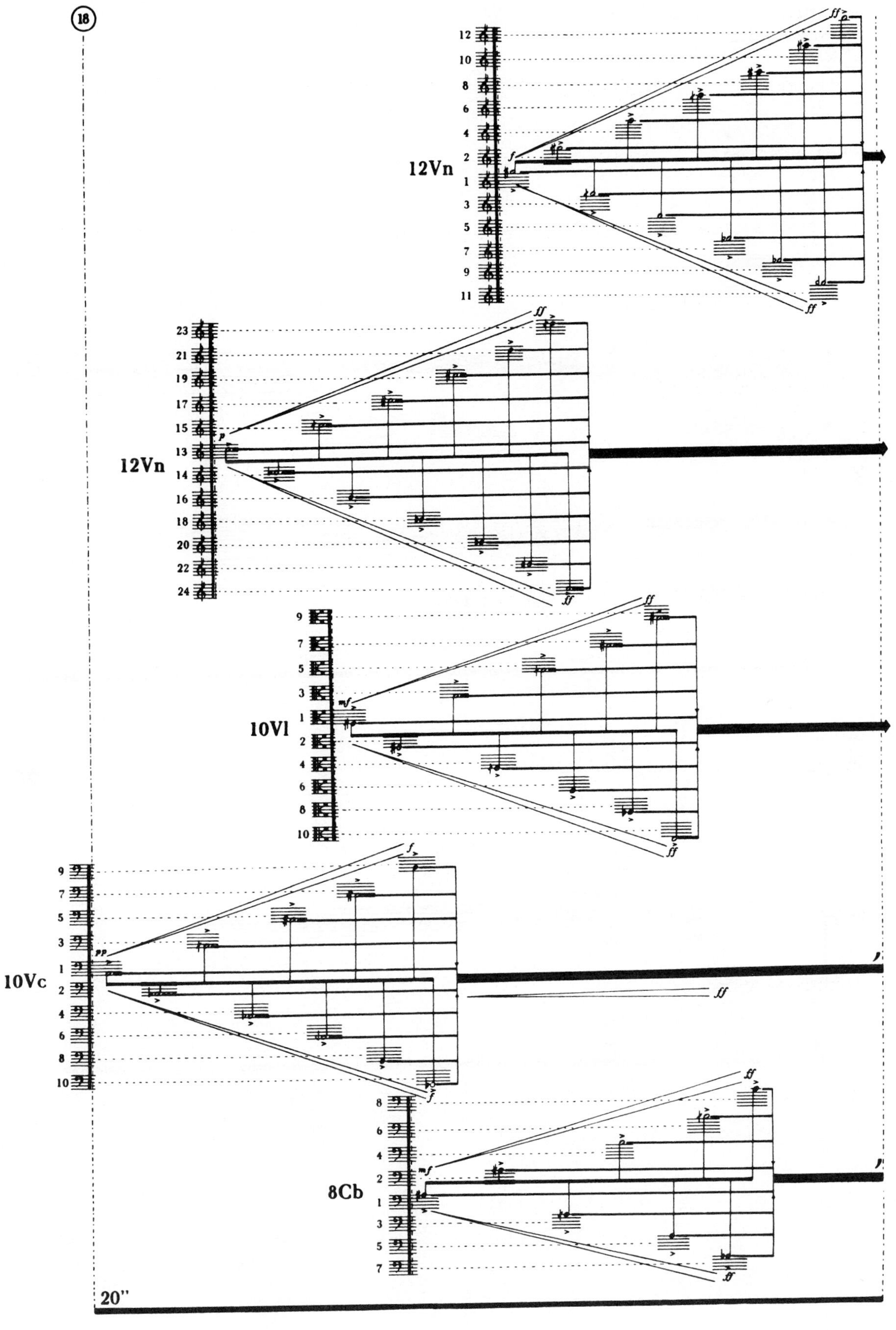
18
12Vn
12Vn
10Vl
10Vc
8Cb
20"

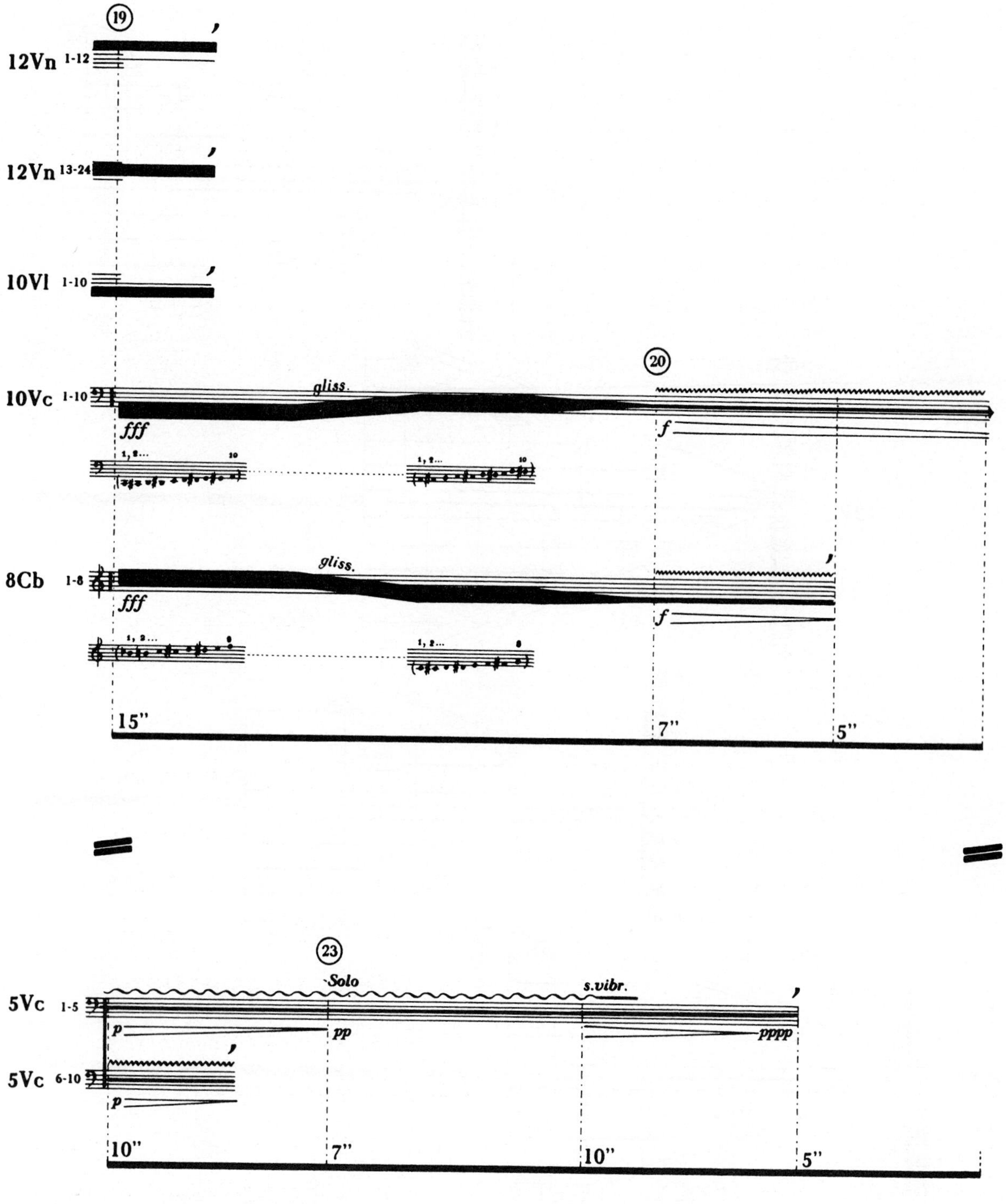

19
12Vn 1-12
12Vn 13-24
10Vl 1-10
20
gliss.
10Vc 1-10
fff
f
gliss.
8Cb 1-8
fff
f
15"
7"
5"

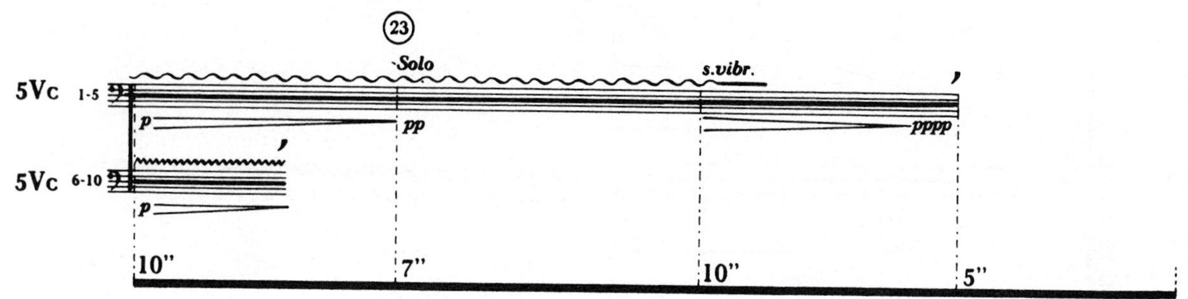

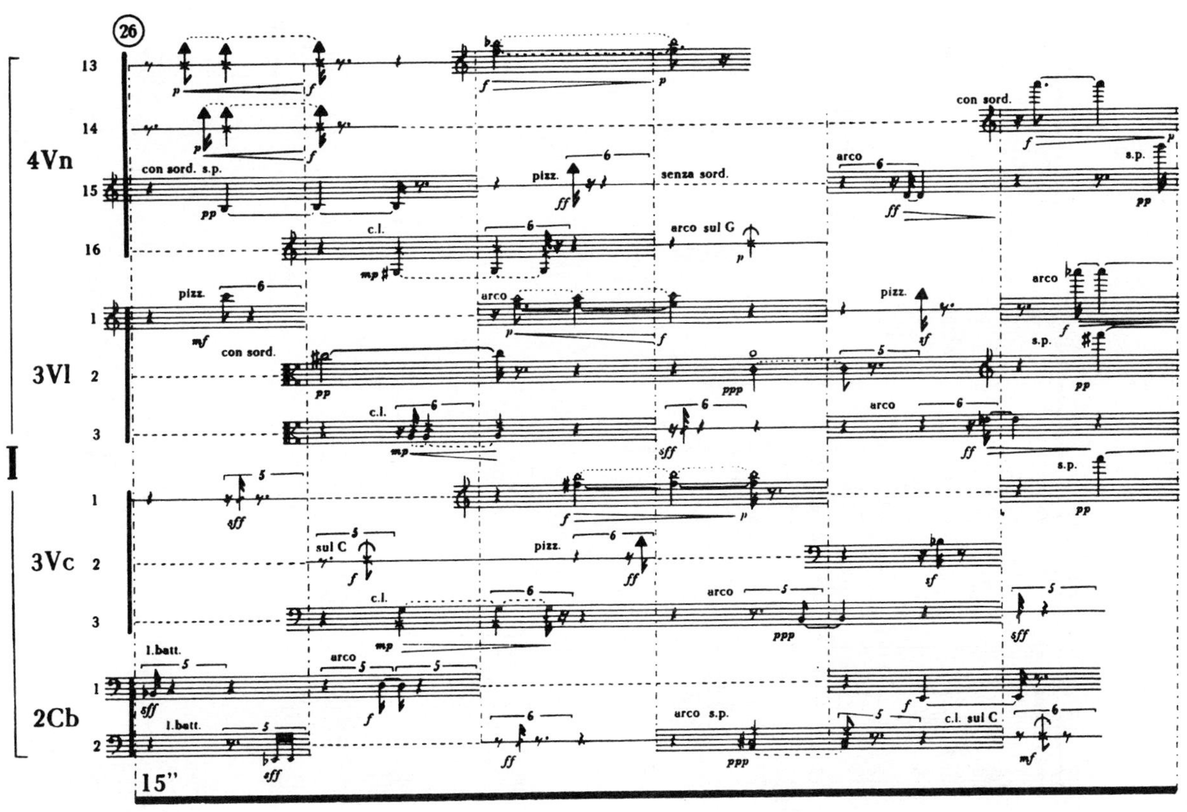
26
4Vn
13
14
15
16
3Vl
3Vc
2Cb
I
con sord.
s.p.
pizz.
senza sord.
arco
c.l.
arco sul G
l.batt.
sul C
15"

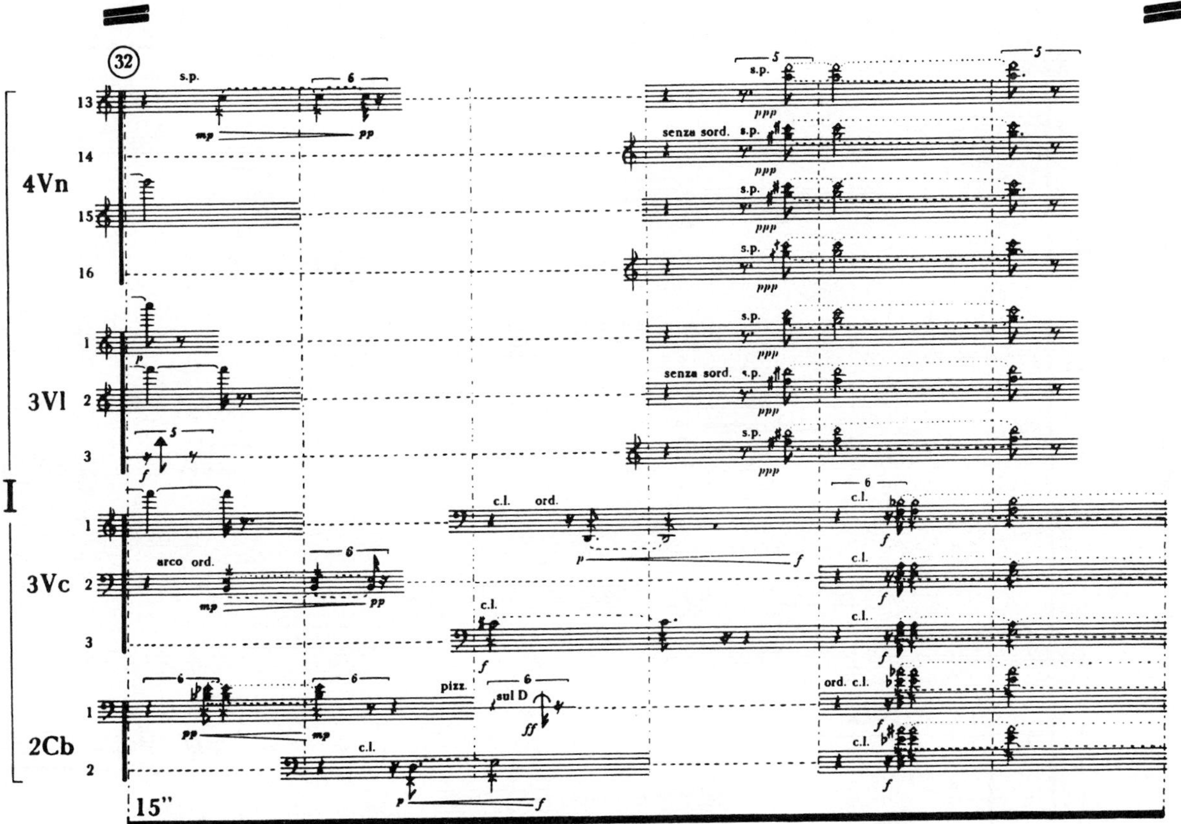
32
4Vn
3Vl
3Vc
2Cb
I
s.p.
senza sord.
c.l.
ord.
arco ord.
pizz.
sul D
ord. c.l.
15"

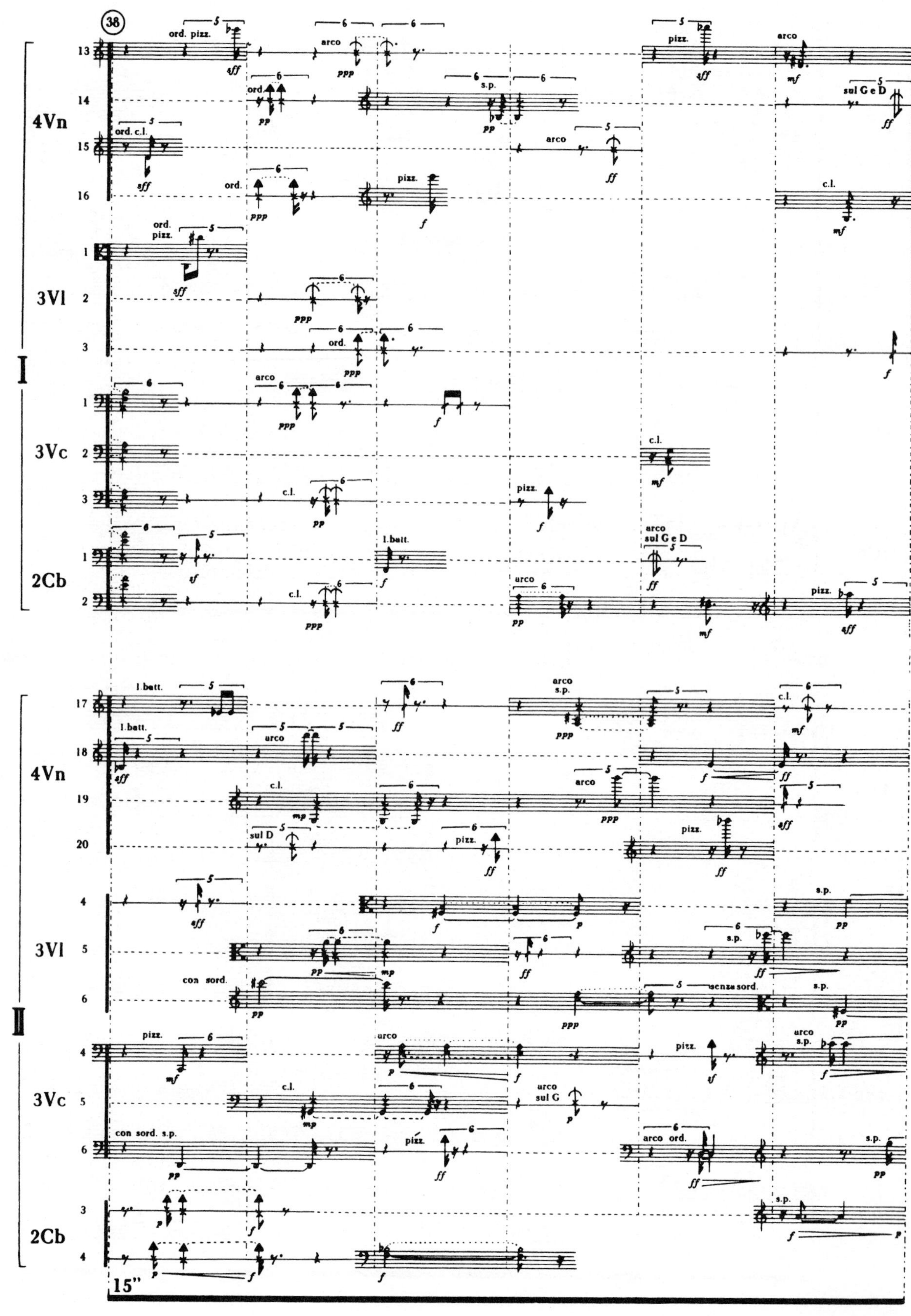
38
4Vn
3Vl
3Vc
2Cb
I
II
ord. pizz.
arco
ord.
s.p.
ord. c.l.
pizz.
c.l.
sul G e D
l. batt.
con sord.
senza sord.
sul D
sul G
arco ord.
15"

44
4Vn
3Vl
I
3Vc
2Cb
4Vn
3Vl
II
3Vc
2Cb
4Vn
3Vl
III
3Vc
2Cb
pizz.
arco
c.l. batt.
c.l.
s.p.
sul D
ord. c.l.
con sord.
senza sord.
l batt.
15"

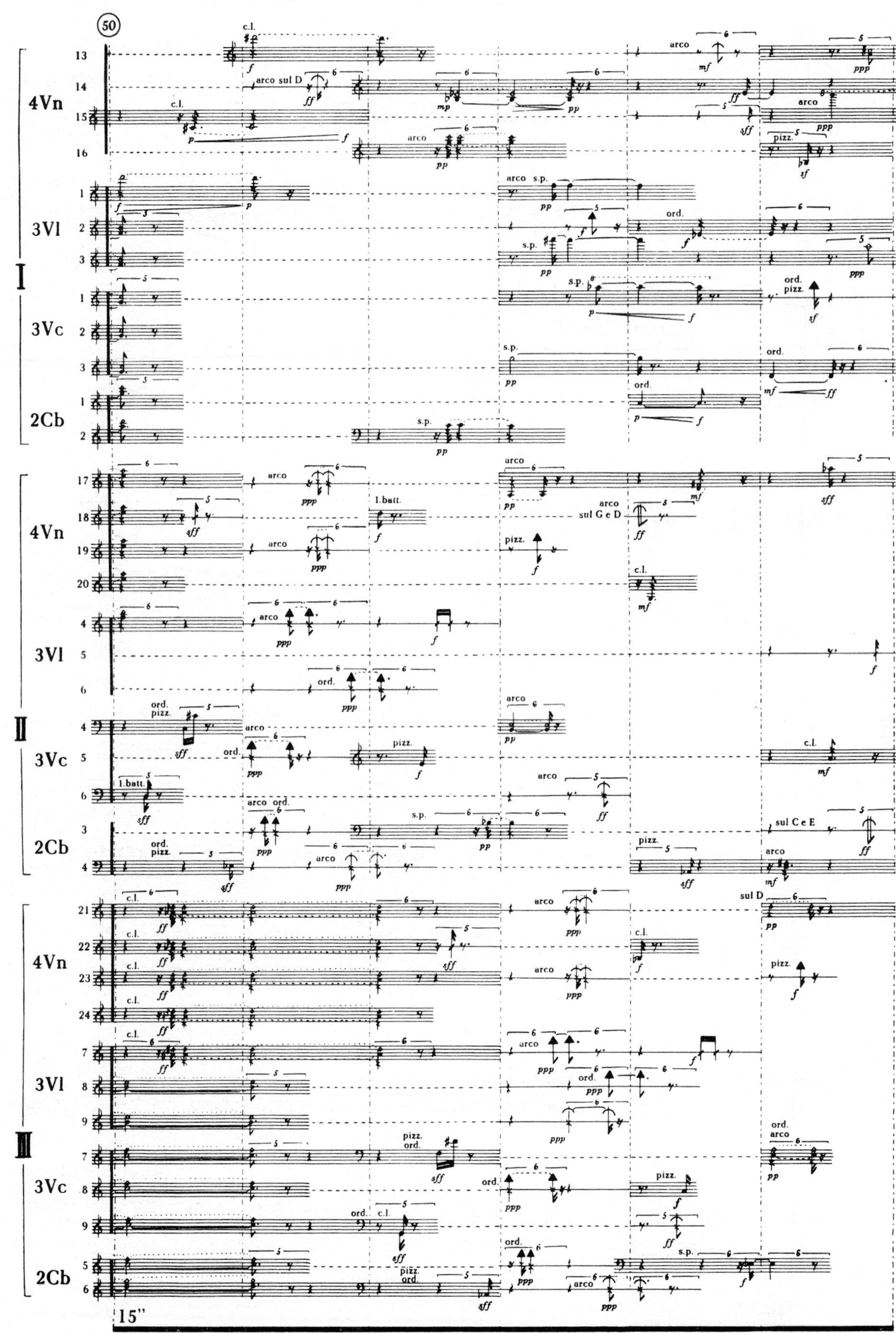
50
4Vn
3Vl
3Vc
2Cb
I
II
III
c.l.
arco sul D
arco
s.p.
ord.
pizz.
l.batt.
arco sul G e D
sul C e E
sul D
15"

56
arco
1.batt.
arco
pizz.
4Vn
3Vl
I
3Vc
2Cb
ff sempre
s.p.
pp
ppp
arco
ff
pizz.
f
p
II
1.batt.
ff sempre
III
mf
sff
c.l.
ppp
10"
pizz.
f
ff sempre

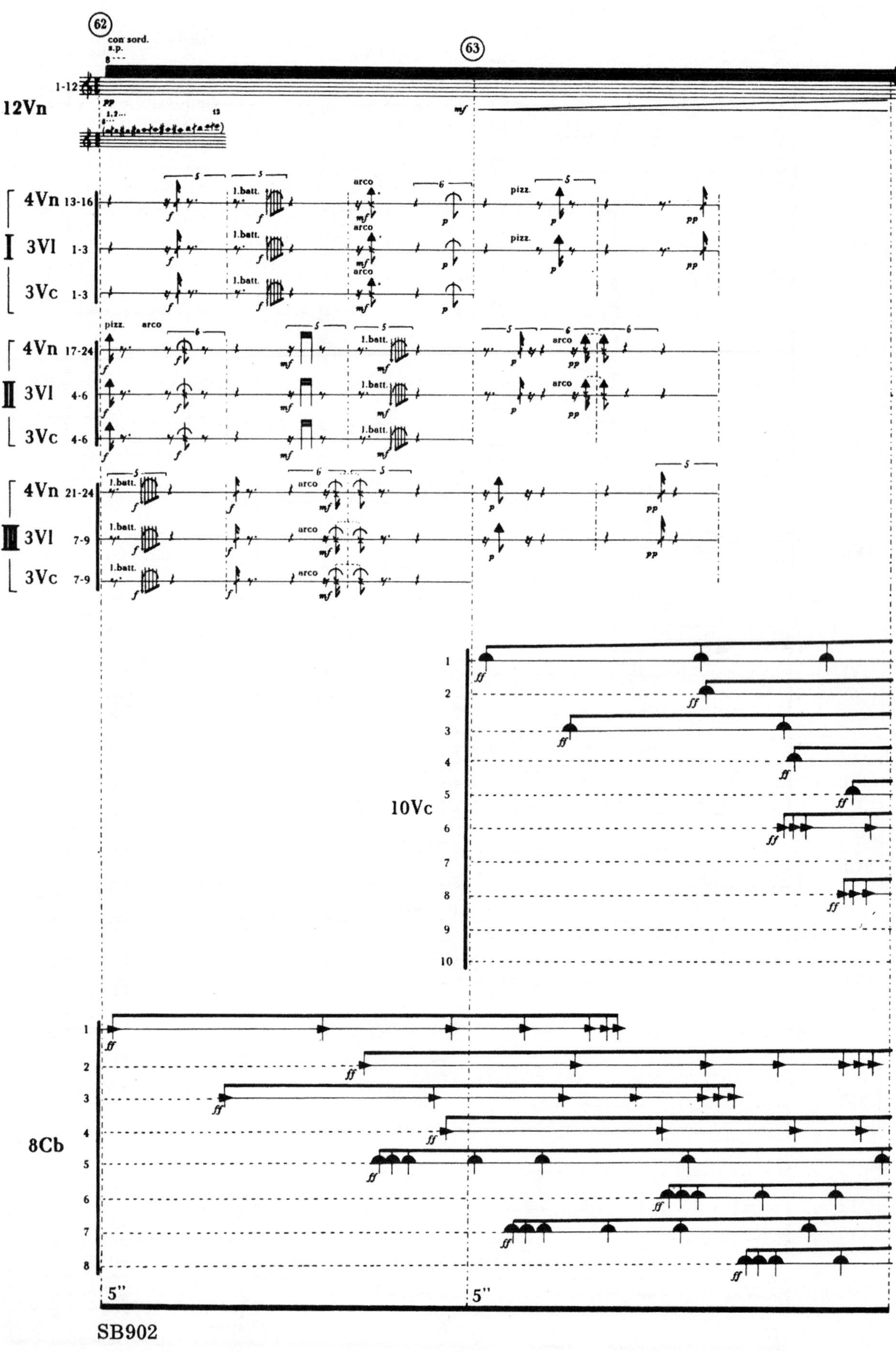
62
63
con sord.
s.p.
12Vn
4Vn 13-16
I 3Vl 1-3
3Vc 1-3
4Vn 17-24
II 3Vl 4-6
3Vc 4-6
4Vn 21-24
III 3Vl 7-9
3Vc 7-9
l.batt.
arco
pizz.
10Vc
8Cb
5"
5"

SB902

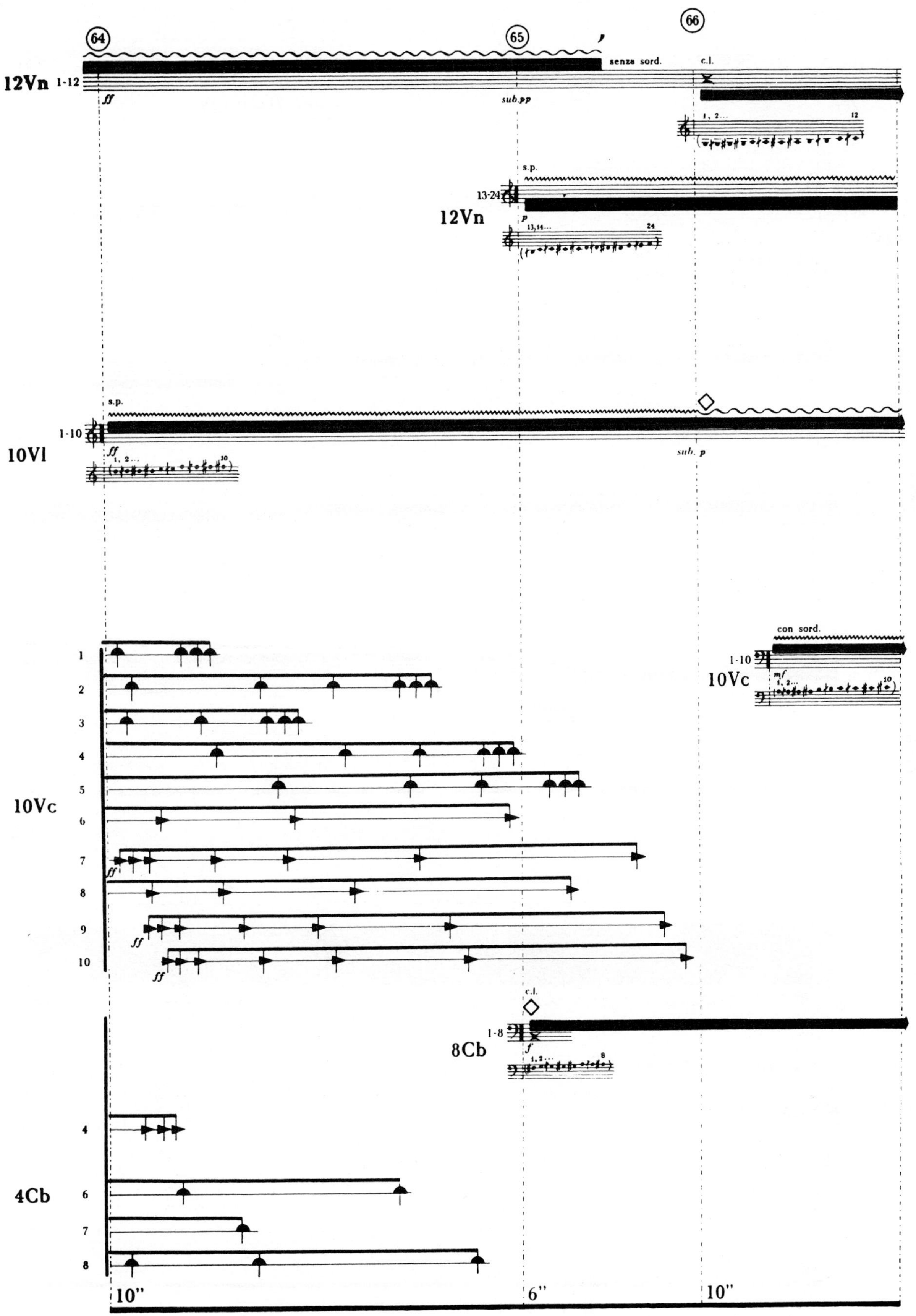

64
65
66
senza sord.
c.l.
12Vn 1-12
ff
sub.pp
s.p.
13-24
12Vn
p
10Vl
1-10
sub. p
con sord.
10Vc
mf
c.l.
8Cb
1-8
f
4Cb
10"
6"
10"

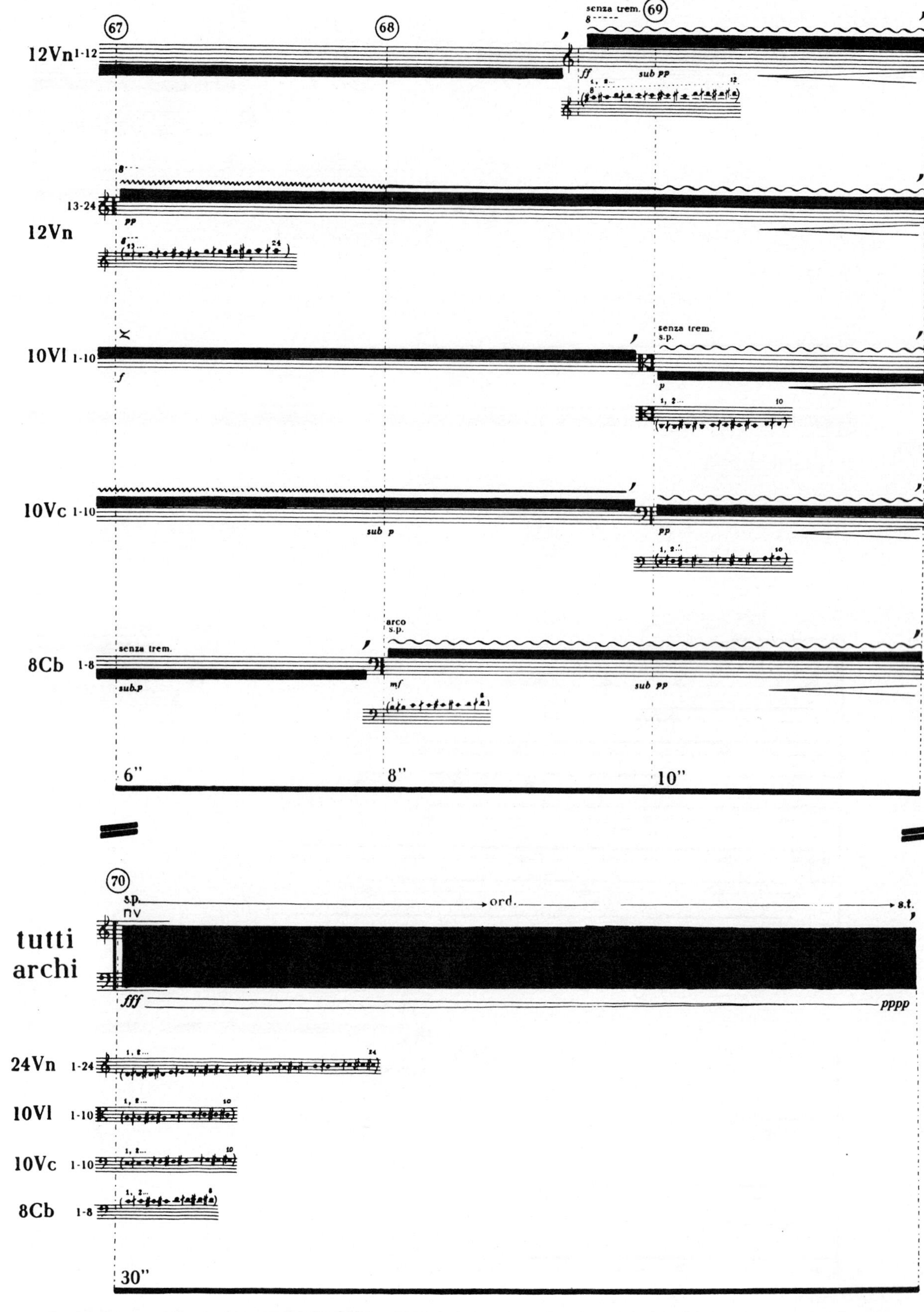
67
68
69
12Vn 1-12
senza trem.
ff
sub pp
13-24
12Vn
pp
10Vl 1-10
f
senza trem.
s.p.
p
10Vc 1-10
sub p
pp
8Cb 1-8
senza trem.
sub.p
arco
s.p.
mf
sub pp
6"
8"
10"
70
s.p.
ord.
s.t.
tutti
archi
fff
pppp
24Vn 1-24
10Vl 1-10
10Vc 1-10
8Cb 1-8
30"

Twelve-Tone Music and Serialism after World War II

204

Milton Babbitt
Composition for Piano No. 1 (1947)

Milton Babbitt's lively Composition No. 1 shows conclusively that a work written using the procedures of strict serialism and the twelve-tone method can produce music that is engaging on every level, not only the intellectual one. Babbitt's brief piano piece has the jazzy, impulsive swing of an Art Tatum improvisation, merged with the strictness of a two-part invention by Bach. Schoenberg is lurking nearby too, as evident where Babbitt extends Schoenberg's twelve-tone method into new areas. Babbitt juggles all of the restrictions of serialized composition and still tosses off a brilliant and witty work, as though with ease.

The tonal organization of the piece is controlled by the row B♭ E♭ F D C D♭ G B F♯ A A♭ E. This and related row forms are easily traced in the individual lines played by each hand. But Babbitt also creates a deep structural scaffolding for the piece by choosing durational values, dynamics, points of attack, and articulations according to an integrated system. The result, in Babbitt's terms, is a work having "total structuralization," or what we now call "total serialism."

On the basis of changes in texture and surface design, the composition can be divided into six sections (at mm. 9, 19, 29, 39, and 49). These are laid out as a palindrome: the rows of the last section, for example, are retrogrades of the opening ones transposed by a tritone. Babbitt increases the degree of symmetry by giving the row that was played in the left hand in the first section to the right in the sixth. In the chart that follows, the basic ("prime") rows are abbreviated as P, inverted rows as I, retrograded rows as R, and retrograde inversions as RI. Transpositions of rows are indicated by a following number, from 0 (an untransposed form) to 11 (a row transposed up eleven semitones). The basic, untransposed row form (P-0) is, by definition, the first one heard.

	Section 1				**Section 6**			
r.h.	P-6	R-0	RI-7	I-1	P-0	RI-1	I-7	R-6
l.h.	P-0	RI-1	I-7	R-6	RI-7	I-1	P-6	R-0
	1	3	5	7	49	51	53	55

The inner sections are likewise paired so that the rows of the fifth part are a retrograde of the second; the fourth reverses the third. Although the rows are ordered as palindromes, that relationship among the six sections is not especially audible, because each passage has its own melodic character.

Milton Babbitt
Composition for Piano No. 1 (1947)
CD 13/3

I

These pieces are intended for performance as a single unit.

Accidentals affect only those notes which they immediately precede, except when notes are tied (♯♩‿♩)

The sign ⌐ ¬ denotes the duration of *una corda*.

The following tempi may be substituted for those indicated in the first and third compositions: 96 instead of 108, and 112 instead of 126.

13
mf
p
f
mp
mf
mp
f
mf
p
f
mf
mp
p
mp
f
f
mf
mp
p

25
mp
p
f
mf
mp
p
f
mf
f
mf
mf
mp
p
p
mp

36

46
f
p
mp
(♩=108)
pp
mf
ppp
ppp
mp
mp
pp
p
p
ppp
pppp

205

Igor Stravinsky
Agon (1953–1957)
Bransle Double

Stravinsky's *Agon*, created for George Balanchine and the New York City Ballet, calls for twelve dancers. Unlike some of the most famous nineteenth-century ballets, this has no story line. The choreography is abstract in conception and presents the dancers in a purely objective "competition." *Agon* is the Greek word for competition.

As he composed the ballet, Stravinsky was working his way from the style of Neoclassicism—the musical language that he had used since the 1920s—to twelve-tone serialism. The result in *Agon* is a provocative mixture of tastes and compositional techniques. Much about the score reminds us of the composer's Neoclassical past. He imitates French courtly dances from the Renaissance and Baroque periods, such as the "bransle double," a fifteenth-century French circular dance in which the participants held hands.

Stravinsky's residual Neoclassicism is apparent in the music's strict rhythms and severely anti-Romantic orchestration. As in the Neoclassical Octet (no. 180), the orchestration of *Agon* rests upon clear oppositions of sound groups. For example, in the Bransle Double, which occurs toward the middle of the short work, Stravinsky divides the orchestra into three distinct groups: the trumpet and trombone, five-part strings, and the woodwinds (the piano, used sparingly, generally plays with the woodwinds).

In this passage, Stravinsky's objectivist past is updated to accommodate the twelve-tone and serialist language of Anton Webern, whose music Stravinsky is said to have studied while writing this composition. Through an extensive use of octave displacement, the sound suggests a Webernesque pointillism in instrumental color. Also in this section the twelve-tone row C D E♭ F E A G A♭ B♭ C♭ D♭ G♭ controls the entire tonal organization. Its presence is clearly apparent in the line played in octaves by the violins in the movement's opening measures.

A	B	A	Coda
336–351	352–364	365–372	373–386

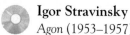

Igor Stravinsky
Agon (1953–1957)
Bransle Double
CD 13/4

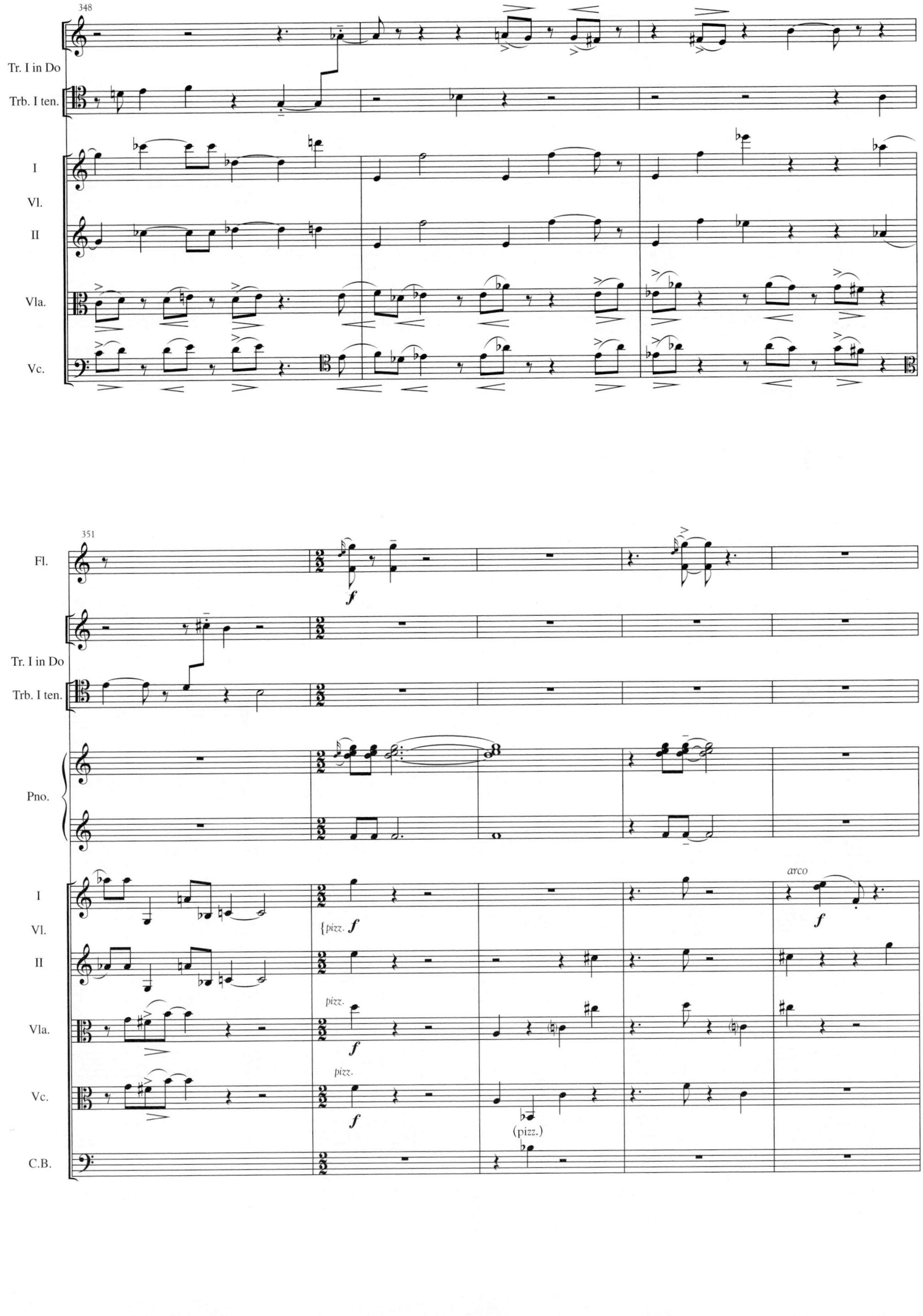

351
Fl.
Tr. I in Do
Trb. I ten.
Pno.
I
Vl.
II
Vla.
Vc.
C.B.
pizz. ***f***
arco
(pizz.)

356
Fl. I. II
I
II
Cl. in Si♭
bas.
a2
Pno.
pizz.
I
Vl.
II
{arco
(pizz.)
Vla.
361
Fl. I. II
I
II
Cl. in Si♭
bas.
Trb. I ten.
Pno.
I
Vl.
II
{pizz.
Vla.
Vc.

366
Tr. I in Do
Trb. I ten.
I
Vl.
II
f

Cl. in Si♭ II
C. Fag.
Tr. I in Do
Trb. I ten.
I
Vl.
II
C.B.
marc. in p
p
con sord.
poco sf
(pizz.)
poco sf

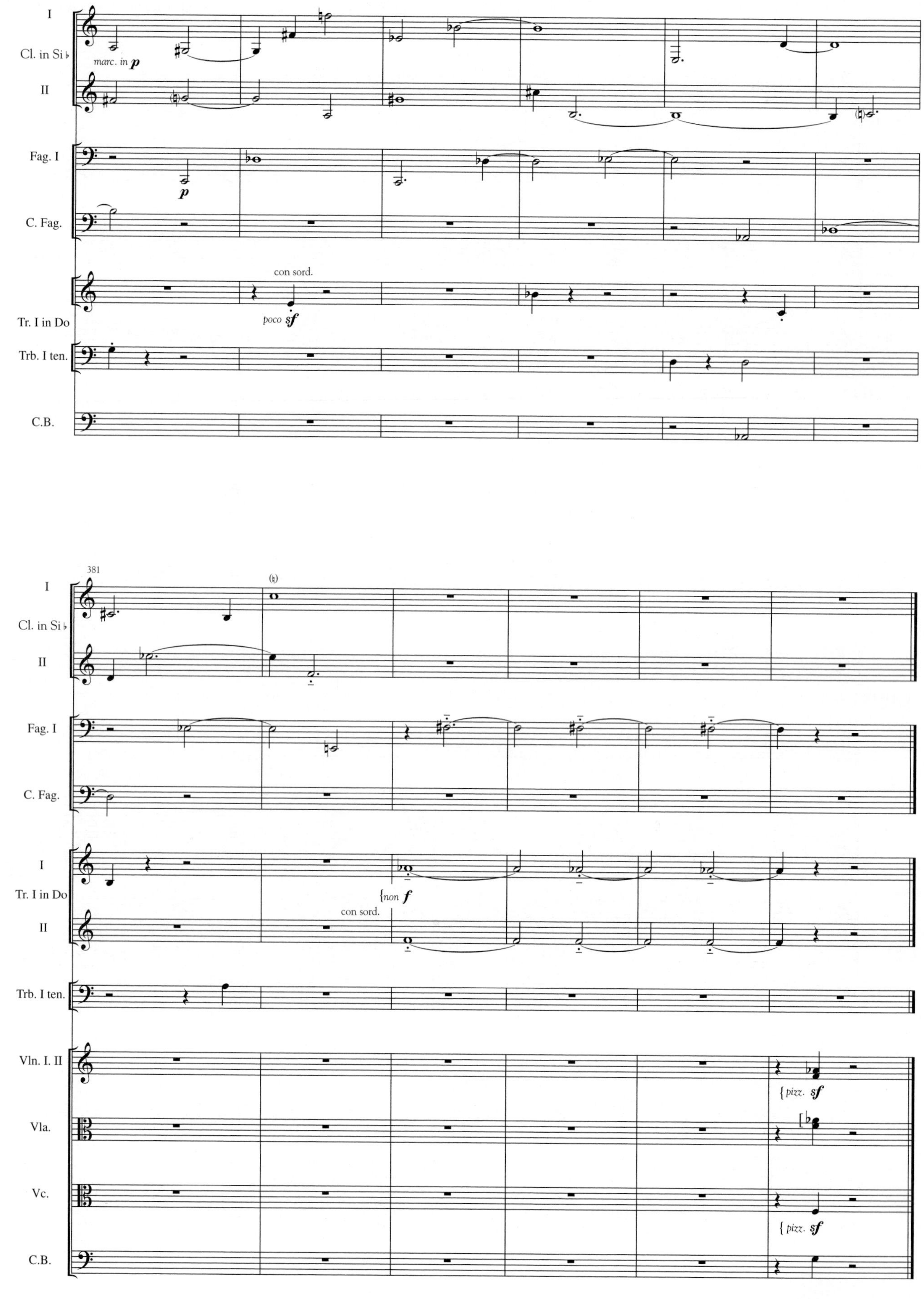

381

I
Cl. in Si♭
II
Fag. I
C. Fag.
I
Tr. I in Do
II
{non f
con sord.
Trb. I ten.
Vln. I. II
{pizz. sf
Vla.
Vc.
{pizz. sf
C.B.

206

Pierre Boulez
Le marteau sans maître (1955)
"L'artisanat furieux"

Pierre Boulez's *Le marteau sans maître* (*The Hammer Without a Master*) was one of the most influential and often imitated works of the decades following World War II. It projects the audacious modernism that Boulez demanded from new music, a modernism that Boulez believed to be required by the spirit of the time. In its medium of voice and chamber orchestra, *Le marteau* alludes to Arnold Schoenberg's *Pierrot lunaire* (see no. 176), which Boulez had declared to be Schoenberg's finest composition. But Boulez's novelty of style and compositional method make Schoenberg's music seem downright old-fashioned in comparison.

In the third movement of *Le marteau*, "L'artisanat furieux" ("The Raging Proletariat"), Boulez calls on the alto voice and alto flute to perform a surrealistic and macabre poem by René Char. The meaning of Char's poetry—which is obscure to begin with—seems of less importance to Boulez than the sounds of its words and the isolated and often conflicting images that they evoke. These word-sounds are floated into a virtuosic and ornate duet between voice and instrument. Their sounds and gestures are so similar that the listener can easily lose track of which sound is generated by which source.

Pierre Boulez
Le marteau sans maître (1955)
"L'artisanat furieux"
CD 13/5

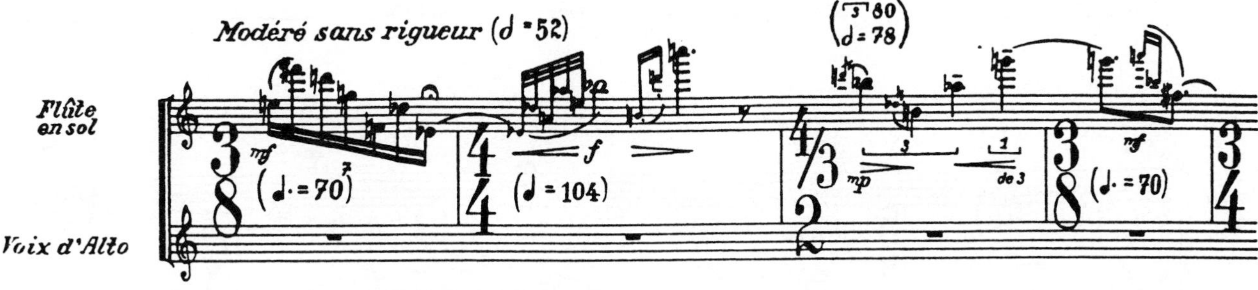

flatterzunge
quasif
Fl. en sol
Voix
(♩= 104)
quasif
4 pour 5
bord
du
pour 4/5
pour 6
(♩.=70)
clou
ff sub.
f sub.
Et
ca - da-vre dans le pa-nier
(♩=104)
de 3
cresc. al - - - - ff
tenuto senza dim.
senza dim.
(3+1+3)
(3+2+3)
Et chevaux de la - bours

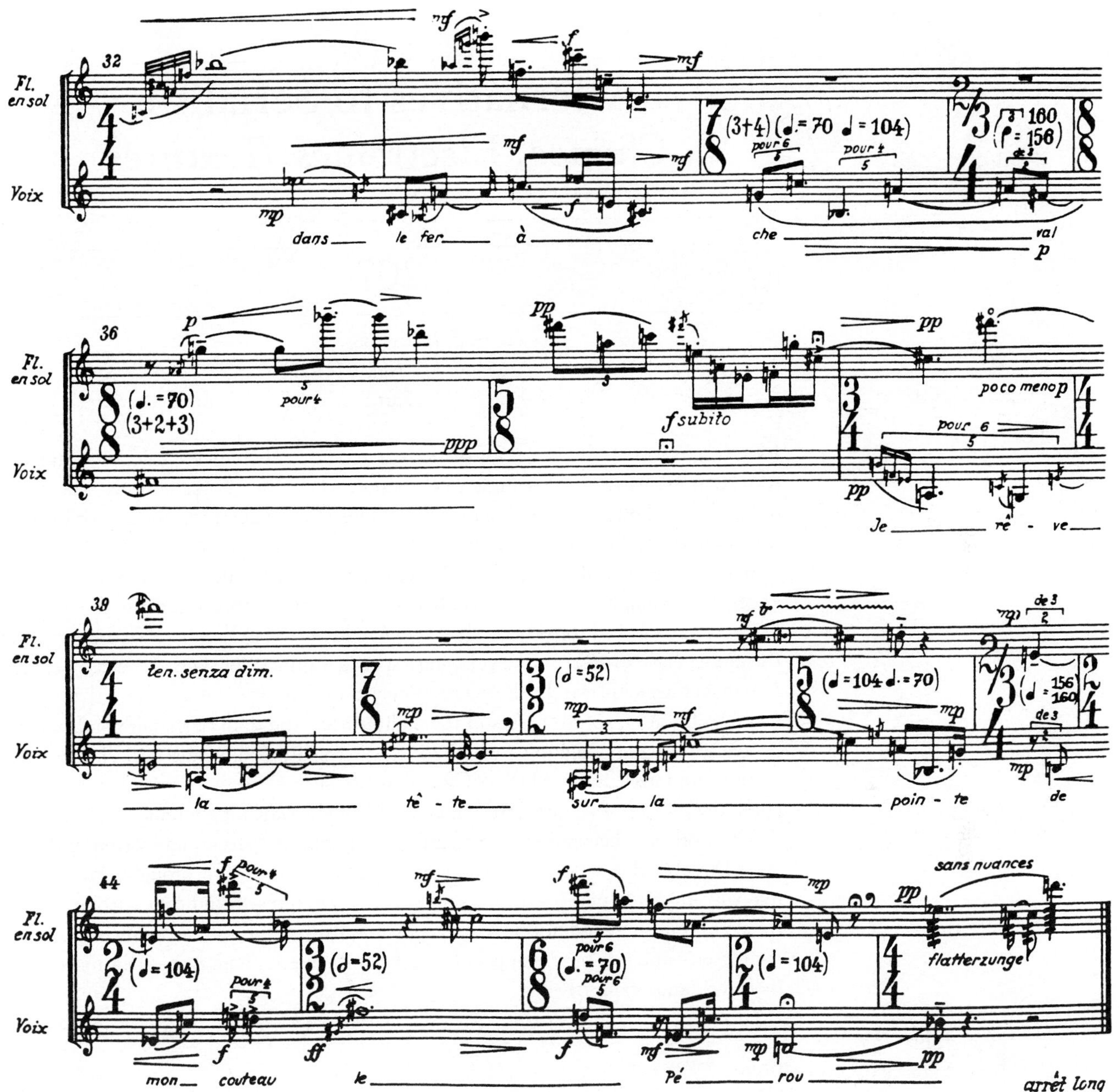

L'artisanat furieux

La roulotte rouge au bord du clou
Et cadavre dans le panier
Et chevaux de labours dans le fer à cheval!
Je rêve la tête sur la pointe de mon couteau
le Pérou.

—René Char

The Raging Proletariat

The red caravan beside the prison
And a body in the basket
And work horses in the horseshoe!
I dream with my head on the point of my
Peruvian knife.

Alternatives to Serialism
Chance, Electronics, Textures

207

John Cage
Music of Changes (1951)
Part I

John Cage's *Music of Changes* for piano is an example of chance music, or what Cage termed music with "indeterminacy of composition." The choice of notes, durations, dynamics, and other such elements was dictated by chance procedures, not by writing music that reflected the composer's taste and musical ideas.

But as Cage himself later realized, *Music of Changes* still reflects certain of his preferences. For example, he set up his chance operations so that moments of silence—places where musical tones were absent—were likely to occupy much of the surface of the music. Cage in 1951 was developing a special fondness for silence because here nature makes itself known. In the silent moments of a musical composition, the listener can turn his attention to noises in the auditorium—the hum of the air conditioning, people tittering or coughing—which for Cage constituted a whole new dimension of material for music. Since *Music of Changes* is a large work that occupies nearly an hour and is divided into four parts, the audience has ample time for contemplation.

The work first became known thanks to the special skills and devotion of the pianist David Tudor, whose transcendent technique and insight brought attention to many avant-garde piano works of the 1950s. Cage himself said that without Tudor, the composition would not have been possible. Whatever we may think of Cage as a composer—and it is nearly impossible to be ambivalent about him—this music is no mere academic exercise.

John Cage
Music of Changes (1951)
Part I
CD 13/6

176
RITARD.
(NO E♭ SUSTAINED)
100
11

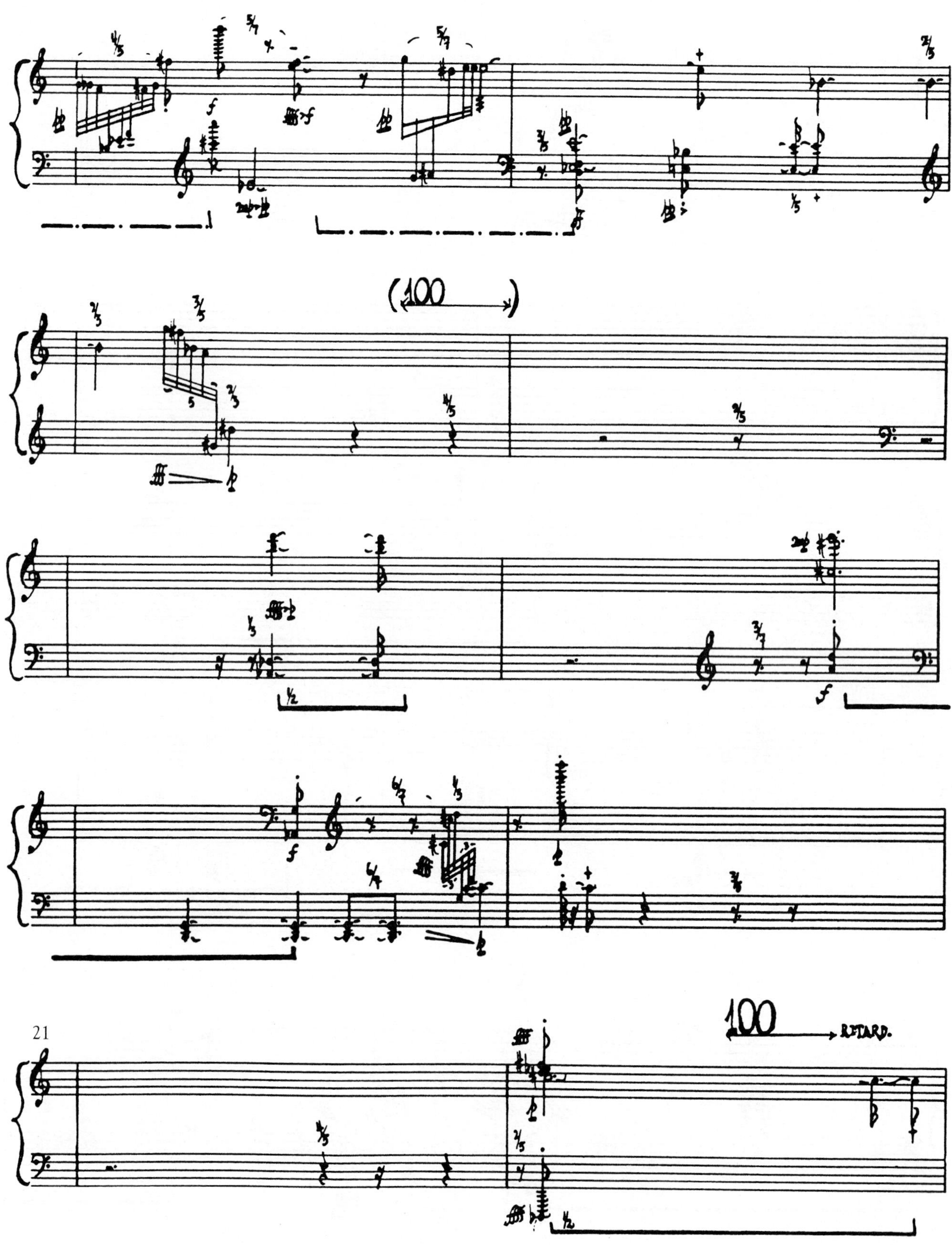
(100)
21
100
RITARD.

58
58
31

58
ACCEL.
76

41
ACCEL.
L.H.
R.H.

51
108
108

108
61
108
ACCEL.
184

71
184

81
184
RITARD.
63

208

Olivier Messiaen

"Mode de valeurs et d'intensités" (1949)

When World War II ended in 1945, Olivier Messiaen was thirty-six years old and living in Paris, where he was known as an organist, composer, and teacher of music. His works to that time had received relatively little attention, especially because they seemed out of tune with Neoclassicism, which formed the paradigm for modern music in France before the war. After the war, Messiaen was inclined to experiment with new musical resources. He tried his hand at a version of the twelve-tone method of composition, and brought many preexistent materials, such as birdsong, into his new works. As his outlook on music gained in legitimacy, he attracted the attention of younger composers, such as Pierre Boulez and Karlheinz Stockhausen, both of whom became his students.

In his "Mode de valeurs et d'intensités" ("Mode of Rhythmic Values and Dynamics") Messiaen experiments with the possibility of composing a piece in which each note of the chromatic scale is unchangingly linked with a specific register, duration, attack type, and dynamic level. Before composing, Messiaen assembled the twelve pitches for each of the piece's three strata into row-like arrangements, although these rows are not used in a strictly serial fashion. After Messiaen determined the pitch order for each stratum, he assigned all the other elements to each note, according to his precompositional arrangements.

The result delighted Messiaen's students, who saw in the system a way of dispelling traditional musical textures and achieving a static array of ever-changing points of sound. The composer himself, however, eventually retreated from this style of composition. "Mode de valeurs" remains a singular—though influential—composition in his oeuvre.

Olivier Messiaen
"Mode de valeurs et d'intensités" (1949)
CD 13/8

Modéré

PIANO

11
8
ppp
f
pp
p
mf
fff
sff
ff
mf
ppp
mp

25
ff
pp
f
mf
p
sff
ppp
sfff
8a bassa
8a ba
8

37

8
ppp
f
mf
f
ff
p
sff
mf
51
mf
ff
pp
sff
f
ppp
mf
ff
ppp f ff

64

77
8ª bassa
8ª bassa

89

8
101
8
8
8

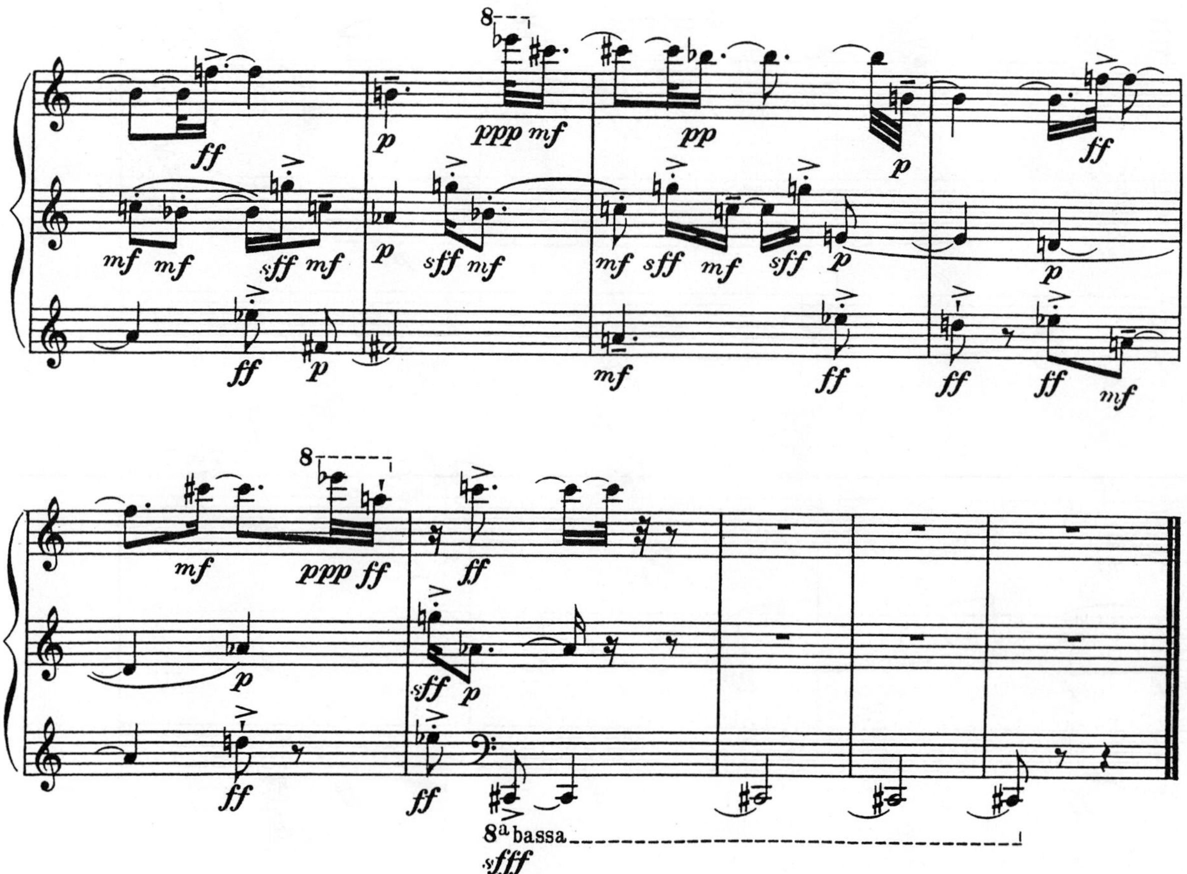
8
ff
p
ppp mf
pp
p
ff
mf mf
sff mf
p
sff mf
mf sff mf
sff
p
p
ff
p
mf
ff
ff
ff mf
8
mf
ppp ff
ff
p
sff p
ff
ff
8a bassa
sfff

Music in the 1960s and 1970s
Live Processes, Minimalism, Metric Modulations

209

Luciano Berio
Circles (1960)
"stinging"

In his *Circles* for soprano, harp, and percussion, Luciano Berio explores new ways of handling the traditional genre of the song. In the older conception of songwriting, a composer creates an accompanied vocal melody that enhances the expressivity of the poem. Berio searches instead for a middle ground in which percussive noises, unusual vocal utterances, and word sounds can mingle as though equals. In this area, music is freed from any strict subservience to the meaning of the words or the need to draw attention to their emotional qualities.

Berio takes apart the words of the poem "stinging" by e. e. cummings and finds equivalences in the noises that can be produced by instruments and voice. In his hands the voice becomes an instrument of amazing flexibility. A new type of expression emerges from the music, which connects with the poetry in dynamic and unexpected ways. While the voice sings the text, the harp is also playing, but both parts operate independently of each other. It is not until the voice completes the text that various percussion instruments are added.

When Berio composed *Circles*, he wrote for a specific voice—that of his wife, Cathy Berberian (1925–1983). Born in the United States, she studied and worked for a time in Italy, and in 1958 gave a remarkable performance of John Cage's *Aria with Fontana Mix* in Rome. When she finally had her American debut at Tanglewood in 1960, she sang *Circles*. She possessed a voice of incredible versatility that could change instantaneously from a high, clear operatic sound to the growl of a sultry nightclub singer. Numerous modern composers, including Igor Stravinsky, wrote works for her voice.

Luciano Berio
Circles (1960)
"stinging"
CD 13/12

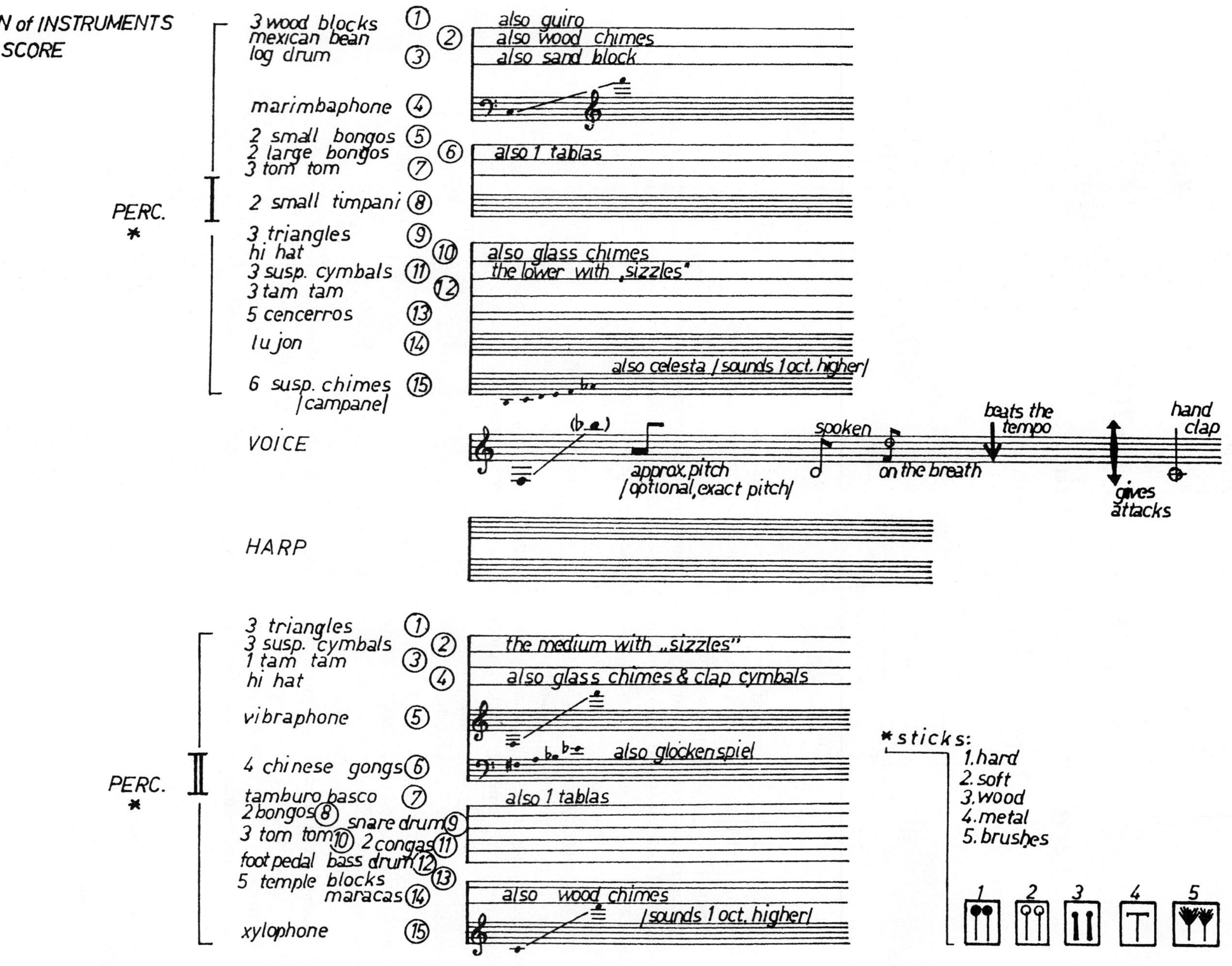
POSITION of INSTRUMENTS
in the SCORE
PERC.
*
I
3 wood blocks ①
mexican bean ②
log drum ③
marimbaphone ④
2 small bongos ⑤
2 large bongos ⑥
3 tom tom ⑦
2 small timpani ⑧
3 triangles ⑨
hi hat ⑩
3 susp. cymbals ⑪
3 tam tam ⑫
5 cencerros ⑬
lujon ⑭
6 susp. chimes
/campane/ ⑮
also guiro
also wood chimes
also sand block
also 1 tablas
also glass chimes
the lower with „sizzles"
also celesta /sounds 1 oct. higher/
VOICE
approx. pitch
/optional, exact pitch/
spoken
on the breath
beats the tempo
gives attacks
hand clap
HARP
PERC.
*
II
3 triangles ①
3 susp. cymbals ②
1 tam tam ③
hi hat ④
vibraphone ⑤
4 chinese gongs ⑥
tamburo basco ⑦
2 bongos ⑧
snare drum ⑨
3 tom tom ⑩
2 congas ⑪
foot pedal bass drum ⑫
5 temple blocks ⑬
maracas ⑭
xylophone ⑮
the medium with „sizzles"
also glass chimes & clap cymbals
also glockenspiel
also 1 tablas
also wood chimes
/sounds 1 oct. higher/
*sticks:
1. hard
2. soft
3. wood
4. metal
5. brushes
1
2
3
4
5

♩= 58·66·80
I voice
harp
stin· ·ging gold (d)
LASCIA VIBRARE SEMPRE
swarms (ms) u· ·pon the spires (ts)
sil· ·ver chants (ts) the li· ·ta·nies (is) the

great bells are rin· ging with rose (s) the lewd fat bells
and a tall wind is drag· ging the sea

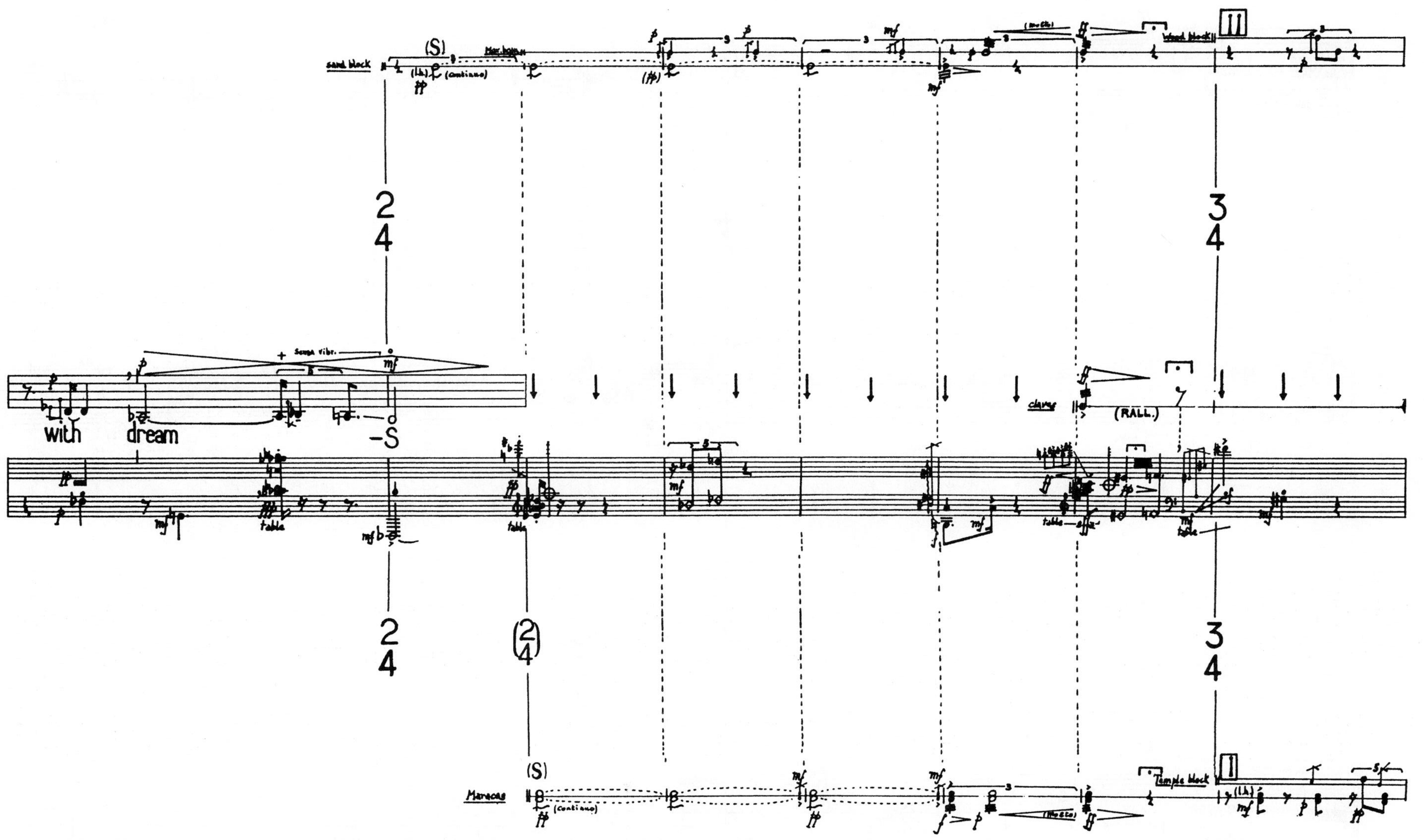
sand block
(S)
(continuo)
Wood block
senza vibr.
with
dream
-S
claves
(RALL.)
tabla
Maracas
(continuo)
Temple block

Log drum II
Marimbaphone
(RALL.)
table
attacca subito
Xylophone

210

George Crumb
Ancient Voices of Children (1970)
"¿De dónde vienes?"

In *Ancient Voices of Children,* the American composer George Crumb continues the search for innovations in the medium of live performance. This quest occupied many leading composers in Europe and America from the 1950s through 1970s. Although working in the medium of the song, Crumb bypasses the traditional trappings of the genre in favor of a dramatic and symbolic interchange among words, ideas, and tones.

The layout of the score in the third section of *Ancient Voices of Children* is one of many challenges for the performer (see pages 1800–1801). Its appearance not only suggests the movement's circular, repetitive form, but is also symbolic of the meaning of the entire work, which uses poetry by Federico García Lorca to create a cycle of birth, death, and rebirth. Crumb draws upon an expanded and richly colorful palette of sounds, made in unusual ways by the singers and players, to evoke the meaning that lies abstractly behind the work. The pounding rhythm of the Spanish bolero in the percussion dominates this dance of life.

Although the music sounds improvisatory, every event and entrance is precisely notated. At the beginning of the song (across the top of the score), the soprano sings nonsense syllables into the piano. Once the harp, electric piano, and percussion enter, she turns to the audience and the "Dance of the Sacred Life-Cycle" begins. There are five events, labeled A to E, that occur in succession, and the cycle is repeated three times. In Crumb's highly original notation, each cycle is identified by superscript numbers following the letters. For example, event D is present only in the first two cycles; events B and C are present in all three. Crumb carefully indicates the beginning of each event through a system of arrows cues. As complicated as the score initially looks, the effect is musically persuasive.

¿De dónde vienes, amor, mi niño?	Where are you from, Love, my child?
De la cresta del duro frío.	From the hard frozen mountain.
¿Qué necesitas, amor, mi niño?	What do you need, Love, my child?
La tibia tela de tu vestido.	The warm cloth of your dress.
¡Que se agiten las ramas al sol	Let the branches rustle in the sun
y salten las fuentes alrededor!	and the fountains leap about!
En el patio ladra el perro,	In the courtyard the dog barks,
en los árboles canta el viento.	in the trees the wind sings.
Los bueyes mugen al boyero	The oxen low for the ox herder,
y la luna me riza los cabellos.	and the moon curls my hair.
¿Qué pides, niño, desde tan lejos?	What do you ask for, child, from afar?
Los blancos montes que hay en tu pecho.	The white mountains of your breast.
¡Que se agiten las ramas al sol	Let the branches rustle in the sun
y salten las fuentes alrededor!	and the fountains leap about!
Te diré, niño mio, que sí,	I will tell you, my child, yes,
tronchada y rota soy para ti.	I am torn and broken for your sake.
¡Cómo me duele esta cintura	How painful is this waist
donde tendrás primera cuna!	where you shall have your first cradle!
¿Cuando, mi niño, vas a venir?	When, my child, will you come?
Cuando tu carne huela a jazmín.	When your flesh smells of jasmine.
¡Que se agiten las ramas al sol	Let the branches rustle in the sun
y salten las fuentes alrededor!	and the fountain leap about!

—Federico García Lorca

George Crumb
Ancient Voices of Children
"¿De dónde vienes?"
CD 13/13

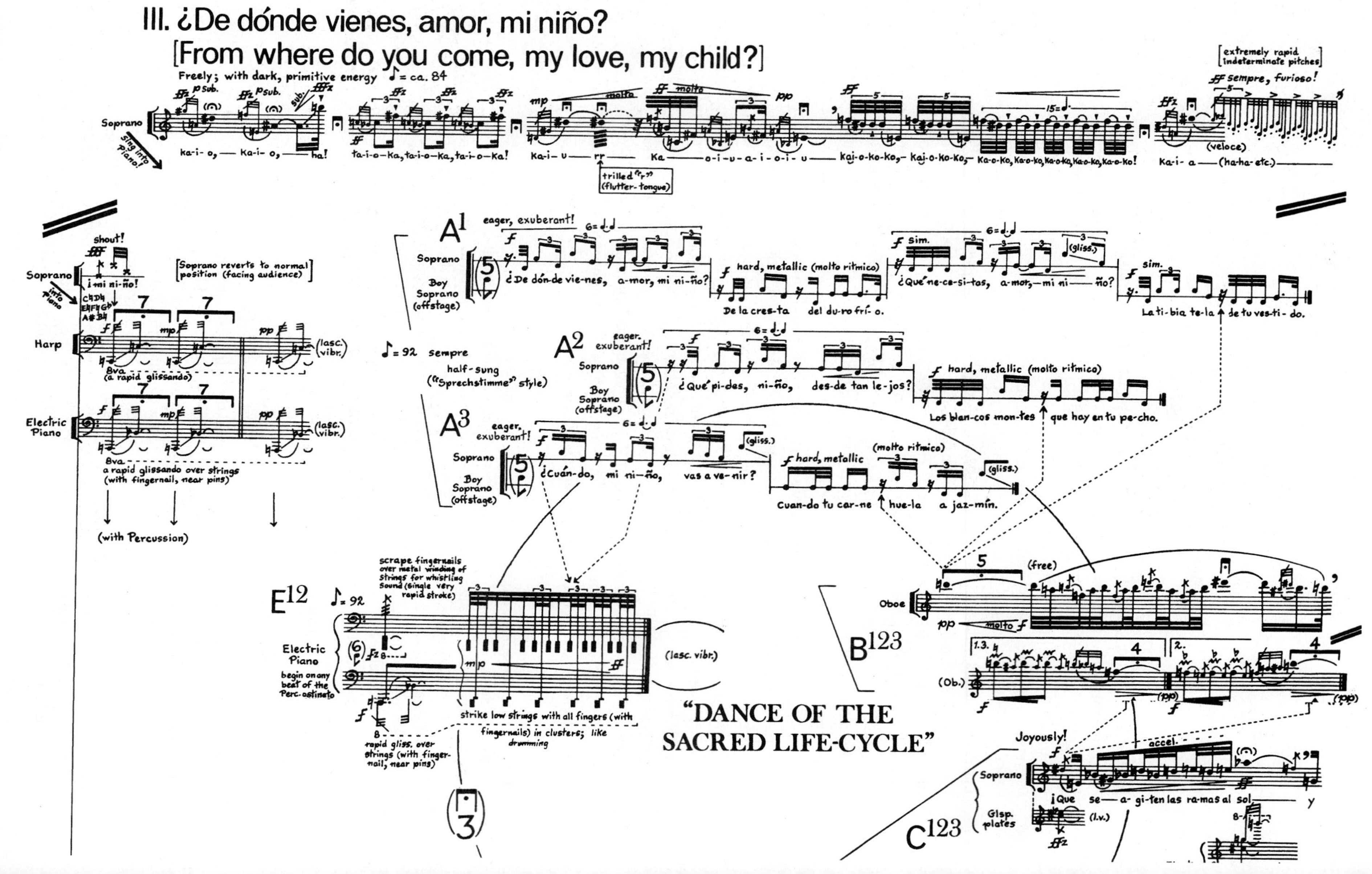

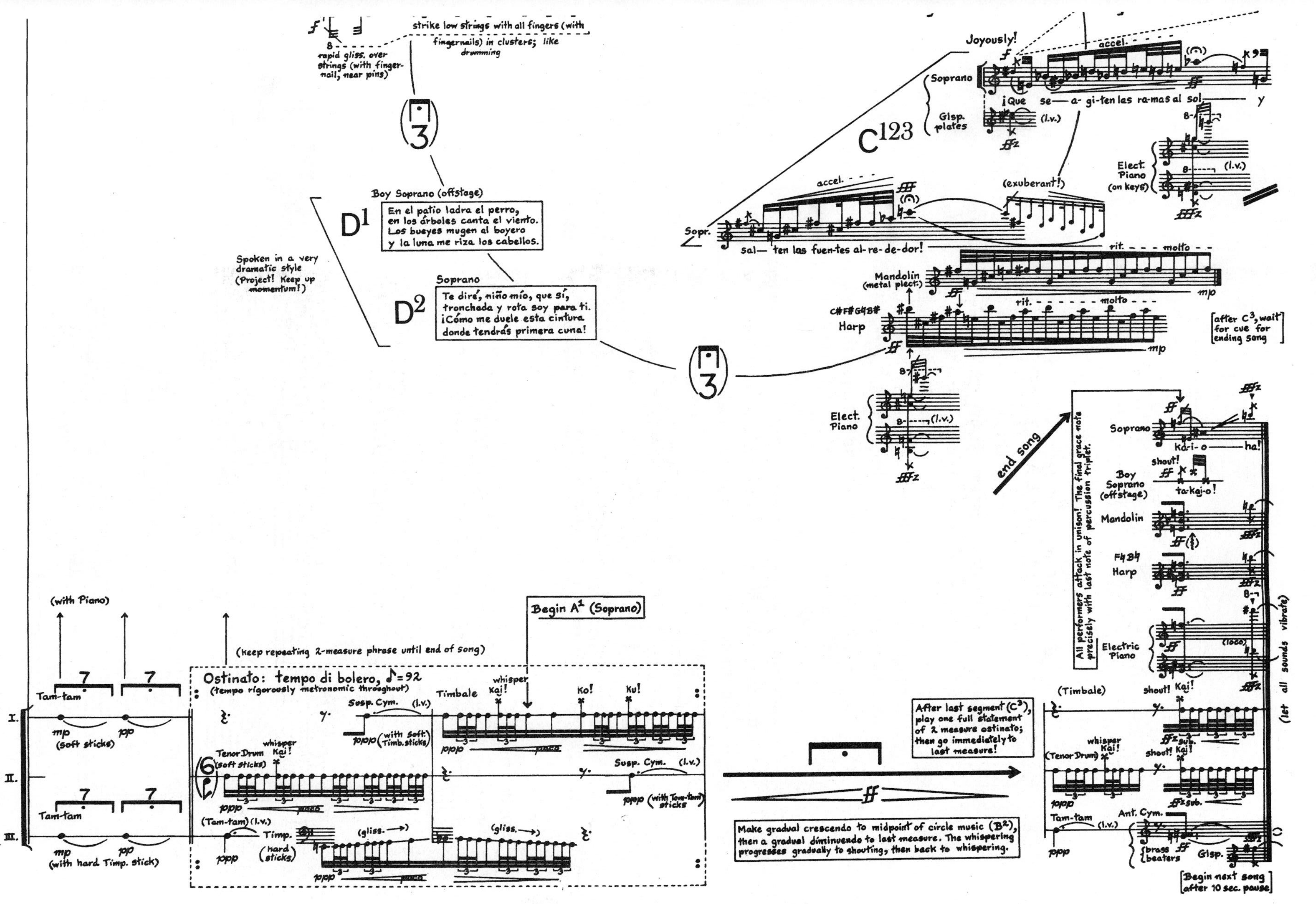

rapid gliss. over strings (with fingernail, near pins)
strike low strings with all fingers (with fingernails) in clusters; like drumming
Joyously!
accel.
Soprano
Glsp. plates
¡Que se— a- gi-ten las ra-mas al sol— y
(l.v.)
C123
Elect. Piano (on keys)
(exuberant!)
Sopr.
sal— ten las fuen-tes al-re-de-dor!
Boy Soprano (offstage)
D1
En el patio ladra el perro,
en los árboles canta el viento.
Los bueyes mugen al boyero
y la luna me riza los cabellos.
Spoken in a very dramatic style (Project! Keep up momentum!)
Soprano
D2
Te diré, niño mío, que sí,
tronchada y rota soy para ti.
¡Cómo me duele esta cintura
donde tendrás primera cuna!
Mandolin (metal plect.)
rit. - - - molto - -
C#F#G♮B#
Harp
mp
[after C3, wait for cue for ending song]
Elect. Piano
end song
All performers attack in unison! The final grace note precisely with last note of percussion triplet.
Soprano
Ka-i-o ha!
Boy Soprano (offstage)
shout!
ta-kai-o!
Mandolin
F♮B♮
Harp
Electric Piano
(loco)
(let all sounds vibrate)
(with Piano)
(keep repeating 2-measure phrase until end of song)
Begin A1 (Soprano)
Ostinato: tempo di bolero, ♪=92
(tempo rigorously metronomic throughout)
Percussion
I.
II.
III.
Tam-tam
mp (soft sticks)
mp (with hard Timp. stick)
Susp. Cym. (l.v.)
pppp (with soft Timb. sticks)
Timbale
whisper Kai!
Ko!
Ku!
Tenor Drum (soft sticks)
Susp. Cym. (l.v.)
pppp (with Tam-tam sticks)
(Tam-tam) (l.v.)
Timp. (hard sticks)
(gliss. →)
After last segment (C3), play one full statement of 2 measure ostinato; then go immediately to last measure!
Make gradual crescendo to midpoint of circle music (B2), then a gradual diminuendo to last measure. The whispering progresses gradually to shouting, then back to whispering.
(Timbale)
shout! Kai!
(Tenor Drum)
Ant. Cym.
brass beaters
Glsp.
[Begin next song after 10 sec. pause]

211

Elliott Carter
String Quartet No. 2 (1959)
Introduction and first movement (*Allegro fantastico*)

The music of the String Quartet No. 2 by Elliott Carter rests on the composer's idea of a dramatic interplay among instruments. "The instruments are type cast," writes Carter, "for each fairly consistently invents its material out of its own special expressive attitude and its own repertory of musical speeds and intervals. In a certain sense, each instrument is like a character in an opera made up primarily of 'quartets.'" At a later time the composer stated that he had in mind characters from Verdi's operas *Aida* and *Otello*. The personality of each instrument has been variously described. For example, David Schiff, one of Carter's students, notes that the cello could be considered impetuous, self-indulgently romantic, or hysterical. As in a true drama, the personality of the role depends in part upon the personality of the performer.

These distinctions in roles are especially evident in the introduction and first movement (*Allegro fantastico*) of the quartet. In the brief Introduction, the four string parts relate as near equals, but in the *Allegro fantastico* the first violin charges to center stage. Here he or she plays in an extroverted manner, leaving his or her compatriots to weakly imitate this arrogant behavior. Listeners to this drama of musical personalities will need all of their powers of concentration to follow the high-speed and quickly changing interactions.

Although the composition has sometimes been referred to as "Four Players in Search of a Quartet," it quickly garnered critical acclaim. First performed by the Juilliard String Quartet in March 1960, it received the Pulitzer Prize later that year and other awards soon followed.

Elliott Carter
String Quartet No. 2 (1959)
Introduction and first movement (*Allegro fantastico*)
CD 13/14

Introduction

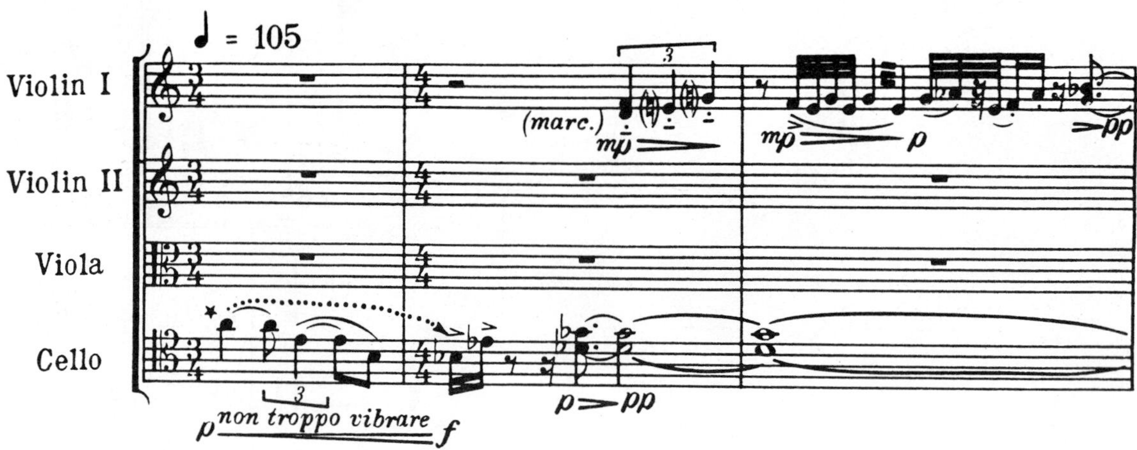

5
pizz.
(pizz. normale)
(pizz. normale)
arco
f molto espr.
mf espr.sost.
p sub.
marc. ruvido
più f
f espr.
gliss.
espr.
f sub.
p - pp
= 140
f marc. ruvido
arco
f marc. stacc. corto
mf sub.
f molto espr.

15
mp
mf
leggiero con fantasia
p
pp
(Tempo giusto)
stacc.
f
mf
f
p
pp
17
mf
mf
f
f
(f)
ff sub.
molto espr.
(f sempre)
mf
f
ff sub.
ff sub.
21
p sub.
pp
ff
p
mp
pp
(f)
p
mp
pp
f
p
p
mp

29
Subito meno mosso (♩ = 112)
marcatiss.
attacca

35
I.
Allegro fantastico (♩ = 112)
Solo to 134
fmarc.
pizz.
III f
sul tasto, secco
mf
pp
senza vib.
sul tasto
mf

p
mf
scherz.
espr.
molto vib.
p
f
p

42
f
p
pizz.
III p
sul tasto
pizz.
normale
molto vibrato
espr.
mf
senza vib.
sul tasto
tasto
p espr.

47
arco
mf marc. sub.
normale
mf marc.
mp espr.
non troppo
51
f marc.
p espr.

57
f marc.
fp
pp
mf
ppp
ff
f
p
♩ = ♫. = 112
𝅘𝅥𝅯 = 𝅘𝅥𝅯 (𝅘𝅥𝅮. = 186.7)
62
scherzando
mp

68

pizz.

f marc.

arco

in fuori

f espr.

poco

cresc. molto

f non troppo

71

marc.

75
(♩ = 140)
leggiero
mf
p
pp
pp leggiero
in fuori
80
ben in fuori
(pp)
mf marc.
mp
cant.
mf

85
mp ben cant.
ppp
(♩ = 140)
89
94
sub.

marc.
(p sempre)
f sub.
98
= 70
= 163.3
p tranquillo
pizz.
mp
mf-p
arco
pp
105
p tranquillo
pp leggiero

110
gliss.
pp
p
mf
fp
f
sf
mp
détaché
= (♪. = 163.3 sempre)
117
f in fuori

123
mf
mp sub.
mp
f
mf
f
mp>p
mp
f - mp
f
espr.
mf
f
>mf
in fuori
f > mf
p
f - p
f cant. espr.
127
mp
mf
mf
f
mf
mf
mf
mp
mp
mf
mf
f
mp
f
mf
mf
f
mp
mf
f
mf
cresc. poco a poco
130
ff
p sub.
ff sub.
mf
f
ff
pp
pp
ff
p
ff
p > pp

212

Steve Reich

Clapping Music (1972)

Steve Reich's *Clapping Music* is an example of what the composer calls a "phase" composition. This was Reich's main contribution to the early development of Minimalism—a style of new music appearing in the 1960s in which a minimum of musical materials are extended by a gradually changing ostinato pattern. In compositions using the phase technique, two similar sources of sounds (taped or instrumental) are first heard playing an ostinato in unison. One of the two parts progressively advances ahead of the other—they "come out of phase"—and this process creates changing rhythmic patterns. *Clapping Music* fits this definition perfectly: The musicians begin clapping the same pattern in unison, but phase shifts occur by an increment of one eighth-note from measure to measure. While "clap 1" remains constant, "clap 2" moves its pattern one eighth-note to the left in each measure. According to Reich himself, these shifts "create the sensation of a series of variations of two different patterns with their downbeats coinciding."

Whereas many compositions begin with a musical gesture in the mind of the composer, this work began as an abstract idea—an exercise in "phasing." The composer has said he considers the composition an étude, a nineteenth-century term for a study piece. As in all such pieces, a succession of different patterns emerge as the progress of the phase moves forward. Some of these resultant rhythms are asymmetrical, but listen also for the seventh measure, where a regular pattern in triple meter suddenly appears.

Steve Reich
Clapping Music (1972)
CD 13/15

♩ = 160-184 Repeat each bar 12 times/Répétez chaque mesure 12 fois/Jeden takt zwölfmal wiederholen

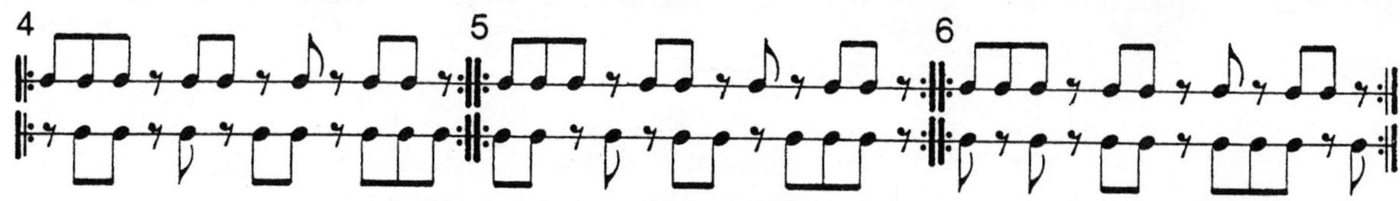

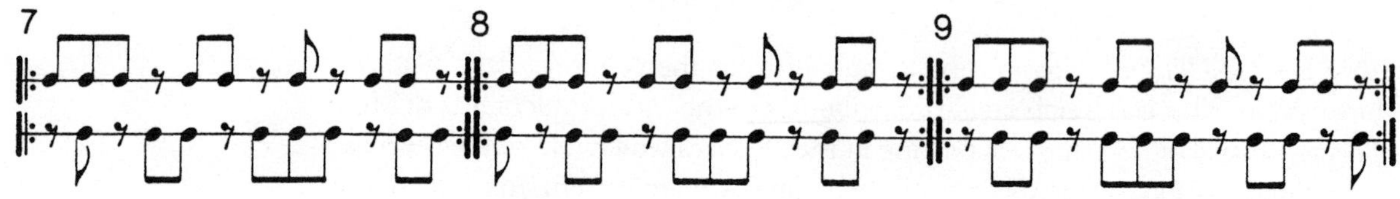

Returning to the Known
Music of the Recent Past

213

György Ligeti
Hungarian Rock (1978)

In his *Hungarian Rock* for harpsichord, György Ligeti playfully mixes styles. By calling upon the harpsichord—an instrument of the Baroque era more than of the twentieth century—the composer suggests a revival of the past, but other aspects of *Hungarian Rock* are squarely rooted in the modern period. Ligeti dedicated the composition to an acquaintance, the flamboyant Polish-born harpsichordist Elisabeth Chojnacka, who was its first important interpreter. (More than eighty composers have written harpsichord music especially for Chojnacka, including Krzysztof Penderecki and Iannis Xenakis.) Recordings of this composition have been made using piano and barrel organ, as well.

The form of *Hungarian Rock* is created by using continuous variations upon a recurring bass line and its harmonic progression, which recalls the Baroque chaconne and reinforces the spirit of a revival of early music. The bass line is a one-measure pattern that is repeated without break until eight bars before the end. The ostinato is stretched into a four-bar pattern in which the short bass figure is harmonized four different ways. These chords impart a colorful, but tonally ambiguous, harmonic progression to an otherwise repetitive pattern.

But other aspects of the work suggest jazz. Above the relentlessly recurring bass, the harpsichordist's right hand spins out its ever more complex variations, much like a jazz improvisation over a steady blues bass. The asymmetrical meter, similar to Bulgarian folk music, is augmented by a hint of Latin jazz. Woven into this mixture of old and new, high art with popular culture, is the harmonic language of the twentieth century, with its free dissonance and chromaticism.

The publisher of Hungarian Rock granted permission to reprint only a portion (about one third) of the composition. The recording, however, is complete.

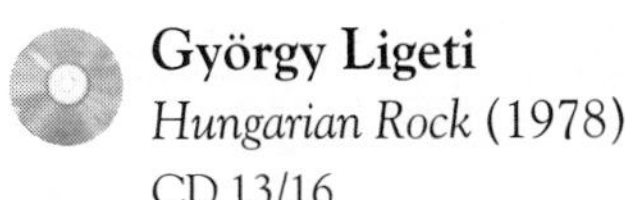
György Ligeti
Hungarian Rock (1978)
CD 13/16

12

214

John Adams
Nixon in China (1987)
Act 1, scene 1, "News"

The opera *Nixon in China,* by John Adams (music) and Alice Goodman (libretto), created a new type of opera based on current events. Many composers in the past have written operas based on relevant contemporary themes. But these topics were almost always brought to a more general than temporal level when they were imported into the opera house. This opera, on the contrary, deals with a specific recent historical event, and Adams and Goodman suggest that opera can become a form of reportage. Their subject is the 1972 visit of Richard Nixon to communist China, an event whose great historical and political significance was enriched by the starkly contrasting personalities of the American politicians and their Chinese counterparts.

In "News," an aria from Act 1 of *Nixon in China,* Richard Nixon and his diplomatic party have arrived in Peking, and the President sings about the importance of his visit, accompanied by the strains of Adams's Minimalistic music. Afterward, the Americans meet the elderly Chairman Mao Tse-Tung, and Pat Nixon visits monuments of the city and meets Mao's wife, Chiang Ch'ing. The political event was rich with comic possibilities that were not overlooked by the composer and librettist. We see one such example in the opening strains of "News." The Chinese premier Chou En-lai attempts to introduce the Deputy Minister of Security, but President Nixon is absorbed in his own thoughts. "The whole world was listening," Nixon says, all the while deaf to Chou's words. The opera ends as the politicians reminisce nostalgically to the sounds of old-fashioned dance music.

For this aria, Adams uses a free ternary form with a concluding episode. Beginning in A♭ major, Nixon sings "News, news, news" at an ever-increasing pace. The frenetic accompaniment and constantly shifting meter energize the repetitive vocal line. The **B** section begins with the mention of "the Eastern Hemisphere beckoned to us" (m. 542), the harmony drops down to D♭ major and the meter shifts from a simple to a compound subdivision. With the repetition of "Sea of Tranquility," Nixon almost drifts into a reverie, but suddenly remembers his purpose, and the **A** section returns in measure 582 with the teletype-style accompaniment. There is a sudden lurch to F♯ minor in the episode beginning in measure 654, as Nixon's paranoia emerges with "the rats begin to chew the sheets."

Adams and Goodman returned to the opera of current events in *The Death of Klinghoffer* (1991), which deals with a darker episode in American history—the murder of Leon Klinghoffer in 1984 following the hijacking of a cruise ship by Palestinian terrorists.

John Adams
Nixon in China (1987)
Act 1, scene 1, "News"
Nonesuch CD 79177 or 79193

While the introductions are beginning, the President begins to sing, and, as he sings the joy of anticipated triumph becomes the terrible expectation of failure. The Chinese and American official parties in due course leave the stage. The brilliant sunshine dwindles to the light of incandescent lamps.

377
Nix.
News, News, News, News, News,
383
Nix.
News, News, News, News, News, News has a, has a, has a,
389
Nix.
has a kind of mys - ter - y:
Has a, has a, has a kind of
395
Nix.
mys - ter - y:
When
8va loco
8va loco
mf

400
Nix.
I shook hands, When I shook hands_ with Chou En-lai, When I shook hands with
405
Nix.
Chou En-lai on this bare field out - side Pe-king_ just now, the whole world was
409
Nix.
lis - ten - ing. The whole world was lis - ten - ing. Lis - ten - ing.
CHOU
May I- May I-
f
mf
f
414
Nix.
Lis - ten - ing. And though we spoke
sim.
ff
p subito

419
Nix.
qui - et - ly, And though we spoke qui - et - ly, And
424
Nix.
p subito
though we spoke qui - - - - - - - - - et - -
mf
p subito
428
Nix.
ly the eyes and ears of hisss-to-ry, hisss-to-ry,
433
Nix.
hisss - to - ry caught ev - ery gesss - ture -
CHOU
May I in - tro- in - tro -
f

437
Nix.
Caught ev - ery gesss - ture–
Caught ev - ery gesss - ture and
Chou
duce,
May I in - tro - duce the
441
ev - ery word,
trans - form
3
Dep - u - ty
Min - is - ter
of Se - cu - ri - ty.
sim.
446
ing us as we, trans - fixed,
Trans -
The Dep - u - ty

451
Nix.
form - ing us as we, trans - fixed,
Trans - form - ing us as
Chou
3
The Min - is - ter -
456
Nix.
we, trans - fixed, made hisss - to - ry.
Hisss - to - ry.
As
(Brass)
sfz
sim.
461
Nix.
we made hisss - to - ry.
The eyes
mf

466
Nix.
and ears of hisss - to - ry, As
sfz sfz sffz sffz
sim.
f
471
Nix.
we made hisss - to - ry.
f
ff
sim.
f
ff
476
Nix.
On our flight ___ o - ver from Shang - hai
8va...., loco
(Picc.)
f
sim.
p subito
sempre secco
sim.

482
Nix.
The coun - try - side looked drab and grey.
8va......, loco
f
487
Nix.
"Brue - ghel," Pat said. "We came in
8va...,
8va.....,
8va..., loco
f
p subito
492
Nix.
peace for all man - kind" I said,
8va.......
mf
mp

497
Nix.
I said, I said, I said, I said, "We came in peace for
8va
(Sax.) f
mf
mp
503
all man - kind" and I was put in mind of our A -
8va ...., loco
8va ..., loco
508
pol - lo as - tro - nauts sim - ply a - chiev - ing a
mf very short
sim.
513
great hu - man dream. We live
p

519
Nix.
in an un - set - tled time.
We live
mf
Ped.
525
Nix.
in an un - set - tled time.
Who, who, who, who,
f
mf
Ped.
531
Nix.
who are our en - e - mies?
Who, who, who, who,
f
mf
Ped.
536
Nix.
who are our friends?
Who are our friends?
f
Ped.

541
Nix.
The East - ern Hem - i - sphere_ beck - oned to us, and
ff
p
sim.
547
we have flown east of the sun, west of the moon
553
a - cross an o - cean of dis - trust
pp
(Ped.)
559
filled with the bod - ies of our lost; The
p

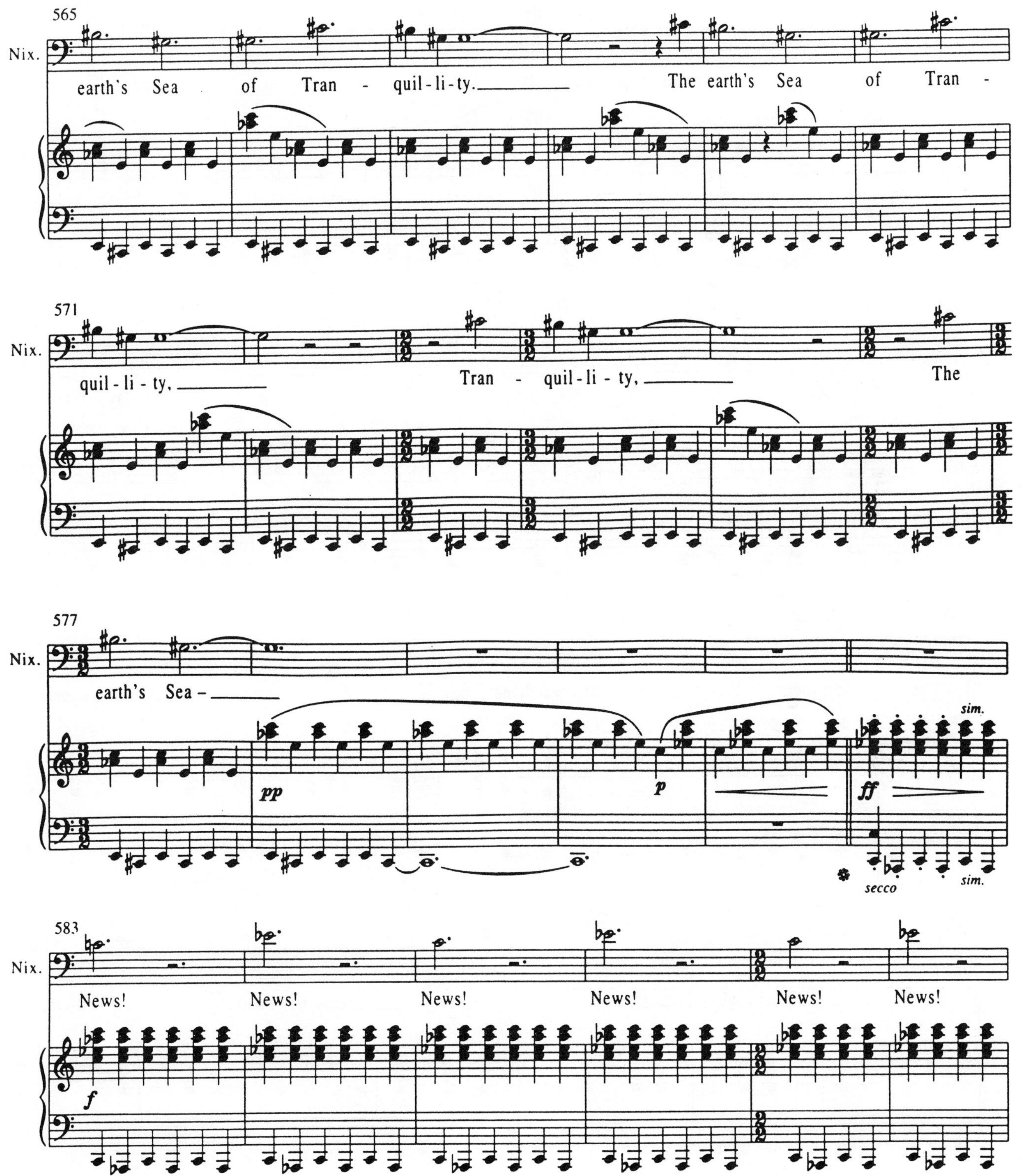
565
Nix.
earth's Sea of Tran - quil-li-ty. The earth's Sea of Tran -
571
Nix.
quil-li-ty, Tran - quil-li-ty, The
577
Nix.
earth's Sea –
pp
p
ff
sim.
secco
sim.
583
Nix.
News! News! News! News! News! News!
f

589
Nix.
News! News! It's prime time in the U. S. A. It's prime time in the
f
595
Nix.
U. S. A. It's yes - ter - day night. It's yes - ter - day night.
600
Nix.
Yes - ter - day night. They watch us now; The three main
p
sim.
sim.
607
Nix.
net - works' col - ors glow liv - id through drapes on - to the
3

614
Nix.
lawn.
Dish-es are washed and home-work done, the
(Brass, harmon mutes)
p
pp
621
Nix.
dog and grand - ma fall a-sleep,
A car roars past
mf
p
mf
628
Nix.
play-ing loud pop,
is gone.
p
f
p
Relax tempo slightly, but not suddenly
(𝅗𝅥=144)
634
Nix.
As I look down the road I know A -
p

639
Nix.
mer - i - ca is good at heart. An
644
Nix.
old cold war - ri - or pi - lot - ing towards an un - known shore
650
Nix.
through shoals.
f
mp secco
sim.
sim.
656
Nix.
The rats be - gin to chew the sheets. The rats, The rats be - gin to chew the
(Tbns., plunger mutes)
p

661
Nix.
sheets. The rats be-gin to chew the sheets. The rats, the rats be-gin to chew the
Spoken at random by each individual in a low, very soft voice with a slight pause between each repetition.
Male Ch.
The rats begin to chew the sheets.
f p
666
Nix.
sheets. The rats, the rats be-gin to chew the sheets.
Male Ch.
There's murmuring
p f p
671
Nix.
9:6
7:6
3
3
There's mur-mur-ing down be-low. There's mur-mur-ing, There's mur-mur-ing,
Male Ch.
Now there's murmuring
p f p ff p

676
Gradual relaxation of tempo
Nix.
mur - mur - ing.
Now there's in - grat - i - tude!
Male Ch.
fade out gradually
Gradual relaxation of tempo
sfz
p
f
681
My hand is as stead - y as a rock.
(niente)
sim.
(Tbn.)
p
f
p
686
A sound like mourn - ing doves reach - es my ears,
𝅗𝅥 = 138 Steady tempo
693
No - bod - y is a friend of ours.
The na - tion's heart - land
sfz
p

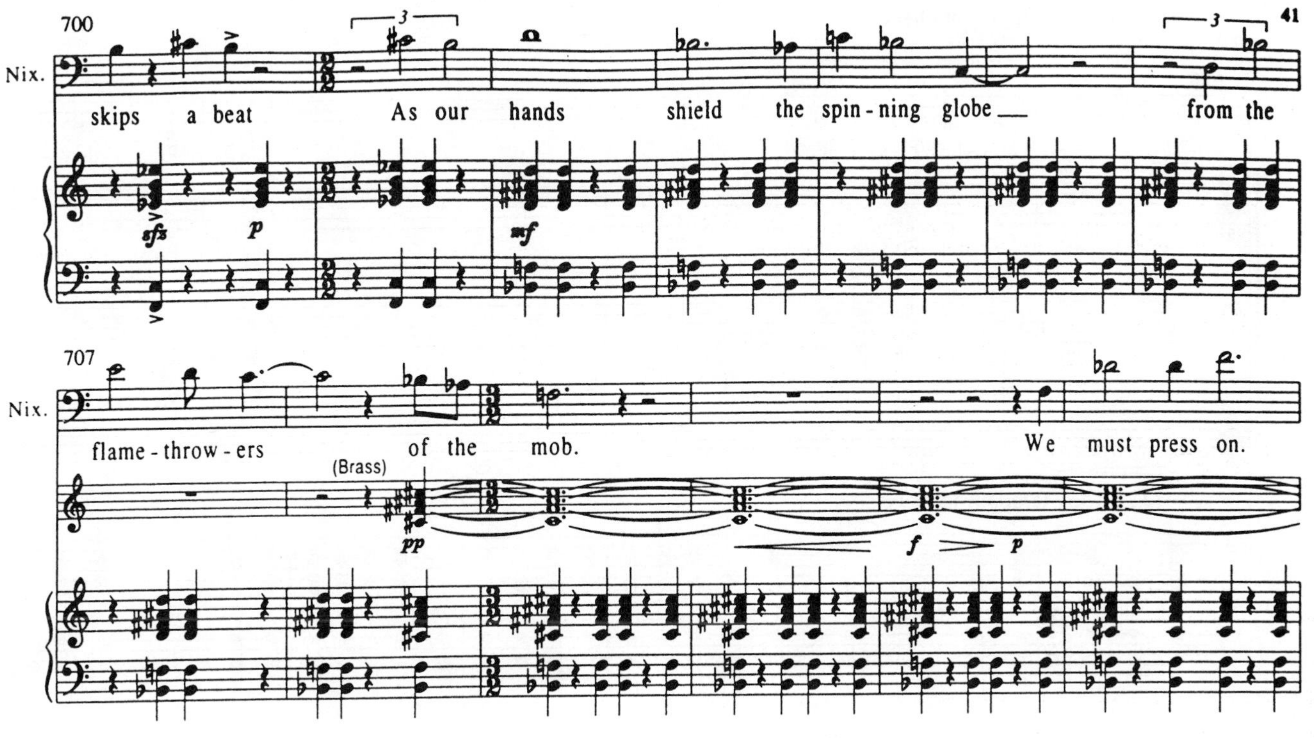

A telephone rings twice offstage, is picked up offstage. In a moment Henry Kissinger interrupts the President to tell him that Chairman Mao wishes to meet with him.

𝅗𝅥 = 122 Steady tempo from here
719
KISSINGER
very softly
Mis - ter Pres - i - dent -
Mis - ter Pres - i - dent -
S
A
very softly
Mis - ter Pres - i - dent -
Mis - ter Pres - i - dent -
T
B I
B II
very softly
Mis - ter Pres - i - dent -
Mis - ter Pres - i - dent -
p
𝅗𝅥 = 122 Steady tempo from here
mf
(p)
725
NIXON (sotto voce)
What?
Oh, yes -
Slightly relax tempo
Kis.
Mis - ter Pres - i - dent -
S
A
Mis - ter Pres - i - dent -
T
B I
B II
Mis - ter Pres - i - dent -
mf
p
Slightly relax tempo
731

215

Joan Tower

Fanfare for the Uncommon Woman, No. 1 (1986)

Joan Tower's *Fanfare for the Uncommon Woman*, No. 1, is the first in a series of orchestral fanfares that trumpet the accomplishments of women in music. Since the Baroque era, women have always been prominent performing artists. Recall the achievements of the seventeenth-century singer Barbara Strozzi, or the greatness of the nineteenth-century piano virtuoso Clara Schumann. But prior to the twentieth century, women composers were an anomaly. There were many reasons for this limited success: one of them is that women typically enjoyed far fewer educational opportunities in music than did men of the same time. Another is that society did not encourage women to have a profession outside the home.

In the twentieth century these restrictions have gradually eased, and today women often outnumber men on the faculty of music programs in universities and conservatories of America and Europe.[1] Joan Tower is one of a growing number of outstanding contemporary female composers, standing beside such other prominent figures as Libby Larsen, Judith Weir, and Shulamit Ran as the creators of new musical ideas. In her series of *Fanfares for the Uncommon Woman*, Tower tips her hat to these contemporaries and pioneers: The fanfares, she writes, celebrate "women who take risks and are adventurous." The Houston Symphony commissioned this work and played the premiere early in 1987. Tower dedicated the fanfare to the conductor Marin Alsop, who conducts the recording included in the CD for this text.

The title of Tower's fanfare, as well as its orchestra of brass and percussion, pays tribute to Aaron Copland's *Fanfare for the Common Man* (1942). The opening passage is based on chords built upon the interval of a fourth. By measure 6, the trumpet harmony is a first-inversion quartal chord. (Another example is the chord played by the French horns in mm. 40–42.) When the trombones enter after the Copland-esque drum beats in measures 11 to 14, they play a three-part chord built on intervals of the fifth.

[1]While this is true for many individual institutions, according to the College Music Society the gender division among the 38,100 music faculty in their database was 61.8 percent male, 36.5 percent female, and 1.7 percent unidentified. The College Music Society, *Directory of Music Faculties in Colleges and Universities, U.S. and Canada, 2003–2004* (Missoula, MT: The College Music Society, 2003), vii.

Joan Tower

Fanfare for the Uncommon Woman, No. 1 (1986)

CD 13/17

♩ = 69 (♪ = 138)

Trumpet in C 1, 2, 3 — *mf*, *cresc.*, *p cresc.*

Horn in F 1, 3, 2, 4 — *mp*, *cresc. poco a poco*

Trombone 1 2 3

Tuba

Timpani — *ff*

Percussion

Snare Drum (hard sticks) — *mf*

ff Medium Bass Drum (soft sticks)

Large Tamtam (soft sticks)

Med. Cym. (soft sticks) — *mp*

ff Large Bass Drum (soft sticks)

7
Tpt. in C
Hn. in F
Perc.
(S.D.)
(Med. Cym.)
(cresc.)
cresc.
10
Tbn.
High Cymbal
Med. B.D.
Tamt.
Lg. B.D.
dim.

15
Tbn.
Tuba
Timp.
Perc. 2
(Tamt.)
mf
p
cresc.
22
Hn. in F
a2
ff brassy
Tbn. 2
fp
Low Cym. (soft sticks)
Perc. 1
Med. B.D.
28
(a2)
(Low Cym.)

32
(a2)
Hn.
in F
a2
Tbn. 3
Tuba
mfp
Timp.
mp
Med. B.D.
Low Cym.
Perc. 1
mf
p
36
Tpt.
in C
mp
mp dolce
(f)
Medium Gong
mf

42
Tpt. in C
Hn. in F
Tbn.
Perc.
cresc. poco a poco
p
mp
mf
mp
High Gong (soft sticks)
p dolce
Medium Temple Blocks
pp
46
cresc.
a2
p cresc.
High Cym. (hard sticks)
(Med. T. Blk.)

50
Tpt. in C
1
2
3
f
Hn. in F
(a2)
Tbn.
Tuba
Timp.
Perc.
S.D.
High Cym.
(S.D.)
Med. Cym. (hard sticks)
Low Cym. (hard sticks)
Med. B.D. (soft sticks)
p
mf
55
a2
mf
cresc.
fp
f mp cresc.
S.D.
Med. Cym. (soft sticks)
p cresc.

59
Tpt. in C
Hn. in F
Tbn.
Tuba
Timp.
Perc.
a2
(a2)
3.
hard sticks
(S.D.)
High Cym. (hard sticks)
Low Cym. (soft sticks)
Med. B.D.
(Med. Cym.)
Low Cym.
Low B.D. (soft sticks)
62
1.
High Cym. (hard sticks)
Low Cym.
Med. B.D. (soft sticks)
Sus. Cym. (soft sticks)
Lg. B.D.
Tamt. (soft sticks)

65
Tpt. in C
(a2)
mf cresc.
Hn. in F
cresc.
Tbn.
(Low Cym.)
Perc.
(Tamt.)
70
Tuba
High Cym.
Triangle
Tamt.

75
Tpt.
in C
Hn.
in F
mf cresc.
Tbn. 2
Tuba
f
Timp.
soft sticks
p
cresc.
Perc.
(High Cym.)
Gong (soft sticks)
mf
(Trg.)
Low Cym. (hard sticks)
p cresc.

79
Tpt. in C
Hn. in F
(a2)
a2
Tbn.
Tuba
Timp.
Perc.
S.D.
(rim shots)
(High Cym.)
T. Blk.
Tom-toms
82
hard sticks
(S.D.)
Med. B.D.
p cresc. molto
(T.-t.)
Low B.D.

216

Arvo Pärt
Berlin Mass (1990)
Credo

In the last few months of 1989, the people of several Eastern European countries rose up in a peaceful revolution against their communist governments. The defining moment came on 9 November of that year, when East Germany opened its borders to the West. Thousands of citizens gathered at the Berlin Wall, the symbol of the Iron Curtain, and began tearing it down with sledgehammers. East Berliners drove their cars into what had been the forbidden western sector. They were showered with flowers and food, and families that had been divided for a generation were reunited. Shortly thereafter Leonard Bernstein conducted a performance of Beethoven's Ninth Symphony with an orchestra and chorus consisting of East and West Berliners, changing Schiller's text from "Freude" ("Joy") to "Freiheit" ("Freedom"). The political reunification of Germany occurred on 3 October 1990. It was a heady time. Arvo Pärt's *Berlin Mass* was first performed in May 1990, during a "German Catholic Days" festival in Berlin, and right in the midst of all this joyful turmoil.

Since the mid-1970s, the Estonian-German composer Arvo Pärt has focused primarily on choral works that use sacred Latin texts. These compositions are appropriate for the concert hall as well as for Catholic services of worship. The text of this work is that of the traditional Ordinary of the Mass, to which Pärt adds movements whose words are proper to the Feast of Pentecost. Pärt mixes styles, reinterpreting the serenity of Renaissance polyphony through the thinking of a twentieth-century modernist.

Pärt sets the text in a syllabic and homorhythmic style that makes the words crystal clear. The rhythm of the musical lines respects the meter of the Latin words. But other aspects of the composition stem from a predetermined plan. Voices enter and exit without regard for text phrases or even words—see the tenor and bass lines in measure 11 or the soprano and alto entrance in measure 29. Short duets alternate with brief passages for four-part chorus. Further, the duet sections also alternate in timbre: The first, third, and fifth duets are for tenor and bass voices, while the second, fourth, and sixth are for the sopranos and altos. This alternation continues without exception throughout the entire movement.

The voice parts are also interrelated by a style that Pärt calls "*tintinnabuli*" ("bells"). He uses this term to describe a contrapuntal texture in which some lines are diatonic and melodious (the bass and alto in the following *Credo*) and others bell-like in their limitation to the three tones of a tonic triad. The music that results has a static quality that for many suggests the spirit of Minimalism. Note also the mechanical procedure by which Pärt varies the basic melody first heard in the bass in measures 1 to 11. Upon each repetition of this line, pairs of notes from its beginning are resituated at its end. When all of its notes have been rotated, the movement ends. Pärt carefully calculates this procedure so that the musical form concludes simultaneously with the completion of the *Credo* text.

Arvo Pärt
Berlin Mass (1990)
Credo
CD 13/18

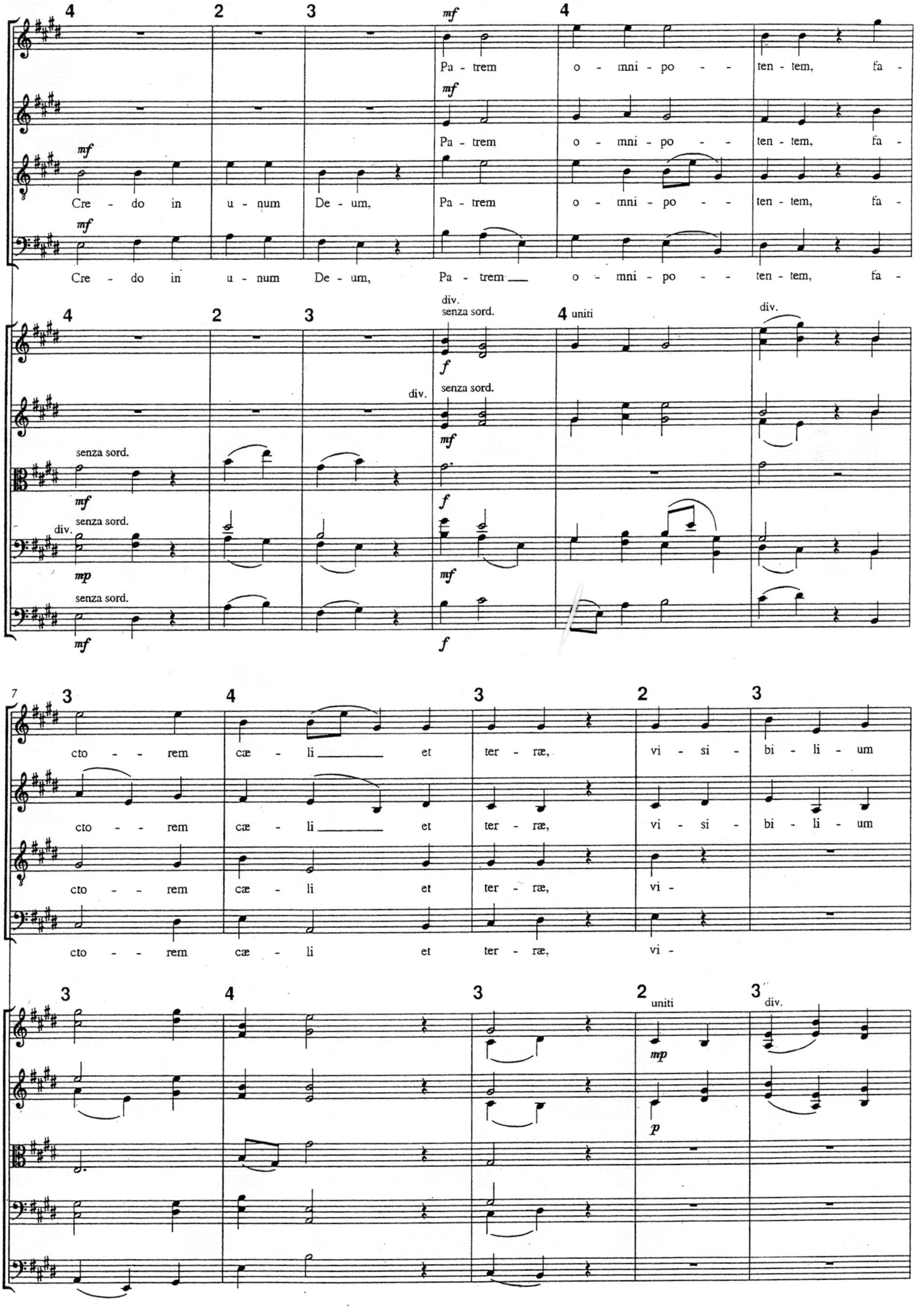

Credo in unum Deum, Patrem omnipotentem, factorem cæli et terræ, visibilium

12
4
5
2
3
S
o - mni - um,
et in - vi - si - bi - li - um.
Et in u - - num
A
o - mni - um,
et in - vi - si - bi - li - um.
Et in u - - num
T
Et in u - - num
B
Et in u - - num
4
uniti
5 div.
2
3
Vl. I
f
Vl. II
mf
Va.
f
Vc.
mf
Cb.
f
17
4
2
4
S
Do - mi - num Je - sum Chri - - stum, Fi - li - um De - i
A
Do - mi - num Je - sum Chri - - stum, Fi - li - um De - i
T
Do - mi - num Je - sum Chri - - stum, Fi - li - um De - i u - ni -
B
Do - mi - num Je - sum Chri - - stum, Fi - li - um De - i u - ni -
4
2
4
Vl. I
Vl. II
Va.
Vc.
mp
Cb.
mf

22
3
2
T
ge - ni - tum, et ex Pa - tre na - tum an - te
B
ge - ni - tum, et ex Pa - tre na - tum an - te
3
2
Va.
mf
Vc.
Cb.
27
4
6
4
3
S
-mni - a sæ - - cu - la. De - um de De - o,
A
-mni - a sæ - - cu - la. De - um de De - o,
T
o - mni - a sæ - - cu - la. De - um de De - o,
B
o - - mni - a sæ - - cu - la. De - um de De - o,
4
6
4
3
Vl. I
f
Vl. II
mf
Va.
f
Vc.
mf
div.
uniti
Cb.
f

31
5
2
S
lu - men de lu - - mi - ne, De - um ve - rum de De - o
A
lu - men de lu - - mi - ne, De - um ve - rum de De - o
T
lu - men de lu - - mi - ne,
B
lu - men de lu - - mi - ne,
Vl. I
uniti
mf
Vl. II
uniti
mf
Va.
div.
mp
Vc.
Cb.
37
3
4
ve - - ro, ge - ni - tum, non fa - - ctum,
ve - - ro, ge - ni - tum, non fa - - ctum,
- ctum,
- ctum,

41
5
3
S
con - sub - stan - ti - a - lem Pa - tri: per quem
A
con - sub - stan - ti - a - lem Pa - tri: per quem
T
con - sub - stan - ti - a - lem Pa - tri: per quem
B
con - sub - stan - ti - a - lem Pa - tri: per quem
Vl. I
Vl. II
Va.
Vc.
Cb.
div.
unite
mp
mf
f
45
4
2
4
o - mni - a fa - cta
o - mni - a fa - cta
o - mni - a fa - cta sunt. Qui pro - pter nos
o - mni - a fa - cta sunt. Qui pro - pter nos
uniti
mf

49
S
A
T
B
ho - mi - nes et pro - pter no - stram sa - lu - tem de - - scen - dit de
Vl. I
Vl. II
Va.
Vc.
Cb.
uniti
mf
div.
54
cæ - lis.
Et in - - car - na - tus est de
uniti
div.
mp

58
2 3 2 4
S
Spi - ri - tu San - cto ex Ma - ri - a Vir - gi - ne:
A
Spi - ri - tu San - cto ex Ma - ri - a Vir - gi - ne:
T
Spi -
B
Spi -
uniti
Vl. I
mp
uniti
Vl. II
mp
Va.
mp
Vc.
Cb.
63
3 2 3 4
S
Et ho - mo fa - ctus est. Cru - ci - fi - xus
A
Et ho - mo fa - ctus est. Cru - ci - fi - xus
T
fa - ctus est. Cru - ci - fi - xus
B
fa - ctus est. Cru - ci - fi - xus
div.
uniti
div.
Vl. I
mf
div.
Vl. II
mp
Va.
mf
Vc.
mp
Cb.
mf

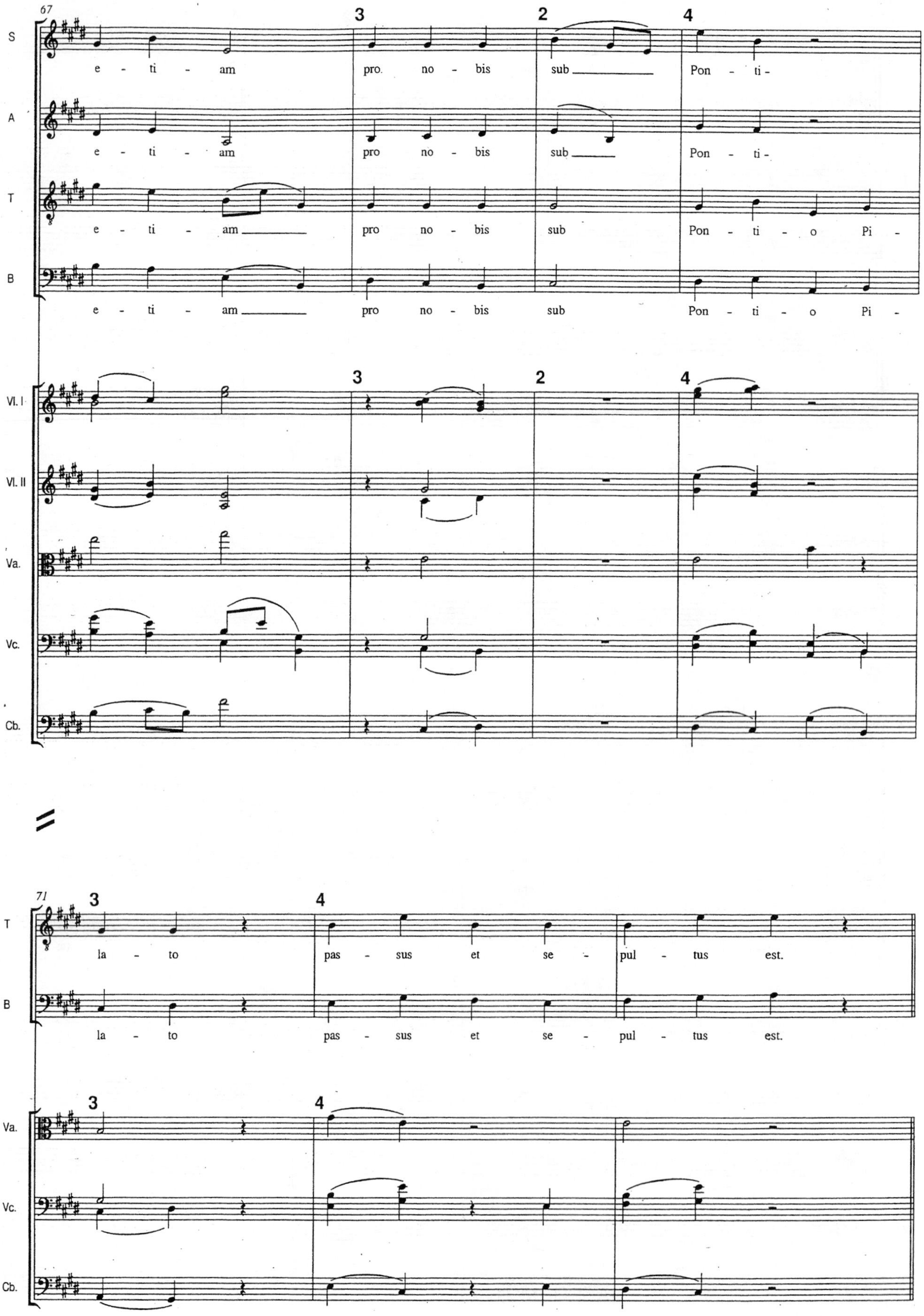

67

S: e - ti - am pro. no - bis sub Pon - ti -

A: e - ti - am pro no - bis sub Pon - ti -

T: e - ti - am pro no - bis sub Pon - ti - o Pi -

B: e - ti - am pro no - bis sub Pon - ti - o Pi -

3 2 4

Vl. I

Vl. II

Va.

Vc.

Cb.

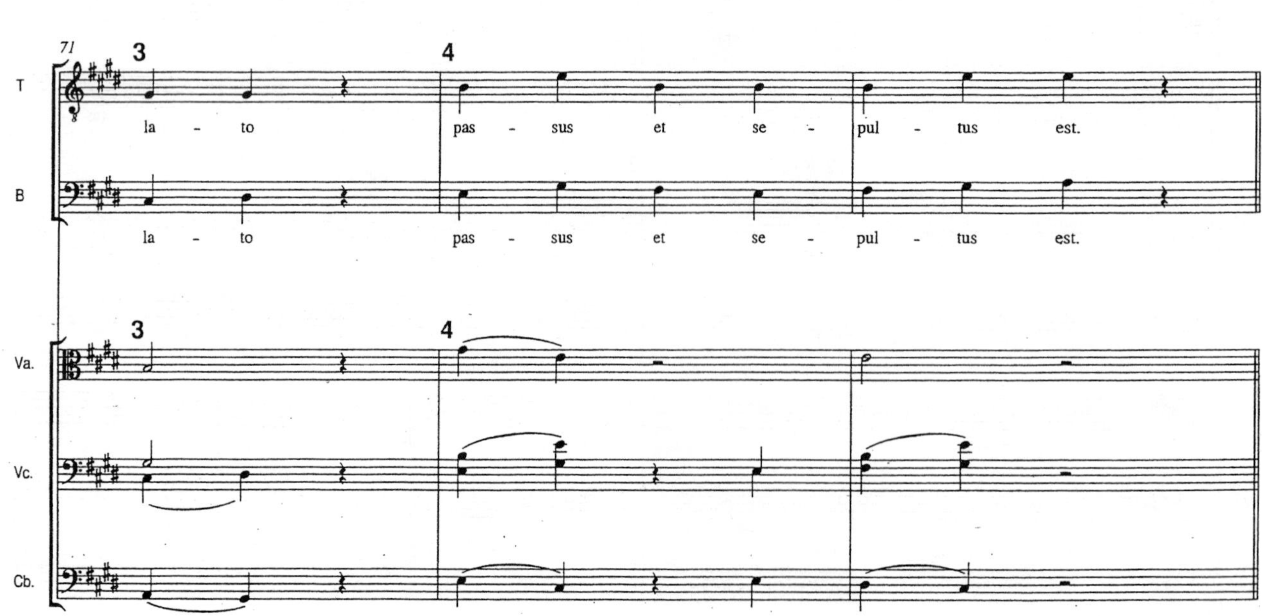

74
3
4
S
A
T
B
Et re - sur - re - xit ter - ti - a di - e, se -
Vl. I
Vl. II
Va.
Vc.
Cb.
f
mf
78
2
3
cun - dum Scri - ptu - - ras. Et a - scen - dit in cæ - lum,
Et a - scen -
div.
uniti
mp

83
4
5
S
se - det ad dex - - te - ram Pa - tris. Et i - te - rum ven -
A
se - det ad dex - - te - ram Pa - tris. Et i - te - rum ven -
T
- te - rum ven -
B
- te - rum ven -
Vl. I
Vl. II
Va.
Vc.
Cb.
mf
f
87
2
S
tu - rus est cum glo - ri - - a, iu - di - - ca - re
A
tu - rus est cum glo - ri - - a, iu - di - - ca - re
T
tu - rus est cum glo - ri - - a, iu - di - - ca - re
B
tu - rus est cum glo - ri - - a, iu - di - - ca - re
uniti
div.

91
4
3
S
vi - - vos
A
vi - - vos
T
vi - - vos et mor - tu - os, cu - ius re - gni non
B
vi - - vos et mor - tu - os, cu - ius re - gni non
Vl. I
Vl. II
uniti
mf
Va.
Vc.
Cb.
95
2
4
2
4
S
in Spi - - ri - - tum
A
in Spi - - ri - - tum
T
e - rit fi - nis. Et in Spi - - ri - - tum
B
e - rit fi - nis. Et in Spi - - ri - - tum
f
div.
mf

99
S
A
T
B
Sanctum, Dominum et vivificantem:
Vl. I
Vl. II
Va.
Vc.
Cb.
5
4
3
uniti
div.
103
2
qui ex Patre Filioque procedit.
qui
mf
mp

108
2
3
4
5
S
Qui cum Pa - tre et Fi - - li - o si - - mul ad - o -
A
Qui cum Pa - tre et Fi - - li - o si - - mul ad - o -
T
et Fi - - li - o si - - mul ad - o -
B
et Fi - - li - o si - - mul ad - o -
Vl. I
Vl. II
Va.
Vc.
Cb.
f
mf
unite
uniti
112
S
ra - - tur et con - - glo - ri - fi - ca -
A
ra - - tur et con - - glo - ri - fi - ca -
T
ra - - tur et con - - glo - ri - fi - ca - tur:
B
ra - - tur et con - - glo - ri - fi - ca - tur:
div.
uniti
div.

115
2
3
5
T
qui lo - cu - tus est per Pro - phe - tas. Et
B
qui lo - cu - tus est per Pro - phe - tas. Et
Va.
mf
Vc.
mp
Cb.
mf
119
3
5
4
3
S
- ctam, ca - - tho - li - cam et a - po -
A
- ctam, ca - - tho - li - cam et a - po -
T
u - nam, san - ctam, ca - - tho - li - cam et a - po -
B
u - nam, san - ctam, ca - - tho - li - cam et a - po -
Vl. I
uniti
div.
mf
f
Vl. II
uniti
div.
mp
mf
Va.
f
Vc.
mf
Cb.
f

123
S
A
T
B
sto - - li - cam Ec - - cle - si - am. Con - fi - te - or u - num ba -
sto - - li - cam Ec - - cle - si - am. Con -
Vl. I
Vl. II
Va.
Vc.
Cb.
div.
uniti
mf
mp
127
pti - - sma in re - mis - si - - o - nem pec - ca - - to - rum.
pec - ca - - to - rum.
f
6
3
4
2

132
S
A
T
B
Et ex - spe - sto re - - sur - re - cti - - o - nem mor - tu-
Et ex - spe - sto re - - sur - re - cti - - o - nem mor - tu-
Et ex - spe - cto re - - sur - re - cti - - o - nem mor - tu -
Et ex - spe - cto re - - sur - re - cti - - o - nem mor - tu -
Vl. I
Vl. II
Va.
Vc.
Cb.
uniti
div.
137
A - - men.
o - rum, et vi - tam ven - tu - - ri sæ - cu - li. A - - men.
f

Credo in unum Deum, Patrem omnipotentem,	I believe in one God, the Father Almighty,
factorem caeli et terrae,	Maker of heaven and earth,
visibilium omnium et invisibilium.	And of all things visible and invisible:
Et in unum Dominum Jesum Christum Filium Dei unigenitum.	And in one Lord Jesus Christ, the only-begotten Son of God;
Et ex Patre natum ante omnia saecula.	Begotten of his Father before all worlds.
Deum de Deo, lumen de lumine, Deum verum de Deo vero.	God of God, Light of Light, very God of very God.
Genitum, non factum, consubstantialem Patri:	Begotten, not made, being of one substance with the Father;
per quem omnia facta sunt.	By whom all things were made:
Qui propter nos homines et propter nostram salutem descendit de caelis.	Who for us men and for our salvation came down from heaven.
Et incarnatus est de Spiritu Sancto ex Maria Virgine: et homo factus est.	And was incarnate by the Holy Ghost of the Virgin Mary, and was made man:
Crucifixus etiam pro nobis: sub Pontio Pilato passus, et sepultus est.	And was crucified also for us under Pontius Pilate; He suffered and was buried:
Et resurrexit tertia die, secundum Scripturas.	And the third day he rose again according to the Scriptures.
Et ascendit in caelum:	And ascended into heaven,
sedet ad dexteram Patris.	And sitteth on the right hand of the Father:
Et iterum venturus est cum gloria	And he shall come again, with glory,
judicare vivos et mortuos:	to judge both the quick and the dead;
cujus regni non erit finis.	Whose kingdom shall have no end.
Et in Spiritum Sanctum, Dominum, et vivificantem:	And [I believe] in the Holy Ghost, the Lord, and Giver of life,
qui ex Patre, Filioque procedit.	Who proceedeth from the Father and the Son;
Qui cum Patre, et Filio simul adoratur, et conglorificatur:	Who with the Father and the Son together is worshiped and glorified;
qui locutus est per Prophetas.	Who spake by the Prophets:
Et unam sanctam catholicam et apostolicam Ecclesiam.	And [I believe] in one holy Catholic and Apostolic Church:
Confiteor unum baptisma	I acknowledge one Baptism
in remissionem peccatorum.	for the remission of sins:
Et exspecto resurrectionem mortuorum.	And I look for the resurrection of the dead:
Et vitam venturi saeculi. Amen.	And the life of the world to come. Amen.